Also by John Calvin Batchelor:

THE FURTHER ADVENTURES
OF HALLEY'S COMET

THE BIRTH OF THE PEOPLE'S REPUBLIC OF ANTARCTICA

John Calvin Batchelor

THE BIRTH OF THE PEOPLE'S REPUBLIC OF ANTARCTICA

The Dial Press • New York

Published by
The Dial Press
1 Dag Hammarskjold Plaza
New York, New York 10017

The author acknowledges his general debt to
Kevin Crossley-Holland's *The Norse Myths* (Pantheon,
1980), and to the following Penguin Classics: *Beowulf*,
trans. Michael Alexander, 1973; *Egil's Saga*, trans.
Hermann Palsson and Paul Edwards, 1976;
King Harald's Saga, trans. Magnus Magnusson
and Hermann Palsson, 1966; *The Vineland Sagas*, trans.
Magnus Magnusson and Hermann Palsson, 1965;
Njal's Saga, trans. Magnus Magnusson
and Hermann Palsson, 1960.

Also, the author acknowledges his specific debt to Penguin
Books Ltd.: Excerpt from *Beowulf*, trans. Michael
Alexander (Penguin Classics, 1973), Copyright ©
Michael Alexander, 1973. Reprinted by permission of
Penguin Books Ltd.

All scriptural quotations are from The New English Bible,
Copyright © The Delegates of Oxford University Press
and The Syndics of the Cambridge University Press, 1961, 1970.

Design by Francesca Belanger
Maps by David Lindroth

Library of Congress Cataloging in Publication Data
Bachelor, John Calvin.
The birth of the People's Republic of Antarctica.
I. Title.
PS3552.A8268B57   1983   813'.54   82-22182
ISBN 0-385-27811-X
9 8 7 6 5 4 3 2

To my Mother and Father

Contents

Contents

A mind that seeks to understand and grasp this
is therefore best. Both bad and good,
and much of both, must be borne in a lifetime
spent on this earth in these anxious days.

BEOWULF

THE KINGDOM OF FIRE

My Mother ▪ My Father ▪ The Nobel Prize Ball ▪ My Father's Crime ▪ Brave New Benthamism ▪ Mord the Hard-Fisherman ▪ Lamba Time-Thief ▪ The Fire

My Mother

I am Grim Fiddle. My mother, Lamba, first spied me in her magic hand-mirror late in the evening of the spring equinox of 1973. She was dancing by herself at the time, at the rear of a shabby beer hall called THE MICKEY MOUSE CLUB, located in the foreign quarter of Stockholm, the capital of the Kingdom of Sweden. She was midway between the music box and the bank of telephone booths. She was not under the influence of any drug, though my maternal grandfather was a Lutheran preacher. There is no further explanation of Lamba's vision forthcoming. Mother was a Norse sibyl.

My conception followed immediately. There is minor confusion as to the precise sequence. My father, Peregrine Ide, an American draft dodger, was seated in a cramped manner in the last of the telephone booths. He was talking with America. One of my godfathers, Israel Elfers, also a draft dodger, was standing nearby, playing a pinball game called Pirate King. Israel later claimed that my father was weepy and very drunk. Peregrine does not seem to have been aware of Lamba until she crashed atop him. Her demands were unambiguous, as was Lamba, a seventeen-year-old beauty, fine-haired and long-legged, with an unhappy depth to her features. Also, I was told, Lamba exuded a powerful scent. Her manner was brutal and possessed. Lamba forced herself on Peregrine. Their embrace was artless. They obviously did connect. And Lamba left just enough, and the right sort of, blood on Peregrine for him later to speculate that she had been virginal, thereby redoubling his fleeting sorrow for this sin of the flesh.

Israel said he did not at once grasp the scene. When he did, he pulled another of my godfathers, Earle Littlejohn, the Ivy League hockey legend, over to the booth, providing my first biological moment with the privacy offered by Earle's enormous backside. Lamba is said to have wailed. In order to conceal the affair further, Israel enlisted my final godfather, Guy Labyrinthe, another Ivy hockey legend, to join him in a vigorous rendition of "America the Beautiful." They were eventually accompanied by a folk singer acquaintance, Timothy, on mouth harp.

Finally, the assembled increasingly uneasy with the battle inside the booth, Lamba ended the escapade by crying out the Norse name "Skallagrim Strider!"

Peregrine's first sensible comment to Israel afterward was simply the American modifier "Grim."

I was born in Stockholm as well, in early December of the same year, in Lamba's sparse bedroom on the first story of the small quayside cottage belonging to my grandfather, the Reverend Mord Fiddle. Mother was attended by Grandfather's chess partner, Dr. Anders Horshead, and by a midwife, Astra, who was plump and cunning, and who was also one of Lamba's secret sister sibyls. Thus, at a diminutive seven pounds odd (which might not be much more than the weight of the hand that writes this), healthy, red-faced, and ugly, with a sea-green umbilical cord attached to where it should have been (I mention this to dismiss notions that I am any other than of woman born), I enjoyed the mystical comfort provided by logical positivism, Lutheranism, and paganism. My birthchamber was so crowded by conflicting schools of thought, I marvel at my ability to assert myself. It was a sudden lesson in the contradictions that then darkened the fair, chill Kingdom of Sweden. My maternal people are a handsome, clean tribe, but I have often thought this might be heavenly compensation for the melancholy that taints their lives.

Grandfather did not witness my dive into contretemps. He was downstairs in his study praying loudly and drinking quietly. He had not slept well the last three months of Lamba's time, haunted by images he associated with his wife Zoe's desertion, and now Lamba's infamy. He looked the robust but suddenly drowned fisherman—his blue eyes like smooth stones, his heavy beard like frayed rope. As he heard my first cry, he reached to find the resolve to bellow back, as if singing the lower range of this Fiddle duet; and what he returned me was not idle, was a portentous message that he had found in his come-what-may Lutheran style, by flinging open the gigantic Fiddle Bible and, with his eyes shut, tapping his finger on the page once for luck and twice for righteousness. He thundered in that Judgment Day voice of his:

"My Son, fear Lord God and grow rich in spirit, but have nothing to do with men of rank! They will bring catastrophe without warning! Who knows what ruin such men may cause?"

This is from the Book of Proverbs. It was staggeringly well chosen; and I have long suspected that Grandfather found it with one eye open, as that splendid Norse scoundrel, one-eyed Odin, would have done. I have never improved upon its wisdom, nor will I soon. What ruin indeed, Grandfather?

For it so happened that Mord Fiddle, a man of very high rank in the tyrannical wing of the Swedish Lutheran Church, was mortified by my birth. That his dim-witted eldest should have conceived a bastard was shame enough. He saw Lamba's disgrace as his own flagellation. But the matter was worse for him than that. Lamba had conceived so far out of wedlock that she claimed she had no clue who the father was, what the father was, what color or religion the father was. Grandfather was numb before fate. Not only was I to be his living curse, but also I could be any wretched shape and color of curse. And being a true son of Norse pessimism—his own father, Gunther, a dismal trawler captain who had anticipated all the days of his life the North Sea storm that drowned him—Grandfather expected the worst. He feared that I would be a Jew. And if not that horror, he feared that I would be dark-skinned. And if not that horror, he feared that I would be American. These might seem random demons, yet one must consider that for many years Grandfather had been hard-pressed to make sense of western civilization. He was a fiery preacher of the coming Kingdom of Heaven ruled by Him whom Grandfather called "Lord God." Prior to his relatively plush appointment to the preaching post of one of Stockholm's most conservative churches, Grandfather had labored twenty-one years sailing, sledding, and skiing the most remote precincts of the Swedish realm on the Gulf of Bothnia, preaching the Word to convicts, misanthropes, and madmen. His colleagues called him "Mord the Hard-Fisherman." He had christened his own ship *Angel of Death*. After all this time in the wilderness, he had become convinced that the coming Kingdom looked a certain way, meaning white-skinned, clean, and well-stocked with lumber and fish. During his few years in Stockholm, he had had reason to reconsider his vision; he had not. One might attempt to excuse Grandfather's irrational attachment to his earliest perceptions of heaven by arguing that he was stuck back in the Gulf of Bothnia, and in the gulf of time, before the heartbreak caused by his beloved Zoe's desertion. Grandfather would be the first to refuse such a defense. He was persuaded, out of the pride that was his worst sin, that if the Jews, or the dark-skinned races, or the Americans, or a combination of same, ever gained control of the West, or of at least the North, then Stockholm would suffer and would deserve (perhaps even would welcome, like suicidal hermits) the same conflagration that consumed so many of the Bible's infidel cities.

I confess in detail Grandfather's shameful delusion, because it became a self-fulfilling prophecy, the bigot harvesting what he sowed. I note also that the fruit was the most bitter for Grandfather because it did not proceed from hatred, which requires some passing knowledge of one's adversary, instead was engendered by his absolute ignorance, his bottomless fear of the unknown. Grandfather did not hate Jews, Negroes, Arabs, Orientals, Indians, Americans. To my knowledge, he had never talked with one. Accordingly, they terrified him. And I submit that, for reasons having to do with his innate fear of hedonism, luxury, eroticism, fleshly profligacy, Grandfather did not fear the Jews or the dark-skinned races with anything equivalent to the hardness of his heart when confronted with the spectre of the Americans who were then pouring into Stockholm, on the run from the American tyrant, President Richard M. Nixon. Grandfather feared the Americans so much that he was willing to suspend his common sense about blasphemy—he had, as a seminarian, preached resistance at all costs in the face of German and Russian blasphemers—and to proclaim from his pulpit that Nixon was fit punishment for the American sinners. He said that he grieved that so many of the rascals escaped their horned chief executive.

My grandfather was a godly man. I loved him despite himself. He was also cruel, narrow-minded, vindictive, and too often hysterically vain. He preached the God of Love, the Sermon on the Mount, and the parables of Jesus with the same intensity with which he opined unjust, merciless politics. He could be a thunderous bully; he could be a dauntless ally. His strength was his resolve, his weakness was his lack of a sense of proportion, which could become a lack of a sense of decency. He stormed through a life of shame and triumph. Grandfather was as relentless as he was ruthless, was as vigilant as he was an ever-dangerous trespasser. He was shrewd, sudden, articulate, and long-remembering. Grandfather was fury itself. He got what he gave, and much more. It is not for me to judge him finally. Over the length of my life I have had to dispute nearly everything my grandfather said about Mother, Father, and peace of mind; and yet I know I am lucky for having been obliged to run such a long-winded course. All along the way I have found treasures.

Dr. Anders Horshead was first down to pronounce me an average boy. This meant that I was not hook-nosed, chocolate, or radically not-Norse. Radar, my maternal uncle, then twelve but already given to the angelic keenness that would carry him on to the stage as the sort of Northman playwrights celebrate as tragic heroes, came down next to say he was going to chapel to give thanks for Lamba's health. Radar was not then permitted to forget the lie that his sickly birth and youth had caused his mother's death (a deception by Grandfather that fooled no one but the fools that cared for such gossip). Grandfather and Anders Horshead then emptied a fresh bottle of vodka in order to toast—and this was very Norse of them—what had so far been avoided.

By daylight, and the first of a heavy snow, Grandfather exhausted his peculiar joy and returned to stoical fretting. "What should be done with the little bastard?" said Grandfather. (I do not know he actually said this; it pleases me that he might have. More likely, he called me "it.")

"Don't talk so," said Anders Horshead. "Let nature be."

"I would sooner it burn in Hell than let her keep it."

"You've a fine grandson. I envy you," said Anders Horshead.

"She's not right! Something must be done! Shall be done!"

Lamba was not half-witted. She was a precocious, motherless child who mocked her father's will and enjoyed letting him know the pleasure she took in so doing. She did not intend to quit her commitment to rebellion merely because the act of giving birth had momentarily overwhelmed her powers of defiance. She did require a fortnight to recover, the nursing of me preoccupying her until Grandfather, in his cruel way, reminded Lamba of her plight. Once the couple was chosen, and my adoption process so far along that all that remained was a rubber stamp or two,

Grandfather pushed into Lamba's room and told her what was about to be done. Lamba lay passively. She wept, did not sniffle or wipe her eyes. She reached beneath her pillows in order to bring forth her magic hand-mirror like a weapon. Grandfather bolted, appalled at the reminder that his only daughter might be a witch. He left Radar in charge while he waded through a new snow to his office in the rectory of the Pillar of Salt Lutheran Church. He telephoned his spiritual advisor, Thorbrand of the Supreme Lutheran Council, to tell him that the deed was done, the future was set. He was right. He was wrong. By the time Grandfather returned home, past dark, I was gone, not to be seen again for many ominous years. Lamba never crossed Grandfather's path again. Radar wept inconsolably. Grandfather called on the police, on Anders Horshead, and then returned to his study to call on his Lord God and, in prayerful repose, on his deeply missed Zoe.

Lamba had bundled me in the usual swaddling clothes and walked to the foreign quarter on the other side of the city. It was Christmas week (though not Christmas Eve). Stockholm was decked in its finery, natural and commercial, its fourteen islands dusted with a fresh snow atop a heavy crust of ice, its streets filled with as many sleds as automobiles, its evergreens buffeted by the arctic winds that whined through the small stone closes of the oldest sections of a city part quaint, part deliberately futuristic. Back then, Stockholm was always aggressively organized. In winter, it also seemed serendipitous and not entirely credible. With only a few hours of sunlight, the twilight that predominated was that much more dramatic for the on-again, off-again flurries. And the deep night was philosophical. Lamba plowed a furrow through a city of ice and stainless steel, singing nonsense songs to herself and to me. Lamba was resolved, but not unafraid. She was not that far from childhood's nightmares, and in those dreams (and also at the zoo) she had seen the telltale yellow eyes of the Norse wolf, poised to strike from out of the darkness.

One might assume she could have taken a bus. She did not, and not only because she was an operatic girl. The recent border wars in the Middle Eastern kingdoms had precipitated an embargo that even then condemned the North to a dim panic. Public transportation was erratic. Shops closed early. My first Christmas was not well lit or well heated. Considering the other problems I endured, such as maternity, paternity, survival, the fact that there were more candles than light bulbs on Christmas trees might be superfluous. It was instead prescient of fratricidal chaos to come.

Lamba shoved into the crowd at the entrance to the very same shabby beer hall, THE MICKEY MOUSE CLUB, where I had been conceived. Some were taken aback by a snow-flecked golden girl gripping a bundle that could hardly have been bread. A few of the women suggested the worst aloud: "It's dead." Lamba did not appear that desperate. The eerie depth to her features intimidated the curious at the last moment before interference. She was a beauty but, in cold lights, could seem overdone and spooky. Her mission reinforced her intrinsically bizarre manner. After all, Mother was magic.

THE MICKEY MOUSE CLUB was a series of concentric ovals, the inmost being the bar, the next being the booths, the outermost being the cafeteria line and auxiliary items, such as the music box, the pinball machines, and the telephone booths. Lamba moved to the bar to inquire in Swedish of the dwarfish bartender, Felix, as to the whereabouts of a tall, hairy, red-bearded American dressed in blue jeans, plaid shirt, vest, and Irish cap, who made telephone calls at the back. Felix told her half of America was tall and the other half lived on the phone. Did she have a name for him? Lamba backed away from the stares. She weaved her way back to the Christmas tree set up by the music box. Some women jumped in her path for fear she might deposit me amid the presents. Lamba continued on to the very phone booth of the act. She placed several calls to her sister sibyls, the last of which, to Astra, secured a room for us for the night. Lamba was a practical pagan. She was prepared to return to the beer hall as often as it took. Under the circumstances, she was finding me the best home available. Mother never, never planned to abandon me.

Peregrine came in late, since it was the first week on his first job after more than a year in Stockholm. He and Israel had fallen into part-time employment selling snacks during, and cleaning up after, a game at the rink of a semipro ice hockey team, the Slothbaden Berserkers. It was filthy work, and it paid slave wages, yet Peregrine and Israel were glad to get it. Like most of the Americans in Stockholm—draft dodgers, deserters, thieves, bad characters—Peregrine and Israel did not have work permits. The King's government might let them stay, because Sweden prided itself on its so-called neutral status, but the King's government would not readily let them work. There was bureaucratic wind about clearance, waiting lists, adjusting the labor pool. In the end, there were half a million foreign workers in Sweden; very few of them were American exiles. It does not matter profoundly, I know, except to make the point that Peregrine and Israel were as much political prisoners in Stockholm as they would have been had they gone to jail in America for draft resistance. They had very little money left from their impetuous flight the year before. They were desperate men. Some of their kind, corrupted by the insanity that was the Vietnam war, had already descended into drugs, crime, or worse. Peregrine and Israel had avoided such an end by luck and by the quick thinking of Guy Labyrinthe. Guy and Earle Littlejohn were "money properties," in ice hockey slang. The sly owner of the Slothbaden Berserkers, Eystein, wanted Guy's balletic talent and Earle's pugilistic talent more than he cared to obey the work laws of the Social Democratic Party that ruled at the King's behest. Peregrine and Israel thus had jobs that paid one American dollar an hour, three nights a week, eight hours a night; it was penury, but it was better than the long fall into drugs and self-loathing. Still, some quick comfort was necessary to endure the irony of having been matriculated by Yale University as preparation for mopping vomit beneath temporary bleachers. Peregrine and Israel came straight from the rink to bathe their realization in good Norse brew.

Past midnight, THE MICKEY MOUSE CLUB was packed with sorrowful American boys, most too self-pitying to care about more than the flock of Swedish girls who offered sex and sympathy with certain conditions. Israel was quick to claim a booth near the Christmas tree, on the opposite side of the room from the panderers and gangsters. Israel signaled Earle, who was nursing a bandaged left arm from the evening's combat, to insert his bulk and to wave his wound in order to open up the table enough for Peregrine and Guy close behind. Israel then volunteered to struggle through the crowd to the bar for beer, mostly because he hoped to catch the attention of his heartthrob, the poetess Molly Rogers. This raised the issue of finance. Peregrine groaned, emptying his parka of a few wormy krona and a carefully wrapped love letter. Earle said he had fifty k. somewhere, reaching with his bad arm. Guy stopped him, then carefully poked to produce Earle's billfold, which had only thirty k., Earle having forgotten he had paid the penalty on their late rent that afternoon. Peregrine sank deeper into his seat to reread his letter.

Israel returned without Molly Rogers. Guy took note of Israel's longing. Israel changed the subject, seizing upon the evening's game and Earle's wound, the result of a well-thrown but untimely cross-check. Israel then produced a four-day-old copy of *The New York Times* that he had bartered American cigarettes for at the rink, and the four turned to debate more somber games. They never talked ice hockey in those days, when there were the totems of Richard Nixon and Henry Kissinger to curse. Besides, the Slothbaden Berserkers did not play ice hockey; they played "goon." It was the American influence. The American and Canadian National Hockey League was a joke but also a fad in Sweden. Guy and Earle, having attended an NHL training camp before they were drafted, shipped to Vietnam as riflemen, tempted to commit crimes and to desert, were celebrities because of their supposed talents at "gooning." Guy hit and scored. Earle just hit and hit. Violent as the Berserkers seemed, however, especially with bearish Earle on defense feeding Guy flying on the right wing, they still played a boy's game. Off the ice, the bruises were badges of showmanship, not reminders of brutality. That night in late 1973, the beer hall was filled with young men who carried permanently the scars of true brutality. Israel once told me that the only time as a young man he had not cared about what happened to the New York Rangers was the year before, when President Nixon, and his prime minister, Henry Kissinger, had ordered bombers over Hanoi for Christmas.

The news from New York was promising. Kissinger, a strong man and a liar, had accepted the Nobel Peace Prize in Oslo two weeks before (on my birthday). His co-winner, Le Duc Tho, a Vietnamese strong man and liar, had shunned the affair altogether. Israel announced to Earle that getting the Nobel Peace Prize was a jinx equivalent to being featured on the cover of *Sports Illustrated*. Earle, who encouraged others to think of him as slowwitted, which was not true, said he liked Israel's idea. Guy grum-

bled about Israel condescending to Earle, and then opined that
Israel was failing to take a dangerous man seriously just because
he was Jewish. The Jews, Guy pressed, were less absurd and more
effective than Israel allowed. Guy was of French-Canadian de-
scent from the very poorest section of upper Vermont. He had a
compact, quick, rugged body and a similar disposition. He also
had a bitter sense of history and was a thorough radical libertarian, bred in the same mountains that gave America the romantic
anarchists who followed Guy's personal saint, Ethan Allen. Guy
was an advocate of the violent overthrow of all governments. His
opinion was to hang them before they hanged you. Israel shrugged
at Guy. This was their oldest, most comfortable argument. Israel
knew that he took Jews seriously, especially German Jews like his
own father and like Henry Kissinger. Israel shifted the flow of
the dialogue, with one staccato reading of a headline and lead
paragraph, to the ongoing tragedy of Richard M. Nixon, president of the United States of America for the last fifty-nine months.

"Never nail him, not as long as he's got the tapes and we've
got the Senate," said Peregrine. Father referred to the amazing
story that Nixon had tape-recorded himself in his own secret
chambers as he conspired to subvert the constitution of the Republic he was sworn on a Bible to defend to the death. The story
is much longer, of course, most of the rest propaganda for subsequent petty tyrants. I admit my impatience. It was a long time
ago, and though Nixon's reign meant everything for my family's
fate, it seems to me now more folly than tragedy. No, that is unfair to my father: Nixon was ruin for him and his friends, was the
immediate cause of their agony in exile.

"I'm not sure anymore," said Israel to Peregrine, sniffing the
front page of the newspaper for what he called "the odor of corruption." Israel added, "Nixon's not straight no more."

"Like he took a shot in the head?" said Earle.

"Yeah, puck in the chops," said Israel. "I'm hopeful."

"I don't see any hope," said Peregrine. "It is what it is—"

"—when it is," finished Israel, scowling. He was annoyed with
Peregrine. Father had soured on them. His heart was breaking,
because his heart belonged to an American woman he was not
permitted—a "full-stomach nightmare" according to Israel—
namely, Miss Charity Bentham.

Of a sudden, Timothy the folk singer squeezed through to the table, sat like a pixie on Earle's huge knee.

"You owe me ten k.," said Israel, palm up.

"Got some news I was thinking I could trade for my debt," said Timothy. "You guys might not like it. Deal?"

"English there," said Israel. "You speak it, we speak it."

"Deal then," said Timothy. "A little Ingrid came in about nine holding a real live baby-manger-type infant. Asked Felix about a tall Yank with a red beard, wears Irish caps, makes phone calls."

"Dear God," said Israel.

"What is this?" said Peregrine.

"Maybe I saw her before," said Timothy. "Maybe nine months back, climbing out of a phone booth with you."

"This is no lie?" said Peregrine.

"Would I sit on the animal and jive you guys?" said Timothy.

"What happened to her?" said Peregrine.

"She went to the back. I saw her sit in a phone booth, *the* phone booth, you know? That was a while ago," said Timothy.

"Slow, slow, slow," said Israel to Peregrine.

"I'll go," said Peregrine heavily, resignedly.

"We all go," said Israel. The four made a wedge through the swirling revelry. They found me asleep beneath the seat upon which I had been conceived. I was soaking and hungry, but I slept unbothered by the racket of revolution around me. I slept as deeply as a human being can sleep that close to innocence. I slept in anticipation of the fabulous, which did arrive, in the guise of four weary Americans in exile from everything but their heart's truth.

I have often wondered, had I cried out before Father found me—because I was willful and not really innocent at all—whether someone might have become annoyed enough to call the authorities, who would then have surrendered me back to Grandfather and thence, stamp, stamp, to strangers. I might now be a clerk, or a fisherman, or a choir singer—anyone. It was an early dose of incomprehensible luck.

I have also always wondered where Lamba had gone. One possibility is that she left me there, safe and asleep, in order to search the beer hall for Peregrine, no simple quest for a homeless beauty amid drunken ne'er-do-wells. Another possibility is that she was standing outside the telephone booth watching over me through the glass, watching for Father's red beard and Irish cap above the crowd. Either way, she certainly kept close by. Perhaps, when she spotted Peregrine and his friends standing aghast outside the booth, she realized there was no need to intervene. And there is the vital consideration that Lamba might have known what was going to happen to me. I mean all of it, from telephone booth to telephone booth to finish, which even I am yet to know. Mother claimed she could see into the future, could, as the Norse said, thieve time. I have never doubted her. Nor have I ever doubted that Mother saw Father open that telephone booth before she left me.

My rescuers were stunned into an awkward candor. Peregrine groaned the more. Israel gestured to heaven and consoled Peregrine. Earle scooped me up and cradled me in his sling. Guy pawed me in order to determine my sex. He was rewarded with a small piece of paper tucked in my linen, upon which was printed the following information, in English: "I am Grim Fiddle."

My Father

One is too easily tempted to reconstruct one's conception, birth, and childhood. I have indulged the former two; I shall not the latter. My childhood was decent, not entirely logical, and as loving as one could wish. After lengthy lamentations, Peregrine did keep me, his bastard blond son. In so doing, he later admitted, he kept his sanity as well, and his three comrades. I provided those four pilgrims what they lacked much more than money or security. I gave them purpose. Peregrine, Israel, Guy, and Earle bound themselves together to become my family. And with the generous help of more maternal sorts, such as Molly

Rogers, we survived the torrents of the Vietnam war and the torpor of what came after, which was no peace.

On the last day of April 1975, Peregrine's twenty-seventh birthday, the last helicopter lifted off the top of the besieged American Embassy in South Vietnam, thus finishing more than twenty years of American war-making in Indochina. Thereafter political chicanery obliged Nixon's successors to offer duplicitous amnesty to the thousands of American men who had chosen jail or exile rather than complicity in the illegal (Israel said "unconstitutional") American war in Vietnam. I have no need for more specificity other than to report that Father and his friends had spit in the eye of the bald eagle once and were not shy to do so again when that bald eagle offered, in its talons, a remorseless deal. My family would not concede there was any justice in the deceitful posture of the Republic that had driven them into exile. They swore on Bibles, on newspaper headlines, and on a petition of redress that we posted to the White House, signed in our blood (mine, too, though I was just three), that we would not go home again until the government of the United States of America admitted its crimes, arrested and prosecuted the true traitors, saboteurs, and assassins, and repatriated us with the respect due us. This may seem vainglorious and naive. It was. My family was bound to, and trapped in, its highest ideals. We were right. America was wrong. My family was hardly the first that has had to endure exile long after the causes of alienation have been obliterated by historical revisionism. I refer to the bulk of the American public. I refer to the Jews.

I also admit that my family's decision to remain in Stockholm was not entirely ideological. Guy and Earle were wanted by the sheriff of an American army infantry division in connection with the suspicious deaths of an American MP and a Vietnamese policeman in Saigon in 1972. The details were ambiguous and tragic. And Peregrine and Israel were wanted by the Federal Bureau of Investigation for questioning in connection with a theft of services from Pan American airlines and with the reckless endangerment of several flight attendants—a hunting knife was involved—on a flight out of Kennedy International Airport in 1972. These details were also ambiguous and tragic. My family needed sanctuary as long as it was available. Some might have said they were criminals.

They thought of themselves as fugitives. They were my family, and I loved them dearly.

We lived secretively in a slummy rented apartment (no one challenged them about me, but they worried continually—I was their shrine) in Stockholm's foreign quarter, until Guy and Earle secured enough money against future gooning for Eystein to rent us a dilapidated double house near the ice rink. Later, through a poet friend of Molly Rogers's named Orri Fljotson, Peregrine and Israel were introduced to a wealthy and mysterious art dealer, Thord Horshead. Thord had many secrets, the very least of which was that he was one of the two ringleaders of a Baltic smuggling enterprise, running liquor, small arms, and wonder drugs into heavily-tariffed Scandinavia and not infrequently through the Iron Curtain. There was never anything concealed about Thord's attitude toward me, for he smothered me with generosity and patience. He overcame Peregrine's objections and moved us all into the back wing of a sprawling manse he maintained at the edge of Stockholm as an art gallery and, covertly, a shipping and receiving office. For many years, Thord's benevolence went unanalyzed but not unappreciated. We might not have survived without him. Thord was our protector. He was also our link to Swedish culture, as he introduced us to the most exotic elements of a society we defensively skirted.

Thord was the one who advanced Peregrine and Israel the capital to enjoin their first and last attempt at American entrepreneurship, a summer camp for boys called Let's Go Viking! I have forgotten whose idea it was, why exactly it failed. It is enough to say that Peregrine and Israel administered, for ten years, a summer camp for American children mostly of Norse extraction whose parents wished to indulge their offspring in the legends of the Vikings. Israel explained to me that American parents did not provide their children with real childhoods when a safe fake one was available for a price. In America, Israel said, it was called "preparation" and was most desirable when most extravagant. He must have had it right, for with just a few advertisements in American magazines, we collected a bag of applications. Using Thord's legal status as a prestigious art dealer and his extralegal apparatus as a smuggler, Peregrine and Israel purchased a run-down wharf and abandoned buildings in Vexbeggar, a Swedish fishing village some leagues south of Stockholm. Vexbeggar was appropriate for an ersatz Viking camp, because it had already been converted by speculators from an antique cluster of shacks into a summertime resort for indolent captains of industry. My maternal people had lost their famous sense of austerity somewhere in the late twentieth century's political compromises between the left, the right, and what Israel called the lazy and had become—for several fleeting decades of luxury—little more than swindlers and malingerers. Vexbeggar's town fathers regarded Let's Go Viking! as crass American profiteering. I feel there was envy, too, at least initially, because one of the reasons we failed was the yearly increases in tax assessments.

Peregrine and Israel, through Thord, purchased costumes, a forge, a small trawler rigged as a yawl, an imitation of a six-meter Viking boat called a *karfi* that Thord had found at a Norse carnival, and all the other props necessary to fashion the camp of a make-believe Viking chieftain—we called him Gruff-the-Ruff—circa the eleventh century A.D. It was historical when it had to be, but was mostly a Viking camp in the same manner, I was told, that a famous American amusement park had re-created other historical tableaux called Frontierland and Jungleland, and my favorite, though I suspect Israel made this up, Ghettoland.

I do not mock our Vikingland, because it provided me with a childhood entirely of fantasy and fun. When summer came, with its white nights and warm Baltic breeze, I became the most precocious student of Let's Go Viking! More, I worked hard to help Peregrine and Israel hold the attention of the tedious, hollow boys we attracted. I soon grew more expert than my mentors and was by the end a snob in all matters Norse. With my mind free of modern education (I did not legally exist, so they did not dare enroll me in school), it was the happiest course for me to fill it with the arcane lore of what is called the Age of Migration. I lived what Peregrine could only show me, what Israel could only give me books about. I made myself into a spear-chucking, boat-making, sword-swinging, rune-carving, cain-raising warrior. The truth was, I had within me the genesis of a full-blooded shape-changer. Back then, however, it was all joy and spontaneity, nothing dark.

During the long winters in Stockholm, my self-education was supplemented with the curiosities of my family, which, being kind,

American, and frozen in boyishness by an accident of history, mitigated my infidel urges actually to go Viking. In my daydreams, I plundered Faeroe Islands merchantmen, razed Saxon farmsteads from John O' Groats to Land's End. But daylong, I was obliged to endure Earle's opera records, Guy's stories of dashing French triumphs, Israel's Socratic philosophizing about things in general, and Peregrine's reading aloud of the great and, as he said, "correct" novels of the world. Sometimes it sounded like D'Artagnan playing Twenty Questions with Huck Finn (the most Norse of American heroes), but I did acquire a wider view of life than permitted by Icelandic sagas. In all, my family tried to culture me. I think now they probably pushed me further into my fantasies. They thought me too much fun to control with measured strokes. And once I had acquainted them with my grandest notion, they readily cooperated, helping to transform me into a chubby-cheeked, ruddy-faced, curly-locked miniature of Beowulf Himself, slayer of Grendel and mother, hero of Viking heroes. If I seem less than a twenty-first-century man than should be the case, if I seem one whose thought is quaint, anachronistic, misinformed, out of step, I reply that I learned how to shape a short sword on an open forge before I learned how to work a telephone, that I charted the exploits of the Norse from Scandinavia to Iceland, Greenland, Markland, Helluland, and Vinland before I learned that Christopher Colombus was a Jew (according to Israel). And thinking back now, there was a most fortuitous result to my eccentric education: it was that during my Norse studies I tentatively solved the puzzle set by Mother—whom none of us then knew or knew whereof—when she exclaimed, at my conception, the Norse name "Skallagrim Strider!"

The boys' camp closed. Sadder, Earle, badly injured in a fist-fight with the Trondheim Trolls, had to miss three seasons. Eystein did not believe in sick leave. At home, Earle was vexed by his back and disconsolate with Guy away for weeks at a time; he calmed himself by teaching me everything he knew about ice hockey. My passion for the Viking Age was displaced by the thrill of learning how to handle a two-on-one breakout, when I was the one defenseman and the two were twinkle-toed Canucks, the only people besides the Norse who live for ice hockey. I was growing quickly, developing to Earle's delight along the lines of a bulwark defenseman—trunk-legged, wide-hipped, long-armed, supple and very solid on ice. Earle trained me exhaustively. He said he thought he had discovered the answer to the right and left wings of the Montreal Canadiens of the NHL, a supreme compliment. It frustrated him hard, then, that I could not live on ice. We were pressed for funds, despite Thord's munificence, and I had to work part-time jobs with Peregrine and Israel. Guy was our only reliable provider, and it was never quite sufficient, what with Earle's physical therapy expenses. Guy was selfless; his money could not lift his despondency. Even given that he could not make the overseas road trips with the Berserkers, it was the rare month that he could spend a fortnight with us and Earle. It was true that Guy loved Earle above all things temporal, and that Earle loved Guy above all things temporal. I say this because it was not for many years that I learned their love was considered by polite society (not us, to be sure) to be unnatural. When I did discover—from other boys at pickup hockey games—that love between men, homosexual love, is considered sick, I was confronted by one of my first adult mysteries. Nature is creation, I argued with Peregrine and Israel, and creation is all there is, so how can what is be unnatural? Peregrine would shake his head and Israel would laugh.

I must speak of Peregrine before I get on. Father was another of the mysteries for me as a child. Israel told me that no man sees his father clearly, because he himself stands in the way. In other words, I should look to myself to see Peregrine. This might be the whole of it. A few facts will help. Peregrine was born the eldest son of a professional soldier, Leslie Ide, who was himself the son of a clerk for a railroad. Peregrine's mother, Jane Peregrine, was an Irish Protestant, a younger daughter of a Londonderry haberdasher, who met and married Leslie during the Second World War, soon after the Allied invasion of France. Peregrine and his several brothers spent their earliest years moving from army base to army fort from northern Europe to North America. The boys were excessively attached to their mother, since Leslie was much away at war, or somesuch, and since the family moved to a new home every two years. Peregrine's earliest loyalty was to what he called a "wee bit of Eire" and to Jane's imagination, which was energetic. Jane wrote women's romances for an American publisher. The one I recall best concerned a three-hundred-year-old Irish witch who attempted to assassinate every English oppressor of the Irish from Oliver Cromwell to Winston Churchill, failed each time, was gruesomely executed for her daring, and was then reincarnated in another beautiful, sinister Irish patriot. It was brutal for a romance. Israel told me the mind doctors in New York City would have made much of Jane's influence on her eldest child, my father. I note that Peregrine could chat with a lovely blarney, and he truly believed that if not for misfortune, he would have no fortune at all.

Peregrine was shaken when Leslie enrolled him in a military school, Washington Crossing Military Academy, on the upper Delaware River between New York City and the state of Pennsylvania. I doubt the Cross, as he called it, was as draconian as he remembered. His problem was that, in America, military academies were considered places of last deposit for the delinquent sons of the well-to-do. Any boy, like Peregrine, who found himself in an academy not because he had been a rascal but because his father thought military science and Spartan discipline worth knowing was reduced to futile rage. The result of Peregrine's incarceration was that he, and his eventual bosom chum, Israel Elfers (who, Israel told me, as a New York City Jew, was as much out of place at the Cross as poetry), became young geniuses at defiance and swashbuckling escapades into the surrounding farmland. The headmaster of the Cross, one of Leslie's comrades-in-arms from the Second World War, Fritz "No-Neck" Fitzgore, thought Peregrine and Israel's conduct suggestive of wild dogs. Peregrine and Israel came to be called the Bucks County Bowsers. By their seventeenth birthdays, those two knew what there is to know about being on the run.

Yale University did not change them. By 1966, when Peregrine and Israel entered Yale (to their fathers' relief, to the consternation of Fitzgore, who had written them good recommendations only because it looked good for the Cross), the Vietnam war had transformed all of America into the dynamic of a military academy. A boy was either in his dormitory studying, or he was en route to Vietnam, or he was on the run. Israel told me that he and Father knew the score, and that it was not straight B's to law school. He said it was run for your life before they ran your life down. At the last, Peregrine did not graduate from Yale, as did

Israel. Father committed a wild act of defiant vanity. I think he attacked another student, over a woman I shall soon discuss; he might have attacked the woman; or he might have attacked the police who tried to restrain him; or he might have told the dean what he could do with his presumption to interfere between a man and his woman.

This is not getting closer to Peregrine's heart. Peregrine was more, and more contradictory, than the sum of his iconoclastic episodes. He was quick-tempered, generous, cantankerous, moody unto black despair, devoted to his loved ones with a passionate steadfastness, and as rational in construction as he was irrational in conflict. He was what Israel said was a full-grown naif. The truth of it might be that he was arrested, fixed in time somewhere between adolescence and manhood by unrequited yearnings.

The pagan Norse would have called Peregrine an unskilled shape-changer. He forgave easily. He apologized quickly, too quickly. He made many mistakes, did not understand that he could atone for them, often suffered foolishly in order to make a show of his remorse. He wept more than one might suspect; he did laugh, not easily. He never forgot a kindness; he could not forget or get over a treachery. He was uniformly suspicious of what he understood as fate, and sometimes spat after hearing the word *destiny*. His defeatism, as Israel called it (that was encapsulated too neatly with his pet epigram, "It is what it is when it is"), often seemed superficial, reflexive, cosmetic, more a disguise for his moments of panic and frustration.

Peregrine was politically simpleminded. He had cruel opinions. He had a very bad temper. He had wild solutions. Peregrine said that he hated anyone who claimed the right to command him. I think it was that he confused authority with tyranny. Still, he was what the Norse would have called a Dragon-Worrier, which was what we did call him—my influence. Father was never more animated than when recounting to me the biographies of what he called America's most famous thieves, liars, and mass-murderers, who were also many of America's most famous statesmen. I often thought, even then, that he and Israel enjoyed defaming their favorite monster, Nixon, more than seemed ingenuous. Over the years, those gloomy hate sessions worried Guy to the point that he stopped participating. Peregrine's response was to redouble his curses against America and what it had done to him, to puff himself up even more into a self-possessed and angry, angry, angry man.

Father was also a lonely and unhappy man. Peregrine lived day and night, summer and winter, with a heavy heart and a longing that he transformed into a malady. Indeed, overarching sorrow is so much a part of Peregrine for me, I still have difficulty imagining what he must have been like before exile in Sweden, when he swaggered through long, rich American days. He had been a bounder and a lover. Then Charity Bentham, his heart's desire, had gone forever, and with her, Peregrine's will to pursue happiness. There were women in his life in Stockholm. I overheard them talking about this or that girl, and there were many nights when Peregrine or Israel or both would stay out all night. But Peregrine never brought anyone home to me, as Israel would let Molly Rogers stay with us. Molly sometimes teased Peregrine about his attitude toward her sisters, and she was not met with playfulness. If and when Peregrine engaged in sexual intercourse, it must have been left at that, eroticism, not intimacy or love. It was as if he believed there was no woman in Sweden for him, because he believed his heart irreparably broken, incapable of loving again. I know it is generally understood that time can heal such wounds. For my father, either this was not the case, or else he chose not only to refuse the cure by pretending to stop time in 1973, at my birth, but also to aggravate his disability by reminding himself, as if with a chant, that he had been wronged, cheated, ill-used—in all, betrayed by fate.

I misunderstood all this discrimination between sex and love and brokenheartedness then, of course, but I perceived the symptoms of love gone wrong. Peregrine had a habit of sighing very deeply of a sudden, like a last breath, of just sitting there watching the sun set and then letting out a groan. He could also lapse into dreadful silences. He often walked out of the cinema, especially during motion pictures that Israel characterized as exploiting the trivialities of romance. I recall once, while Peregrine was reading aloud to me one of the nineteenth century's most accomplished sentimentalists, perhaps Thackeray, perhaps James, that Peregrine dropped the book and fell down in front of me, as if in great pain, but without a sound. He lay there, tears streaming down his face, soaking his beard. It was the worst spell he ever had in front of me. It scared me badly. I ran for Israel in the kitchen; and he coaxed Peregrine upright again, then took him for a walk along the canals. I was not invited along, watched them from the window: spindly Israel supporting burly Peregrine as a nurse might assist an invalid. Israel told me later, "Forget it, kid."

I did not, nor should I have. Peregrine did seem to improve over the years, as if he had made peace with his condition. That was no truce. That was a devastation. He quit trying, a man who came to prefer the malady to health. He forgot humor, self-respect, hope, a better day, the gift that was his life. He only wanted to remember, and to torment himself with his memory of, that long-lost American woman named Charity Bentham.

Though it was over forty years ago, and half a world away from me now, that woman's name still stirs and saddens me. Charity Bentham. If this is credible, she was my father's heart. For me, she is the crossroad where my own story parts from Peregrine's. It is of Charity Bentham, and of her violent entrance into my life, that I now must speak at length.

The Nobel Prize Ball

It was the eve of my seventeenth birthday, as burning cold and still as the Norse creation, when my life, as well as the lives of all those I held dear, changed irreparably and forever. It was also the night that it was revealed clearly to me for the first time that my family was accursed with exile, and that for such people, outlawed and outlanded, there can be no going back, there can too readily be bitterness and more defeat.

I assumed that Peregrine, Israel, and I were lucky to have obtained temporary jobs as servants' servants for the Nobel Prize Ball to be held that evening in the King's castle. Twenty-five hundred very important celebrants were°expected in the Great Hall by 10:00 P.M. Ours was heavy and dirty work. I thought Peregrine's mask of dread was due to our labor. In truth, his mind was his face, as the Norse said. No one had told me Charity Bentham was to be there. I thought, in my childish way, that Peregrine could have been more festive; but it was not like me to resent Father's moods, since he changed them as often as his caps. I was happy. Earle, home again at midseason with his bad back, had promised me a surprise birthday present. More, Israel compensated for Peregrine's surliness by outdoing himself with anecdotes about "the good old counterculture days" when "clowns were kings," and with jokes about the King's new castle then still under construction on the exact site of the burned-down Royal Palace. Israel mocked it as "quick-dry Baroque."

Our gang-boss kept us busy hauling furniture and carpets up from the storerooms to the Great Hall, so there was no time to coddle Peregrine. We had been hired for our brawn. Israel, who knew what deeply hurt Peregrine, was preoccupied with the extra weight he had put on his belly over the years. We did bear up better than most. We really needed the money.

By the time we stopped to change into our livery for the ball, we were giddy with aches and sweat. Israel and I shared a bottle of Norse brew and examined our foolish party clothes, black frocks and waistcoats with shabby white linen and silly ties. Israel and I looked sober in comparison to Peregrine. Father's pants were inches too short, and with his full red beard, his shoulder-length hair, and his fixed scowl, he appeared ridiculous. I started to tease Peregrine. Israel shushed me.

One of the King's retainers, a fat man named Rinse, did taunt Peregrine as we filed into the service assembly room. Peregrine reacted out of proportion to the offense. He turned dark, shook, muttered. He grabbed his stomach the way he did when overwhelmed by temper. Rinse backed away. Peregrine seemed a man in an insane rage. Israel reached to calm him. Peregrine tossed him off with one backhanded sweep, as if he did not know him, as if he did not know what he had become in his fury. I saw murder in my father's eyes. It made no sense to me. I moved to offer love. Israel pulled me away. We stood apart from Peregrine, who, alone in the midst of several squat oafs from Stockholm's simpleton population, seemed to talk to himself. I watched him yank a blue booklet from his frock, roll it into a tube, tap it against his breast.

I could not ask Israel for an explanation, because the Nobel people burst in to line us up and read instructions for the evening. They were officious and overbearing. Israel smirked at them and got a withering stare from a small, unattractive overseer, Mrs. Bad-Dober, who persecuted us the rest of the night. Since we were separated from Peregrine, Father was assigned to the cloak room in the entry hall, while Israel and I were sent to the Great Hall. We were to heft trays of food and drink from the dumbwaiters to the King's retainers, who were the only ones meant to circulate among the guests.

Later though, at the edge of the Great Hall, our gang got a rest break because the dumbwaiter lines fouled. The ball was in symphonious progress, and we crowded into an alcove to listen. I was tired and content, and idly pressed Israel about Peregrine. He looked at me sadly, took a big breath, flicked his gray beard, and told me part of the truth.

Back in America before I was born, Israel said, Peregrine had been very much in love with Charity Bentham. They had met at Yale University and continued their romance while Peregrine and Israel dodged the draft for two years. She was good to them, wayfaring youths, and permitted them to stay with her, feeding them, loving them. When the decision was made to flee rather than be arrested for draft evasion, Peregrine had to leave her behind. She drove them to the airport. It was Christmas 1972, and Nixon and Kissinger had unleashed the total destruction of the American bombers on the Vietnamese. It was a time of colossal abandonment. Charity wanted to escape with them, but they did not know where they were going. Israel said, "It was tough on her, since she and your Dad, they were very very close."

Once Peregrine was in Stockholm, he and Charity corresponded every day. They telephoned once a week. Peregrine's family, at the direction of his enraged father, had cut him off, as if he did not exist, and Charity was Peregrine's only hold on his history. Nevertheless, Peregrine insisted Charity carry on with her life. She returned to Chicago and entered graduate school. They made plans for her to join them after her degree.

"Then I came along and ruined it," I said.

Israel said, "No! Peregrine loves you more than himself, more than he ever loved Charity. It would hurt him if he heard you say that. It's why he's never told you this. You changed plans. That's the truth. Without you, we'd've gone all the way down. Always remember that. Peregrine and Charity, it was rough, but it never would have worked after we ran. I don't care what Guy says. Not on this planet. She was a good woman, but people change. She couldn't have made it here. You know your Dad, the original pilgrim. He stuck it out. He's a real hero. He never would deal with those people, though he wanted to because of her. Oh, yeah, he loved her, and she loved him. They were young. They got caught in a war."

I asked Israel if this was why Peregrine cried so much. Israel said that Peregrine had not yet worked out his sadness, that it was frozen in his heart. Israel said that Peregrine had not done anything wrong, and yet he had lost a woman he loved a great deal. "I've been hoping he was through it," he said, "no, I guess I knew he wasn't. He's still fighting. I don't know if I could take what he's had to."

I asked Israel what happened to Charity Bentham. He again told me part of the truth, and not nearly enough for me to see the danger ahead. He said Charity Bentham had earned herself a happy life. She married a man who was a classmate of Israel's and Peregrine's at Yale. His name was Cesare Furore; he became a rich and powerful architect and builder. Charity graduated with a prestigious degree in economic science and became a famous professor in Chicago. "She writes megabooks," he said, "does television, dines at the White House, which is as white as ever. Old Charity, she's hot. If she's been smart, she's forgotten Peregrine. I figure she hasn't thought of him in a decade. Oh, maybe now and then, when she speaks at Yale or flies out of Kennedy Airport. All the people we knew, not just Charity, they stayed with it back home. They belong. We got lost—me, Peregrine, Guy, Earle, all of us."

I told Israel hesitantly that I did not understand. It seemed like such a long time ago. It explained some things about Father, his depressions, why he never talked about women as Israel did, but it seemed to say nothing about Peregrine's anger that night. I was frustrated. I guessed, "Is she here, at the ball?"

Israel sighed. "You want life to make sense? You want it fair? Yeah, I guess you do. Me too. It's this." Israel averted his eyes and continued, as if talking to himself. "Old Charity, she played it big. She went and got herself elected a guest of honor tonight. She finally made that trip to Stockholm. Peregrine and her ought to have some kind of reunion. I hope he handles it well down in the cloakroom. Maybe nothing will happen. It'll be some scene, though; she hands him her sable and he hands her a check. Peregrine's told me he'd never do anything to hurt her. What a life!" He turned back to me, touched my shoulder, said, "You see, Grim, Charity once did something that wasn't right, a long time back, but it sticks in the gut. It was cruel, considering how bad we had it. I think I understand why she did it. It could have been handled better. Peregrine didn't act all that well either. How can I say this? How can I tell you? He's your Dad!"

I tried to be grown up. I asked what we could do for Peregrine, though I still did not understand the problem. Israel made an odd sound in his throat, turned away. There was a pause. He continued in a tense whisper, "You won't understand this. There's a lot I've skipped over. And you need a few years yet watching this comedy we're in, where if you step out-of-bounds just once, you can't get back in. Like poor Peregrine. He's ineligible, forever. But I want you to hear it from me first. Oh, God, Grim, we haven't got what Peregrine needs. Maybe no one does."

Israel slumped against the wall. I was frightened. Something was deeply wrong. I believe I did then sense that he was trying to protect me from despair; however, I did not realize it was the hopelessness of complete and unpardonable exile. I also did not realize he was concealing the full details of Peregrine and Charity's history. The lesson might be, never protect those you love from the truth. I had learned much. I had always known that Father had an unhappy life; I had learned enough from Israel to begin to see that Father had, and had made himself have, a crippled life.

The dumbwaiter was cleared. We were spotted loafing. We scooted back to the triteness of hauling sweetmeats. The rush of guests swept us into a pace that did not abate for hours. I could only smile at Israel as we passed each other with trays. When I did get a chance to think again, it was because Rinse ordered me to the wine cellar to deliver a special key. I weaved through the Great Hall toward the back stairway, and thus enjoyed my first close look at the ball.

The crowd dazzled me, the men in their tapered black coats and brilliant white linen and the women in all colors and cuts of gown. They danced stately waltzes around me. They seemed well loved, well pleased. There was a particular group—taller, healthier, more arrogant—that I guessed were Americans. This was my first exposure to what Israel called the ruling class of my paternal people, so I set a long course to pass by them. The women were diverse, some fair like most of Sweden, others dark and more alluring to me. It is true that one young woman did fascinate me to the point that I stopped to study her as the crowd separated between us. She was sleek, large-boned, tall, olive-skinned, and had thick black hair down to her waist, which she had filled with combs. She had a pouty doll's face, black almond-shaped eyes, with a large mouth and a long smooth neck, like a swan's. I thought her beauty itself. It is an image that I have treasured all my life, and though it does not replace my last picture of Cleopatra, it remains supreme.

The dancers closed about me, and I was forced on. The wild smell of the gathered disoriented me. I stumbled against a side table. I knocked off several glasses, a flower arrangement, and a pile of papers. In the mess was a blue booklet like the one I had seen Peregrine grasp. It was entitled "Meet the Laureates." I made my escape with it. It had finally come to me, slow-witted youth, that Israel had identified Charity Bentham as a guest of honor at the ball.

She was a Nobel Prize winner. I found the entry, which I did not have time to read until after I delivered the key to the King's retainer in the wine cellar and been told to get quickly back to my post. I was intimidated, rushed through the service corridors, missing many turns. I thought myself clumsy. I was actually over-excited by my discovery. It was luck that brought me to the lift bank—good luck or bad, I am not sure—and as I waited for the lift, I read.

Charity Bentham was born and raised in Chicago, in the American Middle West. Her father, Increase, was a Presbyterian minister; her mother, Dorothea, was a professional choir singer. Her three younger sisters, Constance, Chastity, Hope, were married and were either attorneys or business executives. Her baby brother, Trinity, was deceased. Charity Bentham graduated from Yale University's law school and had a doctorate in economic science from the University of Chicago, where she was at the time a member of the faculty. Her list of publications was very long. Her books included *Brave New Benthamites,* which won an honor I cannot recall, and *The Pleasure and Pain Principle in World Markets.* Her most famous work was *The Greatest Good,* which seemed to have won every major award and to have been translated into every major language.

Charity Bentham was a celebrity, the hostess of a television series called *The Twenty-First Century;* and there was a paragraph about the United States government committees that she had either served upon or chaired. The committee I recall most ironically was The President's Special Commission on Resettlement Crises.

And Charity Bentham's relationship with the American government was not simple. She was married to an architect and builder named Cesare Furore, the brother of a former senator from the Middle West who had been nominated as his party's candidate for the presidency of the American Republic. Cesare Furore was described as the developer of futuristic urban communities around the world; the most famous was in Mexico—called Cleopatrium.

There was mention of Charity Bentham being descended, through her German-American mother, from the Royal Family of Great Britain. Of course, there was also prominent mention of her being descended, through her father, from the family of Jeremy Bentham, the eighteenth-century English philosopher.

Also, Charity Bentham was the mother of one daughter, Cleopatra, and the foster mother of several Spanish-American sons.

Charity Bentham was said to be either the first or second woman to be awarded the Nobel Prize exclusively, and was by far the youngest woman, at forty-four, to be so honored. The Nobel Prize selection committee citation read:

"In awarding Professor Bentham the Alfred Nobel Memorial Prize in Economic Science, the committee cites her tireless work assisting the developed nations in dealing humanely with less fortunate nations, and her profound and far-reaching contribution to international harmony."

If my memory is correct, this quotation is irony to an appalling extreme. Charity Bentham, as I was to learn, was the philosopher in the late twentieth century who most concerned herself with the despair of the vanquished, the outlanded, and the exiled. And yet she did so as a privileged member of the community that cast out the unwanted. I shall not explain further here. There is a story to tell that makes my opinion come alive in infamy and reversal. But I feel I must emphasize that nothing about what that woman did and said to achieve her Nobel Prize is unimportant to my life, and to my confession. Fate made her mind my enemy. Luck made her passion and her children my allies, and my victims, and my betrayers.

The lift arrived to interrupt my study of Charity Bentham's letter thanking the Nobel Prize selection committee for her award. She seemed, in her letter, very smart and very happy. This was the woman Israel called "hot." I pictured a goddess, granite-hard and all-knowing, like Frigg, Odin's wife and first among the Norse goddesses, but this distortion was because I understood little of her biography. I did congratulate myself for what I presumed was an adult understanding of Peregrine's anguish. Here was Father's first and, from what I believed to be true, only love, who had risen to incomparable heights in America while he had remained a bottom-dweller. In my sentimental way, I supposed I could feel how Peregrine must feel—hurt, ashamed, afraid, robbed. It did not occur to me that such emotions in an immature man like Peregrine, who believed himself persecuted by ghosts, could lead to far worse than self-pity.

As the lift delivered me to what I thought was the first story of the castle, I considered how bizarre it was that Charity Bentham was said to be descended from royalty. I wondered if Peregrine had known this pretentiousness when he courted her. I imagined it would have disgusted him, descendant of German and Irish swineherds. I did not think that such strangeness might have compelled him to possess her, nor did I think that his possession might have proceeded to marriage. I never asked myself what it was that Israel had "skipped over" in his version of their romance. I did wonder if her royal blood was true, since Israel had told me that the worse snob in America could at best lay claim to ancestors that had been either too incorrigible or too wretched to have remained in Europe. The America that Israel described to me was a huge, fertile, noisy, greedy land of outcasts from the collapse of European, Asian, and African decency, rushing like lunatics to construct a new and greater amalgamation of indecency. That was where Charity Bentham flourished. That was where Peregrine could never go again. I asked myself, what would such a woman make of my father, after all her victories and all his defeats.

Stupidly, I got off the lift on the first floor, in the servants' corridor beneath the grand staircase. I panicked that I might lose my wages for truancy. I charged out of the small grillwork door and into the milling celebrants. I blushed at the stares of the women in the Earl of Gotland's party. I could not rush the staircase. I tried stealth, ducking my head, edging along the wall, it not occurring to me that no six-feet seven-inch gold-maned ice hockey prodigy in ill-fitted livery does anything unnoticed. The stares became more intense. I shrank closer to the wall.

It was luck again, and perhaps bad luck, that one of the few people in the hall who did not notice my awkward chagrin was Peregrine. He was slumped at the end of the bar top in the cloakroom, his hands folded piously before him, his head bent in the most tender pose, his attention fixed upon the willowy, gray-haired, glimmeringly gowned lady of charm and authority before him. They chatted and smiled. Peregrine Ide, pauper, fugitive, servant's servant, flirted with his long-lost Charity; and Charity Bentham, heiress, stateswoman, and honored guest of the Kingdom, flirted with her long-lost Peregrine.

Israel was not pleased when I told him what I had seen. We did not have time to debate. Rinse rushed over and threatened dismissal. I saw Mrs. Bad-Dober scowling in the distance. We took a cue from the simpletons and feigned obliviousness. We huffed and puffed until midnight, when our gang got a half-hour tea break, because the King's speech was due to interrupt everything.

I wanted to get as close to the dais as possible, hoping Charity Bentham might be there. Israel grabbed me and pulled me along with the other workers to the rear service stairs, where, on the chilly landing, everyone relaxed with tobacco and quiet.

"*Surprise, mon guerrier!*" cried Guy, charging up with a birthday cake held high. Behind him came Molly Rogers and Thord Horshead, followed by Thord's lover, Orri Fljotson, and Orri's younger brother, Gizur, called Sail-Maker, both of them with armfuls of drink and utensils. Last up the stairs was the immense shadow of Earle Littlejohn, his arms crossed oddly. They sang to me a suggestive limerick to the tune of "Happy Birthday," in English, Swedish, and French. I was embarrassed, because many of the simpletons joined in the shouting. Israel pounded me on the back; Molly and Guy, pulling me down to their height, kissed me wetly; and Orri—a ravenous man at five feet tall—demanded we cut the cake. I asked, "How did you get in here?"

"Trifling matter, birthday boy," said Thord. Thord's English was peculiar, learned mostly from eighteenth-century English novels. He was tall, wraithlike, bright and gentle, might have been pretty were his features and person less elongated. His great talent was patronage. As art dealer, he was owed favors by most of the well-placed members of the homosexual community in Stockholm. As "extraordinary tradesman," his term for smuggler, he simply owned every other third-level official in the government. He could get what he wanted when he wanted it. There were limits, but not for social functions. His taste was for the shadows, however, so though he wielded a carte blanche in the then casually carnal and corrupt Kingdom of Sweden, he exercised his power eccentrically. The only man I knew who did not approve of Thord's manner was Guy, but Israel assured me that this was just one of Guy's personality quirks, nothing mean-spirited.

Once we were arranged on the landing like a picnic party, Molly had me blow out the candles. Orri and Gizur took charge of distributing hats, cake, and wine. I leaned against the balcony next to Molly, Israel's great love, whose affections Israel had finally secured exclusively for himself, though they had yet to marry. Molly was a bosomy red-haired woman, irrepressible and never anything but even-tempered, though she wrote dark verses; she held me bent forward to keep kissing me on the head, mussing my mane, which was then my vanity. It occurred to me to tell her that seventeen years old made me a man. I did not, accepting her pinching in silence, eating the cake with my fingers.

"What wish?" said Israel.

"I'm not telling," I said.

"A lass to sport with for many a season?" said Thord.

"*La femme! L'amour! La vie!*" cried Guy.

"Certainly not," I said.

"Aren't we the serious one?" said Molly.

"How about two of them?" said Earle, stepping from the side to pull two squirming animals from his coat, handing them over. I squatted up to hold them, two eight-week-old husky puppies, both bitches, part Chinook and part wolf, with large floppy ears, ferocious tails, and soft tongues that attacked the sugar on my hands.

"The blonde is Goldberg," said Earle, "and the white is Iceberg. Their momma is a sled dog. Their daddy is missing."

"When did you name them that?" said Israel. "Whoever heard of a husky called Goldberg? Iceberg I rather like."

"I like them both very much, thank you all," I said, struggling with them. They had smelled the cake; Molly caught Iceberg as she dove for it. Goldberg yelped as I grabbed her hindquarters. We gorged ourselves, and Earle fed the pups so much cake that they overdosed on sugar and passed out in my lap.

By then, Israel had talked with Guy and Thord about Peregrine and Charity. Their faces were fixed with worry. If I had been bolder, I might have joined them, asked them what we could do to make Peregrine feel loved. But I did not press them, choosing to act. I jumped up with Goldberg and Iceberg tucked in my waistcoat and announced, "I'm going to show them to Father."

"Not now," said Israel. He might have elaborated on his intuition had not Rinse then appeared on the landing.

"Who are these people?" he shouted. "Guard!" he called, gesturing as if we were all assassins. The simpletons, whom we had won with the cake, tried to shout Rinse down. This made him crazier.

Deft Guy, whose craft it was to think in motion, advised a general retreat. Thord ignored Guy and tried to deal, taking some large bills from Orri (as a serious art connoisseur and cautious pirate, Thord never carried cash on his person) in order to bribe Rinse, which might have worked had several castle security men not then arrived to assert themselves officiously.

In the confusion, all the hired help, dressed in black, slipped unchallenged by the security men. Israel jerked his head at me, meaning I should follow along. I raced ahead, intending to get to Peregrine in the cloakroom. What I would do then, I did not think. My conduct was rash and clumsy. It was also decisive, for Earle had taught me to follow instinct first, never to stand still and risk being overrun. Ice hockey is not wisdom, of course; at seventeen it was half of all I knew (the rest being Beowulf and Norse lore). With my puppies against my breast and a stomach full of cake and worry, I pushed back into the Great Hall, heading as directly as I could for the staircase. I got full across the room before a woman's strong voice from the dais distracted me.

"This wonderful night would not have been possible without the unquestioning love and selfless help of my family." Charity Bentham was at the microphone. She was ringed by radiantly proud men and women, obviously her family, and by two in such ornamentation they had to be the King and the Queen of Sweden. On the dais behind them were other opulent dignitaries. All seemed exceedingly happy (that is, Good). At that moment, as I squeezed as close to the corner of the dais as possible, looking over the thousands of wealthy, well-informed, and well-pleased citizens of the most well-fixed nations of the world, I realized how intimidating property, class, blood, and knowledge can seem to those whose lives have been without such, or who have been excluded from such by accident or cruelty. I was a very young, very underinformed twentieth-century man, and I did not begin to understand how truly powerful those in that hall were. Yet even in my ignorance I was overwhelmed. Their smell, their hum, their bright eyes and vitality seemed to push me back against the wall, into the stone, out of the castle. I felt what it is to be a full-grown man and yet be insignificant—ineligible, as Israel had said. Perhaps I felt invisible, although not in the scientific sense. I mean invisible as Israel explained it to me, as how American Negroes, or European Jews, or any number of discarded, destitute, forgotten people have felt insignificant, ineligible, invisible in history. I felt as if I did not matter, did not exist, was not ever to be cared about, loved, respected, missed, mourned. It is a frightening thought, whenever you have it, whatever it is, and the more so if the first time is at the edge of a cavern filled with such visibility. I think what protected me from being crushed by the realization of my meaninglessness was my youth. At seventeen, robust and curious, one is, or should be, full of hope. That I was a penurious bastard, without mother, country, education, legal status, prospects of any reasonable sort, did not challenge me. There was something that did, and it also confounded me. It was their—I mean the assembly's—apparent kindness, benevolence, sweetness. Those people were among the men and women who can be said to be the masters of the earth, and of mankind. They were power and authority. Yet they stood relaxed, amiable, polite, cheery. Their smiles were lovely, and most certainly charitable. They held the power of goods and knowledge, and they dispensed from their holdings. Yes, they were a charitable lot. I did not understand what that truly meant then. Their benevolent might fooled me. I was a young fool, and still might be a fool, yet now I understand charity.

I add that even with all the above gray thinking, I never lost sight of the profound difference between those men of rank and my family. They were in the King's castle as guests. Israel, Peregrine, and I were there as help. We had rights, and chances; in comparison to those of the inheritors, we were kitchen knaves.

"And lastly, my lover, my companion, my strength, my friend, the father of my child, and the man without whom none of it would have been half as much fun, my husband, Cesare Furore," finished Charity Bentham, taking the hand of a darkly handsome man, only slightly taller than she, broad and powerful. There was final applause. The King spoke up again to introduce the next laureate.

The Benthams and Furores made ready to descend the dais by the ramp not ten feet before me. I studied them: first, a small lady whom I took as Mother Bentham, she being helped down by a very pregnant woman whom I took as one of the sisters. Then came an attendant handling a wheelchair bearing a sick-looking man who held himself as if he had had a stroke—the Reverend Increase Bentham. Two more attractive women followed close behind, both arm in arm with escorts. I noted that the Bentham family characteristic was that authoritative fix to their features, which was easily taken for haughtiness or extraordinary piety. Each sister had a prominent nose that was not her mother's.

The Furores took the ramp. I watched Cesare Furore. He was most attractive. Thord might have opined that he was overdrawn, a theatrical profile, studied, stunning. His manner in contrast seemed casual, anything but melodramatic. He was especially affectionate toward Charity Bentham, keeping her hand close to his heart, kissing it once—all quite Mediterranean of him, as my novel-reading had taught me. Cesare Furore held his wife intimately as he reached back to take the arm of the very same tall, dark, doll-faced young woman with the swan's neck whom I had favored earlier. This temptress was Cleopatra Furore. I was not then informed enough as to the volcanism of fate to comment: like fool father, like fool son. There is also the Bible's talk about the sins of the father being visited upon the sons, and my passing knowledge of the Greeks reminds me of their warning: Know thyself, if you dare. The Norse have it best in my case: A man with an appetite for longing will get a stomach full of trouble.

Peregrine vaulted onto the ramp. He slammed Cesare Furore. He grabbed Charity Bentham by her shoulder, spinning her away from her husband and daughter. He shook her. He screamed at her. I could see Peregrine above me as sure as I ever saw anything. His face was twisted, as if in a great pain. He seemed aflame. It was passion. I was fixed in place, like everyone else, by the intensity of Peregrine's attack. Charity Bentham stared at him in disbelief. It must have occurred to her that this might be the man who would end her life. Peregrine shook her harder. Her combs fell out, her braided hair flying wildly. She opened her mouth, could not speak, as Peregrine screamed the more—unintelligible things, mad words, sounds from the dark. Cesare Furore recovered first of all of us, reaching to protect his wife. Peregrine kicked him down.

The officials on the dais were slow to realize the threat. An ancient German laureate's amplified voice initially drowned Peregrine's ranting. That did not last. I have father's lungs. I know what can be done when we lose control. Holding Charity Bentham like plunder, he screamed a wave of hurt and bitterness, for all to hear, to judge:

"You are my wife! You lied! You are mine! I never gave you up! That was your doing! I never agreed! They wanted it! They tricked me! Tell them! Tell the truth!"

Charity Bentham was helpless. She wailed forth tears so big that they drained all dignity from her being. She seemed in a silent terror, as if not surprised, rather as if caught in her own nightmare.

"Tell your lover who I am!" screamed Peregrine. "Tell them all! I am your husband! That paper is nothing! He doesn't exist! Tell them or I swear I will kill you! As you've killed me! I am dead! Do you understand! You left me to die alone!"

By then the officials had signaled the security forces. From all directions, they converged on Peregrine. Two slipped from the dais and tried to get hold of him without damaging Charity Bentham. Peregrine tossed them aside by using her body as a truncheon. He seemed increasingly desperate as he backed down the ramp, holding Charity Bentham high above him, screaming, "Don't you see what it's been for me? How do you think I survived? I only had one thing to live for! I lived for you! I thought you'd come back to me! When you were free of them! I thought they'd trapped you! I would have fought for you! I've been here! Where can I go? Why didn't you come for me? All I ever wanted was for you to say you loved me! You didn't have to give up anything for me! You could have kept your things! You just had to say that you loved me! But not him! I can't stand that! How could any man take such a thing? Please, Charity, please, dear God, please! Help me!"

Peregrine stopped shaking her. He lowered her to the ramp. He hugged her to his breast. She stood there limply. Slowly she regained herself, coming to life. She reached around Peregrine as best she could—he dwarfed her, though she was not small—and hugged him back. They stood there together, weeping, shuddering.

The security guards closed from above and below. Charity Bentham clung as fast to Peregrine as he to her. The guards pried them apart. Peregrine did not react until they had taken her a step back. Then he exploded, flailing angrily, lunging toward her. Two guards jumped him from behind, pulled him from the ramp, and rolled him to the floor. Musicians scattered from the pileup.

Peregrine held his own—he seemed superhumanly strong—until two more guards joined the fray. This was clearly unfair. I forgot myself.

"Father, it's me," I said, springing to his defense, grabbing one guard by his coat and flinging him backward, checking another with a sweeping hook of my leg.

"Don't hurt him," cried Charity Bentham from above us.

"Get out," Peregrine shouted to me from the floor. He twisted against an armlock. I prepared, watching my back, to kick them away. I might have carried the day. I was half a foot taller than my largest foe, as skilled in close combat as any. Often afterward I daydreamed about what I might have done to save Peregrine from his fate. I do believe I felt then, for the very first time, the darkness inside me—the beginnings of shape-changing. It was not to be. I had forgotten my puppies. Goldberg and Iceberg evacuated my waistcoat, one rocketing high, the other low, both yelping. I stood stunned, calling them back.

The guards took advantage of my surprise to take me down. My dogs, to their undying fame, stood by their man. Had they been even half-grown, those two, having been close to me for a quarter of an hour, would have killed to defend me. As it was, at only eight weeks and dopey on sugar, they harassed my enemies ferociously, sending up a howl worthy of a pack. For one glorious moment, it was four on four; me, Peregrine, Goldberg, and Iceberg versus them. Then they reinforced, and we surrendered.

My Father's Crime

I was dragged through the crowd, down corridors and staircases, into the bowels of the castle. I was vaguely aware of the angry faces staring down at me. There was a cursing and crying out in the ballroom, followed by a pervasive stillness, the sort of shock that follows a public furor.

I realize that I seem to fear the facts. Even after more than four decades, in another century, another millennium, it is not possible to recall that night without regrets so deep that I bow my head and pray forgiveness for the damaged, which all of us were, and for the culpable, if any were. Ignorance of one's contribution to a crime does not excuse one, or the crime, or anything. I should have seen. I should have guessed. I was there, at the center, and I could have tried. What? Something quick, something apt. It is I who should apologize to Peregrine. He needed help, he begged for help, and not my boyish sort, Robert Louis Stevenson and a leap from the rigging. He needed respect, steadfast sympathy, patience, calm love. I provided only the sham of indomitable camaraderie. It was a cheat. I cannot dismiss the thought that my interference in Peregrine's affairs somehow prolonged his ordeal and led him to compound his wrong with far worse.

They took us down three levels. As I have mentioned, the King's castle was still under construction. There was not yet a security complex. Workmen had finished the formal parts of the castle first, had left the auxiliary aspects incomplete. There were stacks of lumber, piles of brick and stone. We finally passed into a long, narrow, well-lit lesser hall that I took as a promenade. Three of the walls were up, the fourth only blocked out.

As we came in, a group already there turned to watch. I spotted Rinse, and behind him Israel, Thord, Earle, and several guards. Rinse did not see me; I did not see Guy, Molly, Orri, or Gizur, who I supposed correctly had avoided detention. Israel saw me, did not wave. I could not acknowledge him, my arms trussed behind me. The guards were furious with me and Peregrine,

yanking us across the room and into an antechamber at the right.
The guards arranged a straight-backed bench and slammed us
down, passing the short chain of the handcuffs through a slat of
the bench. We were pressed. together, bent over and twisted sideways. We were surrounded by security guards in garish, leather-
upholstered uniforms. Their chief, a beefy man who more whis-
pered than talked, introduced himself as Skaldur, told us were
were in a lot of trouble. Skaldur left in a contained fury. Peregrine and I sat silently for a time; a laugh from outside (Thord's
as he cajoled for understanding) startled Peregrine.

"I'm sorry, I'm so sorry," he said to me.

"I shouldn't have taken the penalty, huh?" I said as jovially as
possible, referring inanely to an ice hockey concept.

"This can't ruin your life, too. Why did this have to happen?
What's wrong with me? Now what am I going to do?"

Skaldur returned, leading Charity Bentham and Cesare Furore into the room. Peregrine flinched at this, tried to stand, was
pushed down roughly by a guard.

"That will be enough of that," said Cesare Furore in English.
He held himself so commandingly that the guards snapped to attention. I could see that his powerful build and angular features
made him a center in a crisis. He was overbearing, overmuch,
unless one was sympathetic to him. Skaldur must have been, for
he repeated Cesare Furore's order in Swedish, then dismissed all
but two of his men. The others filed out and shut the door, but
because the wall was not completed, I could see them through the
superstructure.

"Did they hurt you, Peregrine?" asked Charity Bentham.

"Let the boy go, please?" said Peregrine.

"We must answer questions," said Skaldur.

"We're not going to bring charges, Peregrine," said Cesare
Furore in a warm, paternal voice.

"Then let him go," said Peregrine.

"Where are my pups?" I tried.

"It's my fault, all of it," said Charity Bentham. She had regained herself, standing apart from her husband. Her hair was
still mussed, her cosmetics ruined, which made her seem more
vulnerable than was the case. Her compassion seemed genuine.
That haughty Bentham look could mislead. She continued, "I

should have explained to you earlier, Peregrine. We aren't what and who we were. Meeting you tonight like that, it was wonderful, exciting. But I didn't mean to upset you. What I said up there, about Cesare, it was only a speech. I didn't prepare it with you in mind. How was I to know you would be here? We're old enough now to forgive each other. Will you forgive me?"

"I won't listen to your lies! Adultery!" cried Peregrine. I felt then that I did not know Father. Everyone jumped at his outburst, the guards outside flinging open the door. Skaldur reached over to take Peregrine by the shoulders. Past the guards, through the door, I could see Israel. It was just a flash, but I could see them all being escorted out of the chamber, much laughing and good humor from Thord and one of the guards. I supposed at the time, correctly, that they had been brought down for questioning like us, and since they had committed no crime, and since Rinse was a liar, they had been released. I wanted to call to Israel and Thord for help with Peregrine, then thought better of it, intuiting it was best to keep our transgressions separate and our familiarity a secret. I was right, though I wish now that I had risked it, cried out, bolted, done anything foolhardy.

Cesare Furore arranged two chairs before us. He indicated to his wife to sit, and when she hesitated, he sat himself neatly and began evenly, "We've known each other a long time, Peregrine. Twenty years? More. What's happened is no one's fault. People do grow apart. Things intervene that keep us from our dreams. This isn't unusual. It doesn't have to continue. A long time ago, when we first met at school, you told me—we were celebrating, after a Harvard game—you said, 'It is what it is when it is.' Do you remember? We'd gambled on a sure thing and lost. The game ended in a tie. I didn't like what you said at the time. I've reconsidered since then."

Cesare Furore went on like this about several other collegiate incidents, all cleverly nostalgic, finally returning to his theme.

"If you still believe what you told me, then what has happened to us must make sense to you. We're old and dear friends. You and I have a lot in common. At least, we have had. Nothing has happened to keep us apart now. We aren't enemies. We can work together on this. You know that anger isn't a solution. What happened tonight, it is regrettable but totally understandable. You

were overcome. We can learn from the past. It is possible. Your concerns are natural. I think this is all very sad."

"Is this your son, Peregrine?" said Charity Bentham, sitting opposite me. She took Cesare Furore's hand. Why did she have to do that? I do not excuse her. It was stupid, might have been cruel. I took my lead from Father, would not answer them.

"Let the boy go, Cesare," said Peregrine, seemingly under control again. "You can do anything you want to me."

"We don't want to do anything to you," said Cesare Furore. "You and your son, if he is your son, this boy, are free to go. Isn't that correct, Mr. Skaldur?"

"What is your name?" said Charity Bentham to me.

Peregrine rattled the chains. He didn't want me to name myself. Is this proof he knew what he was going to do? I think not. He was frightened, was being cautious. Cesare Furore thought Peregrine was objecting to our cuffs, ordered Skaldur to remove them. Skaldur hesitated, then compromised with his caution, releasing me, leaving the cuffs on Peregrine, so that he was free from the bench, not free to go.

"I want my dogs back," I said.

"Go on. Get them. Get out," said Peregrine. "Tell Izzie not to wait up, you know? It's gonna be right, in the end."

I stepped shakily to the door. Charity Bentham leaned back in her chair and studied me. Skaldur opened the door, looked hard at me, then told the guards to return my puppies and to escort me to the service exit. I tucked them back into my waistcoat. They had relieved themselves on the floor nearby—all that sugar—and the room reeked. It would have been funny if not for Peregrine's posture. I turned to see Father's face just as the door closed. He looked exhausted, stiff, hurt, and had one quality I could not identify. It was resignation. The last I heard, Cesare Furore had started talking again.

I walked through the archway, urged on by a guard behind me. Israel had straggled back from the rest and lingered at the exit, arguing with Rinse. It was a ruse, for as soon as he saw me he broke off and signaled me to follow at a distance. Once clear, Israel grabbed me and we sped around the corner, down the access road, and into Thord's waiting sled. Earle hugged me, the puppies squealed, we all laughed at our escape. Orri drove us

straight home, where Guy, Molly, and Thord welcomed us with tea and inquiries. I told them what I had witnessed in the Great Hall and what I knew of Charity Bentham and her husband. Thord made telephone calls through the night. That was how he heard the news. We were at breakfast. I do not remember my first reaction. I do not want to try.

Peregrine Ide murdered Cesare Furore. He strangled him. He crushed his windpipe. He hanged him, holding him at arm's length above his head, using the short chain of the handcuffs as a garrote. As best he could that first morning, Thord pressed his informants in government for details. The newspaper reports were slow in coming and so sensationalized as to be worthless. Also, there were ghoulish rumors on the radio; there was unrestrained slander on the street. And over the next weeks, there followed Byzantine political machinations attendant upon the crime, the trial, and the sentence of life imprisonment without parole. Briefly but devastatingly for all, Sweden became hysterical over the murder in the King's castle by a so-called alien indigent. It is enough here to say that the remnant of the American exile community that had stayed on in Stockholm through the 1980s (either detained, jailed, or, like my family, wanted elsewhere) was soon to suffer for Peregrine's crime.

I heard little of the infamy directly, since I left Stockholm the afternoon of my seventeenth birthday, escorted by Orri to the closed-down boys' camp at Vexbeggar. Israel said it was a precautionary move. It was actually crucial, because the authorities were soon searching Stockholm for "Peregrine Ide's accomplice." I was suddenly as much a fugitive as Peregrine had ever been.

Since it seems to me now revealing of itself, I report the following of what happened in that anteroom, on that night, after I left Father. It is fragmentary, pieced together from several sources, only one of whom was an eyewitness (Skaldur, whose statement to the court was surprisingly sympathetic to Peregrine). Peregrine never again spoke of that night. Charity Bentham would not, or could not, talk about it with me.

Cesare Furore had continued making appeals to Peregrine. Peregrine would not respond. I imagine he sulked, as was his way when he had been childish. Charity Bentham asked Cesare Furore to leave Peregrine be, saying that if Peregrine wanted to solve

his problems, he was the man for it, that he probably preferred to confront his past by himself. If that is what she said, she was perceptive. Cesare Furore ignored her advice and burdened Peregrine with facts.

Israel had told me only part of the truth. Peregrine and Charity Bentham had married the very same day Peregrine and Israel had fled America; they had consummated their marriage in Charity's ancient Volvo, parked discreetly in an airport lot. Israel stood watch. Later, Charity's father, Increase Bentham (who, Israel told me, had detested Peregrine, thought him a fraud and ne'er-do-well) had the marriage annulled. Cesare Furore said that Increase Bentham had bungled the annulment, that he had forced it on Charity while she was on the mend from the news, conveyed in a letter from Peregrine, that he had a bastard son. Cesare Furore explained that he had checked the annulment papers and acted carefully. He instructed his lawyer—after his own marriage to Charity—to have Peregrine cited for deserting his wife. When the suit was brought to the attention of the court, it was possible, though messy, to have Peregrine, as a fugitive from justice, declared no longer Charity Bentham's husband. I might be conflating legalisms here, confusing one state's statute with another state's codicil. It does not matter. Peregrine never contested the annulment, had in fact refused to communicate with Charity after his one confessional letter—in shame, I suppose, for being the father of me. In the end, Cesare Furore thought, as a final security, to remarry Charity Bentham some years later.

Cesare Furore concluded that either way it was argued, annulment or desertion, Peregrine and Charity Bentham were no longer married, had not been married for years, and had possibly never been, legally speaking, more than "unconsummated marriage partners" (the Volvo episode being legally challengeable, something about it not being a place of residence). Cesare Furore promised Peregrine that there had been no acrimony in his legal actions against Peregrine, that he had been acting correctly to protect his wife, his daughter, and all their futures.

Peregrine interrupted, "I have no future."

Cesare Furore answered, "I am sure we can move on that. My brother, as you might know, has served in the Senate. My family is not, and I am not, without influence in Washington."

Those were said to be Cesare Furore's last words; this might be apocryphal, a newspaper editor's idea of drama. Peregrine attacked him. He grabbed him by the throat and hung on. The two wrestled from one side of the room, crashing through the flimsy superstructure and into the promenade on the other. Skaldur ordered his men to get them apart; they were either idiots or impeded by the woodwork. I cannot portray the contest blow for blow. I cannot believe the newspaper reports were anything but lies. It is fair to assume that Cesare Furore did fight back. It is not clear if he knew right away that he was in the death grip of a man made insane by passion, longing, injustice, vengeance, hopelessness, self-hatred. Having seen Cesare Furore just before, I doubt if he understood how sick Father was. He might have thought he was dealing with a runaway child. He actually was baiting and fighting with a man in a delirium of despair and remorse, who felt himself a trapped, mortally wounded animal. More, I argue now that Peregrine was likely so ashamed of what he had done to Charity Bentham on the ramp, of what little he had to show his lost wife for those eighteen desperate years, that he had wanted to destroy himself, and that his self-loathing had been deflected upon the persecutor at hand, Cesare Furore, who had stupidly invoked the idea of "Washington," Peregrine's blackest, most fantastic foe. Peregrine hanged a man, yes; he must have also thought he was hanging 1972, Nixon, the Selective Service Act, the Congress, men of property, all that he believed had condemned him unfairly and totally, had left him, as he said, a man without a future.

This is not to excuse Father. He did an ugly and wrong thing, a criminal thing. He suffered for it the rest of his life. He suffered for it immediately as well. The guards—with Skaldur screaming orders, with Charity Bentham begging Peregrine to stop—pounded Peregrine from all sides. Peregrine cleaved to his crime. Do I seem to favor Peregrine's supernatural strength in murdering Cesare Furore? I do not mean it so. He was my father. They beat him mercilessly. They smashed him with bricks and boards. They fractured his skull, broke his ribs, shattered his knee, trying to cut him down. Cesare Furore tore at Peregrine's face, and did gouge Peregrine's left eye so badly that it later required two torturous operations before it had to be removed in the King's prison.

Skaldur, in desperation, produced a pistol and shot Peregrine twice in the back. That the bullets did not kill Peregrine outright was not only a miracle but also an act of fate that preserved Peregrine for further punishment. The bullets did stagger him, and he dropped Cesare Furore. Peregrine went to his knees. The guards dragged Cesare Furore's body away from Peregrine. Peregrine would not go down and, lunging forward, crawled toward Cesare Furore on that shattered knee, screaming oaths so mad and dark I shall not repeat them. The guards encircled Peregrine, momentarily disoriented by his macabre perseverance. Peregrine's bloody face was said to have radiated an aura of demonic lust. That is nonsense.

Charity Bentham fell upon Cesare Furore. Peregrine screamed at her, "You're mine!" At that, fearing he would attack the woman, the guards pummeled him flat. Peregrine lay broken and alive, not an arm's length but a lifetime of defeat from his beloved Charity Bentham. And Charity Bentham lay insensate atop her second husband's corpse. She was alive also but—and this I say because I swear by it—eternally undone by her own proud, ambitious, duplicitous heart, that had loved two men, and betrayed two men, and cursed two men.

Brave New Benthamism

I n hiding in Vexbeggar for nearly five years, I had abundant time, and more abundant persuasion, to study Charity Bentham. I was embarrassed that I had not understood her prodigious learning. I felt that if I could puzzle all of her out, perhaps I could also understand why Peregrine lay alone in isolation on the King's prison island near Stockholm. Back then, I am not sure that I did more than further confuse myself as to the way of the modern world where, according to what Israel said, "if you step

out-of-bounds just once, you can't get back in." Now I can tell this
about that woman's mind, because I truly believe it has meant
everything for what has happened to me and mine, for where I
am today, here, alone, less angry than argumentative about what
I have learned.

Charity Bentham was a utilitarian. She advocated the principle of utility, or goodness. She maintained that only Good is Good,
that only Good is desirable, that the correct action among many
possibilities is the one that produces the greatest amount of Good,
and that one can recognize what is Good by the fact that Good
causes happiness, while that which is not Good causes unhappiness. She further maintained that common morality, common decency, and common sense are intrinsically utilitarian concepts.
Rational men and women are said to know that only by doing
Good can one be happy and make others happy.

I caution those who find, on first glance, that utilitarianism
seems trivial. It is not that. It seemed to me, at first, very clever
and above all else a practical way to live. For crucial example,
ethics is a profoundly important kind of philosophy; the business
of ethics is to recognize good and to do good, a most desirable
endeavor. According to utilitarians, only utilitarianism provides
ethics with a rigorous method both to recognize Good and to do
Good. Utilitarians opine that utilitarianism comforts one while at
the same time it guides, advises, assesses—providing a rich tradition with which one may resist and overcome the enemies of reason and reasonable men. These enemies are said to be habit,
prejudice, custom, ritual, instinct, feelings, or any other characterization of nonintellectual ethics, which are collectively called
"deontological ethics." (Deontology is the study of moral obliga-
tion and is regarded as stuff and nonsense by utilitarians, who are
exceedingly sensible people.)

In sum, utilitarianism is said to confirm the enlightened man
as the superior man and, more importantly, as the right man.

How does it work? With simple arithmetic, and also with what
Jeremy Bentham (the eighteenth-century founder of utilitarianism, and Charity Bentham's ancestor) called the "hedonic calculus." Jeremy Bentham proposed that experiencing Good could be
measured in units of pleasure, each assigned a positive 1, and that
experiencing what was not good could be measured in units of

pain, each assigned a negative 1. Jeremy Bentham declared that neither a unit of pleasure or a unit of pain can be analyzed, but that both can be easily recognized.

When one is confronted with a decision, one need consider how many units of pleasure (positive) and pain (negative) each possible alternative action will engender; and then one need only compare the sum for each action, choosing the action that produces the largest sum, the greater or greatest Good.

It might seem that assigning units of pleasure and pain to one's conduct is arbitrary and silly; however, it is just because the hedonic calculus requires discretion, awareness of limits, and a temperate worldliness that, say the utilitarians, utilitarianism appeals to men and women who have nothing in common with each other but their utilitarianism. Utilitarianism might seem sloppy, piecemeal, even timid; it is still argued to be more useful than any other sort of ethics in coping with modern experience. More, utilitarianism in its many aspects—act, rule, universal, ideal, et cetera hair-splittings—is said to be best not as a descriptive ethics (what must be done, what should have been done) but as a normative ethics (what ought to be done, what might have been done). It whispers before the fact. It reigns after the fact. It is fueled by caution, dispassion, endless reconsideration, wordy objectivity. Utilitarians shift their positions, opinions, judgments, proscriptions, according to and depending upon perceived circumstances. The overwhelming characteristic that emerged from the scrupulous debates—Jeremy Bentham versus J. S. Mill versus Henry Sidgwick versus G. E. Moore versus Charity Bentham—was that these were extraordinarily pragmatic people. They did not want an ethical example that stood apart from history, as they said did Judaism, Catholicism, Marxism. They wanted a system that adapted with history—come what may.

With utilitarianism, everything is in the example. So I offer, for example: Charity Bentham married Peregrine Ide, which I assign two units of pleasure; Peregrine abandoned Charity, which I assign two units of pain. The sum is zero. Charity Bentham then married Cesare Furore and gave birth to Cleopatra, which I assign three units of pleasure; in order to do so, Charity had to unmarry Peregrine, which I assign two units of pain. The sum is positive 1.

A utilitarian, comparing Charity's historical action to her choices, would say that she acted correctly, with utility.

There are two objections here. The first might come from the deontological ethicists. These people, who argue that an act is right or wrong in itself, regardless of consequences (e.g., divorce is always wrong), would say that Charity's marriage to Peregrine was fine and that her happiness afterward was not significant, that her unmarrying Peregrine was wrong (or "cruel," as Israel said), and that her subsequent marriage to Cesare compounded her wrong, as did everything consequent of her second marriage—love, birth, fame.

Utilitarians would answer deontological criticism thus: Charity's marriage to Peregrine was meaningless, since it produced no Good. In correcting her miscalculation, Charity produced Good, and produced more Good than not correcting it would have produced. Therefore, Charity was right, under the circumstances, though perhaps not as praiseworthy as she might have been if she had married Cesare initially. However, praise and blame do not signify.

The second objection might come from what I call the sentimentalists, those who consider the heart before they regard the intellect. They might say that Charity was a dear fool to marry Peregrine the very day of his flight, that she was more right than wrong in unmarrying Peregrine afterward (especially since she was probably deeply hurt by the news that Peregrine had a son), that she was blessed in making such a good marriage to Cesare, and that she should have anticipated that, though her conduct was proper and understandable, there were aspects of the affair that made her appear less than kind and virtuous.

Utilitarians would answer sentimentalists thus: stuff and nonsense. Folly, pridefulness, fortune, kindness, and virtue do not signify.

Charity Bentham did not win her Nobel Prize because she married Peregrine, or because she bore Cleopatra. She was famous because she applied her utilitarianism and intelligence to what she called "Brave New Benthamism."

"The New Benthamite holds," wrote Charity Bentham in the preface to her *New Benthamite Reader,* "that the State desires Good. The State conducts itself correctly when it engages in activity that

produces Good, and produces more Good than if it had not engaged in this activity, and produces the greatest Good to be gained
from this activity."

Charity Bentham followed this to its logical conclusion, and
innovatively beyond, taking her lead from Jeremy Bentham's thesis that the basis of the State was the principle of utility. Jeremy
Bentham had opined that the State was a construction resulting
from the fact that its citizenry sought, with the hedonic calculus,
happiness for themselves and their fellow citizens.

Significantly, Jeremy Bentham argued that the State was no
superbeing, no Leviathan, with a mind and motives of its own.
Rather, he wrote, the State was the sum total of its citizens' pursuit
of Good, was what a later follower of Jeremy Bentham's philosophy, or Benthamite, would describe poetically as "of the people,
by the people, for the people." Men and women ceded authority
to the State, Jeremy Bentham concluded, not because they feared
the State, but because in so doing they increased the Good resulting from the exercise of the authority of the State. And the amount
of Good was always in proportion to the number of citizens supporting the State: democracy produces more good for a citizenry
than benevolent despotism; tyranny produces more good for a
citizenry than anarchy.

It was clear to me why Jeremy Bentham had wielded profound political influence in the eighteenth century on both the
early American Republic and the fledgling French Republic. More,
I understood why Jeremy Bentham and the Benthamites (especially the English philosopher, John Stuart Mill, who renamed the
movement utilitarianism) became the philosophical heroes of the
liberal democracies of the nineteenth century, particularly for the
United States of America and for the United Kingdom of Great
Britain and Ireland, both of whom exported their utilitarian forms
of government to their colonial empires. The historical development (either by evolution or revolution) of sophisticated capitalist
and communist states, so far from detouring from the principle
of utility, tended to institutionalize it in suggestively prosaic man-
ners, hence the abundance of people's republics, democratic
republics, unions of socialist republics, and parliamentary mon-
archies. Utilitarianism seems the basis for the twentieth-century
State.

Charity Bentham seized on this result and, with scholarship and what could be considered some philosophical sleight of hand, developed it for her own purposes, that is, New Benthamism.

She acknowledged that the State was not a Leviathan. But then she proposed that there was wisdom in inquiring why it was that a State's citizens preferred to anthropomorphize their government, such as the Americans' Uncle Sam, the Britons' John Bull, the Russians' Bear (or Party). This was romantic fantasy, Charity Bentham admitted; yet it was so persistent an aspect of international politics since the Enlightenment that it must be regarded as a popular expression of yearning toward a way of thinking of the world. Given mankind's penchant for (perhaps utter dependence upon) analogy, Charity Bentham argued that a State's citizenry thought of their State with reference to other States as one extraordinarily large person amid other extraordinarily large persons. The State was not demonstrably a Leviathan, she added, but since men thought of it as a Leviathan in relation to other States, was it not appropriate to pursue this idiom? It seemed the will of the people, and the lesson of modern history, said Charity Bentham, that men and women thought of international diplomacy as if it were being conducted by superagents (States) operating with the principle of utility.

Thus, a State was a utilitarian. A State desired only Good. A State, operating with the same dynamic as the lowest of its citizens, acted to increase its happiness, its pleasure. A State should be assessed in terms of the effectiveness of its utilitarian conduct, as to whether its conduct was appropriate in terms of the Good produced in comparison to other possible actions. It was therefore meaningless to speak of a State as moral or immoral, as legal or illegal, as decent or indecent, as virtuous or vice-ridden, as human or inhuman, as godly or blasphemous.

This all seemed removed from me at first reading. As with traditional utilitarianism, everything about New Benthamism is in the example. So it was not until Charity Bentham discussed the United States of America's conduct with regard to the Vietnam war, 1955–1975, that I realized the weighty and, yes, sinister significance of Brave New Benthamism.

Following the French Republic's (Paris) abandonment of its Indochina colonies in 1954, the United States of America (Washington) was confronted with three choices in Southeast Asia. Washington could have supported the Republic of South Vietnam (Saigon), for two units of pleasure, Washington's and Saigon's, while at the same time opposing the Democratic Republic of Vietnam (Hanoi), for one unit of pain, Hanoi's: a balance of positive 1. Or, Washington could have remained neutral toward Saigon and Hanoi, for no pleasure or pain: a balance of zero. Or, Washington could have supported Saigon and Hanoi, for three units of pleasure, though this would have led to such severe contradictions for Saigon and Hanoi that there would also have resulted two units of pain: a balance of positive 1.

With this model, Washington's historical decision supporting Saigon and opposing Hanoi was viable. Though it did not produce the greatest Good, there was no greater Good.

Once Hanoi revealed its desire to destroy Saigon, Washington's support for Saigon, positive 2, was offset by Washington's military opposition to Hanoi (war), negative 2: a balance of zero. There was no Good to be gained by remaining committed, in Vietnam. According to Charity Bentham, Washington's historical decision to remain supportive of Saigon and belligerent toward Hanoi was neither immoral, illegal, indecent, sinful, inhuman, nor blasphemous. It lacked utility.

Washington's decision to remain in Vietnam was explained by American leaders as Good because, they asserted, to withdraw as Paris had would permit not only the triumph of Hanoi, one unit of pleasure, but also the destruction of Saigon, one unit of pain, the probable destruction of the Khmer Republic (Phnom Penh) and the Kingdom of Laos (Vientiane), two more units of pain, and the weakening of Washington's armed forces, another unit of pain: a balance of at least negative 3. As American leaders, for two decades, exhorted, Washington's decision to remain in Vietnam achieved the greatest Good.

In time, as it appeared that Saigon, Phnom Penh, Vientiane, and the deployed American armed forces could not resist Hanoi without excessive support by Washington, the utility of the international relationships had to be recalculated. This was a gradual, contradictory process, Charity Bentham conceded, involving the Union of Soviet Socialist Republics (Moscow) and the People's Republic of China (Peking) and many others. It would be fair to sum up, argued Charity Bentham, that Washington was eventually placed in such a position wherein its support of Saigon and belligerence toward Hanoi resulted in several units of pain. To remain in Vietnam was bad. To withdraw from Vietnam was bad. The wise statesman could see that to withdraw as Paris had was less bad than staying, or more Good. The principle of utility indicated that Washington should abandon Saigon, Phnom Penh, Vientiane, and its armed forces, four units of pain, that Washington should make peace with Hanoi, two units of pleasure, and that Washington should seek other ways to offset further the pain of the situation. In utilitarianism this often means that one should enlarge one's model.

That Washington historically did this, by rapprochement with Moscow, two units of pleasure, by entreating Peking, two units of pleasure, was strong evidence, wrote Charity Bentham, that New Benthamism dominated modern diplomacy, that it was the modern political ethic.

To those who would cry out that war is outrage; that Washington's conduct in Vietnam was a disgrace; that Saigon was a corrupt tyranny that ruled by torture; that Hanoi was the spiritual leader of Vietnam, though it too ruled by torture; that the American leaders who persisted in supporting Saigon despite a popular uprising among draft-age Americans had to do so by trampling on reason and imposing a legislative dictatorship, thereby violating human, natural, and especially civil rights, thereby alienating the citizenry from its own elected officialdom to the point where the democratic process was dismantled and only chance exposure of Nixon's misdeeds saved the Republic; and more; Charity Bentham replied: stuff and nonsense.

Utilitarianism denied such concepts as social contracts, natural rights, human rights, civil rights, inalienable rights. These ideas depended upon deontological systems—ones that claim that theft, torture, murder, and war are always wrong—and are therefore subject to the contradictions—the stuff and nonsense—of habit, prejudice, custom, ritual, instinct, and feelings. Social contracts are said to be legal fictions. Inalienable rights are a logical contradiction. And civil rights must remain continually amendable in order to comply with the ongoing pursuit of the Good—they are never inviolate.

At this point in my study, it was apparent to me that New Benthamism was what Peregrine and Israel would call "the bad guys." New Benthamism had made a dispassionate system of everything that Father and his friends had fought against and been crushed by. It was the practical philosophy of a pragmatic elite. Its genius was that it was matter-of-fact. Its strength was that it explained the international status quo with what amounted to a defense of that status quo. As Israel liked to say of the ruling class, New Benthamism had its cake and then it had the crumbs that had fallen to the floor.

I discovered it was much more insidious. It seemed that there was a certain problem that had once worried thinkers about the principle of utility. How, critics asked, does one keep utilitarianism from becoming simply self-love? The utilitarians proposed in defense what they called "generalized benevolence," which is a way of thinking that tends to keep a person's pleasure in proportion to others' pleasure. The utilitarians added that if a person's self-love conflicted with another's, then the larger the model—the more agents involved in a conflict—the more likely each person was to shape his or her need to conform to the group's. This was not self-sacrifice. It was cunning self-promotion. Pleasure yourself but do not overdo it, or, as the Greeks said, moderation in all things. The happier everyone is, the happier each will be.

Charity Bentham adapted generalized benevolence into her theory of New Benthamism. At that time I thought her adaptation to be a supplement to the system. I have since learned that it was in fact the linchpin, the absolute center, of New Benthamism. She called her version the Charity Factor. A State should first identify its best interest in a conflict, she said. But then that State should consider other States' concerns. It was the wise State, the powerful State, that sought its goals with charity toward other States.

Charity Bentham wrote that the Charity Factor has many names: the communist countries called it "friendship gifts"; the capitalist countries called it "foreign aid"; the nonaligned countries called it "mutual assistance"; international treaty organizations such as the United Nations called it "emergency relief." What I did not understand then, and what makes the Charity Factor so crucial to the whole, is that it is, over the sweep of time, usually more applicable to international conflict than military war, trade war, disarmament, and peace treaties. The Charity Factor is what wise and powerful States do to foolish and weak States. It is foreign policy during the state of affairs called peacetime, when small wars, civil wars, and blood feuds smolder, when the larger wars are said to be mutual suicide. What I understand now is that the Charity Factor is as militant as a battleship; it is as useful to national aggrandizement as conquest and occupation. For the beaten, the lost, the diseased, the exiled, the undone, the Charity Factor is the only hope and the only enemy. I mean to stress the paradox. I have much more to say, in time.

In the Vietnam war, Charity Bentham explained, Washington's self-love was to maintain Saigon and to defeat Hanoi. When this position was abandoned, Washington acted with charity. It bribed Hanoi, dispatched conciliatory diplomats to Peking and Moscow, dismembered its armed forces, and offered refuge—of sorts—to the defeated Saigon. Washington's real strength was said by Charity Bentham to lie in its ability to act with charity and to encourage commensurate charity by Hanoi (which failed to offer it rigorously, degrading Saigon, Phnom Penh, Vientiane, alienating all Indochina, blundering into confrontation with Peking and subservience to Moscow) and by Peking and Moscow. Deontological critics of Washington afterward condemned this charity as concessions. They were not that, Charity Bentham argued, rather they were efficient power plays. The wise State understood that the happier other States were, the happier it would be.

Not surprisingly, Charity Bentham criticized traditional world-scale cliques, like the Free World, the Communist Bloc, the Third World, the Arab League, and the numerous subordinate defense organizations, as distorted versions of deontological systems already discredited as prejudicial because they depended upon habit, custom, religion, feelings. More, she said, the politics of confrontation (sometimes called "firearms races") would always fail to achieve its goal because it did not act with either the principle of utility or the Charity Factor. It was best, she said, for a State to stand alone, to keep its own counsel, and to depend upon the world-scale equivalent of common sense, called "the balance of power." Charity Bentham concluded that if each State conducted itself with the principle of utility, then the give-and-take of diplomacy would dispose all parties in a conflict to cooperate. There were no genuine allies or foes. There were only States with needs that simply had to promote the Good, with an a priori belief in charity, in order to achieve "the greatest Good."

I admit I have conflated Charity Bentham's work, avoiding her biographical essays on the ancient Epicurus, the Enlightenment's Locke, Voltaire, Hobbes, and Hume, and on the nineteenth century's Hegel, Comte, and Marx. I have also bypassed her analysis of the New Benthamism inherent in the foreign policy of the twentieth century's Theodore Roosevelt, Lenin, Neville Chamberlain, Mao, and Charity Bentham's favorite statesman, Henry Kissinger (who wrote the introduction to *The Greatest Good*). I have ignored the economic models for her arguments, and her papers discussing the legitimacy of enormous corporations functioning as quasi states, and the need to repeatedly resubmit what at first appear inequitable (painful) situations to ever larger models of utility (e.g., the territorial wars in the Middle East were regionally harmonizing). I give her great due here, though, for her prose was always tactful, cautious, temperate.

Still, with regard to her economic science, which was why she had won her Nobel Prize, I admit I did not then comprehend its worth and cannot now say that there ever was, or is, anything to such wind but smoother ways of rationalizing historically disproportionate ownership of property—why some work too hard and eat too little, why others own children and their future.

For this disinclination, I plead ill education and impatience. After what I have seen and done, it is a matter of merit to me that I do not rant thereupon. Charity Factor. What arrogance. What heartlessness. It reminds me of nothing so much as the tale of the Norse ogre who lived at the edge of Jotunheim, the land of the giants, and whose wife was renowned for taking in, and feeding, and giving succor to orphans who fled the wars between the gods. When this ogre came home at night, drunk and lustful, he would eat the soft flesh of the children to whom his wife had given refuge, until he was nearly insensate. Then he would stumble to his wife's bed, blood-soaked and self-satisfied, and would grumble to her as he fell upon her, "Now that I've had my way, you can give those left all the charity you want."

I say this here and for now about Brave New Benthamism.

What Grim Fiddle thinks does not matter. What Grim Fiddle has done about what he thinks, there is the proper subject for his passion.

Mord the Hard-Fisherman

In my third year at Vexbeggar, the news from Stockholm grew ominous. I had been comforted that summer by Molly Rogers on vacation, but in the fall she hurried back to Israel to keep him from dangerous, irrational acts. They wed soon after, perhaps the result of a near breakdown by Israel. I was never sure and never asked, since I missed the ceremony, and afterward it seemed irrelevant. Molly sent me verse about the ordeal, "Quiet Israel Quiet," and it reassured me that the marriage had been the proper culmination of a twenty-one-year courtship, Earle giving the bride away, Guy crooning old folkie favorites, the manse draped with Thord's elegant friends.

Israel's honeymoon only temporarily interrupted the gloom in his letters. Israel took it very hard that Peregrine suffered alone in the King's prison—since none had ever dared visit him for fear of reprisal. The King's Spies were much on the highways then, suppressing those who were called seditious troublemakers but were more properly identified as aliens, that is, brown-eyed foreigners.

This shame needs brief explanation. Like other countries in the North, Sweden never recovered from the shocks of the wars in the Middle East. As widespread egalitarian propriety decreased, chauvinism and concomitant bigotry flourished. I have no desire to explicate this formula. I am sure the New Benthamites justified it at great length. It is enough to say that my mother's people came to place a misinformed emphasis on their own heritage, especially on their folklore and their so-called aristocracy, a corrupt lot who responded to this miraculous resurrection with pomposity and wrongheadedness. A spastic feudalism was imposed on a people who had been free of such stupidity for three centuries. Fashion dictated assemblies, processions, balls, baroque etiquette, and a boastful endeavor to remake what had been a struggling industrial state, become slightly inert with socialism, into a painted court in the midst of a much reduced subsistence economy and actual starvation. There was nothing logical about the transformation. The Earl of Gotland could share a horse-drawn carriage (the affection for automobiles disappeared with the petroleum supplies, was replaced with equestrian affectation by the elite) with a chief engineer from the Kiruna iron mines. It was the ridiculous leading the ridiculed. In their covetousness, the only thing all segments of the citizenry could agree on was bigotry. There developed a witch-hunting not seen since the Dark Ages. The Kingdom of Sweden became a stranger to reason.

I know Sweden was not alone in such degenerate politics. That was no comfort to the laborers and hangers-on from the Middle Eastern and African kingdoms (and some from European republics drifting toward anarchy) who were driven from their homes to the streets, and from the streets into what were called halfway camps, from which they were provided passage out of the country on merchantmen leased by the King's government. Pogroms swept Sweden of the dark races first, then of the less dark, the yellow, the sallow, and finally of those few Jews who were caught once again in history's spasms.

The triumph of successive pogroms did not satisfy the most extreme chauvinists, a political party called the Loyalist League for Swedish Homelife, or Loyalists. There seemed an escalating need for ever more cruel measures against shadows. In America, Israel told me, this battle would have been understood as red-blooded Americans versus Them; in Sweden, it was the blue-eyed Norse versus Them. I do not care how it compared to historical race wars. It was hellish. Families were arrested and separated unless they complied with ad hoc relocation programs organized by vigilante groups and permitted by the King's silence. The few desperate men who dared to resist the witch-hunters were maimed

or murdered. And there was always the fire that they used to
burn out the intransigent.

The random hangings and seeming suspension of habeas
corpus panicked the few libertarian groups, one of whom, the
Cartesian League for Reason and Decency, organized small rallies
in Stockholm. This was in the late 1980s. Sadly, the Cartesians
were unable to agree on a single strategy. Denouncing racism and
murder is admirable; it also lacks specifics, such as naming the
guilty. At the last rally, the Cartesians presented many diverse
speakers, who confused the crowd with poetry and high ideals.
The crowd chanted "Crush Infamy!" meaning the King's government. This resulted in a chain-swinging match with the mob dispatched by the Loyalists to bait the Cartesians. The riot that
followed blocked streets and shattered shop windows. It was pre-
dictable mayhem. That was the night the old Royal Palace was
burned down, along with four blocks of the foreign quarter—THE
MICKEY MOUSE CLUB included.

The next day, the Cartesian League was suppressed by the
King's Spies, a thousand-year-old Norse tradition of security police revived by the King's government in order to assuage the
Swedes' persecution fantasies and to complement the aristocracy's
power fantasies. All financial contributors to the Cartesian League
(Thord Horshead among them) were notified that they were under investigation for conspiracy to foment treason. It cost Thord
heavily to escape that net. There were many nasty turns in all this,
such as an undercurrent of Loyalist prejudice against homosexuality and possibly sexuality in general. What is important here is
that the Cartesian League contained more than a few of the
Swedish and American radicals from the War Resisters League of
the 1960s.

In time, the Loyalists directed their loathsome rhetoric against
the small American exile community. Soon enough, all Americans
in Stockholm, regardless of their politics, came under attack. The
Swedes chose to forget the King's onetime Social Democratic government's opposition to the Vietnam war. Peregrine, Israel, Guy,
and Earle were anachronisms. The word was passed that they and
their kind were under suspicion, along with everyone else not cer-
tifiably Norse. This blanket slander was helped by the fact that

many of the Americans had police records dating back to the 1960s, and many of them were genuine gangsters, still dealing in contraband and rackets. I do not overlook the fact that my family enjoyed the succor of a Swedish smuggler.

The Loyalists denounced the whole of the American exile community with a part of it, an old trick, Israel assured me. Whenever the King's Spies arrested a thug who happened to be an American, the politicians would haul the stars and stripes through their foul mouths. This resulted in a precarious existence for the Americans, some of its impetus dating from as far back as the American embargo on European technology in the early 1980s. Nevertheless it might well have calmed down if not for a gruesome crime in the halls of the King's contrived splendor—Peregrine Ide murdered Cesare Furore at the Nobel Prize Ball.

Peregrine's trial delighted the Loyalists. They aroused their faithful by emphasizing Peregrine's seeming lack of remorse. The King's prosecutor, a Loyalist sympathizer, insisted that Peregrine tell the court why he had murdered. The defense counsel, provided by the court, tried to prevent such testimony; but Peregrine spoke anyway, in a whisper, his larynx damaged permanently in the murder:

"I—because I wanted to."

When the King's court sentenced Peregrine to life imprisonment, the Loyalists exploded with hate. They demanded Peregrine's life be forfeit. They wanted his heart cut out. They wanted his head fed to the fish. They wanted him to die in screams. I do not exaggerate. They said these things, repeatedly. I heard worse on the radio. And since there had been no death penalty in the Kingdom since the defeat of the German blasphemers, the Loyalists achieved the neat trick of increasing their power by demanding from the King's government what it could not sanction. There was still an inherent decency in Sweden that no amount of cant had been able to overcome. The King, who was not as stupid as he seemed, even went so far at his birthday address to declare, "I shall not wash my hands of this man's fate."

This was ill-advised imagery. The Loyalist mobs chanted "Fiend! Fiend!" in reply to the King's bravura; it was not clear if they meant Peregrine or the King or both. The Loyalists manipulated the King's dilemma. Peregrine became the goat that one could flail without restraint, knowing the whole while that one was actually castigating the King's government. Whenever the Loyalists were denounced by the good men left in government for another of their race riots, the Loyalists screamed about the moral corruption of the "American fiend's protectors." The illogic was intentional. The politics were effective. The Loyalists wrapped themselves in piety, dared anyone to mention the blood on their hands. The contest became as religious as it was political. There was talk of the need for an evangelical republic in order to restore order and what was called godliness to the land.

There was one Loyalist leader whose gift for demagoguery soon lifted him into the position of holy strategist for the movement. This was apt, if opportunistic, for he was the head pastor of the wealthiest and most aristocrat-packed Lutheran church in Stockholm. His power grew as the King's government weakened, since he represented himself as the spokesman for, the embodiment of, the traditional Norse ideas of purity and vengeance, which he claimed would return the country to harmony. He was chief of those calling for a national oath of Christian fealty, and for a referendum on the question of making Sweden an Evangelical Republic. He was a fearmonger of the first rank, a genius at mass hysteria and at denouncing his detractors as demons. Also, he could throw himself completely into deranged calls for Peregrine's death. His name was Mord Fiddle.

"Me and Moll were down shopping on the quays last night," Israel wrote me in the spring of my fourth year at Vexbeggar, "and we got rousted by a marshal for a Loyalist rally. It was a taffy pull. We went along, wanting no trouble from the thugs. They had the square fixed up like a birthday cake, with a chorus of one million eight-year-olds singing 'Jesus Loves Me.' That stirred them up, definitely a gooseberry crowd. I had to keep telling myself they were the same folk with the taste for arson. Old Adolf, he was partial to torchlight and kettledrums. These people are more for harps and pinwheels.

"Then a couple of minor angels got up on the platform to remind us how wonderful we are. Sublime homes. Sublime children. Sublime duty. This is dopiness like who'd believe? Where is sense? What happened to it? It was just here. They burned out four tenements last week. In the daytime. They don't like the night, claim it's for wolves. Is it this bad back home? I can't believe I'm on the same planet. Moll tells me I can't let this get me down like I was. I haven't got the rage I used to, something inside is broken. I promise I'm trying. I'm definitely off the drinking. I just want to run and keep on running. How did I get so far out of goose step?

"Once the angels wrapped up their act, the crowd got heavy and male, mums and kids trundling home to make gingersnaps. The attention shifted from the platform to this podium set up on the bow of a ship tied up along the quays. There was an organ roll from somewhere, and their head witch doctor popped up from below and strode to the podium. They call him 'Mord the Hard-Fisherman.' He's about twenty feet tall, with a funky white beard and hair down his back in braids. He had on preacher clothes. Back home this is what they call presidential timber. The man is a spellbinder. Evil spells, bad spells, but there it is. He has magic. I can't say most of what he said, his Swedish was too fast and colloquial. It was a fearsome noise, and wild, you know? He kept his real madness till the end. Then he started in on poor Peregrine."

I won't record what Israel wrote me of Mord the Hard-Fisherman cursing Father. It was hideous. It was Mord Fiddle who first said that if the King washed his hands at all, it would be to cleanse them of innocent blood, not of Peregrine's, whom Grandfather called "that assassin." It was Mord Fiddle who first waved the white handtowel—to dry the King's hands, he said—that became the favorite of the Loyalist mobs, they waving those towels over their heads, chanting for executions, deportations, crimes against the helpless, and especially for Peregrine's head. And it was Mord Fiddle who toppled the King's government—more of that shortly. According to what Israel wrote me of that day on the quays, the issue was at the point where the Loyalists believed they could force an election. Mord Fiddle alluded in his speech to the raising of a vigilante force—"Evangelical Brigade"—to storm the King's prison and relieve the King of his burden of Peregrine Ide.

That Mord the Hard-Fisherman was my grandfather, that it was he who against nature and conscience had driven his daughter and grandson from the nursery, never occurred to us. The surname Fiddle was not rare in Sweden, or in the North. Indeed,

Peregrine and Israel had always thought that my name on that piece of paper was a sad joke.

It seems blind of us now, but really, we had so many problems, why should such a farfetched coincidence of surnames have seemed significant? What is more, I was not then fully informed of the details of my conception and birth, and Israel was almost as ignorant as I was. There was only one person in the Kingdom who had facts enough to act, and she was as far from a philosophical disposition to politics as my dogs, high-minded wolves, were to the leash. However, Mother was not one to pass by an opportunity for melodrama. I have often thought that her reentry into my life was less luck than premeditated showmanship.

Lamba Time-Thief

Vexbeggar had been a modest fishing village centered on its Lutheran church until speculators had transformed it into a seaside gambling resort for the idle rich. It was shaped like a fishhook about a natural inlet, the bulk of the saloons and casinos shoved up against the lower part of the J, the housing complexes spreading back from there. Our dilapidated camp—two bunkhouses and a mess hall—stood at the extreme upper part of the J, at the tip of shantytown that itself was back from the harbor. The poorest and most unwelcome of the resort's domestics lived there, heaped like driftwood on the tides of fate.

Because the bank would not buy it back from us, we had our own pier, jutting about forty yards into the Baltic. The Asians and Africans loved to fish from it, so it never appeared as sorrowful as the rest of the camp. After Molly returned to Israel, I closed up the inland houses and moved into the storage shack at the end of the pier, where we had tied up our ersatz six-meter Viking boat and our old ketch. My room, on the first story (an attic really, walls shaped by the pine roof), overlooked drifting hulks, abandoned warehouses, our two sad vessels, and the few craft tied up that far from the yacht club. It was damp up there, but with insulation and innovation it was tolerable in winter and heavenly in summer. I cooked my meals on a stove Guy had installed on the ground level, and used most of the shack as a kennel for Goldberg and Iceberg and the guests who followed them home frequently. Most of their friends were canine and male, and of consequence both had litters their third years; however, by that fourth year the human and feminine came regularly to my door.

I was shy, necessarily secretive. At first, the daughters of the year-round domestics pried into my affairs. I learned to say "boy" and "girl" and so forth in Turkish, Korean, Urdu, and Brazilian Portuguese. In the summer, there were also the intriguing nymphs from the resorts whom I chanced upon along the harbor walks. I had more than my share of fun, made a fool of myself in many tongues, learned some unbelievable things about females, spent spring nights wishing I was not alone and autumn nights wishing I was, and generally blundered my way through first love, second love, just fun, and what Molly called "serious crushes." The summertime girls knew things I could not accept and never understood. I disguised my ingenuousness by telling outrageous Norse tales and by making up even more absurd stories about my father, Perceval, and his comrade, Moses, who had both been killed in action in Vietnam.

In brief, I moved from fumbling novice to casual heartbreaker. The wintertime girls had names: Lilli, an American halfbreed from Cam Ranh Bay who corrected my errors about the Vietnam war; Ananda from Bangladesh, who introduced me to Eastern eroticism; and Ethel-Bethel, the most sincerely devout Christian I ever met, who was from what once was called Mozambique (I have no knowledge of its name now). The summertime girls also had names: Gunnhild, who was called "Lace-Cuff"; Liva, who was called "Fine-Hair"; and the ultramarine-eyed Unn, whom I called "Sly-Eyes."

Sly-Eyes was the only daughter of a life peer, a minor count from the western dairylands. She was a major influence on my libido, three years older than me when we met, leaving me feeling too old when we parted. That last summer at Vexbeggar, I thought of Sly-Eyes as my Charity Bentham, for she was smarter, sexier, sneakier than all the rest. That was youthful fancy. I was yet to meet the real thing. Still, while she was there, Sly-Eyes twisted me about her vain self. Everything about her seemed to me careful, ladylike, gorgeous. I did love the way she smelled. She could make me do anything, including dressing properly enough to attend the dissolute parties at her father's shore house. And the more I feared her foolish friends, the more I clung to her. Lilli, in an uncharacteristic aside, said that Sly-Eyes was a pale snake in my tree of life. That was overmuch, though Sly-Eyes tempted me greatly. She taught me envy, jealousy, pettiness. She ran with a bad lot; her other suitors called me, to my face, a fishmonger. And I took it, because I thought that if I challenged them they might question my identity. My safety remained in my apparent thickheadedness. I hung at the fringe of that bright crowd, waiting for Sly-Eyes to bore herself with the pretty boys. She fancied me her Norse outlaw, as in the stories I told her. I was her "Grim Evening-Wolf," hiding from the relatives of my victims. She said this innocently, without sense of the burning half-truth.

One weekend under the harvest moon, Sly-Eyes and I fought over how much wine she could drink and still remain ladylike. I broke a bottle against the carriage of one of her feyest suitors. She refused my appeals for reconciliation the rest of the month. This did not annoy me, because I was very busy washing dishes at three different restaurants for funds I needed. By the new moon, I had lost patience and retreated to my shack to plan how to win her back. I aimed to make her regret that she had toyed with Beowulf-Come-Again, King of the Weather-Geats, slayer of Grendel and mother, bested finally by the unnamed dragon guarding an ancient gold-hoard.

I gathered my harness from the tattered remains of Vikingland. I dressed my dogs as well, decided not to take along the three pups I had kept of their litters. We were decked in as much iron and wolf fur as we could heft. I let my hair down, combed out my red beard, coated myself in grease and fish oil. I looked and smelled unholy. I had not dressed the warrior since we had closed the camp ten years before, and my full-grown bulk made it no masquerade. I figured this would scare Sly-Eyes into submission. It scared me enough—examining myself in the polished helmet—that I mention that I carried no weapons that night. I was only crudely sensitive to my power then, intuited enough about the strange darkness inside me to avoid provocation.

I knew from my friend Dede Gone, an angry Turk and fellow dishwasher, who also delivered groceries to the rich, including Sly-Eyes's shore house, that she was giving a party that Saturday. My dogs and I approached her house—a cakelike affair set on stilts on a low cliffside amid other equally pretentious roosts— from the wooded plateau behind. In position by moon-rising, I climbed up a pinetree from which I had spent many embarrassed, delightful evenings watching people in their baths and so forth. I had first seen Sly-Eyes from that perch, since it was directly in line with the sun deck off her mother's cluttered living room. I planned our howling entrance at midnight. Sly-Eyes had unwittingly prepared a surprise for me.

Just before midnight, Sly-Eyes and her best friend, Asgerd, the daughter of a scoundrel who actually called himself the Duke of Vexbeggar (the King had made life peerages a lucrative game), swept onto the sun deck and waved the partygoers to attention. There were cheers. At fifty yards I could not hear what they said. Soon they had turned off the electric lights and distributed candles around the deck's railing. They also arranged large pillows in thronelike display at the edge of the terrace.

From out of the revelry and firelight, two cloaked figures appeared through the screens to the side. The larger figure sounded a long, high-pitched whine. It stunned the party, and shocked Goldberg and Iceberg, who commenced answering whines. I waved them to silence, checked the crowd to see if they had noticed. Instead, they were transfixed by the whining figure, who threw back her cowl to reveal a bloated face, caked with white powder, distorted with artifice. She had greased her hair back so that it hung to her shoulders like snakes. She carried a wooden staff a foot taller than herself, and this was a large woman; she used it to clear a circle about the pillow throne. In her sweep she paused, seemed to fix her eyes directly on me. It is not credible that she could have seen into a dark wood, as one generally uses the word *see*. I ducked. When I looked again, the smaller figure had fixed on me. Her eyes were bright in the candlelight. She stood as still as a statue. I knew something was wrong. Then, with a histrionic spin, the smaller figure dropped her cloak and began a dance around the pillow throne.

The small woman was a prophetess. Such performers abounded in the Kingdom then, for they suited the chauvinistic need for Norse folklore. Sly-Eyes and Asgerd had hired a sibyl to titillate their guests. From the looks of her I knew thay had paid a high price. The sibyl was dressed magnificently, a dark mantle adorned with polished stones, a gem necklace, a touchwood belt from which hung several lambskin pouches, black calfskin boots, and a lambskin hood. Her head was shaved, as was popular then among the spooky. I was enchanted, as were the partygoers. And as she danced, faster and lighter, clapping her hands while the hag banged her staff on the deck, the sibyl seemed to descend into herself. Watching her was like being drawn into a cave, or a chasm, or something misty, ashen, foreboding. It was as exhilarating as it was frightening. She danced so passionately that it did not seem a carnival act, more as if she were pleasing herself and we were being permitted to attend. She was erotic and fierce. She was magic. After all this time, recalling that dance, I confess truly, she was stupefying. If you can hear me now, Mother, you were very, very good.

A short time later, my dogs and I sneaked up to the house and then inside the service entrance. Because the servants were also fascinated by the show on the sun deck, the kitchen was empty. We were untroubled getting into position outside the pantry door. I could hear the sibyl singing warlock songs to charm the spirits of the dead. She had a striking voice, fragile, authoritative, wounded, woeful. I concentrated on interpreting her words as best I could with what I knew of Old Norse. I supposed it was part of her act. She sang of "black seas," and "red seas"; she sang of "islands reaching to the sun" made of "wind and blood"; she sang of "black and hurt half-men." When she stopped, the silence was followed with moans.

"Approach and declaim," said a gruff-voice—the hag.

Sly-Eyes and Asgerd asked trivial questions about love. The sibyl answered one in three in a monotone, not unpleasant, not vital. Several of the fancy boys called out vulgar requests. The hag warned them not to offend the spirits of the dead now gathered here to reveal the future. The hag also warned that it was folly to inquire of one's own end, as the truth could be ruinous. That rocked the party. Finally, one man dared politics: "Who killed the couple at the rathskeller?" This referred to a recent crime in Vexbeggar that had been distorted into racial bigotry by the press.

"The wretched and the righteous," said the sibyl.

"Was it Turks?"

"The spirits say the men of the Great City do violence to themselves," said the sibyl.

"What should be done with the Turks?"

The sibyl refused to answer. The crowd, stirred by her mystery, ventured increasingly dark inquiries. The sibyl replied to a few, always with foreboding imagery. I knew that none understood her learning. They had missed her reference to the "Great City," which was what the ancient Rus (Norse peoples, for whom Russia was named) called modern Istanbul. I surmised that the sibyl was something more than a trickster. I did not begin to believe that the spirits told her what to say. I thought her quick and clever. That she held the crowd spellbound I explained by considering the black fatalism of the Norse. I was wrong, for then Mother called to me, as casually as if I had always been hers to beckon.

"Skallagrim Ice-Waster, son of Out-Lander, Wolfman and Rune-Carver, seek your destiny."

I crashed from my hiding place. I felt compelled. My dogs thought me frightened, reacted with sisterly whines. This was too much for the skittish in the crowd, who thought Goldberg's squeal was an angry spirit of the dead. There were screams. This upset the dogs, who, because I did not calm them quickly, began the wild barking of a wolfpack. I yanked on their harness. Several guests hurtled over us. The dogs panicked. It was not the entrance I had envisioned, stampeding over tables, sofas, screens. We trampled as we were trampled. We caused havoc, the crowd tumbling pell-mell to flee this Norse spirit come to punish his degenerate posterity. It was a wicked prank. I did like it. There had been so little silliness in my last few years, it seemed fair. I bellowed as the dogs howled. I was finally hauled to the ground as Goldberg and Iceberg went for a lake of gooey cream spilled on the sun deck. In the quiet, I measured the field. We had carried the night, and two walls with it. Sly-Eyes lay on a couch, weeping.

"You are not what you could be, Skallagrim Ice-Waster," said the sibyl—Mother—seated above me. I certainly did not know this was Mother; it seems contrived to refer to her otherwise.

"I hope I didn't ruin your fee," I said.

"You are my fee. Speak your face."

"Do you really know who I am?"

"I know your future. This is not your future," she said, waving her hand over the destruction. "Your father is your future. Your wolves are your future. Tell me of Skallagrim Strider."

"Yes, yes," I said, charged, controlled. I was under a mother's power, which was such a novel experience for me that I confused it with her magic. It may be true that motherhood has powers beyond the natural, and it may be true that one who experiences his own mother's nurture discovers the extraordinary. I note here that my mood that night was visionary. It passed, and later I would fall back onto the muddy course of reason; right then I told her what I knew, and many things I did not know I knew, of a Norse outlaw whose name was spoken portentously—in passion and hope—at the moment of my conception.

"Skallagrim Strider was a chieftain, originally from Ireland," I began. "He was exiled from Iceland for the slaughter of his wife's family. The legend says that he sailed to the sun with forty outlaws. The legend says that he became King of the South, where his sons still reign."

"No!" Mother called, leaping from her pillow throne. She was livid, as if I had bungled my education. I knew the legend of Skallagrim Strider as well as anyone. I had studied the Icelandic texts religiously in order to piece together that sorry, amazing tale. I supposed that she wanted more than bookish deduction.

Born Grim, son of Thrain Otterson of Falconess, near the Fort of Hurdles (modern Dublin: as Peregrine once joked with me when I told him of Skallagrim Strider, this was another tale of blarney and lost opportunities, of men making a success in order to make a grand failure), he was called "Skalla," meaning bald, because of his early loss of hair, and he was called "Strider" because of his luck (the crucial concept to the Norse, all-telling) as a navigator in the storms of the Irish Sea and English Channel.

Skallagrim Strider was the grandson of the notorious Otter Black-Nose, whose assassination was avenged by his brother, Eyvind Fast-Sailer, who was then forced to flee Ireland for Iceland to escape vengeful factions. In time, Skallagrim Strider's good luck attracted the King of Ireland's greedy attention, and, getting the bad luck that goes hand in hand with the good, Skallagrim Strider was forced to flee Ireland. He too found refuge in Iceland, which was then still a young colony filled with political and fratricidal refugees from Norway, Sweden, Denmark, Lapland, Normandy, and other Norse kingdoms washed by the North Sea.

Skallagrim Strider settled with the wealthy descendants of Eyvind Fast-Sailer, by then called the Men of Red River, in western Iceland. Skallagrim Strider was adopted by Eyvind Fast-Sailer's eldest son, Alfstan the Peacock, whose own son had been killed in a duel at twelve. At Alfstan the Peacock's direction, Skallagrim Strider married a wealthy widow, Dotta Long-Hands, from Laxriverdale in northwestern Iceland. He soon became a bountiful farmer and serious poet, as well as continuing to enhance his reputation as a wild outlaw, going off once a year ("going viking") in summer, after the common law assembly, the Althing, to plunder his old enemies in Ireland.

After several years, it was revealed that Dotta Long-Hands loved another man (there were actually two contradictory saga fragments, one saying that she loved her own brother, another saying that she spurned her husband because she could not accommodate him physically in the sex act). Skallagrim Strider acted ruthlessly. He left her bed, made her a prisoner of the farm. He remained away on summer adventures for longer periods. He broadcast her infamy, boasted how he would not take another wife until Dotta Long-Hands begged his mercy. She was a bright, vindictive woman. She convinced her family to carry her back to Laxriverdale, which they did, in secret and with full knowledge of the risk.

To avenge this humiliation, Skallagrim Strider conducted himself with cold logic. First, at the Althing, he demanded huge reparations in gold from Dotta Long-Hands' family, knowing they would not and could not oblige him. With the false pretense of not being able to obtain justice peacefully, Skallagrim Strider then led his forty best men to Laxriverdale one spring and murdered Dotta Long-Hands and her entire family, more than four-score people. He also killed the livestock, burned the fields, poisoned the wells. Even for a Viking raid it was a ghastly act of vengeance.

The lawgivers at the Althing, pressed by an outraged Christian faction, ruled that Skallagrim Strider and his men be banished forever, forfeiting all their lands and claims.

One account, another saga fragment, indicates that Skallagrim Strider and his best men took to their best longship, a "wavecutter," and sailed to a small settlement in eastern Greenland, which they were soon forced to leave because of more mischief with a prominent settler's wife. They then sailed southwest to the fledgling settlement of Vinland (somewhere on the North American continent), where they lived for many years, peacefully if disconsolately, among the *Skrælings,* or wretches, who were actually the North American Indians. Growing infirm and melancholy, Skallagrim Strider and his remnant took to their wave-cutter one last time and sailed south, to the sun, where the *Skræling* legends had told them that there were calm seas and rich lands and warmth for their old bodies. Skallagrim Strider thus disappeared from the sagas.

There is a map fragment, however, from a sultan's library in Istanbul, that dates from Byzantium and the Great City. It was signed "Men of Red River." How it came to Istanbul cannot be known with certainty, though it is possible that Islamic traders from as far east as the Philippine Islands and as far south as Madagascar could have carried it to the Great City to trade with the wealthy court scholars. The map fragment shows a sailing course from "Vinland" into the "Sea of Sun." The course touches on "Sandland" and "Boneland" and "Serpentland." It ends in what is called "Nightland," which is also called, in a rune poem at the edge of the map fragment, "the wall of blizzards and behemoths." Of course, without longitude or latitude markings (since the Norse sailed dead reckoning, perhaps assisted by noontime and North Star sightings), the map's geography is not truly decipherable.

The poem on the edge of the fragment, however, introduces a whole new concept to the saga—the hint of an apotheosis. The poem seems to say that the legend of Skallagrim Strider and the Men of Red River ended in the south, where Skallagrim Strider was crowned the King of the South by the animals living there. His children were said to be half man and half beast.

I recited the tale slowly to Mother. I finished, "And his sons still reign there."

"No! No!" called Mother again. She grabbed the staff from the hag (who was Astra, Mother's mentor) and raised it over my head. With a grunt, she dropped it on me. I was knocked sideways. I rolled over, sat up, the room spinning. Mother clubbed me again. I fended it off the third time, grabbed the staff from her hands, and flung it off the deck.

"His sons do not rule there! You are his only heir!" called Mother. My dogs growled at her. She hissed at them. Mother was the only living thing who ever cowed my dogs. They hid behind me. I recall being frightened of her powers just then, for the first and not the last time.

"This is my prophecy," she continued. "You shall rule the South as king. Flee the fire. Seek the ice. You are Ice-Waster. Follow the counsel of Skallagrim Strider. He will guide you. Listen to him. Follow your heart. Listen to it. It will protect you. The black and hurt half-men of the wall of blizzards and behemoths await your coming, Wolfman and Rune-Carver. And hurry, hurry, hurry!"

I pleaded for more intelligibility. I felt her words, but could not accept them.

"I am Lamba, called Time-Thief. The spirits of the exiled and unavenged have told me your future. Heed the hardest heart. Trust the fisher-of-men. Your destiny is with the cold and the cruel."

I was uncomfortable now, probably angry. She was pushing me too far and too fast. I stiffened. I scowled. I flaunted my defiance. I think now she might have been trying to protect me from the truth, which she could see and which was then too unacceptable to say aloud. She was wrong to protect me from the truth, even if it was the worst imaginable. I forgive her that; it might have been mother-love, a sad bargain, a bad bargain, part of her fate to have given birth to an heir of magic, wonder, crime. I suppose that she realized then that I was about to reject her completely, for she paused. She stepped back. Astra covered Mother with her robe. The two stood to the side, chatting in Old Norse, too quietly for me to hear. Mother turned back to me to whisper, "This is what I can tell you. You are not yet what you could be, Skallagrim Ice-Waster. Remember that if you fail, it was fated and is no fault of yours. Remember that all things are not set. You are loved. As long as you are loved, you are safe from shame. Also, you are lucky."

Mother danced away. I was dumbfounded. I wanted more. And yet I did not want more. It is no easy thing to demand to know the future, one's own destiny. I shook my head—it was too much for me. I got to my feet. Mother and Astra vanished into the shadows. I did not pursue. I kicked rubbish and cursed the night, the sky above me, black and star-packed. I barked at my dogs to follow me. They whimpered, joined just then by another female whom I had forgotten in my temper.

"Oh, Grim baby," said Sly-Eyes, moving across the room, weeping, acting, manipulating. "What am I to tell Mother?"

"I wouldn't know about mothers," I said, turning my passion on her, forcing my advantage, warrior claiming his bride of mischief. Sly-Eyes responded in kind, and it was easy to dismiss for the rest of that night, and for many self-indulgent nights afterward, that my future was said not to be there in silk and woman's heat, was instead somewhere far beyond the constellations of the northern sky, on the track of a thousand-year-dead outlaw, at the end of which I would come to rule the cold and the cruel.

The Fire

I did nothing about what Mother foretold. I did have wild dreams, of herds of animals, of immense blue pools covered with sunbursts. There were also feelings of loss, or irreparable damage, and, contradictorily, a sense of swirling adventure. I was not a player in these phantasms, more an observer, or most accurately: a listener to descriptions of vivid events. This passive role—listener—was based on what I knew of Norse lore, in which the spirits of the restless and unavenged dead are said to whisper to the living in their sleep. There were indeed aspects of the images that made me think the scenes were of long ago. I thought them like pictures I had seen of Iceland, those volcanic ridges cut by glaciers and washed by ashen clouds. That was not Iceland. I pushed all this aside at the time. It was not that different from the rich, boyish fantasy life I played out in my daydreams. I was very young and very easily persuaded. I told myself that the sibyl's prophecy had engaged my yearning for such experiences. I certainly never saw fire in those dreams, and this must mean that the only born child of a sibyl inherits nothing practical of her gift. The first I considered fire as a foe was with Israel's letter at summer's end.

"They outdid themselves last night," he wrote, referring to the Loyalist League for Swedish Homelife. "Me, Guy, and Earle hiked up along the canal after curfew, across from gooktown. We couldn't believe those sad little creatures on the other side were human. Whole families were huddled along the canal bank. Guy figures they are the ones who keep moving all day to avoid the roundups. We were walking up toward the smoke when we heard these insane screams. Some of those poor bastards take their own dogs and hang them and set them on fire. Guy says it's because they think the screams will scare away evil spirits. Behind the dogs an entire block was on fire, a real monster. Within half an hour, sparks lit up the shacks along the canal. It was one of the so-called safe fires, since it couldn't jump the canal. But there were firemen on our side in case a gust launched some cinders. There were Loyalist lackies, too, passing out handbills that said the fires were a 'blessing' because they 'rid the city of filth and infestation.' Guy read it to me, and when he saw my face, he got so angry he made a move on the Loyalist. Earle kept him in control but not by much. I can't let this upset me again. You should know that bit about 'filth and infestation' is what the Nazis said about us chosen people.

"We got home about dawn. We figured we'd seen forty tenements go in three hours. I was too upset to sleep, so I went down for the paper. There was talk at the shop of a Loyalist rally later that morning. They wouldn't tell me details, but I got that some of the boys were planning to hijack the van transferring the suspected arsonists, all gooks, from the north of the city to the prison island. They kept talking 'Norse justice.' I did what could have been a stupid thing on the way out. I asked them what century it was, since I'd lost my watch in the swamp. They didn't get it."

Israel continued in this exhausted tone. I was so drained that I had to read the last paragraph three times before I understood he was telling me a secret, in a colloquial code of sorts, in case the King's Spies were reading Thord's outgoing mail.

"And take special care with your rehabilitation of her. The surf is up that time of year. We don't want any sickly passengers to catch their death. Get plenty of sleep yourself. Be good to strangers with long legs. Peace and Love, I."

I puzzled out that this could only be referring to a rescue of Peregrine with our ketch from the King's prison island. I raced from the post office, down the harbor walk and over the fences into shantytown. I was on the boat immediately, measuring, inspecting, estimating. She was in bad shape, without serviceable engines, with rotting bulkhead and mainmast, with tattered lines and sails. I might have given up if I had been anything but a dreamer. She was still afloat, I told myself, and with hard work, a fair wind, abundance of luck, she could make Stockholm harbor, and from there, perhaps cross the Baltic to Poland. There was a new rebellion there, and anything was possible for homeless outlaws in a land turned from extremism to anarchy.

Over the next few weeks Israel's letters continued to encourage me, with cryptic asides and buoyant double-talk. I invested the money Israel sent me in ill-fitting sails, in used lines, in a new boom for the mainsail. I used my savings as well, abandoning my longtime fantasy to steal up to Stockholm, bribe my way in to Father, and, if he agreed, to save him from his pain by killing him.

I do not hesitate to confess this, because the question remains if it might not have spared Peregrine and so many more of my loved ones—all of them—of far worse than whatever I would have had to endure as a father-murderer. I was too young, too angry, too romantic, and in that state life seems easy because it seems clear-cut. Could I have put a knife in my father's heart? Could Peregrine have found the strength to resist suicide so offered? There is no end to this speculation; I defer. Yes, I imagined Peregrine's death; yes, I imagined my release from his crime.

The possibility of Peregrine's rescue gave me great joy. It

seemed a gift. I worked tirelessly. Yet there was never enough time for what had to be done. Fate was not patient. September in Vexbeggar ended with labor troubles at the casinos and hotels. Soon there were pickets, scabs, thuggery, and strike committees. The news from the rest of the coast was more of the same turmoil. The government overreacted and stationed troops near Vexbeggar. There was a crucifixion of a striker in one of the inland villages. The strikers, who were mostly foreign workers, formed a secret militia. There was strutting and cruelty on both sides. I watched it from afar, hearing stories from my neighbors in shantytown. We all sensed something bad coming. By All Saint's Eve, which the Lutheran Norse ignored but which the mostly Roman Catholic alien population celebrated with processions, Vexbeggar was prepared for the worst.

I was just returning from a trial run on the ketch. I had a volunteer crew of Dede Gone, a now unemployed dishwasher and militant striker, and his three younger brothers: Wild Drumrul, Little Dede Gone, and Kazur Gone, called Goggle-Eye for his wandering left eye. They were gritty Turks from Cyprus via a Greek labor camp and an American intervention in a massacre on Rhodes. They had grown up in fishing villages ignorant of the industrial age. This meant they were superb inland-sea sailors. They taught me how to navigate a leaky, sluggish ketch with bad sails and a useless motor. How pathetic my ambition seems now. Yet, filled with boyish hope, I aimed for glory.

Dede Gone spied smoke as we wore around the shoals. We heard the alarms as we tied up below my shack. The one-legged fisherman, Gino, who survived in a tent at the end of the pier, called to us that there was rioting in town. Dede Gone started off immediately to join his strike committee. I called to him that he was no good to us as another martyred soldier of Islam. He stopped to wave. Wild Drumrul, then fifteen, understood his brother's risk and asked him not to go. Dede Gone ordered him to stay with me. He called to me in English, "Love my brothers like your brothers."

The fire started near the school. Soon enough, the flames spread along the edge of shantytown toward the well. The smoke thickened with the nightfall. The boys and I, with Goldberg, Iceberg, and the three of their male pups that I had kept, climbed

atop my shack to watch. We could see the burned-out in flight. It
pleased me to see one of the large hotels catch fire. Wild Drumrul
prayed, "Fire, be cool to my brother, and keep him safe."

We heard sirens, roars, and gunfire soon after, which signaled the assertion of martial law and order. The first refugee
column started south. We discussed Dede Gone in sad voices—
they had no Swedish or English, I no sensible Turk, so we communicated in poor German. The three brothers looked so forlorn
there, skinny and shaking with grief, that I considered something
rash. I might have done it if not for a great surprise. A covered
carriage just then emerged from shantytown. It paused at the camp
entrance, then swung around quickly to bear down, six run-to-
ground horses afore, three men and a driver atop, on my shack.

One man leaped down before the carriage stopped rolling.
He was medium-sized, with tight, copper skin and wire-like red-
dish hair; he was dressed in common, nondescript clothes, but his
steel-frame eyeglasses made him appear an arch intellectual. He
jumped to my door and pounded, calling in American English,
"Grim Fiddle! We have messages from friends!"

I called, "Get back!"

I had my dogs snarl. He dropped his hands, stepped back
defensively to the window of the carriage. I noticed the door of
the carriage was ornamented with a coat of arms—an aristocrat's
coach. I would learn that it had been stolen by some of Thord's
colleagues, and had been provided at the roadblock north of Vexbeggar. It had served to convince the troops that its passengers
belonged in the area.

Another man swung down to confer with the first man. This
one was large, all black, with long dreadlocks and a full beard. A
cloaked female figure then appeared from the coach, tall, nimble,
and with an aggressive bearing. She slapped the carriage door
shut, looked up toward me, shielded her eyes from the drifting
smoke, and called in sharp American English, "Come down, Grim
Fiddle. We come direct from Israel Elfers and Thord Horshead."

I had the Turks stay hidden in the attic with the pups. I went
down with Goldberg and Iceberg. I lit the lamp and let them in,
first the copper, then the black, finally the woman. The driver
stayed atop the carriage, being watched by a third man, a squat,
South American type with an automatic firearm cradled in his

arms. The woman strode up to me and stood with an ostentatious curiosity. I recognized the swanlike neck immediately, even though she was older now, full grown and unqualified—broad shoulders, short waist, very long legs, with black, rich hair.

"That is a war out there," said Cleopatra Furore.

"You mean the fires?" I tried.

"Are you ready? Where's the ship?"

"I don't understand."

"There's not time for this. The King collapsed to their demands. They're marching on the prison in the morning."

"Father?"

"We have to move. Where's our crew? We'll need provisions for thirty days for a dozen."

"What? I have some food. But my crew," I paused, calling the Turks. They crept downstairs, crouching in peasant fashion as the pups licked their faces. Cleopatra sighed. She did not have to reprimand me. I felt my failure and tried to explain.

Cleopatra listened to me patiently, nodded, then stooped to stroke Iceberg, saying, "They're what we have. We have all been caught short. Thord Horshead is our last hope. We must be there by morning."

She did not invite debate. The squat one tapped the doorjamb, pointed up the pier. He used his right hand to make sign language. The black drew a pistol. The four of them moved together fluidly, and I reconsidered my assumption that they were mistress and hirelings. I would learn that the three men were Cleopatra's foster-brothers: wiry, copper-skinned Lazarus; mountainous Orlando the Black; deaf-and-dumb Babe—all half-bred bastards like me, sharing the Furore patronym and the fact that at some point in their lineage they had Cuban progenitors.

I walked over to the door to look up the pier. A dark mass of people moved along the main street toward the camp. It was another refugee column. I assumed the troops had cut the south road, had started closing a pincer on both rioters and refugees. This was a roundup. The refugees were in a panic to escape. And I had one of the last ways out of Vexbeggar—the ketch.

Cleopatra touched my arm. "We have to go."

I barked to the Turks to get to the ketch and make ready. I got upstairs to collect my best fatigues, to toss Israel's letters into the sea, to gather the pups. One bolted and fled. I left Goldberg in charge of the other two and chased him with his mother, Iceberg. Orlando the Black stopped me at the door.

"Have you got weapons?"

"I have to get my dog."

"Forget it. We have to fight."

"I've got this," I said, snapping the two-handed, double-edged war-ax that Thord had given me from the wall.

"He is a bloody Viking," said Lazarus.

"I'm going to get my dog," I said to Cleopatra. "You get your people and that stuff there to the ketch." I was out the door and up the pier, Iceberg beside me. Babe was positioned behind a dead horse, his automatic weapon fixed. He had turned loose the team to slow the mob, and though it had helped, the mob had shot down three. The driver had run off or perhaps been killed. I prepared to vault the carcass to pursue the pup, when Babe took me down with a leg hook. I cursed him just as he opened fire, short burst, long burst, short burst.

"Those are families!" I cried. Orlando the Black pounced on me, pinning me down.

"We need you," he screamed. "Those aren't people anymore."

"No! Get off!" He slammed my head.

"Hear what I say. We have to get out," he said. The air was acrid. I sagged. The mob readied to charge. My pup was gone. I thought of Father. I kept Father in mind as I agreed to a retreat, Babe as the rearguard, Orlando the Black and I gathering Lazarus and Cleopatra in the shack. I took up my war-ax and hacked through the back window. I dropped to the floating deck. Iceberg and Goldberg and the two pups followed me. Orlando the Black passed down Cleopatra, then he and Lazarus swung free. Cleopatra started for the ketch.

"There isn't time!" I cried.

"We have to try!" she returned.

"I'm in charge," I said, turning to Orlando the Black. "Get them in that boat there." I pointed to the imitation six-meter Viking *karfi*, *Black Crane*, which had not been at sea for six years. I yelled to the Turks to cut the lines on the ketch and to get to *Black Crane*. I scrambled back to the shack for the sailbag and rudder, finding Babe grappling at the door with two insane Asians. I killed one—I suppose now that I killed him—and Babe bashed down the other. What was it like, my first murder? It was darkness, first and last, all darkness. I struck with the war-ax and can still feel the sensation that ran down the handle into my arm, my heart. It was like nothing. There is no adequate metaphor.

I pushed Babe through the window, tossed the sailbag and rudder down to him, soaked the floor with coal oil. The next moment I was in the stern of *Black Crane,* calling orders. The Turks unshipped the oars. I balanced the craft with people and dogs. I lowered the rudder and kicked off the pier. The mob roared above us. Babe fired two short bursts at the bait shack. I grabbed the gun barrel, tossed the weapon into the sea. Orlando the Black watched me closely but did not move. The bait shack exploded in flames. Once into the inlet we used the oars to fend off the partially submerged hulks. We came about sloppily, and I had to roll half overboard to keep us upright. I could see the pier over my shoulder, the mob stampeding past the fire and onto the drifting ketch. It listed with their sudden weight and crashed back into the pier, tearing loose a pylon, the bait shack toppling over to spread flames onto the rigging. The last I wanted to look, mothers and fathers were heaving their children toward the sinking ketch. No one can swim in the November Baltic.

The next morning, I found Stockholm harbor choked with ships and foreboding. Stockholm is built on islands and peninsulas bunched between an inland lake and a tongue of the Baltic. The channels are crisscrossed with bridges and dikes; heavy traffic was customary there in spring and summer. With the first bad weather, only the main channels were navigable into the markets. That morning, however, the lanes were so jammed there seemed no safe conduct. There were rafts, boats, barges, sailing ships, all manner of steamers and derelicts, some at anchor, or adrift, or aground on the mud flats. It was chaos, no one obeying port rules. I saw strange flags, stranger ships' names. On the barges, badly dressed children surrounded cooking pots. Their faces had looks of sleepiness, upset, also curiosity.

I knew as we cleared the harbor light that the congestion ahead would add two hours to my estimation of arrival at the King's prison island on the inland lake. I shouted this to Cleopatra as she emerged from the sailbag, where she had passed the night. Our crossing had been rough. *Black Crane* was an open boat, machine built, with a shallow draft; she wallowed under sail, did not answer to the helm quickly in even moderately heavy seas. We had bad moments. We had got to Stockholm, but it was much later than she had demanded of me, midmorning. I took the rudder from Wild Drumrul in order to avoid a barge that started to drift into our path. By the time I got us clear, Cleopatra sat conferring with Lazarus.

"Go there," she said, waving weakly into the thick of the main channel. She was seasick, troubled.

"I can make better there," I said.

"Obey her," said Lazarus. I had seen him wince when I had told Cleopatra, on the pier at Vexbeggar, that I was in charge. As he watched for my reaction, I realized that Lazarus resented any authority from me. In the daylight he was stone-faced, his red hair and copper skin making him appear rusted. He seemed knowing, secretive, calculated. Cleopatra gagged then; he comforted her. He nodded some sort of fraternal message to Orlando the Black and to Babe. I had surmised enough of them during the night to know that Lazarus was the one to suspect; Cleopatra, to placate; the other two to avoid. Their high-handedness did annoy me. I had rescued them, yet they treated me as a convenience. I ordered the Turks to get down the sail, unship the oars. Our route was tricky; we repeatedly had to fend off small craft as we pushed deeper into the heart of the city. I discovered that the people on the sailing ships in particular were not Swedes, were instead Finns, Poles, Latvians. It made no sense to me. The large steamers had Asians and Africans hanging from the railings. They heaved debris down on us. Cleopatra kept waving toward the inner quays, below the opera house, by the fish markets. I navigated by keeping quick sight of a church steeple. Once out of the main channel, I saw that the quay road was lined with troops. At various points on the piers, King's Spies, in their crimson coats, shouted down to gangs of glum men in longboats. There were multicolored tags (probably identification papers) on the coats of the men in the boats.

We were ignored from the shore as I poled us toward an opening between two sleek, well-guarded schooners flying Swedish flags. I asked Cleopatra if this was the place; she backed me off with a scowl. Lazarus nodded assent. Orlando the Black and Babe released the safeties on their pistols. Wild Drumrul looked to me for reassurance. I took the rudder and sent Little Dede Gone forward with the line. Three men in black, priestly clothes called to us from the pier and motioned toward a pylon, Little Dede Gone throwing the line, Wild Drumrul playing off the sea wall with an oar. A soldier came to the rail above and peered down, shouting something to one of the Norsemen, who waved a badge that seemed to satisfy him.

The three men handed Cleopatra out, and she ran up the stone steps, followed by her brothers. We waited uneasily in *Black Crane:* the dogs were hungry; the Turks were mournful; I was exhausted and regretful, staring at the dried blood on my sleeve. I tried not to think of Vexbeggar. I thought of Father and what Cleopatra had said of "their scheming."

"Grim!" called Thord from above. "Hurry, Grim!" called Earle.

"Stay with them," I said to Goldberg, meaning the pups and the Turks, as Iceberg and I shot out of *Black Crane* and up to my family. Earle lifted me like a child. He seemed much slower, heavier, although still the brown bear. I turned to get a big wet kiss from Thord, who clutched me close and said, "Forgive me, if you can, please. I did not realize."

I ignored Thord's look of guilt—like a penitent awaiting judgment—and tried to question them as they pulled me across the quay road, past sentries and two waiting carriages, into a small stone cottage. "Are we too late? What is this place? Where's Father?"

"He's alive," said Charity Bentham. She was seated on a couch in the foyer, between a very pregnant Molly Rogers and Cleopatra Furore. Babe stood like a bulbous mastodon behind his mother. I could understand his protectiveness. Charity Bentham seemed to have aged twenty years in five. She looked ruined. She started to speak to me, instead smoothed her skirt, reached out to take Cleopatra's hand. Cleopatra moved closer to her mother in an odd way, more condescending than consoling, as if she were the senior. As I reached for Molly, Cleopatra glared.

"Well timed, eh?" said Molly, mussing my mane, patting her stomach. That was Molly's second pregnancy; her first had ended with an abortion at twenty-four (and was much discussed in her verse). I said there was never a better time; Molly twisted her face and pulled me so close that I had to brace myself.

"Come away, now, Grim," said Thord, pulling me back.

We went to the right, down a short hall, where a petite, beautiful young man stood beaming, beckoning me, taking my hand, saying, "Dear Grim, you are very much welcome. I have missed you. You cannot remember me. I am Radar Fiddle. Your uncle. Lamba's brother. Your mother, you see." He kissed my hand.

It was the first I ever heard my mother's name. I did not have a moment to react, as Thord ushered me through sliding doors into a book-lined study. There, commanding the room, stood a gigantic Norseman, white-bearded, intense, overwhelming, his face fixed with surprise.

"It is true! Lord God, it is true!" boomed Grandfather. Iceberg stiffened; her nape hair rippled; she growled, ready for attack.

"Now keep your bargain!" shouted Israel, moving to Grandfather's far right. He was enraged, desperate.

"Israel, it's me," I said.

Israel moved over and tapped me, saying, "I introduce you to your grandfather, the Reverend Mord Fiddle, leading candidate for despot of the new Sweden."

"Easy, Izzie," said Guy.

"He brought the *karfi*, not the ketch," said Thord.

"There was a riot," I said. "Soldiers. And they rushed us. They threw their children. I had to fight. There was a fire."

"It's okay, Grim," said Guy.

"Yeah, okay, we're getting out," said Israel.

"Tonight," said Guy.

"We need a ship. You said we'd have a ship," said Lazarus. He and Orlando the Black were seated by the window.

"Is there anything?" Israel asked Thord.

"Perhaps, with time," he said. "I can call favors, but there are so many gone."

"We haven't got time," said Guy.

"Oh, Israel, please, please, forgive me," sobbed Thord. "This is my fault. I have been idiotic."

While my family argued among themselves, one of the black-suited men (they were seminarians) stood near Grandfather and translated the English banter. The whole confrontation was likely more disconnected than I recall—Israel's Swedish poor and colloquial, Grandfather ignorant of English—but because I spoke both easily, I have it in my mind as of a piece.

Grandfather raised his arm and pointed at Israel. "You shall have your ship." He spoke with such power and assurance that all turned to him, transfixed. Grandfather was too large for that room, my height and Orlando the Black's breadth, yet massive in more than physical dimension—monumental, a pagan vision of an inexplicable god. He continued, "Leave me alone with my grandson. You shall have what you ask."

"What ship, you murdering liar? Where? When?" demanded Israel, the veins of his temples dark blue, his cheeks puffed red and blotchy.

"Izzie, no, come on," said Guy, reaching out.

"Damn you, Jew, do you know who I am?" said Grandfather.

"Old man," said Israel, even-voiced and utterly contemptuous, "you forget who we are. We raised him. He is ours. What you did twenty-one, twenty-two years ago, is unforgivable, by my God, his God, any God. You degrade all faith to claim yourself a man of God. You turned out your own daughter and you abandoned your own grandson. You sicken me. I won't pity you. No one will."

"Izzie, we need him," said Guy, this time gripping Israel.

"I came here to get my father. That is what I want. If we need these people, then we need them." I paused, realizing I was over my head. "Israel, tell me what I should do."

"What must be done right now is to establish order," said Lazarus, walking to the center of the room. He seemed mannered, aloof, cold. We shuffled in place as Lazarus, with that measured, condescending voice of his, continued, "Now, what ship, gentlemen, and where is it?"

"We can't trust that madman," said Israel.

"We have to trust everyone now," said Lazarus.

"And no one," said Israel bitterly, starting to laugh. Lazarus smiled at that, not as if happy, rather as if amused by the gloom.

"My ship, damn you, out there!" spoke up Grandfather. "I shall sail her for you. Wherever you want to go. Anything you want. What I want is the boy. Now go and leave me with him for a moment. I do not ask for pity, or for anything you have. Only the boy. I gave my word. I shall keep it, as Lord God is my judge. Go!"

When we were alone together, Grandfather put his right hand on the Fiddle Bible and went to one knee. Without explanation, he began a version of my birth and abandonment, the whole of which I have already recounted from several sources. I do not recall him using my mother's name. What most distinguished Grandfather's tale was that he was merciless in his criticism of his own part. He spoke as if in a dream, exhorting, whispering, thundering. I was enchanted, and frightened, and gripped. He had a magic tongue. And he used it to heap dark, lurid metaphors on the name of Mord Fiddle. Yet all through his confession, he kept that demagogic hubris of his at the fore. Grandfather was a man who could curse himself in a bold, heroic way, so that his humility seemed illusory, unearthly; it was certainly not entirely believable. In truth, he was proud of his fury and what it had wrought.

As Grandfather's confession closed, it occurred to me that he was not really regretful about what he had done. This was all the discernment I could bring to Grandfather's performance at twenty-one, a boy before a force of nature. I know now that he was without sorrow for anyone, especially himself. His self-abnegation was more ritual than revelation. Kneeling there, one hand on the Bible and the other alternately touching me or reaching upward for emphasis, Grandfather brandished the weapon he made of theological rhetoric. He was negotiating beneath the eyes of heaven, or, to be blunt, he was scheming for what was before his own eyes.

"This is the truth!" he said after half an hour, more, it was a timeless speech. "I have been wrong about you! I shall **not make** apology! I shall not! I repent, yes, I call on Lord God to forgive me. I shall atone. I know what I have done." He halted then, studied me. I tried to think, tried not to avert my eyes. He broke the silence with a resolved tone, "You are a fine boy, Grim Fiddle. All that I have achieved is nothing compared to you. You are my grandson. Mine. I shall give all this up if I can have you back. I shall do that! I have earned this. I must have my grandson!"

"You are my grandfather?" I managed to get out.

"Tell me, boy, tell me, Grim Fiddle, that you will stay with me."

"Can you help my father?"

"He sinned!" said Grandfather, and it is hard to think how any other man on one knee could have spoken with such condemnation. "He sinned against Lord God."

"Yes, I know. He's suffered for it." I controlled myself. I would not cry. "He doesn't have anything, just me. I don't have much. My father—"

"Do you know who I am?" he interrupted. "What I have done this day?"

"You are the man Israel calls the Minister of Fire."

"Does he? That is what he would say, the Jew. Hear me close! This morning, your father was sentenced to death for what he did. I cannot reverse that decision. His execution is imminent."

"Please!" I remember then touching him, for one of the few times ever. "If you are my grandfather, help me. Help my father. There must be something you can do. Will you?"

"I am the only one who can save him," said Grandfather.

"Will you?"

He braced himself. The negotiation he had enjoined with Israel had been nothing before the profound deal he fought to close with me and for me. Now the paramount bargain was struck. My memory is that he said "Yes."

"Thank you, sir," I said to his assent.

"Don't talk so! Remember this, Grim Fiddle. Make right by doing right. What men say of you does not matter. You shall be judged swiftly and finally by Lord God."

Grandfather pulled me down to one knee beside him. He prayed for us, a long, deep, militant psalm that began, "Lord God is my light and my salvation, whom should I fear? Lord God is

the refuge of my life, of whom then should I go in dread . . . ?"
Then he got us both to our feet, handed me the Fiddle Bible
(which is here at my hand as I write, and from which I have
learned that Grandfather chose Psalm 27 that day, which ends
with good counsel, "Wait for Lord God, be strong, take courage,
and wait for Lord God"), and then he took me to the window. He
pointed to a tarpaulin-covered two-masted schooner tied up behind *Black Crane*'s single mast—a big, lovely, fierce-looking ship,
what the ancient Norse would have called a "wave-cutter." He
asked me if I could handle her. I told him I had never managed
so large a ship in open sea. He told me that he meant from there
to the King's prison island, that night, near midnight. I gave a
boastful nod. With that Grandfather pounded me on the back
and told me he had waited all the days and nights of his life to
have a son who could captain *Angel of Death*. I balked at the name.
He did not notice, already throwing on his coat, throwing back
the sliding doors to announce to the assembled his plan for the
rescue of Peregrine Ide, who had been condemned that very
morning to die that very night by an extraordinary tribunal of the
Provisional Revolutionary Government of the Evangelical Republic of Sweden, a revolutionary vigilante court that had been given
its mandate two days before by one of the leading strong men—
in plain language, despots—of the revolution, the Reverend Mord
Fiddle, my grandfather, Minister of Fire.

The details of the rest of All Saint's Day do not concern me
now. It was a rush to flight from a Norse reign of terror. I learned
as I worked. Not just Sweden but all of the Baltic was afire. In
Finland, there had been a murderous bombing at a rally called by
the government's opponents. And for Estonia, Latvia, Lithuania,
Konigsberg, the anarchistic revolution in Poland (millions starving
as winter approached, crucifixions commonplace, battle-tanks out
of petrol being overrun by teenagers with petrol bombs) had
awakened slumbering Slav chauvinism. There was street-fighting
in Riga, food-rioting in Tallin, and an interminable dock strike in
Leningrad. Panic was omnipresent and pitiless out there. Whole
populations scattered, seeking shelter, asylum, mostly food. Stockholm harbor was filled with those clever enough, brutal enough,

to procure oceangoing transport. The radio crackled with lies in twenty tongues. The news in Stockholm was mostly rumors, and they were dreadful. The King was said to have retired to Uppsala, was said to be very ill. There was strong word that the government had fallen; other talk that the King had abdicated in favor of replacing the parliamentary monarchy with an Evangelical Republic. But there was also talk that the King had denounced the Loyalist League and their so-called Provisional Revolutionary Government, that the King had called them all traitors and insurrectionists, and that the King's illness was in fact gunshot wounds, or perhaps poison. The Prince, at sixteen, was believed a Loyalist sympathizer, and it was equally assumed that he was implicated in a long struggle to wrest the right of succession from his elder sister, the Crown Princess, who had been sent overseas for safekeeping. In all, the weather in Sweden was revolution.

One certainty in Stockholm seemed that the Provisional Revolutionary Government had taken control of the security network, especially of the King's Spies, now called the Evangelical Brigade. A nation of law had become a nation of men, some very bad men. One of the first declarations by the PRG had been posted at the King's castle that morning; it said that Peregrine Ide would be executed on the King's prison island before another sunrise, along with more than one thousand arsonists, rapists, assassins, saboteurs, and other "godless ones." Another certainty in Stockholm seemed that, once the new government was in place, there would be an end to so-called tolerance of so-called undesirable elements; this meant that aliens, half-breeds, and socio-sexual deviants were marked for terror.

All this should explain why, as I directed my family and our new allies, the Furores, to load and ready *Angel of Death,* it was wisest to post Babe, Wild Drumrul, and one of Thord's most loyal lieutenants, Otter Ransom, on guard at the pier. The city was stricken. There were hangings and crucifixions. There were immolations. Stockholm was pursued by demon Purity. There was no refuge there for either the righteous or the wronged. There were sirens, fires, and faraway howls—a larger, more obscene version of what I had fled the night before in Vexbeggar. Columns of refugees wound from the foreign quarter to the quays. Columns of smoke wound from the foreign quarter to spread a stench over the docks, the air sometimes so thick that it was necessary to wear moist cloths on our faces as we worked. The harbor changed for the worse as the day faded, steamers shifting for safer berths away from the smoldering depots, small craft ramming smaller ones, ragwomen in open boats bartering for food, rafts of armed thugs guarding their ships from raiding parties. None hesitated to shoot, and there were bursts of gunfire all day, a few gray lumps, which were probably bodies, to be seen floating in with the evening tide. I thought I saw the worst of mankind that day—far short of it, as I know now. It was still hard on us, more disorienting than any of us admitted. Our known world disintegrated irreparably, and none of our grand assumptions about the intrinsic decency of human nature could protect us. We felt beyond mortal succor. If not for our obsession with delivering Peregrine, I do not rule out the possibility that we would have collapsed with the North. It was a near thing. Molly and Thord suffered a wordless hysteria. Israel started drinking again, passed out at least once, not from spirits, from despair. We had to force Earle to eat for strength, and even sturdy Guy lost his temper at me over stowing a crate. I watched the Furores more suspiciously than was right, and thought badly of Lazarus without call.

Thord took leaving the worst. He saw the rightness of it, and did not grieve for his lost warehouse. He had grown tired of what he had become in his own land—a persecuted deviant, a marked man. But he and the Fljotson brothers, Orri and Gizur Sail-Maker, were the only full Swedes among us, without links to any other culture (Otter Ransom was part Ukrainian). Sadder, Gizur Sail-Maker's young wife had died the year before of meningitis, a disease he insanely ascribed to Sweden's irreligion. He had not been rational since. He wanted us to take along her gravestone; Orri had to lie to him. As Orri's protector, Thord suffered the Fljotson dilemma acutely. More, he could not forgive himself his powerlessness to save us. He felt, with a bleak conviction, that he had brought on our jeopardy by remaining silent about the truth of my birth.

I must include here that I also learned that day that if not for Charity Bentham, there would have been no escape. She was the heroine, and the mystery, had been from the first. Her motives in discarding her widowhood and retrieving her first husband are beyond me. I declare here that Charity Bentham made her own mysterious bargain with her own mysterious conscience, and the particulars that contributed to such seem lost to me now in her love for Peregrine Ide and Cesare Furore. I can guess that she longed for order, decency, kindness, a fragment of happiness; she longed for an end to her self-torment; she reached for peace of mind and found Peregrine and a few more years of love and remorse. I could go on, but what would it serve?

What I do know with some certainty is how Charity Bentham went about gathering back to herself her Peregrine. She did not attend Peregrine's trial. Israel hated her for that, a bias that would create difficulties. Afterward, Charity Bentham bribed Israel's whereabouts from American draft dodgers who had returned to America (Peregrine used Israel's name the night of our joint interrogation, the crucial clue that led Charity to search for Israel). She contacted Israel through agents during Peregrine's first year of imprisonment. Israel spurned her. She persisted by letter. The first plan she proposed for helping Peregrine—having him transferred to an American prison to serve out his sentence—not only was rejected by Israel as self-serving, but also was discarded by Charity Bentham because of the Loyalist campaign against Peregrine.

She then funded two legal appeals on Peregrine's behalf, one in her own name to the King, asking for mercy, another on legal technicalities to the court. Both were overwhelmed by politics. Charity Bentham next traveled to Stockholm to visit the King, the Queen, and the Prime Minister to plead for Peregrine. She even petitioned the President of the United States; for that she suffered the wrath of the Furore family in America. Rather than argue with them, Charity forfeited her inheritance from Cesare Furore, abandoned her teaching and lecturing posts, committed herself to traveling back and forth from America to Sweden to seek a solution. When all this seemed futile, she contacted, again through her agents, the Loyalist League for Swedish Homelife and arranged an audience with Peregrine's chief persecutor, my grandfather, Mord Fiddle. That meeting never took place, for at the last Mord Fiddle refused her, claiming more pressing matters than mercy.

After nearly five years of tireless pursuit that had cost her fame, fortune, family, the respect of her colleagues and the fruits of her Nobel Prize, Charity Bentham was desperate. She shed more than widowhood; she shed patience, pride, law. Learning of the Loyalist move to overthrow the government, and anticipating Peregrine's final peril, she returned to Stockholm at the beginning of the summer. She was near collapse. Her children, Cleopatra and the brothers, were aware of their mother's state and followed her, either to help or to get her safely away.

Charity Bentham pleaded by letter to Israel for his help. He still ignored her, for the same unfair reason—he blamed her for Peregrine's ruin. She took to visiting Thord's manse at odd hours, hoping to catch Israel. She acted like a beggar, stood outside, weeping, waiting.

Thord Horshead finally took pity when he saw that none of the others would challenge Israel, and met with her, permitting her to talk, confess, ramble, beg. That was Thord's way, the listener and not the confider. It is a credit to Charity Bentham that somehow in her wildness she was able to intuit that Thord knew more about Peregrine, me, all of us, than he should have or was telling. She drew the secret out of him. She used that brilliant and by then overwrought mind of hers to open up that large but guarded heart of Thord's. Their roles reversed, she the confessor, he the penitent.

Thord Horshead had kept my true identity from my family for many reasons—fear of candor, fear of rejection, fear of loss, fear of his own motives—at least in part because of his deep regret for disappointing his father, Anders Horshead, the attending physician at my birth. Thord's homosexuality seemed to preclude a natural family; the weight of that had split father and son, more Thord's doing than Dr. Horshead's. Thord adopted me and the rest (and he had sought us out, allowing it to seem a chance convergence) in order to offset his seedless destiny. He had actually learned of my abandonment by Grandfather from his father, had moved to right the wrong. In doing it the way he did—not telling us—he had done more wrong. That is hindsight. It is unfair to him. He took pity on us, the same pity he took upon Charity Bentham before his manse. I was never his son, but I was his child as much as everyone else's in his house, and in Thord's way he fought to keep me and to protect me. Once Charity Bentham discovered the truth, she gave Thord the strength to confront his deception; she showed Thord how he could repair the damage he had done. The two of them found, in their pity and regret, a way to act for the good. I wonder if she called it the greatest good? In any case, she accompanied Thord that same afternoon (this was August, just before Israel wrote me to prepare the ketch) to Mord Fiddle's church, the Pillar of Salt. They were blocked by Grandfather's coterie of seminarians. Thord thereby exercised his power to get where he wanted to get, strong enough even then to penetrate the Loyalist screen. They confronted Grandfather in his own chancellery, under the guise of bringing a petition from Cesare Furore's widow. They told him what they knew to be true. Grandfather rose from his desk, placed the Fiddle Bible down before Charity Bentham, and told her to swear. She obliged. Grandfather then asked her if she had proof. She said she could produce living proof. Grandfather ordered them to withdraw.

That was a month before Cleopatra arrived to fetch me from Vexbeggar. In that time, Charity Bentham had taken control of my family, had ordered them all to prepare for Peregrine's rescue and their own escape. Israel, persuaded at last of Charity's sincerity, furious at the twists and joyful for the hope, argued that something rash must be done, that Mord Fiddle would never admit to what he had done. He counseled that they should expose the connection between Mord Fiddle and Peregrine Ide. Charity Bentham counseled faith and resolve. Her opinion was that Mord Fiddle must be given time to consider the revelation, and that as he did, he would help them.

Grandfather nearly confounded Charity Bentham's wisdom. He followed through, remorseless, determined, hard-set on his plot to establish the PRG and to convene the tribunal to judge and sentence the enemies of his Evangelical Republic. Only then, after Peregrine was sure to be sentenced to death, had he sent for Charity Bentham. That was All Saint's Eve, and she, anticipating her moment, had dispatched Cleopatra and her sons (with Thord's help) to provide proof to Grandfather that he must cooperate completely, unconditionally.

Why did Grandfather wait to the brink? The answer is the man. He primarily saw himself as a servant of his Lord God first. I can suppose that he felt that his duty was to his Evangelical Republic, that only after he had discharged his tasks in a way that not even he could have upset its destiny, did he believe he could step away from his call as Minister of Fire to attend to his own desire. I see the conflict—mask or heart—and make sense of it, if I do not approve. I have made similar choices, to similar dark ends.

More important, why did Grandfather collapse to the truth of what he had done to me? He was neither simple, nor sensible, nor qualifiable, and I do believe that if any man ever born could have stood unmoved, unbent, before such a crime, it was Grandfather. He agreed to rescue Peregrine, and then he agreed to help my family, for a reason that is profoundly simple, equally fetching. It still wins me. He wanted his grandson, Grim Fiddle.

And yet I hesitate at this explanation now that I have written it. It can seem to me now not complex enough, or rather, too straightforward. It makes Grandfather as selfish as he was self-elected. I want him to be more. I want my memory to be more fulfilling. I want to believe that he was not only a great fury, an edifice of self-serving God talk and a flame of self-aggrandizing vengeance. I want to believe that he had a secret, unexamined reason for rescuing Peregrine, one that makes him human, even gentle. Somewhere in him was a husband who had lost a wife, who had driven away a wife, because he had been Mord Fiddle and she had rejected him for it. I cannot speak to the failure of that marriage, though if it can be judged by the antipathy between Lamba and Grandfather, it must have been a bleak conflict of wills. I would like to believe that Grandfather had loved Zoe greatly. The fact pertinent here is that Zoe abandoned Mord. And when she had gone, I choose to suppose, Grandfather had frozen a part of his heart in time—just as Peregrine had done when he had lost Charity.

I argue that Grandfather, as he considered what Charity Bentham revealed to him of me, Peregrine, herself, was able to perceive the misery of Peregrine Ide more completely than could the rest of my family, than even could Charity. I argue that Grandfather understood Father, at least the aspect of Father that had moved Peregrine to murder. I argue that Grandfather, sitting there in his chancellery, wrapped in black robes and blacker mood, might have asked himself what it must have been like to murder out of jealousy and longing and loneliness. If it did happen, it would have been a brief insight. Grandfather was not the sort to offer compassion or to put himself in another man's place.

I have no proof of this, unless it is me, living proof that my Grandfather and Father were of the same bolt of cloth, romantic outlaws, desperate self-deceivers, proud, sorrowful lovers who would not let themselves mend their ways. And their reward for lifetimes of regret was dark confusion, until chance, or luck, or this one woman, Charity Bentham, sacrificed herself to give Peregrine the possibility of love regained, and to give Grandfather the possibility of a new course, hopeful and dangerous, out into the world with his grandson beside him.

It was Charity Bentham who charged this affair, then, heroine and provider, a woman of intellect and theory became a conspirator of action and heart: for she and Cleopatra were to accompany Grandfather, supposedly to witness the scheduled execution of Peregrine Ide at the King's prison that night; for she and Cleopatra were central masqueraders in Grandfather's proposed plan of rescue and escape.

I cast off well before 10:00 P.M. in a cold drizzle and choppy water. Otter Ransom had procured ten liters of fuel from the police yards, so I was able to motor us into the harbor. Grandfather's *Angel of Death* answered to her helm smartly—an elegant, well-built, seventy-six-foot schooner, carrying a jibsail, foresail, mainsail, with spruce masts, an oak keel, a mahogany cabin, registered at sixty tons. I had an exhausted, untried crew—three Americans, three Furores, three Turks, three Swedes, a Ukrainian, and four dogs—and a precious supercargo: Molly, her baby, my father's fate. I set Babe and Otter Ransom at the bow to man one of Thord's fixed automatic weapons and our light. I set Wild Drumrul and Orlando the Black in *Black Crane,* which we towed close behind. I set my hand on the Fiddle Bible.

We anchored a half mile off the island. Grandfather wanted me and four others—I chose Guy and Earle; Lazarus chose himself and Babe—to approach in *Black Crane.* For appearances, we were relatives come to claim a corpse. We were not alone; there was a cluster of small craft just off the floodlit pier, held back by sweeping searchlights and the presence of a company of the Evangelical Brigade. The procedure began with a name called on the megaphone. A boat then bobbed toward the floating raft below the pier, as several chained convicts emerged from the portal at the base of the prison tower abutting the pier. They were hauling a body bag down to the raft. Finally, relatives in the boat reached to be reunited with their dead. We waited hours in that damp, watching as dozens of bodies were processed through, the ordeal slowed now and again because of questions about a corpse's identity. They were headless, after all, and likely so starved that there was no resemblance to the man arrested. The Evangelical Brigadesmen were rigorous. Rings and scars were checked carefully. Mass execution seemed to bring out the shopkeeper in the military, the patron in the bereaved. Guy distracted us by telling stories about Vietnam. Lazarus then told about a gruesome massacre he had witnessed in South America, where he had traveled either as a journalist or observer, or perhaps a student. Guy talked openly with Lazarus; Lazarus seemed sympathetic to Guy's disgust for the American military. Earle asked Lazarus about some of the hand signals he used to communicate with Babe. Their month together seemed to have given the four of them respect for their separate agendas. I mention here—incidentally, because it proved to be less significant than one might think—that Lazarus was a Yale graduate, like Guy and Earle. Orlando the Black had attended the American Roman Catholic university called Notre Dame; he had considered a career as a professional athlete before turning from that to travel with Lazarus, Babe, and Cleopatra in South America.

The wait wore us down. Earle sat beside me, his hands white from gripping the oars. We passed food to a family nearby that had almost succumbed to the cold and their fear. Those poor people, terrified children, weeping and shivering for their fathers and husbands and brothers. We should have helped. We did nothing. Our moment arrived when the megaphone announced "Peregrine Ide!"

Guy handled the tiller. We pulled hard and smooth. We shot toward the floating raft. The searchlight found us. On the shore, I spotted an approaching convict party carrying a body bag on their shoulders. Right behind I saw Grandfather's white hair. He towered over the figures of Charity Betham and Cleopatra Furore walking behind him.

I bent to my oar. We bumped to a halt at the raft. The officer on duty, a short man whose hands were stained with blood from the inspections, challenged us, "Who are you here for?"

"Peregrine Ide," said Guy.

I heard clamoring behind me. I heard Grandfather end a psalm with a flourish: "Hosannah!" I heard the leg chains of the convicts. I turned enough to see the officer stoop to open the body bag.

"No need!" boomed Grandfather.

"Get away!" cried Charity Bentham. She seemed hysterical. Even though he knew it was a ruse—to divert the guards—Babe flinched at the sight of his mother's twisted face.

"Yes, Lieutenant, do not waste your time," said Grandfather. "No Christian burial for this fiend."

"We have a right to him," said Guy.

"Get rid of them!" said Grandfather.

"I cannot do that, sir," said the lieutenant. "My orders say that I must turn over the body to those who claim it."

"I signed those orders!"

"I understand, Reverend, sir, but," tried the lieutenant.

"He's dead, that's enough," shouted Guy.

"You want him? You want this thing?" shouted Charity Bentham at us in *Black Crane,* moving to the bag. "He murdered my husband! He tore out my heart! Tell me how giving him to you will give me back my husband? Tell me how anything matters? He died only once, and I have to live with nothing! Do you hear? I want nothing for him! Nothing!" She kicked the body bag as she screamed. Cleopatra tried to pull her mother back. Babe shook with effort to hold himself in check. Earle took Babe by the shoulders to comfort him.

"They want something?" continued Charity Bentham. She moved her arms under her cloak. "Here! Take it, here!" With that, she slammed a dark object so hard on the raft that it bounced into *Black Crane*. The sound was hideous. Lazarus leaned forward, took the gory thing with both hands, and tossed it into the water.

"Mother! Mother!" cried Cleopatra. I turned full around to see Cleopatra lift her Mother clear of the body bag. How much of Charity's performance was masquerade? Peregrine had indeed murdered Cesare. I was never sure. Cleopatra had surprised me again: she was as strong as she was strong-willed, and as strong-voiced, commanding, "I don't care what you do! Stop tormenting my mother! Have you men no decency?"

"Please, understand," started the lieutenant.

"Do those orders say he is to have a Christian burial?" said Grandfather. "Surely you see this woman has a right to revenge herself. I did not condemn this man to have him shown respect!"

The lieutenant looked to his sergeant. The blood, the mourners, the night—they did not have enough of a will left for this. The lieutenant suggested he send for his captain. Grandfather started to lecture him on the vengeance of Lord God. The lieutenant interrupted Grandfather in order to ask for a solution.

"Give me one of your men, and this vermin here"—Grandfather indicated two convicts—"and we'll feed him to the fish. He needs worse."

"I cannot do such a thing," said the lieutenant.

At that Cleopatra struck the lieutenant in the back, then thrust against him with her shoulder, sending him over the side and into *Black Crane*. He landed hard and rolled toward Earle, but was only stunned, and tried to sit up. Earle reacted with a motion so swift and tight than none of the Brigadesmen saw. Earle struck to kill.

Grandfather immediately began his thunder: "Get that man out of there! Stand back! Sergeant, you will provide us a trooper, that one there, him, get in, you will help me! Get that body aboard! I shall take charge here! Trooper, get in! Ladies, now you! Give way!"

Grandfather stepped into the stern of *Black Crane*, seizing the tiller from Guy. Earle, Lazarus, and I fixed our arms on the raft to steady the boat as we balanced the new passengers. Grandfather bellowed, all rage and righteousness. What a magnificient bluffer; despite everything I had heard of him and seen, I was awed, and just as amazed that by a twist he was on my family's side, more, he was my family. He assumed total charge, getting the convicts and the women aboard, berating a Brigadesman who moved sluggishly, suspiciously, to take position as a guard in the bow, warning the troops on the pier to mind their own, tend their duty, for he was "the Reverend Mord Fiddle, doing the work of Lord God!" That magic tongue overwhelmed them. One wanted to believe him in order to escape his wrath. I think now they permitted us to shove off for their own release. Then again, there is the fact that Grandfather really was the would-be despot of the Evangelical Republic of Sweden; and that in revolution, it is not the prudent man who prevails, rather the fanatical, the tyrannical, the pitiless.

This is to speak prematurely of the phenomenon of a black prince. I have studied this matter as best I can. Grandfather was never in the rank of such as Savonarola, Torquemada, Cromwell, Robespierre. And I can speak with the authority of one who has seen what it is to pretend to self-elected omnipotence. Grandfather's sense of the coming kingdom of his Lord God was always informed, however tardily, by a faith in the possibility of reconciliation. What he helped wreak in Sweden should not be forgotten, though it probably has been by now, another passing disgrace. I cannot say what happened there, in the North, after we fled. I presume that all improved once the passion of insane prejudice ran its course. The Loyalist call for purity was not a masterwork, it was a cowardly surrender. For their shame, for Grandfather's shame, I pray to God for forgiveness. I say this with intimate knowledge of far worse, with liability for far worse, than anything Grandfather and his thugs did there. I must not telescope my story too far ahead. There is much I must record for clarity. It is appropriate here to say that aboard *Angel of Death,* I and my family escaped a kingdom cursed by fire, and that aboard *Angel of Death,* we fell into an age cursed by exile and toward a kingdom cursed by ice, and that it was in so falling that Grim Fiddle was to discover that most profound of human treasures, his own destiny.

THE FLEET

OF THE DAMNED

Hope Abandoned ▪ *The Free Gift of God*
▪ The End of the Earth

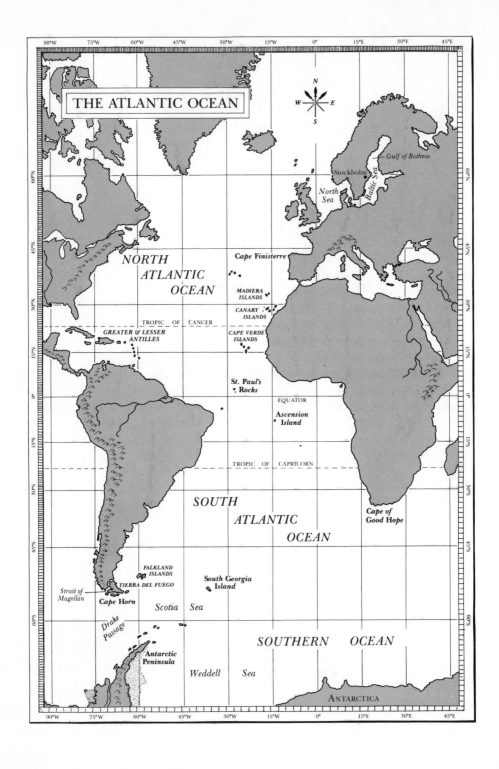

Hope Abandoned

Punishment had transformed Peregrine. And, one-eyed, emaciated, bent, he came back to us more changed than even his physical distortions would suggest. He had rid himself of his anger. He was peaceful; no, not merely that, for there was also his fascination with the sea, the food he ate, whatever we said to him. He had not relaxed—as might a man who has been broken by five years of incarceration—he had intensified about the commonplace. He spoke to me peculiarly with his new self, saying things such as, "No man has a truer son." I had no ready reply, usually smiled, which set him at ease, as if I were the lord and host and he the wayfaring guest. Did he feel impermanent? He made being alive and on board *Angel of Death* seem a reward.

The metamorphosis disturbed me, not unhappily. Before, Peregrine and I engaged in conversations that circled around our love for each other, that were grounded in events, objects, history. After, all we talked about was our relationship. Peregrine had seized upon fidelity, loyalty, devotion, upon what I presume he meant with the single word *true*. Before, Peregrine had only rarely spoken candidly about family, America, Sweden. He had avoided the deepest truth-telling. And his deception had been most damaging when directed against himself. He had made believe more than he had believed. After, he seemed to fasten on that intangible Greek concept, the Truth, as if it were his next breath.

"He got away," said Guy of Peregrine's metamorphosis.

"He got her," said Israel.

Indeed, it was not possible to determine how much of Peregrine's new identity was self-generated and how much was called forth by his intimacy with Charity Bentham. She was with him like a new limb. She held him, sang to him, fed him, helped him on deck for exercise, slept with him in that narrow bunk. She seemed to animate his wasted body. He was my father, and Israel's friend. He was her devotion.

Charity Bentham also changed after the rescue. From what I learned of her conduct beforehand, she had known despair but overall had been assertive, effective, self-generating. Her performance on the pier with the Brigadesmen was typical of her power. On board *Angel of Death* all that disappeared. She gave the impression that if Peregrine left her sight, she herself would disappear. If Peregrine was more loving afterward, Charity was all sentiment, a creature so fragile and vulnerable that one worried the sea might wash her away as she huddled with Peregrine in the gangway. She stopped speaking in complete sentences. She must have talked at length with Peregrine, for I saw them wrapped in conversation. I never overheard her. And as he grew stronger, Peregrine developed a way of speaking for Charity, as if there were two bodies, one voice, one heart. Where was the Nobel Laureate? The answer is that she was in place. She had turned inward. Charity Bentham was an extraordinary human being. Before, she had pursued fortune and power. After, she pursued Peregrine. She applied that will of hers to reawakening a man who should have died soon after his rescue. It was as if she kissed him back to life, adored him, in order to keep him from quitting us. She performed a miracle of love and hope.

And as Charity's hope filled Peregrine, their love conjoined affected all of us on board. We did not become new men, like Peregrine, but there were changes. Israel joked less, spoke seriously, perhaps heavily, to me. He explained how wrong he had been to spurn Charity's help, saying, "I should never have given up on those two." He warned me never to wait for love, as he had done with Molly. Guy was more patient, doting not just on Earle but also on Molly and me and even my dogs, whom he had never much liked. Thord talked less and brooded more, but even he acted pleased to be alive when not upset by Orri's ordeal with Gizur's hallucinations. Earle remained steady, as taciturn as ever, with the change that he spoke up more readily in our shipboard councils; he was fatherly toward the Turks and conciliatory toward the Furore brothers, not waiting for Guy's lead.

We had each changed some, then, not entirely for the better, certainly in concert with our expectations. We congratulated ourselves for having survived the fire. We felt tempered. We had lost everything we possessed and yet held to our community. Those first few days out of Stockholm harbor, we could admire Charity's care for Peregrine, and Peregrine's metamorphosis, and all our reconciliations, and have reason to believe that we were free of Sweden's murder.

Yet we were not so free that one of our number could not easily remind us of our troubles. Cleopatra Furore patrolled our consciences. It was unfair and cruel of her, yet I know now it was in character, and is therefore condemnable only in that we had so many immediate obstacles that we could have been spared her dissent until later. Her brothers seemed to restrain their moods and did cooperate with the business of getting on. Cleopatra alone stood apart, and imperially. She treated Lazarus as her prime minister, the other two as her courtiers. She treated us as vulgarians. Whenever there was gaiety on deck, she would appear in a rush, a cloaked and accusatory look about her, and try to intimidate us into sobriety, which generally worked, even on the gentlest, least culpable of us, Molly.

And why? Guilt alone would have been sufficient. We really had rescued the man who had murdered her father. And we were openly prideful of our action. Yet that was our initial reaction, our affair to digest, and I believe would have eventually settled into a manageable history. Perhaps Cleopatra sensed that the passing of time would make her conduct out of place. And so she did more than silently accuse us. She was belligerent. I was her target. Toward me, she was cynical, manipulative, venomous. I dwarfed her physically, and she was no slight person. In reply she made me feel an intellectual mite. In conversation, between us or in a group, she would cut me off, dismiss me, overwhelm me. She was as eager to mock me as I was to avoid her. She wanted to humiliate me, and went farther on one of the first nights on *Angel of Death:* she cursed me.

"Any woman who could love that man is no mother to me," she said. This is typical of her talk, premeditated hyperbole. "And if you could see as I do, Grim Fiddle, you would know how odious to me is everything that man loves. You are worse than he is."

What did that mean? It was non-sensible, so filled with revulsion as to be pitiable. At the time, though, I thought it impossibly profound and undecipherable. I could not reply. I moved away, afraid of her temper. There was nowhere to hide on seventy-six feet of Norse timber. And she pursued me, running on about how she held me responsible for Charity's love for Peregrine, and Peregrine's escape from death, and all that had happened. It seemed for Cleopatra that I was Peregrine's first and most contemptible crime, the one that had engendered the divorce, the remarriage, and Cleopatra's conception. Therefore, for Cleopatra, I was the germ of all that had befallen the Furores.

Israel several times attempted to explain to me how he saw Cleopatra's attitude toward me. He said that Peregrine had wrongly murdered Cesare Furore and been rightly condemned for it. Charity had delivered Peregrine from his ruin, for her own contradictory reasons. All this confused Cleopatra and gradually came to sicken her. Cleopatra was left with a murdered father whom she wanted to revenge, and an aggrieved mother whom she wanted to help. Then Charity had actually involved Cleopatra in a conspiracy to rescue the man she naturally reviled. Cleopatra had cooperated, reluctantly but effectively. Afterward, she reconsidered her actions and, feeling shame for what she thought was the betrayal of her father, turned against everyone who reminded her of the sadness. With the best and most praiseworthy of motives, love for her father and mother, Cleopatra felt something she was constrained from acting on—revenge—and Cleopatra had done something she could not accept in retrospect, helped to deliver Peregrine. She could separate herself from Charity, and could continue to condemn Peregrine, and could regret her fate. But that was not enough, or at least it did not satisfy her. Her frustration unbalanced her. I recall Israel saying she felt stained by her father's blood. Cleopatra herself became murderous. And she stabbed at what represented to her Peregrine's dark side—the side that had murdered—and this was his bastard, Grim Fiddle.

I remain cautious of all this. It seems too neat to me now, certainly too Greek. Israel would appreciate my suspicion of his theory. If people were so logical, there would be no difference between mankind and the stars. Yes, Cleopatra might have hated me from the first, without need for specific cause, with a general disgust for her condition. Yet she also seemed to have need of me. And I argue now that what she needed was my presence, the fact of me, the eagerness and awkwardnesss of me trying to understand her, pity her, help her. I represented to her not only

her persecuting fate, as Israel said, but also her success at standing up to her tormentors, her father's murderers. I was her pride
of conquest, in that she could feel herself most righteous and indomitable when she could strike at me. I provided her a certain
sense of identity in her confusion of roles, for to revile me was to
demonstrate that she remained unreconciled to her fate. Seeing
me would hurt her, hurting me would hurt her, knowing I was
hurt would hurt her. All this pain, cruelty, hardheartedness would
make her feel justified. It does seem contradictory that one can
cling to pain, and pain-making, as firmly as one can cling to joy
and joy-making. That is what Cleopatra seemed to do, passionately. In this peculiar way, from the first, I was Cleopatra's passion. She lavished on me a nakedness of soul that one would
ordinarily give to a lover. This confounded me as it compelled
me. I risk to argue here that I became Cleopatra's passion as Peregrine had become Charity's. As we were father and son, they
were mother and daughter, by blood, by manner, and by persuasion to love and to hate and to remain unresolved.

This investigation will have to end for now, perhaps for always unless I am further tempted by it. The truth of it might be
that I did not understand Cleopatra then any better than I do
now. I admit my failure to render her. I wish that I had Israel to
turn to, or perhaps a book of these things—crimes of the heart.
That is the depth of it. I was attacked by Cleopatra. She was ar-
resting, dangerous, fast. Perhaps I loved her in defense of my
self. We fought on the battleground of our hearts for the satisfaction of revenging our parents' wrongdoings, for the satisfaction
of conquering each other's very reason for being. We were conceived in a confusion of fate: she could have been my sister, I
could have been her. How could there ever be a finish to our
contest? We both lost as we both won. How I still can feel my fear
of her as I feel my love for her! I wonder if she feels the same of
me. The single conclusion I offer myself, after all this time, is that
our love was, from the first abrupt exchange at Vexbeggar, as
unlucky as it was hopeless.

Grandfather was the first of us to notice the new shame in
the world of men. He had kept apart from us the first few days

out of Stockholm harbor, busy commanding a makeshift crew as *Angel of Death* cleared the Baltic for the Kattegat and Skaggerak and then passed into the North Sea. He was indifferent to our recapitulations and peacemakings. He looked to his ship and to the sea. He gained a clear vision of certain eerie irregularities in the merchant traffic, the shoreline, the sea.

The evening he took me into his confidence was humblingly bright with stars, Castor and Pollux nearly straight above, like eyes of heaven. Wild Drumrul and Lazarus had the watch at the wheel; Orlando the Black, Babe, and Earle had the deck watch. They were bantering playfully as we came on deck. Grandfather, somber and gruff, invited me forward, making it clear he disapproved of the watch's conduct. He sat me down by the foremast. We were soon drenched in a cold mist as *Angel of Death,* trimmed for slow running in a rolling sea, cut a steady course westward. Grandfather gestured above to the Milky Way. He said something odd about signs, in Old Norse. I was impressed and delighted to discover that Grandfather knew the heavens as keenly as he knew the Bible, and in the same way, a celebrant not a critic. He began loudly, "You are a prize! I see that. No man could have raised you better."

"You will like my father. He wasn't always like this," I said.

"No matter now. Do you know what they have in mind?"

"Israel and Guy?"

"That heathen lot. They want me to take you halfway around the earth. To this Baja California. They do not know. I shall not tell them. I shall tell you."

"You're a fine teacher. We're a better ship every day," I started. I thought he meant that his ship's hands were amateurs. Initially I had worried about this, but I could see that *Angel of Death,* even with *Black Crane* lashed down between her masts, was a muscular beauty; she had originally been built for weathering the brutal Gulf of Bothnia. Grandfather once boasted to me that three men and a Bible could sail *Angel of Death* to the moon. I discontinued my defense of the crew, however, when I felt Grandfather's impatience. I asked, "What is it you know?"

"I am not one to quit a rough business," he said, gesturing to the west, "but we have no chance for this Mexico."

"It's where the Furores live," I tried. I was wrong again. He turned on me slowly, his hair and beard matted like stone by the sea spray, his face filled with a dreadful certainty. He wiped his eyes. He studied me. It was not then possible for me to imagine anything Grandfather could not do, or anything that was too rough for him to try.

"You think me a monster. Is that what they tell you? For what I did? My work with the League? A monster?"

I struggled to say I did not understand.

"Speak your face," he said.

"It was ugly, what you did. Yes, you were wrong," I said.

"What I did, what I had to do, what we did—we were saints compared to what is out there," Grandfather said, pointing to the west. "I have served Lord God all my life. I would sooner put this knife into your heart than disobey Lord God. Understand this, Grandson. When Lord God told his servant Noah to build him an ark; and when Lord God told Noah, 'The loathsomeness of all mankind has become plain to me, for through them the earth is full of violence, and I intend to destroy them, and the earth with them'; and when Lord God fulfilled this terrible plan; and when Lord God spared Noah and the remnant after one month and twenty-seven days; and when Lord God told Noah and his to come out again on this sanctified earth and be fruitful and increase there, I ask, then, was Lord God a monster? Is he ugly to you? Was he wrong? Speak right to me. You think Lord God a monster?"

"I do not, Grandfather," I said.

"Then you begin to understand the power and the wisdom of Lord God, almighty and all terrible and all righteous. We of the League did his work. We tried to build us an ark. We tried to save a remnant from the wrath of Lord God for mankind's loathsomeness. We tried and it was worth the trying. Their wickedness is alive, stronger every day. We might have succeeded. It is my failure that I was called away, that I was not strong enough to see our work to the end. It is also my failure that, for my wrong to you, I am brought low. I accept my path. I have you. I do not challenge Lord God's wisdom. I serve it."

"Please, Grandfather, I don't know the Bible as you do," I said, deep breathing, for if ever there was a first moment for me to learn moral courage, that was it, "but didn't Lord God, didn't he promise Noah, after the flood, that he would never send the waters again, no matter how evil man might become?"

Grandfather rumbled; the sound of a mountain moving. And I do believe that he started a smile that was erased by the wind.

"I cannot believe it was as you say," I continued. "And I cannot believe Lord God would do that to people. At Vexbeggar they burned schools and churches. They shot at children. And those poor people drowned their own babies. I think I had to kill a man because of what your League did."

"You fought for your own. That is not wrong. We fought for our own. That is not wrong. Their wickedness, Grim, it is everywhere. Satan takes the soul of any man who does not love Lord God completely. What I have seen! What I have done! What can a boy know of what heathen do to believers in the name of their kind of justice? Their justice. Not mine. I am prepared to admit my error. Show me where I was wrong to fight for my people. Show me, tell me. I was not wrong! I struck at darkness, as you did at Vexbeggar. You call me ugly and wrong. The darkness is worse than anything you have seen. You do not know the dark. It is not that sky. It is not that sea. It is not what I have done. It is there and there and there!" Grandfather flung his arms south, east, west.

I stood beside him, looked out in the directions he gave. I said, "I see the world, Grandfather. It frightens me. It doesn't hate me. Why should I hate it?"

"You want to see the darkness?" he said, annoyed, ferocious. "Then use your eyes and wits. If you had, you would have seen that German wolf to starboard today."

"What wolf?" I said.

"Do you want to know of that place of theirs, that heathen land, America? Does your father tell you? Does that woman? Have you heard of their infamy?"

"Do you mean Vietnam?"

"Done and gone! Worse than what a boy sees. See it!"

I felt I was missing a fantastic battle. I wanted to see something. I strained. There was still only the world. He put his arm around me, not friendly, a death grip.

"You!" thundered Grandfather. "I want to save you from their darkness! Come with me. We can take that *karfi* of yours and make northwest. I know some good men. Greenland would take us in. We could fish, keep clear for a while longer."

"What has happened? What haven't you told me?"

"There is no refuge. There is no sanctuary. There is no peace. This Baja, this California—lies! We cannot fight them there. We must run, and fight only when we cannot run more. See it!"

He ordered me to leave, not to bother him again until I had made my decision about Greenland. I had no reply, could not imagine what I should say. Was Grandfather mad, as Israel said repeatedly. Or was he trying to tell me something significant in a language I could not interpret? I wanted to establish a sure relationship with him despite his thunder. Grandfather was a man with whom one could be intimate, if he permitted, without ever enjoying an intimate moment. His devotion to me was direct, captivating. He did not want to talk about it, or even show it in any normal manner. I asked myself why he seemed to believe in me so absolutely. He did say he owed me for his wrong to me, for abandoning me at birth. Perhaps his fidelity to Grim Fiddle was a way to express his dedication to the idea of his own destiny, perhaps his faith in me was part of his own discipleship. Then again, perhaps he believed in me simply because he loved me, as a grandfather should love his grandson.

If that was all of it—love—then I can puzzle out more than our bond. I can speak to what I am. For with that love Grandfather passed on to me huge parts of himself. I understand this now, that all the energy, fortitude, perseverance, daring, vision I possess, as well as the pridefulness, hypocrisy, cruelty, and plain dishonesty, springs from the fury in Grandfather; it is also mixed with what I learned from Father of the ironies of loss, surrender, helplessness. As I once learned to respect Father's melancholy, I learned on board *Angel of Death* to respect Grandfather's resolve. My situation on board *Angel of Death* was such that I could no more have denounced and turned from Grandfather than I could have denounced and turned from one of those wearying, mesmerizing, indefatigably brutal prophets of Judah who harassed, cursed, condemned, and finally saved their kinsmen from another period of the same sort of "darkness" Grandfather announced to me. Grandfather was mad, in the rational sense Israel meant. That must be established: Grandfather lacked reason. Yet there was grandeur and savvy in him. It should not be forgotten now, when the heat and rush of those times can seem as long ago as Noah's flood, that those times called forth the extraordinary in creation, like a Leviathan. We aboard *Angel of Death* had my grandfather. I remember Israel joking to me once that if the world really was a stage, then there must be some big parts. Grandfather was a big part. For all his meanspiritedness, he was our deliverer. I learned to believe in him intrinsically. I learned to trust him as a foundation of my faith. I learned to worship him.

I thought hard on his warning, irrational as it seemed. What was Greenland to Grandfather? To the ancient Norse, it had been a desperate refuge, temporary, sad-minded, from which they had usually planned to return to action and retribution. And what of Grandfather's talk of arks? If Sweden was an ark, were there other arks? And what of his "German wolf"?

There had been a cutter to starboard that afternoon. It might have been German. I had seen no threat. On reconsideration, it had seemed to be monitoring us as we slipped into the North Sea. Later that night, after my talk with Grandfather, we did hear thunder to the east. It might have been gunfire. The next evening, we sighted a group of large trawlers to the north, under power and in concert, suggestively belligerent. The following afternoon, we spied wreckage across a wide front, and passing south of it, thought we saw bloated animal corpses, dogs and cattle. Grandfather came to the railing at the sighting. I asked him what he saw now. Grandfather raised his voice so that Israel and Molly would hear, "There was a battle here."

That evening, in our routine council, Grandfather tried to insert himself in our decision-making for the first time. He urged we change course, making for the Atlantic north of Scotland, what would have been a rugged sail that time of year, huge seas and ice floes. Israel was instantly opposed to Grandfather's recommendation and said so gruffly, having me translate his English rather than himself addressing Grandfather in Swedish. It was an excessive display of disregard. This exchange is where I mark the beginning of the spiritual battle for control of *Angel of Death*, a contest in which I would find myself pawn, traitor, and bounty: yes, Grandfather was always in command of the ship, owner and captain; but for those first weeks out of Stockholm, Grandfather was not overlord of his passengers. And this pained him. He listened to my abridged version of Israel's remarks, and then left the galley. I thought him frustrated; he was actually maneuvering, biding his time. The council's resolution—approved by our ruling triumvirate of Israel, Guy, and Thord—was to continue to the English Channel.

A British patrol, two well-armed cutters, intercepted us at dawn. The lead ship sent automatic-weapon fire across our bow before hailing us. They made no attempt to communicate on ship-to-ship radio. I got topside hurriedly. I relieved Earle at the helm, sent the watch to trim us smartly. Orlando the Black was ready to uncover our fixed automatic weapon, and it was only the quick-thinking intervention of Otter Ransom, screaming "No! No!" that saved us from an answering barrage. Otter Ransom had been appointed our weapons officer, and this had already caused disagreements with the Furore brothers, who had been obliged to surrender their firearms to the arsenal. Otter Ransom ordered Orlando the Black and Babe below decks, shouted into the hatch that the two convicts we had rescued with Father were to keep everyone out of sight. I note that those two convicts were not idly chosen for their part in the rescue, had once been some of Thord's best smugglers, a Laplander named Skyeless and a grizzly little man whom Orri called Tall Troll.

Grandfather came on deck and took charge. We ran up our Swedish flag. Grandfather had Israel bring Molly and Cleopatra up to make us appear a pleasure craft; Guy came up without permission. The second cutter closed on us at high speed and sent a wake that listed us suddenly. Guy shook his fist. Grandfather said to stand easy. He then cupped his hands and boomed across that we were Swedish nationals, bound for the Americas. The lead cutter flashed a light across our length, pausing at the tarp covering our automatic weapon. A portly officer in a great blue coat appeared with a bullhorn and called across his name, rank, and ship's nationality. He continued, in a tired way, and warned us not to attempt to land on British soil, including the Channel Islands, and that all British ports were closed to "unauthorized refugees." Guy screamed out, "What's authority, then?" Grandfather nodded in approval and then drowned out the sea with a condemnation of the officer's birthright, his navy, his country, every man who would dare to support a policy that excluded him and his ship. Grandfather demanded to know what right the British Navy had to open fire on a Swedish ship in international waters.

The officer, apparently disgusted by his task, but the good seaman throughout, said one word: "Cholera."

We lost the British when we left the Strait of Dover, but soon spied some French cutters to the southwest. We did not want to risk their accuracy across our bow, and kept far north of the Bay of the Seine while at the same time endeavoring to avoid more British patrols. Our task was grueling, given that we were also struggling with the wind and current from the west. It was an anxious Channel passage. There were nights we could see fire to the northeast, either from ships or from the English coast. And Wild Drumrul, who had the best eyes on board, swore he saw an explosion that tore the horizon with red and yellow flares in the direction of Cherbourg. Each dawn we heard the thunder, which we now had reason to assume was gunfire. There was much wreckage and spotty oil slicks that grew into black lakes which coated our bow with greasy seaweed. South of Plymouth, Guy and Orri, on deck watch, said they saw wreckage with people clinging to it. In that rolling sea, it was not possible to maintain an observation station. Soon after, a gale rose sudden and fierce from the southwest—our fifth blow since the Skaggerak, but our first serious test as seamen—and we were too pressed manning the pumps, shortening sail, making into a heavy sea for four days to care about anyone adrift out there.

What few moments we did have, between fighting the sea and sleeping poorly in that sickening pitch and roll, we used to debate the meaning of what we had seen. We agreed that all of northern Europe seemed to fear the disruptions of the Baltic refugees as much as had Stockholm. We supposed that some precautions were required, given the panic. We had seen enough overladen trawlers, ancient frigates with decks covered by tents, and ship wreckage to be able to surmise the deadly confusion of populations in pellmell flight.

What was not obvious to us was the extent of the exclusion. It was no simple or local policy, much more virulent. We could not see it, not the way Grandfather meant. We had been permitted to pass unharmed. We supposed our fate was common. It was luck. I can have no certain knowledge now as to how many ships went down by misadventure, how many were deliberately scuttled by hired crews, how many were sunk by those cutters. I can guess at a pan-European shame.

What fooled us, what we permitted to deceive us, was that there was nothing overwhelmingly out-of-the-ordinary on the radio, either ship-to-ship or international, to indicate there was an organized plot. At a council, we listened to Lazarus's explanation that the larger the conspiracy the more heinous its implications and the more likely it was to be silent, indirect, bureaucratic, mundane. "Saying no doesn't seem a threat," said Lazarus, "but when everyone says no, it can be a death sentence."

Cleopatra bridled at this. I was surprised, since I had thought Lazarus did no more than express her opinions. She said, "This is the late twentieth century, Lazarus, there are no villains."

Grandfather was hunched in the galley; he spoke across to me as soon as Gizur translated what Cleopatra had said. "The darkness, Grim. Satan smiles."

We passed into the main lanes south of Lizard Point, still struggling with heavy seas as we made for the Bay of Biscay. We intended to make our Atlantic crossing with the northeast trade winds from the Cape Verde Islands. We sighted numerous gleaming freighters carrying on as usual. Another blow off Ushant made us run seaward, away from a battered-looking frigate that, at a distance, appeared dismasted. We were days beating off that storm, and I think the better for it, since those wild Atlantic gales improved our seamanship, forced us to learn to work together, prepared us for the ordeal ahead. It was not until the end of November that we chanced upon our first unambiguous evidence of outrage.

We were east of Cape Finisterre at dawn. I recall it vividly because Earle had urged me up the mainmast to watch a school of phosphorescent fish pass beneath us. Wild Drumrul was already above me, near the top. There, he spied a small vessel adrift up wind to the west. She was also on fire, for within minutes a thickening spume marked her for all on deck to see. Grandfather ordered us about, and we made toward her slowly. We were shocked to see, after half an hour, a small motorcraft shoot away from the derelict and toward the coast just as an explosion ripped the hulk's bow. Someone had managed to launch a jolly, which did not make for us, just wallowed. There were ten bodies in the jolly, eight dead of smoke and burns, one child dead from unknown causes, and a tenth, a small man, dying of a mangled torso. The sea about us was strewn with corpses. Tall Troll, who had a worrisome talent for clear thinking in the midst of murder, estimated one hundred bodies, mostly children. We worried about infection. That officer had said "Cholera." Without agreement, we pulled that survivor on board. He replied to three questions before he died.

"Who did this to you?" asked Lazarus.

"They wanted gold! We have no gold! We have children! We need water! They killed us for gold!"

"Where did you come from?" asked Lazarus.

"The fleet of the damned!" he said.

Israel heard Lazarus's translation, turned away, looked at me, dark-faced, as if he had been shot, and said, "It's not possible. It isn't. Not now."

"Where were you bound?" asked Lazarus.

"Water! They would not give us water! They wanted gold! Get the children to America! I have cousins!"

Grandfather held him tenderly, prayed over him loudly enough to protect us from hearing his cries. The final question the man answered dead. He was not from the Baltic or northern Europe. He was not Spanish, Moroccan, African Negro. He was a Moslem, Lazarus said, probably a descendant of people originally from what was then the Islamic Republic of Pakistan. He spoke Portuguese. Lazarus guessed he was a refugee from the People's Republic of Angola.

"The fleet of the damned," we said to each other. Lazarus said this was a crude translation and could also be "ships of the accursed" or "boats of demons." Wild Drumrul said it would have been the same in Turkish. Orlando the Black added it was the same in Spanish. Guy said it was the same in French. I knew it was the same in Old Norse, Swedish, German. Only in English did it sound stilted, fantastic, hallucinatory. Israel said it was the worst kind of humor, the most appalling sort of joke—completely contagious. He also said it was near enough in any language to the unspeakable.

We tried not to speak of it as we carried as much sail as possible running the Portuguese trades down the Iberian coast. We slept badly, since we established extra and military round-the-clock watches. Otter Ransom gave lessons on weaponry; Tall Troll and Skyeless made plans for dealing with boarders. Wild Drumrul lived on the mainmast, eyes set to the east for motorcraft. We were blacked out at night, during the day kept well seaward of the shipping lanes. We remained in this panic until well past Cape Saint Vincent, when we could be reasonably assured we were beyond shore-based boats.

Orri upset our supper one night by speaking aloud our worst fantasy, to Thord, though we all heard: "But pirates? Off Portugal?"

Thord shushed him. Guy said it was not possible, said that it was unwise with people with as little information as we had to suppose that those Pakistanis had been murdered by pirates operating in daylight in the most heavily traveled sea lane in Europe, Ushant to Gibraltar. Grandfather, sitting nearby, reading the Fiddle Bible, listened to Gizur's translation, then looked accusingly at Guy. Guy returned the stare and said, "It was a freak."

Later, Lazarus took me, Israel, and Guy aside to explain how he had reworked his earlier thesis; he said that it was well within Europe's talent to organize a conspiracy of indifference. He grinned in that self-satisfied way of his, brainy, arrogant; he added that if one took into account the violence of the weather, the sea, disease, and those jackals in the boat, such a conspiracy of indifference could mean murder on a massive scale of all those caught helpless, without a nation, a coastline, an island, a rock to cling to.

We sighted Porto Santo, the small island to the northeast of Madeira, at first light on my twenty-second birthday. We were not celebratory. Peregrine told me, "We'll party when we get to Baja." Israel overheard this, did not conceal his sigh. We needed water, relief. The sea ran dark and the sky closed about us as we wore away to the west to sight Madeira's central mountains, shrouded in a dense mist. We intended to clear the stacks on a port tack and come around to the south of Madeira, to anchor at the Funchal Roads by nightfall. I was delighted with myself, not because of my birthday, rather because I was improving quickly as Grandfather's navigator. I had us exactly on course. It was not to be. A Portuguese cutter boomed out of the lee shore of Madeira to intercept us with unmistakable malevolence. Earle hurried Molly below. Grandfather gave an order and we came about for the southwest. In council that night, Israel and Guy took over an hour to reach the same decision Grandfather already had made about our sailing course. I was bothered that they made such a show of their authority in the command of the ship. But it seemed important to them to be able to tell Grandfather what to do. They ordered Grandfather to continue to the southwest.

Over the next week, we decided to go on two-thirds rations until the Canary Islands. That was our first defeat, and it invited bad turns. We were baffled by light winds, calms, thick pools of gray ooze that seemed to ride the northwesterly swell. We carefully avoided other traffic. We were a day out of Tenerife, the central island of the Canary group and our destination, when we sighted a large mass of dead fish, including several dozen dolphins, belly up, half rotted, riding the crest of a multicolored stain across our front. A fair wind at our quarter spared us the smell, not our doubts. Lazarus, through Gizur, asked Grandfather if this was unusual. Grandfather replied, "Very old." Israel tried to start an argument with Grandfather, decrying his black fatalism. Grandfather shrugged. It hurt me to see those two dig at each other, especially since, out on the ocean, Grandfather outclassed Israel.

It was the same at Tenerife as it had been at Madeira, with the distinction that one of the two Spanish cutters that came out after us did pass close enough to shout across that we could tie up at the harbor's breakwater in exchange for gold. They named an astronomical sum and specified it must be gold, not gems or cash money.

On bad rations, save Molly and Peregrine, we made for the last landfall feasible before our Atlantic crossing, the Cape Verde Islands, a week to the southwest. Goggle-Eye was the first of us to sicken. Hallverd, the young King's Spy (or Evangelical Brigademan) we had taken with us—and had not been able to land—collapsed with a similar fever soon after, confounding us because we assumed Goggle-Eye's poor health history made him exceptionally susceptible to infection. We continued to boil the water, which cut further into our supply. We argued the problem might be the fish we caught, or the flying fish that caught themselves. We ran with the wind and in fear of microbes. If it was cholera, we were finished; so we assumed otherwise, and no one else got sick. There was still no margin left. Israel and Guy declared at a council that we should not turn away from any Portuguese cutter without a fight. We readied ourselves for a struggle which did not come, at least not as we anticipated. We sighted Sal, the northeastern island of the Cape Verde archipelago, at midmorning, and swung well clear during the day, passing Boa Vista and Maio cautiously. There was nothing but mist, dark seas, quiet. We slid into Port Praia, on the lee shore of the main island, São Tiago, at dusk.

The silence was representative. The town was in ashes. Lazarus's spontaneous reaction to the sight of the smoldering wharves— for Cleopatra's benefit, but I overheard—was that there had been another failed revolution that had consumed itself with blood lust. He said he had heard of a "liberation struggle" there in the 1980s, that this must be the latest outbreak. His smugness did not suit the facts. The ruin was total. Studying São Tiago, in that dense weather, under the moonlit profile of those volcanic peaks, it was clear to me there had always been famine and turmoil there, even in good years. It was as clear to me that only man could have reduced everything so maliciously. The few victims we spotted camped at the waterline scampered away like vermin. The muggy doom unnerved us. The near shore was littered with dark lumps being picked over by dogs and birds. The evening's land breeze, as it shifted, poured a stench over us, that sweet, clinging, dizzying smell of death. We moved twice to avoid that stench, finally dropping anchor a hundred yards off an unburned pier. We made our plan quickly: me, the Furore brothers, Otter Ransom, Tall Troll, and Skyeless, plus Iceberg as scout, going ashore in the jolly by relay. We needed water, food, information. I waited on deck for my turn in the boat, did not talk with Israel and Guy, who stood behind me mumbling heavily, nor did I acknowledge Earle as he went forward to man the automatic weapon. I thought my conduct appropriate impertinence at the time, expressing my anger at them for not heeding Grandfather's advice to try for America on a northern route. I see now it was more honestly an expression of disloyalty to my family.

When I got ashore, I sent Iceberg ahead. Not one of us was bold enough to pause beneath the banner that some desperate official had strung like a shroud across the pier's main pylon, which read, in Portuguese, DANGER QUARANTINE. We had vowed we would not be turned away by men, and this meant the diseases of men as well. Lazarus found the other news, once we had gotten off the pier and formed a skirmish line, at Otter Ransom's direction, to walk into town. Painted in black tar across the concrete sea wall was a sinister Portuguese graffito; Lazarus translated literally, "Enter into despair." In English, Lazarus said, that would be "abandon hope."

I thanked Grandfather's Lord God that it was night, sparing us from seeing most of what a tropical climate—we were fifteen degrees north of the equator—does to a massacre, for that is what we found. Iceberg growled steadily, her hair up, teeth bared, blood sense alert. We soaked handcloths in Otter Ransom's whiskey flask and held them to our faces, fended off the flies as best we could.

There were survivors, those either too ill or too beaten to have fled. We stayed on the main avenue, making our way by moonlight, listening to the cries, low and not necessarily human. Iceberg marked the rats. We found signs of a battle near the central square, unburied human parts, burned-out vehicles. We did not examine the heap beside the town hall, instead turned away when we saw the main well was poisoned by corpses. It took us some time to locate an artesian well, down a side street, whose water Tall Troll tasted, pronounced potable. As we filled our casks, a man walked out of one of the huts, right toward us. He was old, withered, drunk. Several other ancients followed him, and they gathered to watch us. Lazarus started a conversation with them. I did not pay mind until our work was done and we were ready to leave. The chief informant gave no name, seemed older than the corpses we had seen. He spoke to me as I approached; Lazarus translated nearly simultaneously, "This is my ghost. I am dead and buried."

The ancient also answered questions: "They came in howls. There were many, many, like ants. We beat them. Then the sickness. They took our food. They came again. They took everything. The shit! They could not eat our food. They ate it and died. What men cannot eat food? My son, he told me these are devils. That was what the priest said. That Hell was full. Satan has returned them to the earth. From long ago, the priests say, the worst sinners, Pontius Pilate and Judas. They were little. They were hungry. From Hell. That is why they could not eat our food. The priest said. We begged them to leave us. They died. It burned! It was Satan. Mother of God, our cathedral burned like a stable. Only the shit did not burn. What sort of shit is it? It moves!"

We ran back to *Angel of Death,* as fast as I hasten to close this episode. I am hard-pressed, even now, to recall the first shocks of those times. Also, I do not want to dwell on Port Praia, because it was not extraordinary. I can suppose there are accounts of worse elsewhere in the Atlantic that are unavailable to me; if not, I shall tell things that make that island seem merciful. We gathered our water. Port Praia gathered nothing.

Goggle-Eye died while we were ashore. He rolled over in his bunk and melted with fever. Wild Drumrul came to the rail to tell me. I looked to Israel for guidance; he ignored me, holding Molly close. Peregrine and Charity were of no use to me, remaining huddled below. We stowed our water casks, then wandered about the deck. We talked in spurts, me to Guy, Otter Ransom to Thord, Lazarus to Cleopatra, then we fell into a silence that matched the night's. Dawn surprised me, a thick soup over the sun, the on-shore breeze stirring the cinders in the ruins into new fires. It did seem as if an evil force raced through Port Praia with a torch. That place drained us of desire. If not for Grandfather, we might have laid in anchor until self-pity finished us. That is a dull sort of exhaustion. One cannot eat, or drink, or think in a reasonable pattern. Perhaps that is why Grandfather could act so effectively. His thinking was not reasonable, part in the present and part in the Sinai, or Palestine, or Babylon, wherever there was a space and time that called forth the prophetic. While we whined about cholera, dysentery, the charnel house that was Port Praia, Grandfather pursued his ministry. He got below, wrapped Goggle-Eye's body in a blanket, weighted it, prayed loud and long over it, then passed it over the side with a psalm (131 in the Fiddle Bible): "Lord God, my heart is not proud, nor are my eyes haughty. I do not busy myself with great matters or things too marvelous for me. No, I submit myself, I account myself lowly, as this weaned child once clung to its mother. O Israel, look for Lord God now and evermore!"

There was a splash. Grandfather sobbed, stood, turned on us, then exploded in a muscular scolding, "You are alive! Sinners, you live!" He strode from the bow to the cockpit, shouting, "Praise Lord God we have lived while one of his children, one of the meekest among us, has not! If we all die now, we have received infinitely more than that poor dear child ever got! Are you thankless fools? Clear way! All hands to stations! Passengers below! Make ready the lines! Up anchor! And praise Lord God! Praise him!"

I threw myself at the mainmast and hauled lines in a fit. I wanted to hurt myself, anything to make me feel alive, to make me forget that old man's, that ghost's, story, to keep myself from seeing what had probably come to me, a true vision, when that old man had said, "Hell was full." So I worked, shouted orders, helped Wild Drumrul with the anchor. We all scrambled over *Angel of Death,* feeding on the energy that was Grandfather. We left the harbor in a daze. The sea was up, and we were rocked hard with double-crossing waves. There was a tightening in the electrically charged air; there were deep reports to the west, not gunfire this time, thunderclaps across the sea. We knew we were heading into a storm. We were for it. We had to clear Port Praia. We wanted bad weather to wash off some of that rot. I understand now that I was in some sort of mind-fever—another hint of the shape-changing that would overwhelm me later in life—which I did not come out of until I paused to pull on my foul-weather gear. While I was in the gangway, Cleopatra came up behind me suddenly. Her eyes were red, her face glowed with a beauty and a fear I remember now as her very nature. It was certainly one of the things that made me love her. The truth, Grim Fiddle says, is that she was my graven image. I stopped before her like a pagan. I started to weep, for Goggle-Eye, for Port Praia, for us. It is the first instance I can recall that we shared an intimate thought, even if it was just to acknowledge that we were too young, and that there were things in heaven and earth that we had never imagined. She broke the spell, asking, "Lazarus won't, can't. What did you find?"

"I can't either. I just can't."

"It is important, Grim. Tell me what you saw. Who did that? You know. What is it? What's wrong? Why won't you tell me?"

"What do you want me to do, describe that? Who did it? Don't ask me, don't ask me again!" I raised up. I raised my hand. And why? Earle must have been watching us; he was instantly there, stepping between, turning her away, blocking me with the same enormous backside that had given me privacy at conception. A swell took the ship, throwing me to the deck. I rolled over and got topside, remained there daylong, driving myself, taking in the sounds of the building storm and of Grandfather's fair-equal temper. It was exhilarating, rejuvenating, and up there I regretted my transgression. I was ashamed of how I had acted with Cleopatra, because I understood that when I had made ready to strike her, her imperious demands, it had not been Cleopatra I was striking out to silence, it had been my own prodigy. I had panicked rather than confront what I saw clearly for what it was the moment she forced me to think. I saw that Port Praia had been destroyed by the exiles and refugees who called themselves the fleet of the damned.

The Free Gift of God

Only Grandfather's metaphor is appropriate to the tempest that swallowed us southwest of Port Praia. We sailed into oceanic valleys of the shadow of death. We had the force of several gales over the deck and were picked up and carried along the crest of the waves like a twig; if we had fallen off line just a touch we would have gone over. I recall one moment that overwhelmed me: I was struggling at the wheel to keep us into the wind, when of a sudden I looked up to see what I thought were clear skies to the east. I called to Grandfather and the rest, that we were saved, that the storm was broken. Grandfather catapulted into the cockpit, wiped his eyes clear of caked salt, and looked up to where I pointed. He straightened gracefully, then he raised his arms high and screamed, "A fine laugh, Satan!" I saw my error. What I had thought were white clouds marking a break in the weather was in fact the white crest of a cliffside of water. *Angel of Death* shot up that wall, dipped hard at the top, then plunged again toward the center of the sea. There were times, as we rode up and down those canyons, that I hoped for an end, relief, release from that vast tomb of salt water. I kept my station, held to life by a power that I realized would let me go when and if it chose. Grandfather told me that storm was a sign from Lord God. I puzzle now if it was not a welcome into our time in the wilderness.

We nearly lost Skyeless on the second day, which was Christmas 1995, as a rogue wave crashed over us, with him and Orri at the boom; only luck and a lifeline saved him, half insane from being snapped back from his grave, his leg smashed up. We did lose Hallverd, the King's Spy, on the fifth day: delirious with fever, he charged on deck and threw himself off the stern; a wave caught him in midair and drove him back half the length of the ship before it pulled him under. We lost the top of our foremast on the seventh day. The sea still whirled as the sky raged, lightning bolts like claws leaping as if from wave crest to wave trough— an illusion that was magnificent and awful. By the ninth day, the first day of 1996, we could not pull ourselves to duty on the foredeck. Grandfather lashed himself to the wheel, ordering the heaviest crew members to take alternate turns holding his legs to provide him leverage against the rudder. We gave ourselves up to fate. Grandfather did not sleep; he prayed, he sang psalms, he argued with his Lord God: "You should not abandon us here! We have not begun to suffer! We are vain sinners! What purpose my work if this is an end? I must deliver him from their ways! Satan cannot take me! I feel your hand cradling me! Test me, break me! I shall not relent!"

When the storm did break, we were straddling the equator, approximately one thousand miles from Africa and a little less from South America. The waves poured us like debris into an unholy heat. With Babe's help, I untied Grandfather and pulled him below. Cleopatra helped us undress him, wash him, lay him out to sleep. We were too exhausted to talk, collapsed in our own berths. I do not know how many days it took us to recover, *Angel of Death* drifting in the humid calm.

It was Wild Drumrul, asleep on deck to avoid the swelter below, who first smelled the smoke; unless it was Iceberg and Goldberg and their pups up top, also to escape the heat, who licked Wild Drumrul to alarm. He awoke me, screaming in broken German, "The fire! The sea is on fire!"

We awakened Guy, Israel, and Thord, and we five stood aghast at the stern. It was midmorning, the sea nearby like green glass. Above, the sky was whitish blue with the heat. And before, at a great distance to the west, there was a shimmering fire line, subtending a ninety-degree angle. A thin smoke hugged the water in the near distance, and as we watched it curled across the sea to wash over us in the light breeze that fluttered our single sheet, then died. The calm was complete. The view was unconvincing, another illusion, and one had to turn away and look again, several times, to judge time and space. There was a fire line there, like ragged red crystal between the green blue sea and the pale blue sky.

We drifted in the strong westerly current toward the burning sea. At twilight, no indication of a wind from any quarter, all of us save Peregrine, Charity, and Grandfather gathered on deck to lounge before that terrible beauty.

"Water cannot burn," said Wild Drumrul to me.

"Is it the coast?" asked Israel.

"I don't think we can see that far," I said.

"Water cannot burn," said Wild Drumrul to Israel.

Full night displayed the Magellanic Cloud above and a spectacular seascape below, the fire starkly clear. We were still dazed from the storm, so I suppose more available to hypnotism. It did not occur to us to think of jeopardy. There was not a harsh word all day. It was Grandfather, emerging past midnight, surly and mighty again, who upset us, especially me. He paced the deck, then turned to drag me to the foredeck, another private conference.

"Greenland! You have not declared yourself," he said.

"I can't do it, please, you see," I tried.

"Knowing what I have said is true? We might have a chance."

"This is my family. You are my family. You said that to fight for what is mine is not wrong."

"Lord God is angrier than I had thought," he said.

"Do you know what that is?" I asked, pointing to the fire.

"You know!" he boomed, springing to the mainmast to preach. "You all know what you see! My children, how long will you not see? You lie there beaten, even as you are sucked into the maelstrom."

"A fire storm!" said Israel, standing up in excitement as I translated Grandfather's idioms. "That is what. Old man, you are crazy, but you do see things. Don't you understand, Guy? Grim says we're in the doldrums. The variables. It's where the junk collects, right? An enormous stagnant pond, between the winds and currents of the North Atlantic and the South Atlantic. That junk, it's been ignited into a fire storm, fed by waste."

"That's farfetched," said Guy.

"So were those pirates. So was Praia," said Israel.

Gizur told Grandfather what they had said; Grandfather stamped the deck. "Your godless science and your perversions have blinded you. Look again, then pray for our delivery from such evil."

"It is Satan," said Gizur, who had fallen under Grandfather's spell more than any of us, his mind weakened, now crumbling.

"That doesn't help anyone, Gizur, that nonsense," said Israel.

"Accursed Jew!" said Grandfather.

"None of that," said Thord, moving to shelter poor Gizur.

"Unrepentant Sodomite!" said Grandfather. "Heed the boy! Hell has burst into the world! Satan has torn creation open! There's the wound! Perdition!"

Guy, Israel, and Thord collected forward to confer. I sensed their digust with Grandfather. It was deserved. He had quit decency again, permitting his genius for metaphorical persuasion— which supported his superhuman resolve in a crisis—to become distorted in the calm, moving him to cruelty, hysteria. It was much the same distortion that had carried him from the Gulf of Bothnia to the pulpit of the Pillar of Salt to the near dictatorship of the North. I saw this, and tried the impossible, to give my loyalty to two irreconcilable parties.

"Whatever it is," I began, "it must feed on the wind. If we try for the trades to the Caribbean, we have to risk being dragged into that. It blocks us. We shouldn't go back there."

"It is Satan, Grim," said Grandfather.

"Shut up, old man, I swear," said Israel.

"Act, for pity's sake, act," spoke up Cleopatra. "What good is your talk?"

As Gizur explained her words Grandfather clapped his hands, well pleased with Cleopatra. We stood there gripped by her cold, obvious fact. Either we found the wind and sailed out of that calm, or the back draft of the fire storm would drag us into the burning sea. We had less choice than I had presented.

Grandfather thundered forth Psalm 100, "Acclaim the Lord, all men on earth, worship the Lord in gladness, enter his presence with songs of exultation, know that the Lord is God!" pausing between his bursts to order us to launch *Black Crane* and the jolly, to take to oars in teams, and, in Grandfather's words, to tow *Angel of Death* "free of the fumes of Hell."

"Pull, children!" Grandfather cried from the bow. "Until you know perdition when you see it, pull! Until you fear damnation more than death and death more than pain, pull!"

And I remember this: while I was going out to my shift and Lazarus was returning from his, I overheard him and Cleopatra; she pointed to the burning sea and asked, "Could there have been a war?" It was an idea that had not occurred to me, for I was ignorant of Lazarus's so-called political science. I waited to hear Lazarus say, "Nothing so easy, wilder, no explanation, none," and then he slumped to her.

We did catch the wind, after three days of rowing that wore us down badly and broke Earle's health. Grandfather thereupon proclaimed his own counsel. Hell was behind us, he said, he would not go back, and as master of *Angel of Death,* he would not risk proceeding east or west into the trades without trying for a landfall to mend the foremast and other minor damage that would worsen in a blow. At our council there was a bitter argument about Grandfather's fitness to continue as captain of the ship. I opened my charts to assist their decision. Guy wanted to go back, arguing the fire would burn out; Israel was wary of another calm, and equally of another storm. I told them we were three degrees south of the equator. If we were to continue without repairs, our choices were: either make for the southeast trades and ride the Benguela Current into an African port along the Gulf of Guinea, risking pirates and cutters; or to ride the trades across the Atlantic to catch the Brazil Current and, bypassing American ports for the same reason we should avoid Africa, try for the Pacific via the Strait of Magellan, the legendary grave of all ill-crewed, ill-equipped ships. I pressed them that making for the southwest seemed safest, and mending our foremast beforehand seemed most prudent. Grandfather's preference for a landfall midocean had two possibilities: either Saint Paul's Rocks to our northwest, an uninhabited desolation; or Ascension Island to the southeast, a British naval station that might be as hostile as had been the British Isles.

Israel and Guy listened and studied, then gave a qualified assent to Ascension for repairs, saying that only then would they decide whether we went west, east, or back north.

This was good caution; it was bad luck. Making for Ascension was another defeat. I am unsure if there were better choices; still, there might have been some other way than I was able to formulate, some other way that I could not see, that would have carried us back inside civilization. I stress this; it is not exaggeration. We knew we were in absolute peril, though we deceived ourselves, though we had known it since first we heard the word *cholera*. It was not something we were strong enough to share at meals. How does one say, "I think we are lost"? I could place us on the chart. Yet we were lost. Somehow, at some point, for a reason I do not yet comprehend (a mystery that compels this story), we on board *Angel of Death* had passed from the inside of civilization, reason, decency, privilege, common sense, and security to the outside of civilization, where there was no sense, only terror, silence, worse upon worse. Did it happen in Stockholm harbor when we stole *Peregrine*? Did it happen when we obeyed the exclusion by the cutters and fled? Did it happen when we ignored the massacre of children off Portugal? Did it happen when we walked through Port Praia in a nightmare? Did it happen when we survived a tempest that would have destroyed us except for Grandfather's bravado and our luck? Had we failed and were we condemned, had we dared and were we trapped, or had we stumbled and were we being tempted? It was this: We were lost to what we had had, by fortunate birthright, back in Sweden and America; and it became necessary to find a new life that was outside, other, incredible. If there was a greatest Good, it was no longer for us.

A week of rugged sailing brought us windward of Ascension Island. Thick weather had closed about us, and the rains were down in sheets, solving our fresh-water problem but keeping us at the pumps. We beat up hard toward where Ascension should have been. A sharp squall picked us up, drove us southward. I was not yet a certain navigator, but good enough to tell Grandfather that unless I was backward, Ascension should be to the east when the weather broke. It was not, more fog and rain. We took a new tack, listened for a foghorn, watched for lights. I reworked my figures. It was twilight, and I was going topside to admit my miscalculations again, when, simultaneously, Wild Drumrul cried, "Land to port!" and we heard the screams.

Did we hear anything? Did we see anything? I must explain that I was assuming that we had missed Ascension during the night. I blamed the squall for driving us more south than I had been able to determine: our instruments were antique, and without the stars to resight (even with them, for the southern heavens were new to me and Grandfather), I was mostly guessing. When Wild Drumrul cried, "Land to port," I quickly supposed that the land he sighted was not Ascension, was rather uninhabited volcanic formations, of the sort that poke up from the mid-Atlantic ridge, treacherous for uninformed sailors like us.

The screams dumbfounded us. The half-moon gave enough light to risk a pass close to the lee of the largest visible peak. Wild Drumrul cried again, this time a new surprise, "Light to port!" He identified the source as a ship at anchor a mile off the rocks. We scrambled to a new tack to take us toward the light. As we came about, there were more screams. We strained our eyes into the dark. We could make out a natural harbor, shaped by two hornstone ridges slanting down into the sea. In that cove appeared a heap of man-made things—boats, barges, rafts, frigates. The waves jammed them against each other, making snapping, thumping, squeaking sounds, some ripping open, some slipping underwater. We studied the ridges for signs of the crews and passengers. The rocks were barren of vegetation. There were no campfires. I called to Wild Drumrul that he must see signs of life. There were none. There were more screams.

"The wind, through the rocks, it's possible," said Israel.

"Speak your blind lies, Jew," said Grandfather, ordering us to shorten sail.

"I can see them!" cried Gizur to Orri, pointing to the rocks.

There was nothing to see. That is accurate. Yet when I swung free of our foresail, I did see something. I asked Babe with a shrug. Though he was deaf, he nodded yes. I asked Little Dede Gone; he ran to his brother. I went back to Grandfather. *Angel of Death* caught the wind and listed. Cleopatra came up top with Lazarus. They were arguing. I turned to them as another scream startled us, a barrage of screams, a chorus in pain.

"What is it?" said Cleopatra, more to me than Lazarus.

"Port of the damned," said Lazarus. He was angry. I understand now that he was jealous of me.

"You don't believe that," I said to Lazarus. "Those are just derelicts piled up here by the storms."

"And you don't believe that," said Lazarus.

Orlando the Black swung down beside us. He looked stern. He spoke patiently. "I see three sharp ridges forming a peak. Ocean, and clouds over the moon. Flotsam and jetsam. That is all."

Grandfather ordered us to stations; we came about one more time. Otter Ransom and Tall Troll readied for combat. We chose not to talk more of those screams, of those shapes and figures on those rocks, which none of us saw, which we only thought we saw, which we sensed. The ancient Norse held that an unburied corpse, especially if death was by misadventure or murder, can seek out the living, can walk and talk and scream, for retribution, for their regrets. Did we see the dead? We were exhausted, frightened, lost. It was the wind. We did see that lone ship's light.

They said they were missionaries. Their ship was a badly dilapidated cargo bomb, nearly a century old, a wooden hull, four masts for sail, and aged diesel engines added at some point in a makeshift reconditioning. It was named *The Free Gift of God*, out of Luanda, which Lazarus told me was the capital of the People's Republic of Angola. At our first pass, several of the missionaries appeared on the forecastle, robed, ebullient, and threw us greetings in English and Portuguese, holding up a crude wooden cross, calling "Hallelujah!" We chose to drop anchor off a small rock formation at a good distance from the freighter's stern, wary of the tide and unseen rocky teeth. Once we had anchored, our cable out forty feet, the weather cleared enough for me to resight our position. I remember no special shock at my discovery that the land behind us was indeed Ascension Island, marked on my charts as populated by four hundred people.

"I never doubted it," said Grandfather when I told him.

I did not go in the jolly with our lead party of Israel, Guy, and the Furores. The Furore brothers returned within the hour in dismal moods. Lazarus said the missionaries seemed Roman Catholic mendicants, a lay order, possibly a rogue order. They offered us assistance and what supplies they had. Lazarus also said they behaved strangely, as if none of what we were witnessing was out-of-the-ordinary. Lazarus said that Israel wanted me, Grandfather, Otter Ransom, Tall Troll, and Wild Drumrul to row over in *Black Crane* as soon as possible.

The Furores brought back with them two of the missionaries: a thin, old man of mixed blood, Father Hospital; and a nimble, middle-aged, very dark Negro, Father Novo Pedro. They spoke Portuguese, had some corrupt, plausible British-English, were dressed in heavy robes and skullcaps, and carried ornate crucifixes. The first thing they did was to announce they were ready to hear our confessions as a prelude to offering Holy Communion. Father Hospital asked me if anyone was in need of the sacrament of the last rites. I translated all this for Grandfather.

"I'll have none of that on my ship!" said Grandfather.

"Are you in need of absolution, my son?" Father Hospital said to Grandfather. Grandfather scowled at him, waved him back as he gave orders to lower away *Black Crane*. I explained to the fathers that we were mostly unchurched, but that my grandfather was a pastor in the Swedish Lutheran Church. They smiled pleasantly. I could see what Lazarus meant by peculiar. I asked Father Hospital, "What happened to Ascension?"

"We are doing Christ's work," he said, going below abruptly.

I pursued, found him greeting Charity and Peregrine. He seemed guileless, simpleminded. Peregrine smiled at him, looked at me and said, "Be careful." Father Hospital and I went up again, came upon Lazarus explaining to Cleopatra what he thought of *The Free Gift of God*. She called over Father Hospital and Father Novo Pedro, then tried to interrogate them: how long had they been here, where had they come from, what they hoped to accomplish. They replied with fragments of mystical evasiveness until Father Hospital took Cleopatra's hand, asked her how long it had been since she had made confession. Cleopatra answered flatly, "Five years," and then she lowered her head and added, "and one month." It had not occurred to me that she had been raised Roman Catholic. I did realize then that she had made her last confession before her father's murder.

Before we got down into *Black Crane*, Lazarus took me aside. I was pleased he seemed to trust me; he had not wanted to tell Cleopatra everything, yet needed someone to tell. "It's a stink over there," he said. "These people, refugees maybe, are down below. We kept clear of the hatches. There is something wrong." I recognized a deep agitation in Lazarus, fear mixed with disgust, and I touched him in sympathy. He pushed me away. I noticed that Grandfather was also agitated. He made the two missionaries sit before him in *Black Crane*, told them through Gizur not to talk to his crew. As we shoved off, I mentioned to Lazarus my puzzlement at what could have moved Israel to send for Grandfather.

The answer was that *The Free Gift of God* was an open grave. It reeked of human waste and putrefaction. We staggered aboard using a cargo net flung over from a plank at the waist. Other missionaries greeted us, more pleasantries and polite invitations, particularly to a chapel on the foredeck. Grandfather rebuffed them with a blast. We found Israel and Guy on the quarterdeck; they looked stunned, ashen, terrified. Israel said that he and Guy had just returned from the captain's quarters, where they had interviewed the missionaries' leader, Father Saint Stephen.

"They're all insane," said Israel.

"They pray over them," said Guy. "You should see it below, hundreds of people! And foodstuffs! In crates, anything you want, medicine, tools, grain. It sits there, rotting, for the rats! They pray over them. Some of those things down there have torn at the crates. Nothing is being done! You ask them why they don't feed them, and nothing!"

"They say they're doing Christ's work," I said.

At this, Grandfather turned to Otter Ransom, said, "Secure *Black Crane*. Clear the deck of those priests. None of them near your men. You and Tall Troll get below and mark the goods still worthwhile. Check that hoist." There was a pause, Otter Ransom looking to see if Israel agreed. Guy said, in a pale protest to Grandfather's presumption, that Father Saint Stephen had offered us whatever we wanted. Grandfather ignored Israel and Guy, pointed to the mast behind us, told Orlando the Black, "Find an ax and get that down. I'll want the top forty feet."

"You can't do that!" said Israel to Grandfather directly, in Swedish.

"How long have they been here?" said Grandfather.

"They didn't say," said Israel, in English to me.

"This ship will never leave this anchorage," said Grandfather.

"Reason with him," Israel told me. I struggled with a translation of Israel's concerns.

"Where is this priest who has frightened you children?" said Grandfather. Israel balked, straining to understand Grandfather's withering Swedish. Grandfather continued, "You think him as mad as me, is that so, Jew? Now you need me. Not because you deserted your country and lived where you were not wanted, not because you forced me to save a fiend who deserved the blade. None of that! You need me because you see the darkness that you have cowered in for decades, and you begin to see what it has come to. To this! I do not intend to hold you up. And I would not help you or your Sodomites if not that you have filled my Grim with a child's need of you, and you use him against me. Look hard, Jew. This ship is no Babylon. At most, it is a hole for Balaam. You are a small, weak, cowardly, unrepentant, faithless man. Show me this priest you fear. I shall show you what he is, and that he is as sane as me, and more sane than you!"

Israel was stiff with rage. Guy tried to soothe him. Grandfather bellowed at Orlando the Black about how to cut the mast for use on *Angel of Death*. This was a naked display of his lack of limits, his cruelty. He dizzied us. We stumbled about him: Guy begging me to shut him up; Lazarus and Orlando the Black con-

ferring secretly in opposition to everyone. Father Novo Pedro appeared and saved us further misery, saying that his brother, Father
Saint Stephen, begged a meeting with "the Lutheran." When I
told him, Grandfather clapped his hands, told me to follow, was
gone with Father Novo Pedro. I looked to Guy, who said I could
go, he would take charge on deck. I said that even I could not
handle Grandfather when he was like this. Lazarus surprised me
by saying he would accompany me, touching his belt oddly,
threateningly. Israel pushed Guy away, looked at me and Lazarus,
disdainful of our concern for him, saying, "I'm not afraid of that
bully! I've got more backbone than any fanatic."

Israel led me and Lazarus into the gangway. He stopped
abruptly, turned to me, defensive, tense. I sensed he was competing for me, and I felt sad for it. He told me that he had made a
bad mistake, out of rashness, when he invited Grandfather over
here, that only the shock of what they had found could explain
his stupidity. He said Grandfather was a savage man, capable of
any crime. He felt responsible for protecting these pathetic people
from him. Israel was in a killing mood himself. I had watched him
deteriorate since Stockholm. I am ashamed now that I had become more trusting of Grandfather's patriarchal brutality than Israel's enlightened humanity. To be fair to Israel, Molly's pregnancy
was a disabling fact. Israel seemed to suffer more than she with
each new peril. Several times I came upon him belowdecks sitting
with Peregrine and Charity; he was pale, weepy, withdrawn,
seemingly inconsolable. I had tried to conceal that I was increasingly suspicious of his opinions. I was not the only one to waver
before Israel's weaknesses. Guy and Lazarus openly challenged
him at our councils, even Earle—whose broken health under-
mined Guy's confidence in the same way Molly's listlessness did
Israel's—spoke against Israel's pronouncements.

Israel told me before Port Praia that he thought what was
happening to us—what I have described as falling from the inside
to the outside—made no sense, was neither a judgment of us nor
inevitable. He said he did not hate Grandfather, nor did he blame
him for our condition; he said that he was certain the opposition
he had encountered all his life was not organized, nor of a piece,
nor did it have a face. He also denied my talk of luck. He said, "I
keep going, we keep on, because we believe we're decent and right

and honest. There is no protection for us if we lose that conviction. That will be the end."

I wonder now about that man, Israel Elfers, who loved me from that first moment I lay in Earle's arms in THE MICKEY MOUSE CLUB, who helped to raise me happily, who taught me what he believed in above all else—decency—who played the gentle uncle for me so effortlessly that it was not until my five years of exile in Vexbeggar that I appreciated what a gift it is to have such parenting: ever patient, ever earnest, never ponderous or heavyhanded. Israel talked to me continually as I grew up. He drenched me with wit, wisdom, and plain fun. When I think of him now, I think of a man in motion, hands waving, eyes darting, a flood of talk—an endless monologue. Israel talked most easily when musing about himself. And before any other kind of portraiture, he described himself as a Jew. A man's idea of himself has weight. Israel's idea was that he was first, always, lastly, a Jew. He also said he was both profoundly comforted and profoundly worried by his birthright. He toyed with the word *chosen,* as in the Jews being God's chosen people. For a quirk that I never penetrated, Israel laughed every time he said that God had chosen the Jews. I can guess that it suggested an irony to him that he preferred to illustrate with those romantic, melodramatic, sometime operatic stories he told about the struggles of the Jews since, as he said, God exiled them from Eden, abandoned Adam and Eve to homelessness and temptations. Indeed, so many of the best stories I remember from childhood were Israel's parables about fantastic Jewish reversals, epic Jewish displacements, beastly Jewish persecutions, that I suspect that much of my ability to confront the sorrow in my story derives not from my Norse learning, rather from my borrowings and innovations of what Israel told me of Jewish history.

Yet there is more to say of him, and there was more mystery to him, than whatever he finally meant to communicate with the idea of Jewishness. He was smart, cagey, kindhearted, political, secretive, motherly, childlike, all things to all he loved, and he loved everyone whom he could tease and who appreciated, even acknowledged, his jokes. There were always those jokes—ridiculous word-games, absurd puns, excited displays of farce involving costumes, props, masquerade masks. That was Israel most of the time I knew him, the jester, the man who could always make me laugh. Beyond that, it did not come to me until after he was gone from me, forever, that his pranks and cracks and gamesmanship were his way of struggling with the despair that threatened him as an exile and that had dragged Peregrine down to his crime. Israel once told me that he thought tragedy was too easy to be deep wisdom, all one had to do was pull up a chair and moan about betrayal, hatred, slaughter, and get the audience to weep at the meaninglessness of murdered innocence. It was comedy, Israel declared, that was the sublime endeavor; for one to get that same audience to laugh in the face of defeat or at their own fears, that was a worthy challenge. Israel told me, "Make laughter, Grim, and you make reason."

Israel stopped laughing at Port Praia. What undid him were his tears for Molly's helplessness and his inability to love her and himself back to strength. He had passed his life laughing and making laughter. His weakness was that he had not learned how to cry and at the same time remain balanced and resolute. I understand why; I rush to excuse. His life had been endless adversity. He had been obliged to reach for laughter again and again, straining to smile, wearing out his humor. He had emptied of smiles. His cup filled with tears. He would not drink it. He thought it poison. He was right. Still, I have learned that one must risk the drink, try endurance. Israel must have intuited this, yet he could not make himself accept sorrow as a meaningful theme. Lost in darkness, he denied the darkness. This might explain his frustration and rage with Grandfather, who could seem the sponsor of the very darkness Grandfather warned against. This might explain more completely Israel's rage at Grandfather—he must have thought it appalling that Grandfather could seem to be winning me to his way of seeing. Israel must have thought he had to show me, had to show himself, that he was right to believe in laughter and that Grandfather was wrong to sing woe.

That was why I followed Israel so close behind in the gangway. He was murderously determined to disprove, to undo, Grandfather. We missed a turn, another, were some few minutes finding our way. We finally had to follow the sound of Grandfather's voice.

There was laughter. I opened the cabin door to duck into an

austere, shadowy tableau, half a dozen men in sooty robes seated about a bare table, among them Grandfather, his back to me, his hands spread before him as if he were gesturing in conversation. The light was from a cluster of candles. The smell was incense, barely covering the stench from below. Grandfather continued to speak right at a man who was not as old, nor as hairless, nor as thin, nor as agonized as I had thought he would be. Father Saint Stephen seemed, in his soft piety, to be a fair and suggestively anonymous version of the sort of priest the Roman Catholic Church, in my readings, favored as voice and authority. However, he was not an ordinary religionist. Indeed, I can make the good guess now that he was an Englishman—his manner, his accent, his contrived passion. He was certainly not an opposite to Grandfather. They shared egotistical discipleship, bore their burdens with pridefulness and impiety. It was Father Saint Stephen whom we had heard laugh, joined by his brethren; they thought Grandfather's Lutheranism an amusement.

"What of their empires?" said Grandfather in German, who did not seem to take offense at their laughter—because, I now suppose, he thought them also due condescension.

"That is the reward, isn't it, Reverend Fiddle?" said Father Saint Stephen, speaking a careful German, looking up to welcome us with a smile. He gestured that we be given benchroom at the table.

Israel marched forward, said, in English, though his German was adequate for the exchange, "We'll take what we need, and go."

"Tell the Jew what you have told me," said Grandfather.

"Where are you bound?" said Father Saint Stephen in excellent and aristocratic British-English. He spoke with the care, tact, dispassion, of an accomplished intellectual. I can also guess now that he had never been poor in his life—he was perfect as the mendicant, which I take as meaning he was playing a part he had chosen, that had not fallen to him. Father Saint Stephen held himself like a painting: original, cold, sincere, calculated.

Israel answered flatly, "Mexico."

Father Saint Stephen continued, "We have heard stories about the Caribbean. The poor souls spoke of their revolution. The Americans are said to have taken a complete vengeance. You are

American? I do not reproach. They made slaves to build their towers of Babel. Now that the cities rise over the plains—purple, is it, or golden—they have less need of slaves. I do not condemn. It is the same east and west. Is this news to you? These are the last days."

Israel reacted oddly to this; he seemed to be talking to himself when he said, "I don't know what you are."

Father Saint Stephen said to Israel, "My son, we are servants of God."

Israel repeated, "I don't know what you are."

Grandfather interrupted to say that the Jew was a fool; there was no use telling him anything. Grandfather added that he would appreciate it if Father Saint Stephen could explain the mission of *The Free Gift of God* to his grandson. He introduced me. Father Saint Stephen began in German. I shook my head no, and he continued in English.

"Your grandfather has set me a difficult task. I introduce myself as did the gospel-writer John, 'I am a voice, crying out in the wilderness, "Make the Lord's path straight." ' "

Father Saint Stephen continued in the measured, sonorous tone of a preacher in his pulpit, "When Our Lord returned from Jordan, he was led by the Spirit into the wilderness for forty days, where he was tempted by Satan three times. Jesus carried no food. He grew weak and angry and afraid in his hunger. Satan challenged Jesus to demonstrate his power by turning a stone to bread. Jesus was not a little tempted, because he loved his life. Jesus took courage, and told Satan that he would never be so hungry as to follow a suggestion made by Satan.

"Satan saw that Jesus was a stubborn, soldierly antagonist. Satan conjured up a kingdom on the wasteland, of utter splendor and power on earth, and challenged Jesus that if he just paid the smallest allegiance to Satan, perhaps crush an insect like this creature here"—Father Saint Stephen plucked up a cockroach—"that Satan would make Jesus king of that shimmering realm. Jesus studied the towers and gems and beautiful bodies, and was not a little tempted, because he was a poor man's son and there had been few pleasures in his life, because he was ambitious for more than he had as a carpenter and pilgrim. Jesus took courage, and told Satan that he had only to worship God, and God alone, and a kingdom the like of which the earth would never see would be his to enjoy.

"Satan saw that Jesus was sly as well as learned, devoted, and trusting in the future as few men are in times of catastrophe. Satan took Jesus by the hand and led him to a precipice that we can suppose hung over the pit of Hell. Satan challenged Jesus to leap into the pit, for, said Satan, if Jesus was the son of God then surely his Father would send angels to catch him as he fell, and surely the angels would obey for fear that a hair on Jesus' body"— Father Saint Stephen singed the back of his wrist on a candle— "should be damaged.

"Jesus looked down into the pit. He was tempted a great deal this time, more than when he was hungry, because he was young and healthy and had confidence in his physical fortitude, and much more than when Satan offered the kingship of pleasure palaces, because Jesus was faithful and knew that the kingdom he had set out to establish made Satan's construction seem sandstone caves. The third time Jesus was tempted to his limit, because he himself wanted to know if God, his Father, loved him as completely as he had been told, because he wanted to know if the angels were quick, because he wanted to know that he could not fall were he deliberately to throw himself into the pit of Hell. Jesus stepped to the edge and raised his arms, prepared to dive. And then he took courage, and then he laughed. Without looking back at Satan, Jesus said that he did not need to test God, his Father, further than this, and that he felt ashamed that he had tested God this far. Jesus said, 'I have been forty days with you, Satan, without food or weapons or security, and yet I still want to live. You are evil incarnate, yet I am still capable of laughter and play.' Jesus flapped his arms as a child imitates a bird. Satan withdrew from Jesus, to bide his time."

Father Saint Stephen stood, went to the cabin door, opened it, pointed toward the gangway that I presumed led below decks. He waited while I summed up quickly for Grandfather what he had said. Grandfather nodded approvingly.

Israel suddenly grabbed my arm and asked me to get out of there with him right away. I did not answer. I confess I was too hungry for knowledge of God and man, to leave then, as I should have. I was tempted by Father Saint Stephen's story, and wanted more, wanted also to test my faith in God and Grandfather and Israel and my own sense of decency. I did not think then, and certainly do not now, that Father Saint Stephen was a devil. Nor was he an evil man. He was weak, in his own way. He had read the Gospels for his own purposes, the way good and bad men have done since Paul, and though Father Saint Stephen's interpretations (or misinterpretations, his black, black exegesis that I shall present as best I recall) had led him and his brethren to vertiginously bad judgments, Father Saint Stephen's opinions were still grounded in a compelling parable, Jesus' temptation in the wilderness. In that sweltering, rolling cabin aboard *The Free Gift of God,* in the middle of the Atlantic Ocean, Father Saint Stephen's sermon offered me raw revelation of what we had chanced upon in the world.

Father Saint Stephen continued to me, "That is what happened in those forty days, my child. Think hard that Satan withdrew when he failed to tempt Jesus to damnation, yet also that Satan is said to have bided his time."

Father Saint Stephen explained that since that day in the wilderness, twenty centuries of blasphemous critics had attacked Jesus' courage. These critics had declared that mankind will worship anything, bird, star, or machine, for bread, power, and security. The critics said Jesus lacked pity, that he arrogantly presumed mankind was as strong as he. The critics said that mankind was desperately eager to forge even one kingdom on the sand to secure peace and prosperity, and that Jesus was irresponsible and pretentious to refuse Satan's proffered kingdom, for Jesus then could have provided, however incompletely, some measure of love and health for mankind.

Father Saint Stephen identified the worst of the critics, the Russians, the Germans, the English, and the Americans, who he said were "the weaklings of the north, impatient and reckless." These in particular claimed that there was so little goodness in the world, the world had become so inhuman, that a leap into Hell might be the only way to test if God still lives. They claimed that if Jesus had doubts enough to accompany Satan to the precipice, then who are we, sad sinners, to presume that God loves us?

In the late twentieth century, these critics had used their attacks to usurp Jesus' power. Father Saint Stephen said they had announced they could nurture mankind better than Jesus ever had. They had established vast earthly empires that had knitted into one kingdom, filled with towers of Babel, offering food and weapons of security to the multitudes. And the rulers of this blasphemous kingdom had told the servants of God that mankind had no more need of God or knowledge of God. They say that God is a hypothesis that has proved unnecessary.

Father Saint Stephen said that the "obvious" has happened. He said that Satan had bided his time and continued to tempt men, and finally in the late twentieth century he had triumphed. The blasphemous kingdom had fallen under Satan's control in exchange for food, power, security. It was not enough for Satan. Satan reviled any man who continued to hunger for more than bread, who continued to turn from earthly power for obedience to heavenly wealth, who continued to refuse to test God and his angels. He said that those people that Satan reviled he had had cast out of the blasphemous kingdom. He said that these outcasts were easy to identify, they were "obviously" the most meek, the most wretched, the slaves, the ones for whom God sent Jesus.

"You ask what happened at Ascension Island," said Father Saint Stephen. "The same that has happened in the Caribbean, aflame with race war, or in the Pacific, where there are famine, tyranny, massacres. Satan slaughters the faithful. It is not enough he has cast them out, now he tempts them to damnation, and they, starving, brutalized, emptied of trust, sin in despair. They flee. How can one hide from Satan?

"And what is to be done?" asked Father Saint Stephen. "Here we are, in a ship we acquired by begging, filled with goods we begged for, because we thought we could nurse these outcasts back to the Lord's straight path. We are not the only ship, or attempt. It is an ancient tale. And in our agony of good works, we were overwhelmed and exhausted. If you had seen what happened here! Thousands! We prayed for guidance! Reverend Fiddle, you know, you understand! And then there was revelation and mystery!

"Jesus has come into our hearts," said Father Saint Stephen, smiling, sighing, gesturing, "to inform us that he has loved his children steadfastly for twenty centuries. He has not forgotten his promise to take us into the Kingdom of Heaven. He knew, however, that if he took us directly into God's love before we had suffered a time in the wilderness, as he had, then we would never understand how magnificent is the Kingdom of God. Jesus has permitted us to suffer, with our free will, to turn from Jesus to Satan. Why? Because he wanted his children to learn the truth that men will live entirely for food, power, security—but that none of this will ever be satisfying! Children will still yearn for righteousness, though they live in palaces and enjoy near immortality and never know fear."

Father Saint Stephen paused again. I could see he was pleased with his sermon. He asked if we would like a tour of the hold. Did we want to see what mankind's freedom and learning had brought? Israel lowered his head rather than meet that man's eyes. They shone with an ethereal recklessness.

"My brothers and I have discovered," said Father Saint Stephen, hand in the air dramatically, "that the most supreme obedience to Our Lord Jesus Christ is not to feed men, not to assist men in establishing order, not to minister to men when they stumble. We have discovered that the goods in our hold, the learning in our minds, the sacraments we can offer to baptize, or marry, or ordain men to continue their lives—that all this is no longer righteous. We have discovered that Jesus is in our hearts telling us it is time, now, immediately, these last days, to help all the little children in the most loving way. The Lord's straight path stands revealed. It is death to this sinful world. We celebrate the most courageous human journey, that of passing into the Kingdom of Heaven!"

"The free gift of God," said Lazarus.

I finished for Grandfather my summary of what Father Saint Stephen had said. Then I added what Lazarus—standing alertly behind Israel—had said, in an even, unsurprised voice. I asked Lazarus what he meant. Grandfather answered for him.

"For sin pays a wage," said Grandfather, quoting the Fiddle Bible, Paul's sermon to the Romans, "and the wages of sin is death, but Lord God gives freely, and his gift is eternal life in union with Christ Jesus Our Lord."

"God bless you," said Father Saint Stephen to me, touching my hand, "and may Our Lord's love come to you swiftly."

"Get away!" said Grandfather at my side, blocking off Father Saint Stephen.

"Mad, completely mad, do you see, Grim, both of them?" said Israel, moving in front of me, shaking his head, relaxed now, certain.

"This is a death ship," I said. "They mean for it to be."

"We suffer the ravages of hellfire," said Father Saint Stephen, "because we must stay behind while the little souls go on to glory."

"Grandfather, do you want me to believe him?" I spoke in Swedish, not wanting Father Saint Stephen to understand how shaken I was. "I cannot, not for anything. I think Israel is right. He's crazy."

"Not that, Grim, think for yourself," said Grandfather.

"We should stop them! It isn't right to give up! We can fight whatever they are afraid of—the British or the Americans, or anyone! Didn't Jesus fight? He should have! It is crazy to quit! This ship is suicide, and that is insane!"

Grandfather spoke to Father Saint Stephen in German, "My grandson wants to stop you." At that, they both started to laugh. The other missionaries joined in. How crazy their laughter seemed. I felt humiliated. I felt angry. Israel gave me what sympathy he could manage, a quick nod of agreement. It was small comfort.

Grandfather saw my upset, and turned, "They are not mad, Grim. Disagree with them, but do not dismiss them. As Lord God is my teacher and judge, they are wrong, not mad, wrong! You must learn the difference and the lesson. Them and their works. It all makes them err again. They worship their works, Grim. And when they cannot purchase their way into Heaven, they blame Lord God, and weaken, and break. Yes, Grim, fight! But you must see that your enemy is Satan. This priest is not the enemy. He is wrong!"

Father Saint Stephen set himself, as if to begin another apology. I can suppose now that what entertained those two was their opportunity to argue the Reformation once again: works, faith, justification, sacraments, Martin Luther, and tireless rhetoric. How revealing of them, and their confessions of faith, that they stood eager to dispute abstractions as if in an ecclesiastical court while hundreds agonized in the hold. They did agree on preening talk.

They did not agree on correct course of action, the Catholic priest to help others first in order to help himself, the Lutheran pastor to help himself first in order to help others.

It was action that settled the confrontation. Father Saint Stephen overreached himself and ushered his end. He might have genuinely believed that Satan ruled the earth—as worn as those men must have been in trying to minister to the so-called fleet of the damned, they might have hallucinated anything. But Father Saint Stephen had chosen to overlook that those were human beings not theological ideas whom he watched die in the ship's hold, whom he watched die madly or wrongly, what matter? And an able brother of those people was present to rise up to destroy Father Saint Stephen's clever talk with certain violence. I mean Lazarus Furore, a fair representative of those late-twentieth-century critics who had reached to establish a kingdom in the wilderness without need of God-talk or God. Lazarus flung himself— exactly like a bird of prey—across the room and against Father Saint Stephen. The two crashed through the table and rolled back against the bulkhead. I did not see Lazarus's knife. Israel screamed, "Not that way!" Lazarus just screamed, unintelligibly, and then ripped. It was a crime of precision. Is the how worth recording? There is a soft spot at the base of the throat. Lazarus found it. He recoiled from the corpse as suddenly as he had attacked. He staggered backward, met no one's eyes, wiped his blade on his clothes, found the cabin door by reaching behind him, and was gone.

I crouched defensively, Israel backed away. Grandfather advanced toward the corpse, said, "Lord God forgive them."

The missionaries reacted sluggishly. Father Hospital looked at me with what could have been either condemnation or compassion. The others lifted the corpse onto the table. They began a prayer in many tongues, at least some of them speaking Latin. I observe now that the effect was babble. Within moments, they conducted themselves as if we were not present.

Grandfather would not permit me to speak. He ordered Israel to get me out. Israel obeyed instantly. We got topside in a rush. Guy met us, demanding information, saying that Lazarus was huddled bloody and delirious in *Black Crane*. Israel outlined the murder. We three sagged on the quarterdeck, then fell into the work crew loading *Black Crane*. I made several trips into the hold for crates, and I admit that I have no memory of what I saw. I refused to see what was down there. It was an hour, or hours— time fails in that sort of shock—before Grandfather appeared on deck. He looked past Israel to Otter Ransom and Orlando the Black, declaring, "I shall have that mast down straightaway."

The End of the Earth

After that defeat, Grandfather gained effective control of his passengers as well as absolute command of his *Angel of Death*. He again bargained with me: he would get my family to Mexico if I would come away with him afterward. I did not agree, I did not refuse, a passive pledge of obedience that I understood as a final act of disloyalty to Israel. I would not speak against Grandfather in our councils that, to our discredit, became an opportunity for dreary exchanges between the factions on board united only in their fear of Grandfather: Earle baiting Thord; Israel shouting down Guy; Peregrine and Charity obtusely silent. Lazarus regained his composure but distanced himself from all including Cleopatra; he became dogmatic, saying the "revolution" had come and we were caught in a worldwide struggle. It may not have been Grandfather's intention, yet he came to rule us in the same way he had once subdued the North, by division, subjugation, dismissal.

Grandfather declared our course was southwest for the Strait of Magellan. He said he would not go back through "the flames of perdition" at the equator, nor would he risk "the legions of Satan" in the Caribbean. It was not bad strategy, even if it was based upon grandiose metaphor. I stood with Grandfather; the Turks stood with me; the Furores with no one; my family dissolved in doubts. Grandfather's will prevailed. We ran the horse latitudes, rode the Brazil Current for weeks; our progress was cautious and erratic, standing well seaward of the coastline and, after we were fired upon by a convoy of freighters, of the sea-lanes as well. We suffered squalls, ghastly heat, innumerable sightings of wreckage and corpses on rafts; we witnessed at least one large sea battle off Rio de Janeiro, gun flashes and deep thunder two nights running; we were chased soon after by two small vessels booming out of the edge of twilight. We no longer hesitated about derelicts or ships in distress. We monitored the radio waves to find more of the same silence we had experienced off Europe. We did see a plume of fire off the mouth of the River Plate; perhaps there are records of catastrophe at Montevideo. We assumed there was only disaster on that coastline.

Grandfather reconsidered his intention not to stop again. He weighed a new notion to make a landfall somewhere on the Falkland Islands, a rugged archipelago several days' hard sail east of Tierra del Fuego and the Strait of Magellan. He worried about the jerry-rigged foremast and the damage to the bow. Worse, a blow off Cape Tres Puntas sent us careening into the South Atlantic, and beating back west ripped our best sails. I encouraged Grandfather's reassessment because of my worry for our health: we were all heartsick; at least one of us, Gizur, was mind-sick (I was not unaware of Lazarus's black mood, just insensitive); and we had infections, malnutrition, Earle's back pain, Molly's listlessness. Grandfather and I conferred over the charts and made a decision. Grandfather did not inform Israel, Guy, or Thord of our new course. I was too ashamed of my collusion with Grandfather to do more than mention that we were bound for a stopoff before making for the Pacific. Grandfather gave his sailing orders. He was obeyed.

We wore around one of the two large islands, East Falkland, keeping well clear in a freakish late summer storm of very dirty rain and heavy seas. By nightfall, we drew opposite where I put the capital of the archipelago, Port Stanley. We stood in close enough for Wild Drumrul to report large concentrations of campfires on the hillsides. At daybreak, a baffling fog closed on us and we put to sea again, hearing very distant booms to the south that we hoped were thunderclaps. At twilight, the fog lifted enough for us to observe several cutters well to port, making for Port

Stanley. We came about to the south, back into fogbanks. We passed where I put the southern shore of East Falkland at moon-rising, and decided to risk one of the out islands. I chose Mead's Kiss, on my chart several miles off the southern cliffs. I was anxious by then, because my charts were too general; I had become acutely aware that one of the chief things we needed for Tierra del Fuego was better sailing information. We circled the lee shore of Mead's Kiss, fighting contrary winds and another squall. There were campfires at several places on the north shore, so I chose what seemed a deep cove on the southern shore, and at dawn, with an opening in the fog, I took the jolly and a party to reconnoiter. I found a dilapidated weather station and a stone-built sealer's shack. At my signal, Grandfather brought *Angel of Death* into the cove. That morning, we ate our first meal on land in more than three months.

The first days we gave to reconnaissance, security, and rest. Mead's Kiss was a four-mile-long triangle of treeless moors, penguin and seal rookeries, and battered cliffs. It seemed pastoral to us, more forgotten than desolate, a sense confused by the many sheep skeletons we found and by an unusual layer of black soot gathered in drifts in the rock crevasses. The campfires on the north shore of Mead's Kiss were those of two large refugee parties. We avoided contact. When some of their number spied on us, we brandished our guns and showed our dogs and they scampered back to their part of the island. It is sad to suppose that they were more frightened of us than of their plight. Their ships were finished.

After establishing our defense, we worked at rehabilitating ourselves and *Angel of Death*. We fixed the sealer's shack against the incessant wind and filthy rains. We fashioned a makeshift dry dock to get to the bow damage, removed the broken foremast to retop it by lashing on the mizzenmast pilfered from *The Free Gift of God*. At Gizur's direction, we mended our sails; at Grandfather's command, we reconditioned and cleaned *Angel of Death*.

Grandfather was blunt that we must leave before the storms that would begin in March. Within two weeks, we were set, except for two essentials: We were very short of fresh food; we had no information of conditions in the Strait. At a council, a reconnaissance to East Falkland was proposed, debated, voted upon in the

affirmative. I was to lead the party. Grandfather dissented impla-
cably. Grandfather had been unseated in his authority over us the
moment we touched land, and knew it, and yet would not acknowledge it. He would not directly denounce Israel and Guy. He
talked through me. He said that our fortnight on Mead's Kiss was
"Lord God's grace," and that we were fools to divide ourselves.
He added, "They opposed me landing here. They oppose me when
I want to leave. They are sheep! Like those bones there, they will
not gather to their shepherd. I say damn them, damn all men who
have eyes and ears and hearts but will not see and hear and turn
to understand Lord God's judgment on the sins of unbelievers!"

Israel and Guy scoffed at Grandfather's advice; indeed, they
seemed reinforced in their opinion by his prejudice against them.
I was more upset by the quarrel than either side was. They were
comfortable in their contempt for each other.

I recall that, soon after the council, I challenged Cleopatra
with Grandfather's declaration that we should not separate. I repeated it exactly. And why? I think that I wanted to engage her
in order to test myself against her mind. I simply wanted to get
her attention. And she shocked me. She was not unmoved by
Grandfather's warning. She spoke seriously of him and what she
called "the Norse reach." I felt proud. She had inadvertently used
my way of thinking of myself. It was as if she admired my seamanship, more, for she seemed to evidence appreciation of my
birthright. Cleopatra did not actually intend her remarks that way.
She meant near opposite, adding, "You and he are crude, proto-
typical in some fashion new to me. You get what you want by
pursuing ends without doubts. I'm curious if it is that you can't
recognize my world or I yours. How can you be certain like this?
I have studied you. You don't hesitate, or flinch, or reverse. You
do this because you say it has to be done, then you do that. Do
you think abstractly? Do you have an imagination? Are you happy
or sad or afraid? Lazarus and I talk about what it could be you
two have or know that makes you like those wolves of yours. Your
dogs live in the shade of your existence. They would sleep on that
fire for you because they believe in you completely. What do you
believe in? Or is it that you are utterly primitive? That to crash
through each experience is what you do, all you know to do, and
I am irrelevantly imposing a pattern on you? Am I making the

mistake of anthropology, presuming you have reasons when you only have reactions? Your Grandfather's 'Lord God' seems to mean something to him. What? He's no theologian. He's a power. You're a power. This fascinates me. If you wanted me, for no reason, because I was there to take, I doubt you could be stopped. Could you be? What would stop you? If we are sheep to you, to your Grandfather, does that make you the wolf? Who could your shepherd be? Do you know what I'm talking about? Mother says that man, your father, he doesn't know what you are capable of. He's been frightened of you for years. Not afraid, precisely, that would be too much. Better to say, under your power. The power of the barbarous. Do you see how the others treat you and your grandfather? When you turn on that face of yours, they get out of your way. I saw it at Vexbeggar. It stunned me. Israel says you saw me at the Nobel Prize ball. Is that where I remember your face from? You can look like a face in a nightmare. You mock civilization when you look like that. I can't solve this. What are you for? What are you reaching for?"

This speech is probably a conflation of many remarks Cleopatra made to me during the voyage; nonetheless, if it is, it touches the themes she reiterated that night. I could not answer her. I felt humiliated. How cruel she was. A man speaks better of his dogs than that. It still hurts to recall her compassionless appraisal of me as if I were a specimen in a cage. It would please me if I could now declare that she was wrong. She was not right.

At the time, Cleopatra's reference to Peregrine's so-called fear of me made me most ashamed—of what kind of son I was and had been on board *Angel of Death*. It was that remorse, for faults I see now were not mine but the result of fate, mixed with my boyish adoration of Cleopatra's intelligence, that turned me once again. I wanted to show Cleopatra that I could act with reason and utility. (New Benthamism was on my mind, although not as now, for I was not bold enough then to challenge Cleopatra on her mother's prodigies and how ruinous they seemed for the outcasts we had encountered in the Atlantic, sacrificed hideously for someone's idea of the greatest good for the greatest number.) I wanted to show Cleopatra that I could think abstractly, could imagine, could choose.

I was a fool, as I tangled myself up again racing between

Grandfather and Israel. Having been finally disloyal to Israel after *The Free Gift of God,* I was willing to be disloyal to Grandfather too. I should have minded Grandfather. He told me what I myself believed. We were lucky on Mead's Kiss. We should not have asked more. I confounded myself. There were good reasons, utilitarian reasons, to follow the council's vote for a reconnaissance to the Falklands. Molly needed vegetables. I needed charts. There was a sound argument that we were being overcautious, that the Falklanders would welcome us not as refugees but as a ship in distress. I know now that all the reason in all the books cannot change fate, or provide a flicker of the wisdom one gains if one heeds a prophetic voice like Grandfather's.

I understand now that those two weeks of Norse luck on Mead's Kiss had lulled us, so that the inexplicable outrages of our Atlantic crossing no longer weighed on us. It was profoundly wrong of us not to concentrate on what we had learned out there, on what was right in front of us, that dirty rain and those ash deposits and those deep, resonant boomings from the south. It is my experience now, as it was not then, that tragedy—I mean drama of catastrophe on a global canvas, like the Greeks' Troy, the Romans' Rome, the Lutherans' Saxony—is like a living thing, with genesis, personality, talents, especially with times when the despair seems to have done. This apparent respite is where the irresolute fail. One is beaten by turning from themes established and explicated. When under attack, one is always in peril, even during the lulls. I shall be specific. It was possible to reconsider our voyage from Stockholm harbor in such a way that our escape from the King's Spies, the German "wolf," the British, French, Spanish, and Portuguese cutters, the massacre at Port Praia, the tempest, the burning sea, Father Saint Stephen, were not simply defeats, were also victories—that we were fortunate, blessed, very, very lucky to have made Mead's Kiss. However, this did not mean that the tragedy was complete. We were still in jeopardy. We were still lost, outside, exiled. It was stupidity to let down our guard. Indeed, if Israel and Guy and Thord and the Furores had one common fault, it was not that they could not believe in goodness, it was that they could not believe in irredeemable and nonrational badness. Cleopatra was wrong. There are villains. Israel was wrong. There is darkness. For all his shameless excesses, Grandfather could look at those villains and into that darkness and endure, more, he could keep fighting for his own. The others looked at darkness and begged parole, pleaded for a peace that did not exist.

I pushed off in *Black Crane* at twilight. I took with me the Turks, Otter Ransom, Lazarus and Orlando the Black, and Iceberg, who had weathered the tropical crossing better than Goldberg and the two pups. Grandfather's final warning to me was clear: he took me behind the sealer's shack, stood me up against a huge boulder protruding from the hillside, and lectured me with an intensity that was a blend of his dread, wisdom, resolve, might, and love. He told me that if there was trouble and I could not get back to Mead's Kiss, or if he was forced to retreat from Mead's Kiss, I was to sail *Black Crane* due south on the sixtieth meridian, and he would find me no matter how long it took, "as Lord God is my witness and judge, I swear." If only I could report equally meaningful exchanges between me and Peregrine, Israel, Guy, Earle, Thord, Orri, Gizur, Molly, even Charity. My farewell was subdued. I was too superstitious to say good-bye. How profoundly I regret that now.

East and West Falkland are like two crabs, back to back, divided by a one-hundred-mile-long and ten-mile-wide funnel of water, bordered by out islands like droppings, especially west of West Falkland. The archipelago lies about four hundred miles off Tierra del Fuego, on a part of the ocean floor that is called the Falkland Plateau. What I knew about the Falklands that day was concise; wind, rain, birds, seals, and a dampness that frosted one's beard. I approached cautiously, intending to swing around East Falkland in three days, my original plan was to circle east through the Falkland Sound and come around to approach Port Stanley, at the eastern most tip of East Falkland, from the northwest.

We crossed what was called the Eagle Passage between George Island and East Falkland without incident but with difficulty, the seas sloppy, the fogbanks and steady wind dangerous in lumbering *Black Crane*. The out islands showed concentrations of fires, and wreckage that was likely other derelict vessels piled up on rocks. East Falkland showed encampments inland. Lazarus made

sense when he said there seemed more fires than there were supposed to be people in the Falklands. And where were the flocks,
I asked, the islands were supposed to be covered with sheep
ranches. I bypassed the first villages we sighted on East Falkland
as we moved into the Sound, more for uncertainty of tides than
for worry. By midnight, we felt more of those very deep rumblings from the southwest. Wild Drumrul used a Turkish word
that I was to learn meant earthquake.

When Wild Drumrul spotted several long boats filled with men
and rowers making for us from East Falkland, we must have been
twenty-five miles inside the Sound. My crew reacted well, no alarm,
steady-handed. We were pressed maneuvering the mid-Sound is-
lets and rocks, because the water was choppy, the tide dragging
us westward. I struggled to keep our bow up to the threat. The
longboats passed us as if we were not there. I counted four craft,
heavily laden so low in the water, pulling in haste toward West
Falkland to the northwest. I liked their look. What a peculiar explanation for a choice that would mean everything to my fate. It
is so; I liked the look of purpose about them: determined, sure,
hard-set, well done. I brought *Black Crane* about and fell into their
wake. We could not keep up with the wind against us, so I struck
sail, put us under oar. Soon after, we heard explosions to the far
east; Otter Ransom agreed with Orlando the Black that it was an
artillery barrage. We pulled across the Sound's centrifugal tidal
rip, returned to sail.

By first light, we had lost the longboats, but we had found an
inviting West Falkland inlet, with what seemed a ramshackle village at its northern end, sprawled between cliffs and rolling moors.
We passed outlying jetties, saw holes that resembled impact craters. It was early morning as we came about to clear the sandbars,
took in sail, pulled into the inlet. We passed two old men working
on sails on the stony beach. At the inmost wharf, there was a
sandbag redoubt, and a flagpole bearing a blue and white pen-
nant showing a yellow sunface. None of us recognized that it was
the flag of the Argentine Republic. What we saw seemed quiet,
not dangerous—deep poverty. My explanation for the fact that
we were ignored is that several other boats came into the inlet
after us, and more were already tied up. There was a festive mood.
When church bells began tolling from the town, I made my deci-

sion to land. We tied up, and Lazarus, Otter Ransom, and I set off for the village. We fell into a rush of men and boys from shacks on the shore, and we were swept along to the village square—muddy holes, plenty of dogs, several rusted vehicles, a church, and a row of stone huts. The bells stopped as a tattered platoon of soldiers in green woolen uniforms emerged from the church doors. I quickly made sense of the scene. There was to be an execution by firing squad. Though we were strangers, there were many there not of the village, and we were overlooked in the excitement. We slid toward the church side of the square, near several ancient-looking nuns—whom I thought out of place, given that the church was Protestant, by the cornerstone, the First Presbyterian Church of West Falkland. There was also a scaffolding there. I tell this about that scaffolding: There were wagon wheels raised above its platform; there were decaying corpses tied on top of those wheels. The crowd became lively, expectant, when the soldiers led out a dozen prisoners chained together in threes.

Lazarus translated the commanding officer's speech to the crowd, whom he called "the vigilant home guard of the liberated village of *2 de Diciembre*." His talk included sufficient references to invasion, sedition, sabotage, and counterrevolution for us to conclude that the Falkland archipelago—two hundred treeless, wind-scourged islands of shepherds and fishermen—was buried in a civil war. Lazarus said the soldiers were Argentines, though the officer also used the word Patagonians, meaning they were from that region of Argentina. They belonged to what was called *"El Ejército de la Tierra del Fuego,"* which means, literally, the army of the land afire, or, figuratively, The Army of the End of the Earth.

"I've seen this before, read about it all my life," said Lazarus. "It's too familiar. It's routine. This town is the front, or was recently. A good guess is that it fell to these troops last December, in a late spring campaign. These *campesinos* are the militia. Our commandant is regular army, a drunkard, to hear him. He's probably assigned to organize the villagers. What war this is, and who the enemy is, well, I can make a good guess."

Lazarus was interrupted as the executions did proceed with a routine. The first trio, a Negro and two gray little men, died badly. The subaltern's pistol misfired at the coup de grace. The commandant was furious with the ineptitude of his men. His temper seemed to amuse the crowd. And once the corpses were cleared, the gathering relaxed noticeably. Women and children appeared from the stone huts. Altogether, the villagers appeared as condemned as the prisoners—beaten down, starving, hanging on. The idea of politics in such a place was ridiculous, what Grandfather would have said was a Satanic jest. The highest form of civilization in 2 *de Diciembre* was the firing squad. The second trio of prisoners was dragged to the posts.

The women behind us let out a wail. I realized then they were not nuns, just hags in black. One stout hag churned across the yard, heaved herself down before the post of one of the condemned, a thin, boyish white man with a mangled arm. The subaltern tried to pull her away. The boy sagged to her, held up only by his bonds. The display seemed to embarrass the commandant. From the graveyard gate, a stocky black-bearded man appeared. He wore a broad-brimmed hat and a clerical collar as would a minister calling on his parishioners; oddly, he also wore excellent brown seaboots. Black-beard made for the hag. He carried a shovel, and it occurred to me that he was both pastor and gravedigger. He moved with a weight and dexterity that attracted me— more animated than the whole assembly. He got the hag up, took her back to the scaffold steps, consoled her like a worried son. It was bizarre yet sad-making. I suppose that explains why the commandant was not alarmed. The subaltern ordered his men to get on with it. Black-beard shouted at the subaltern in Spanish, then walked toward the commandant, turned to the crowd, began a speech in broad English, "What ye've done, there's no forgiving! She raised that boy after his folk was killed by yerr butchers! Ye tortured out his mind! I want ye to know, it's important to myself ye know, I don't see an end to this! Don't want an end! Yerr Republic be a thief! What's ours be ours by right!"

The soliloquy was a ruse, as Black-beard was a masquerade, neither pastor nor gravedigger. He was the enemy. His talk distracted the mob, astounded the soldiers, signaled the attack. Black-beard arched back and swung his shovel, felling the commandant. The square was suddenly awash in ricocheting bullets. Explosions tore apart the church tower and the second stories of the only two real buildings in town. The scaffolding took a direct mortar hit and toppled in pieces. We three broke for the inlet, were cut off by firepower and the hysterical crowd. Otter Ransom dragged me and Lazarus behind the trough of a well.

The assault was intended as a rescue, became a fiasco. The condemned died with their captors. The subaltern waved at the warehouse down the cliffside, the origin of the heaviest fire, and gathered what men he could for a charge that did not lack courage. Two small groups of men firing pistols and rifles then rushed the square from the north side to outflank the militia. The combat was hand-to-hand, fanatical. We had to scramble again, Iceberg right with us, through the shattered church, through falling timbers, over the iron gate, and into the graveyard. We worked from stone to tomb back to a stone-built shed. We were moving away from *Black Crane*. Behind the shed was a sloping heath, beyond that, hillocks and treeless moors. As we rested, Lazarus said he hoped Orlando the Black had pushed off. I said that would make us dead men. He returned that I was a coward, this was "the revolution." I can see now that he was as frightened as I was, that his dogma was disguised panic. At the time, I cursed him, we cursed each other, over the gunfire and explosions.

We did not do more than yell at each other, however, too terrified to swing. It was childish hysterics. I understand now that I despised Lazarus not, as I then thought, because he was a braggart and poseur, or because I did not understand why he had murdered that pathetic priest; I hated him because he was my rival for Cleopatra. I knew he thought me a dumb beast; I thought him a sly cheat. More, I had reason—incidents on board *Angel of Death* I have passed by—to believe that he and Cleopatra were lovers. This seems as inappropriate a revelation here as it was an inappropriate interlude then. We were trapped by massacre. Yet I had deceived myself for months about the two of them. She had shown her condescension toward me the night before. I blamed Lazarus. I was a young man. I had naive fancies. I do even now, without the youth. I suppose that I have delayed until here to mention my longing and jealousy because I have yet to accept completely our baleful, never resolved triangle.

Lazarus and I were interrupted in our squabbling by the appearance in my life for the second time of the very same bold, graceful, sad-eyed seaman who had earlier heralded the battle with a shovel. There should be some more telling way I can introduce

Germanicus. It does not come to me. Germanicus Frazer himself, stockily built, black-bearded, proud-hearted, girded with iron determinism as Grandfather was with his ineffable Lord God, then pushed through the graveyard's postern gate. He had the boy with the mangled arm across his shoulders, and the stout hag in tow. He saw us before we did him, crouched, gritted, waved a black horse pistol to keep us at bay while he weighed his chances.

He began heavily, "I'm Frazer, of the South Georgia Volunteers. I need yerr help. Give it, or I take it. She's bad hurt, he's near dead. I need ye"—he pointed at me—"to carry her. We got to get up there."

"It's not our fight," said Otter Ransom to me in Swedish.

"We have people back there," I said to Germanicus.

"Dead or gone now. With me or divil take ye," he said, shifting the boy on his shoulders. That was not a choice. I got the woman up, and we ran for it. We climbed, dodged, up above the town, back across to the cliffs. Germanicus was stalwart, not suspicious, though I doubt we could have overpowered him. He had the aura of the indomitable; if one has met such, one knows the effect is absolute. We rested at a vantage that showed the inlet. *Black Crane* was gone. Through the mist, we spotted a patrol in pursuit, shooting at us from great range. We got up to the peak of the cliffs, plunged to our fate. We slid the last fifty yards to a boulder-strewn shore. There were four long boats in the shallows, the same ones I had chanced to follow the night before. I cursed my luck. All happened quickly. We three were deliriously winded by our escape, clinging to each other, lost. Germanicus was alert and tireless, ordering the men in the boats to action. We handed over the boy and the hag to a boat already filled with wounded. Their attack had failed so badly that there were only enough left to man three of the craft. Germanicus was second-in-command; his captain was seriously wounded. The company, grizzly, sheepskin-wrapped, heavily armed, was, I would later learn, a guerrilla group from the South Atlantic island of South Georgia, calling themselves the South Georgia Volunteers.

Germanicus went over to his captain, then returned to us. "Be ye beasties?" he asked. I did not understand. (*Beasties* was their word for refugees without refuge, for the washed-up remnant of the so-called fleet of the damned.) I told him we had peo-

ple back in the inlet and also way to the south, that we had to
return for them. He said, "I understand ye, I do. And thank ye
for yerr help. Know this, yerr folk're done. I need ye more, short
four oars in my boat. Frazer tells God's truth. The Patties have
gunboats down the Sound, coming up, sartain."

"We came up the Sound last night," I protested, "from Mead's
Kiss."

"It's done!" he said, gesturing dismissively. I was a head over
him, still he was my match. His anger was not directed, was more
for his wasted men than our defeat. He looked to the three of us,
said, "Ye're drafted into the Volunteers. We shoot deserters. Get
in the boat, lads."

"We must go back," I said. Lazarus and Otter Ransom gathered beside me.

Germanicus softened. "If they're alive, they'll make east for
Stanley. Ye can too. I don't want ye shot. Are ye good Christians?"

I did not reply.

"Thank God ye got here. Help them that need it," he said.

It was a fine, godly point. It carried us into Germanicus's boat.
We pushed out into the Sound, pulled hard northward against
the wind to clear the tidal rip, making for the cover of the mist.
There were many wounded in our boat. One throat-shot-man kept
pulling wildly at my feet. More than once, Germanicus's sergeant,
a meaty, rough man named Motherwell, asked to lighten the boat
by passing over the dead. Germanicus did not answer until, at one
point when we came under nuisance artillery fire from the West
Falkland shore, he scolded Motherwell, "Everyone goes back with
me!" The third boat, with the stricken captain, was too under-
manned to keep pace with us. Germanicus had us slow down, but
the captain signaled we should press on. We watched as the third
boat fell farther back, until it was lost in the mist. Word was passed
by signal from the eastern shore that there was a gunboat coming
down the Sound to intercept us. Germanicus directed us closer to
the East Falkland shore, berating us, "Pull, lads, we no quit!" We
rowed, vomited, rowed, bled and wept and rowed. My hands were
shredded; the cramps in my back and legs were so painful that I
could relieve them only by pulling harder. By late afternoon we
left the Sound for an East Falkland inlet with two forks, one back
south, the other toward the mountains. How we got to shore I do

not know. We were met by more guerrillas at a burned-out wharf before a row of shattered stone huts. They helped us up the hillside to a muddy plateau with a sandbag-built redoubt commanding a view of the Sound. There was also a tarpaulin-covered field hospital, where we collapsed.

I awoke with cramps in my legs and pushed myself to a crouch to ease the pain. As I did I noticed a tall, bent, sticklike man walking among we survivors of 2 *de Diciembre*. He was almost deformed with his twisted posture. He offered us small bits of fruit and some whiskey from a cup, then told us with a beautiful, tired voice more compelling than the wind that he was the chaplain— Longfaeroe, he said. He then began to sing above the groans and death rattles, "Hear our cry, Jehovah. From the end of the earth I call thee with fainting heart. Lift me up and set me upon a rock. For thou be my shelter, a tower of refuge from the enemy. In thy tent will I make my home for ever, and find my shelter under the cover of thy wings. For thou, Jehovah, hast heard my vows and granted the hope of all who revere thy name. To the true king's life add length of days, keep him, keep him!"

He broke off with a gasp, then continued, finishing what is Psalm 61. I wondered what "king" he meant. I hurt too much to think hard. He did lighten my heart. Lazarus rolled over beside me, mumbled, "The end of the earth, did you hear him? They're rugged, whatever they are." Otter Ransom listened to my translation of the psalm, smiled for it. Iceberg lapped my face and, in her nursemaid way, comforted the three of us. I must have slept. It was dark when Germanicus woke me.

"Ye're free of us now. We're back for my captain. I'll not have him on their wheels, the divils. I'm grieved for yer folk. If they make Stanley, it be ours still. Keep to the high road there, east, eighty miles. The hills be bad with the beasties. My advice to ye be to go with the column the morrow."

"Can you give us a boat, or take us with you, when we're rested?"

He tightened his bandoliers, said flatly, "It's finished here."

"We can walk back," I tried.

"So ye say. Frazer tells, what's south of here on both sides of the Sound be Patties. Yerr chance be east, or none. If there's trouble for ye, tell them Volunteers ye served Germanicus Frazer, El-

ephant Frazer's son. He owes ye debt for yerr backs and faith."
He offered his hand; we touched as we could, raw flesh on raw
flesh.

"This is Lazarus Furore, and Otter Ransom, from America
and Sweden," I said. "And Iceberg. I'm Grim Fiddle, Peregrine
Ide's son."

"Luck then, Grim Fiddle," he said, and was gone. It is crucial
to note that Germanicus's captain, whom he never found, was his
older brother, the legendary and beloved Samson Frazer, whom
the chaplain, Longfaeroe, referred to when he sang, "Keep him,
keep him!"

Despite Germanicus's promise that we were free to make our
own way, we were drafted as bearers into the hospital column
leaving the next morning for Port Stanley. We learned something
of the fighting from the guerrillas as we waited to move out. The
South Georgia Volunteers, and what was left of the Falkland Irregulars, were in full retreat from a massacre at Goose Green on
East Falkland's Choiseul Sound the day before Germanicus's raid
on *2 de Diciembre* (whose Falklander name was Port Howard). None
of this should appear grandly military. At most a thousand men
and boys were involved on Germanicus's side—fishermen, shepherds, sealers, whale-poachers. As the guerrillas wanted us to understand, these were the vocations of Jesus' disciples. I suspect
this detail had been forced on them by their preachers, like Longfaeroe, to fuel their fight. It was not a holy war, however, even if
the guerrillas saw it that way. It was primarily a blood feud between those who spoke Spanish and those who spoke English, a
contest for territory and revenge, what Germanicus meant when
he bellowed, "What's ours be ours by right!"

Once he had some facts to add to his intuition and knowledge
of South American history, Lazarus insisted this was less a civil
war than the remains of an imperial conflict. In the nineteenth
century, Great Britain had used its fleet to acquire the Falkland
archipelago, making it the chief component of what was then a
sealer's and whaler's promised land, called the British Falkland
Islands Dependencies—which included the Falklands, South
Georgia, the South Sandwich, South Orkney, and South Shetland
islands, the Palmer archipelago, and Graham Land, also known as
the Palmer Peninsula of Antarctica. The British claim was ever in

dispute by the Argentine Republic, who laid cross claim to the whole of the Falkland Dependencies, and to the Falklands in specific, calling them the Islas Malvinas. I am describing this too carefully for the information I can be sure of, but it does evidence Lazarus's ideological mind, and does pertain to what happened to me there. Bluntly, the Falklanders, who were mostly British descendants, hated the few South Americans settled among them— a racial and religious bigotry. By the late twentieth century, revolutions and reactions on the mainland had upset the shaky political equilibrium in the Falkland Dependencies. The Argentine Republic was certainly the main sponsor of the invading Army of the End of the Earth, who were mostly from Argentina's Patagonian steppes, those whom Germanicus called "Patties."

I have a faint heart for this. It seems as over-simple and miserable recording it now as it was living it then. In every land, for every people, the oldest wounds opened as easily as the fresh ones. Who first transgressed in the Falklands, and why, and where, is lost to me in the cycle of lies, what Israel taught me was the politics of falsehood. I know Germanicus told me the Patties struck first. I imagine a Pattie would say opposite. What matter now? Patriotism, separatism, imperialism, colonialism, adventurism—all fine words, all graves and ruin, north under fire, equator under tempest, south under ice. As Grandfather told me, there was no refuge, there was no sanctuary, there was no peace. As I had seen, there was only flight and exile and abandonment and endurance until one could take no more, then standing or dying—perhaps first giving what one got. There is profoundly more to the politics and ruination of the end of the earth, but that must await further events in this chronicle without whose explanation I realize now, acutely and fully, what happened to me and mine would remain incredible, unacceptable, seemingly less history than fantasy—so dark, I worry that even the light this writing means to me might not be able to show the truth.

I reach too far ahead. There was specific jeopardy for us in that hospital column in retreat across the high moors of East Falkland. The Army of the End of the Earth—I shall henceforth call them as did the South Georgians: Patagonians or Patties—was said to have been reinforced with a heavy-weapons company of regulars on West Falkland, was said to be rushing to obliterate the so-called loyalist resistance (Falkland Irregulars, South Georgia Volunteers) before the fall winds hampered the supply lines from the continent. The loyalists had no hope against gunboats supporting artillery. Worse, the desperate refugees cast up on the Falklands, as *Angel of Death* had been, whom they called beasties, were wandering the islands, killing and being killed. The Patties used the beasties as forced labor, sometimes as paramilitary labor, since many of them were originally from the Americas. The loyalists had three sorts of adversaries then, closing a claw-hand on them: Spanish-speaking Falklanders native there; the Army of the End of the Earth from Patagonia and Tierra del Fuego; and the beasties from everywhere. And how I recoiled then at the notion of calling those poor people beasties, even wince now as I write *beasties;* that was what they called them, what I came to calling them, and I should not hide the shame of it.

The hospital column ordered to traverse East Falkland's No Man's Land was commanded by a captain in the Irregulars, a nephew of the Falklander commander, Brackenbury. He was a butcher who encouraged his men to shoot at will at the beasties who showed themselves to our line of march. I thought this hideous, and also stupid. There were less than a dozen sound men in the column—the bulk wounded, with women and children tending a flock of sheep we drove before us. The treeless moors made our group helplessly naked. We marched and shot all day, up the muddy sheep runs and into the foothills of the gray-green and snowcapped central mountain range. Our line of sight was impeded only by folds in the land and a patchy ground mist. I asked one trooper if our tactics—sniping at the beasties—did not invite trouble from them, whom we could see camped in large numbers way down below us along the north shore of the island. Because of this conversation, later that day the butcher challenged my loyalty and deprived me, Otter Ransom, and Lazarus of our weapons.

After that, we were used as cart beasts, all pain, up and down the rolling tracks, leaving the foothills to make for the big mountains to the east. On the second day, we crossed a rocky waste pitted with bogs and piles of sheep skeletons. The smell of battle drifted over us from the south, and we swung away from a pass and made for a path north of the range. With nightfall, we could see hundreds of campfires below us, above us, all about us. We three were assigned burial duty. When we finished, we were banished to the off-loaded hospital carts and given small rations. We pulled blood-soaked sheepskins over us to keep out the howling winds.

The beasties attacked before first light. Iceberg woke me with her paw. The wind at first covered the shots and screams. The battle centered on the food carts that had been set in the middle of the main camp, fifty yards off from us. They came in waves down the hillside, men and boys and women, filthy and slow-footed, a few weapons, mostly clubs and fists. The melee was savage, awful noises—growls, snarls, whines. We three rolled under an empty cart with Iceberg. We watched the butcher command his men to form a circle around the tarpaulin, where the wounded were laid out. We watched a tide of flesh crash over a wall of flesh. It was cold-making, the wind and the dying, those beastlike noises.

Longfaeroe appeared out of the dark. He carried a torch, led several children and women by the hand. He must have seen Iceberg's eyes flash in reflection of the torch, because he beckoned us to him. He had the women pile crates together, which he smashed with his foot, lit for a fire. This, with all the rest continuing. We stayed under the cart. There was nothing between us and the massacre but heath, wind, and Longfaeroe. He organized the people near the fire, perhaps ten yards from us. He told them to bow their heads. He filled his lungs and sang out clearly, and as he did, first I, then Otter Ransom and Lazarus, crawled over to listen to his prayer: "Rescue me from my enemies, O Jehovah! Be my tower of strength against all who assail me! Rescue me from evildoers! Deliver me from men of blood! Savage men lie in wait for me! They lie in ambush to attack me, for no fault or guilt of mine! O Jehovah, innocent as these be, they take post against us. . . ."

They did pass over us; at least, they let us be. We huddled there, praying with Longfaeroe as the sky lightened to the east. We fed the fire and wept. It was shock, and eventually we did respond to the cries of the wounded. I have no explanation why we were not murdered. I think of Longfaeroe's psalm, 59 in the

Fiddle Bible, which concludes with celebration "when morning comes," and makes much of Jehovah as "the strong tower." I assumed then that Longfaeroe saw himself as a strong tower too. He sat there, stern, wind-whipped, and faced down that murder. I put weight on him for it.

Thinking of that psalm, I ask myself what protected me. It was certainly not true that I was without fault, or guilt, for I had likely killed that stranger in Vexbeggar. Perhaps the lesson I took most completely from that heath at the time was that it was vain of me to try to tally innocence and guilt, good and bad, pleasure and pain in a formula that can explain why some men die horribly, ripped and smashed, and others walk through slaughter unscarred. I saw that there is a divine justice that has judgments beyond my intellect. The Norse in me then, as it does now, offered luck for proof. Though that can seem inadequate, it is all I know to say of the mystery of how I survived that hospital column.

Longfaeroe took command of the remnant. We pulled a single cart. The women led the children. It was not right to leave the dead uncovered. We had to flee, down into the ravine and up with the sun toward another mountain. There is one more aspect of that episode that I must record, for it signified for me a beginning of my understanding of Lazarus, and of myself. It was night again before Lazarus, Otter Ransom, and I could talk intelligibly. We made the fire, tended the worst of the wounded, stood our watch listening to Longfaeroe sing psalms to put the children to sleep.

Lazarus said, "I didn't know it would be like that. I can't make it out. That madman, Saint Stephen, I'm sure he's the enemy. Them and their cant, empty words in cathedrals built with blood, doing 'God's work,' collecting money, while the colonels and the death merchants rob children of any chance—I thought getting them was right. That's what that madman was doing, Grim, I swear it, blessing them while they were tortured! Luanda! Do you know what they've done in Luanda? I don't know. What were those things last night? Were those people? How could it have gotten this bad? They really were beasts."

"They were men, like us," I said. Otter Ransom asked me to explain what Lazarus was saying. I did so, watching Lazarus stir the fire, his eyes glazed, as if the massacre was still there to see.

"They were not men, you are wrong, Grim Fiddle," said Otter Ransom to me. "I have seen killing, more than either of you. My mother's people disappeared in 1941. They never were like that."

Recalling Lamba Time-Thief's portent, I sat forward, said to the fire, "They were half-men, weren't they?" I forbade the thought with a smile that was not humor. I banished the portent, hoping the while my resistance to prophecy would last. I knew I needed Grandfather.

Port Stanley was a smoldering fortress. The town was heaped together on the south shore of a ten-mile-long inlet that was shaped like open scissor blades between cliffs that led up to the second highest peak on East Falkland. The remains of the naval station were scattered at the southeastern tip of the inlet; the port was marked for miles by pillars of black smoke. Pattie gunboats were running in every night to lob incendiary shells, running out again before the shore batteries on the cliff shelves north and south of the inlet could locate and reply. West and north of the loyalist wire were camps of beasties, too desperate for food for the loyalists to keep away with threats.

Ours was not the only hospital column that arrived that afternoon, three days after I was supposed to have returned to *Angel of Death* with food, news, hope. Longfaeroe herded us together as we waited to be passed through the first wire into the wet fields outside the loyalist redoubts, where there was a field hospital. The most modern form of medicine I saw was amputation. We delivered our wounded, fell into a mess line for hot gruel with whale fat. We made our beds at the edge of the field kitchen and a corral of sheep, slept in the afternoon sun. When I awoke, it was twilight and Longfaeroe was gone. We three conferred, agreed we should try to get into the loyalist fortifications to hunt for *Black Crane,* perhaps grab a boat and escape. There was no optimism in our conspiracy. The sentries passed me and Otter Ransom readily, barred Lazarus because of his copper skin. I jumped at this; a sentry clubbed me back, cocked his rifle at Otter Ransom. Lazarus screamed, "Murdering bastards no better than the Argentines!"

They forced us to our knees, called an officer. He took a look, said, "Do your duty." One must understand how exhausted we were; it explains our carelessness, and our change of luck. I used Germanicus's name, I invoked his name, yelling at them how we three had rescued Germanicus and his brother, Samson, from execution at *2 de Diciembre*. I also said we had rescued Reverend Longfaeroe from the wheel and beasties. It did not convince them, did confuse them. We were bound and dragged by our feet through the gate, dumped in a wire-covered pit they must have used for burning sheep remains. We lay there in fetid, maggoty mud through a long night of fireballs on the cliffsides above us. The screams were distant. Port Stanley was an outpost of the kingdom of fire; we had grown accustomed, just lay there and listened to the wind rushing into the vacuum of fire, smelled that gasoline miasma. When they came for us at dawn, we were resigned. I took my last comfort in that Iceberg had guarded our pit nightlong. We were blindfolded, dragged up steps, thrown down steps, pushed against a stone wall. I thought it my end and was not ready; nor was I prepared for the surprise when they removed the blindfolds and we found ourselves in a lamplit cave in the cliff face overlooking the harbor, the headquarters of the combined commands of the Falkland Dependencies. It smelled of whale oil and defeat—crackling radios, maps like grave plots. There was a long pause when we seemed forgotten, then a short gray man, thick arms and legs, a huge hairy head, old and very tired but unbent in a great sealskin coat, turned to me, asking, "Ye them that rescued Frazer boys from Patties?"

He looked into my eyes and saw my half-truth. That face, it tightened to stone. "What know ye of my sons?" continued Elephant Frazer. I replied the full truth, fast and certain, then I started to beg forgiveness. He turned away, told the sergeant to get us out.

"No!" I kicked at the sergeant, shouting at Elephant Frazer. "I lost my friends and boat in that raid. I was wrong to lie, and I'm sorry for it. It kept us alive. We did help Germanicus, and might have saved a boy's life. Germanicus said if my friends were alive, they'd come here. I have to find them. I need a boat, to get back to my family on Mead's Kiss."

"Yerr family?" said Elephant Frazer, spinning back to me.

"Don't we each have families? What's yerrs to me? What's mine to ye? A thousand families out there I can name, three times that I never knew. What help, what boat, when the Patties come?"

"It's all I have, sir, please?" I said.

"Get on! Beggar's fate we've not shot ye!"

"Germanicus Frazer told me to thank God I got here, and to help them that need it. I need your help."

Elephant Frazer relaxed at that. I would learn later that I had quoted him to himself. "God's truth about the parson? Him praying and the beasties let ye be?" I said it was. "And was it ye said we Volunteers no better than Patties?"

"I said it," said Lazarus.

"Ye're no Pattie," said Elephant Frazer.

"I'm an American citizen," said Lazarus.

"Ye're a beastie or ye're a Volunteer, laddie. What ye said, tell Frazer it ain't so."

"You are willing to murder men because they're brown-skinned, and those beasties because they're hungry. You make them beasts. It's true, and there's nothing you can do to me that will change that."

I liked Lazarus Furore then; I loved him for his words, and especially because he did not care to defend himself. He could be a braggart; he was also daring, and if one listened closely, he meant what he said. I liked Elephant Frazer then also. He too did not defend himself. They challenged each other with bitter silence. Neither relented. Elephant Frazer said, "I can't hate you, lad," then he faced me. "Germanicus made ye Volunteers, that's what keeps ye alive, not me, not yerr talk. If ye find yerr friends, I won't help ye more than this. Ye're Volunteers till we're done, then it's every man, every family, for it. If ye run before, we'll shoot ye as beasties. Get on! Ye're in the fire detail. And if ye see the parson, tell him keep singing till kingdom come."

We dug out charcoal-like corpses for two brutal weeks— burned hands, bad backs, soot so thick we tasted it and not the rations. Iceberg distinguished us because she was expert at smelling the living from the dead. One of those living, whom we found under a collapsed building, was Christmas Muir, a sealer; he had come to the Falklands to help his brother's family, had lost his brother to the Patties and the widow and two boys to a fireball. We did not find *Black Crane,* or a way back to *Angel of Death.* We had gained the fortress to lose freedom.

I cannot recall if the cholera broke out before the Patties launched their final drive, or if the crush of beasties fleeing before the Pattie scourge brought the cholera, or if it all happened at once. Christmas Muir, who said he could tell an ill wind from a fatal one, said the verdict on Port Stanley was set. Cholera is a middling dying, not as terrifying as the plague that kills like fire, not as slow as scurvy with the cure so simple but impossible at sea or on the ice. Nonetheless, cholera is a finish. People collapse, cannot eat, excrete so it seems their insides are running out, then melt with fever. I came to appreciate why the fear of it had paralyzed and then dismantled the British Commonwealth, contributing to the abandonment of the Falkland Dependencies. There is a vaccine, and we loyalists had it; it is a temporary clemency, and fixed a timetable for the loyalists to quit Port Stanley before the cholera did the work the Patties might not have been able to do before winter.

The evacuation began with several ships out in convoy every night, risking the blockade to run southeast eight hundred miles to South Georgia. The command drew in the defenders as the port burned and emptied. The Patties must have suffered the cholera as well, because their attacks were haphazard. The fall winds brought hail, huge seas, thick black clouds hurtling from the west. And then there were the seaquakes that rumbled increasingly beneath us, which we learned from Christmas Muir were the result of enormous volcanic eruptions way to the south, beyond the Scotia Sea, on the peninsula of Antarctica and off Antarctica's shore on the South Shetland Islands. I record here the first I ever heard of Satan's Seat.

"Poachin' off Coronation isle, I was, that first summer she let go," said Christmas Muir one night in the shelter, "and 'twere fearsome, sealer's fate. Bergy bits spun like tops and sea shakes, this ice island to beam crumbled up, like cake. We was in the backwash of this shock wave. We got to lee of shag rock, quick, tell ye, fer that tidal wave picked up floes and flung 'em. Ice down there be black now, sort of kicked up, carved in twists. It's meltin' the ice, on Graham Land. That's how'd they called it. Satan's Seat. Big as Hell; hot, ye can fix on that. I never seen it, don't wish it. South Orkney's close as I been, and that ain't the same since the shakin' started. Makes the whales and seals easy, I admit, kind of stunned, don't run on ye. The black ice islands are fearsome, pieces of Hell ten miles long. Satan's Seat."

Otter Ransom listened to my translation, then said he had seen a volcano on Spitzbergen in the 1980s and that though it had closed down the mines and scared the Russians badly, it had not affected the glacier. He supposed that if Satan's Seat was hot enough to melt ice, it must be part of a chain of eruptions.

"Might be," said Christmas Muir, grinning, "lot of wee demon seats, a union meetin' in Hell!" We thought this an excellent jest, which pleased Christmas Muir, a grimy little man, forty years alive and thirty of that a sealer. He liked us because we had saved his life and because the other Volunteers treated him like an outsider too, since he had quit fighting after cutting his brother off a wheel. He liked to spellbind us with sealer talk—broad, imaginary, ten times more than truth—and continued the same next morning about Satan's Seat.

"The worst of it be this. I didn't see it myself, heard it, ye take it as sealer's truth. There's black fumes gushin' out of Satan's Seat, they say, and when the winds—them winds ain't like this here, them be winds!—get it right, that ice blowin' off the plateau like white fire, then that black cloud above Satan's Seat takes shape of a giant figure. Hard to say what. Mate of mine, Norwegian salt, said he seen a man's face with whiskers, wearin' iron, same's them sorts talk of their old god Odin. Odin? He was pretty-headed like that, my mate, couldn't trust him. Others said they saw what they wanted. Mark me, more than some said they saw a face. What I favored fer myself was them that said they seen a ram's head. Blunt snout, big horns curled back. There's more. At night—and night down there be dark, matey, long and dark, six months long and dark, what makes a man sad and filled up with memories, that long and dark night—then that face of that giant black ram glows. He lights up when the sea shakes and the ice islands crack apart—bang! bang!—and the birds filthy with ash scatter off the floes. Big albatross all black and stunned, sink fer swimmin'! That black giant ram's face glows. They say that face has a smile to it.

Get that, he's happy. I'm no good Christian. No time. I don't favor it still. What's damned funny to the Divil?"

The last two weeks at Port Stanley are a single dark episode for me. The attack the first week was from the west, the Patties sending armed beasties at our forward redoubts. The command withdrew us to an inner perimeter, anchored by a shore battery north of the inlet on the cliff's plateau, two concrete wharves seaward protecting a thin rocky beach on the Atlantic, and the stone-built Presbyterian church guarding the quay road. The Falkland Irregulars formed a rescue team to bring in those cut off in the hills to the south; none came back. The second week began with the Patties making an amphibious landing across from the northern scissor blade of the inlet, cutting off the Volunteers holding the headquarters caves over the harbor. The Patties established fireposts on our abandoned redoubts. We traded nuisance fire the next day, watched as the Patties put up wheels with Volunteers and Irregulars lashed and alive above the jetty at the mouth of the harbor. We three, with Christmas Muir, had been relieved from the fire detail. We were armed and assigned to the graveyard of the Presbyterian church, its high wall topped by jagged glass. Rumors said that Elephant Frazer, the new commander-in-chief with the other senior officers dead or wounded in the caves, had rejected a demand to surrender. There was also word that Volunteers were straggling in, that one of the Frazer sons had arrived by boat at the south point of the inlet.

An Irregular officer came at supper to tell us Port Stanley was done. It was our choice to stay or to evacuate in longboats. The six Irregulars chose to fight, took their rations and went back to the wall. We Volunteers counted off by fours, signifying how we would be withdrawn: Otter Ransom and Lazarus counted 2; Christmas Muir and I counted 3.

I do not recall any untoward feelings inside me that night as we waited for a mass attack that did not come. I was hungry, very frightened of dying, very tired, curious if it had been Germanicus or Samson Frazer who had come in. I did think much of how Grandfather would have judged my conduct during my weeks among the Volunteers. I prayed while I huddled from the wind and the rain. I am certain I felt no vengeance, had no more need of killing my enemy than I did of quitting.

The big storm that started during the night slowed the Pattie attack and our retreat the next day. The Atlantic tossed up angrily, belittling any violence we men might do. The number 1's left us, and early in the afternoon the number 2's were called. We three did not talk at our parting—Otter Ransom did smile, Lazarus kept his head down. I sat by Christmas Muir, with Iceberg between us, and watched them run for it. Word came to us at the Presbyterian church soon after that the evacuees were pinned down on the embarkation beach more by nature than by the murderous volleys off the mountainside. Elephant Frazer nearly lost control of the Volunteers then—there could not have been two hundred of us left—because the notion of starting an eight hundred–mile voyage in an open boat in such a storm was hardly less frightening than facing the Pattie wheels. Some volunteers did come back to the church. We heard that one was shot for mutiny.

Christmas Muir and I were called at twilight. We dodged sniper fire over the open ground, our way marked by corpses to the crescent-shaped embarkation beach on the Atlantic, east of the settlement. We found Volunteers pressed so close to the cliff face along the shore that they seemed part of the rock, the surf crashing up almost to cover them. There were pools of burning gasoline from the Pattie fireballs floating on the wave crests, and with each new rush of the sea the flames threatened to scorch the men. Out to the left, I could see the evacuation boats being brought up one at a time around the point, risking the Pattie bombardments from the west.

I got down on the beach and was assigned a place in line. I boosted Iceberg up on my shoulders to keep her from the surf. It was then—turning and twisting away from the cold water—that I spied *Black Crane*. They were bringing her about the far wharf and into the breakers toward the beach. She was manned by Volunteers, no sign of Orlando the Black or the Turks. I pointed her out to Christmas Muir. "It's my boat!" I screamed.

Christmas Muir looked quickly, said, "Don't, matey. Stay in line, stay in line. Don't, it's mutiny if you go out there."

I would not control myself. I dropped Iceberg and we ran for *Black Crane,* out of turn, against all discipline. Just as suddenly, Orlando the Black and Lazarus emerged out of the cliff face ahead of me; they waved and pointed at me. We all were shoved back against the cliff by a wave, and when the sea drew back to expose beach to run on, I struggled again toward *Black Crane.* Orlando the Black boomed, "Go back. No!" I waded through the water near him. He and Lazarus wrestled me against the rock as a new wave poured upon us. They started to laugh with relief at reunion, but their joy disappeared when they realized my intention.

I said, "I have to get to her. It's my boat!"

Orlando the Black pleaded, "Germanicus Frazer brought us back, Grim! Don't do it! Wait your turn! We're together! Little Dede Gone is dead with fever. But Germanicus Frazer saved me and Wild Drumrul! He'll kill you if you try it! It's their boat now!"

I pushed him aside as the surf took us again. Lazarus tried to hold me, could not, cried, "Think, Grim, it's no use! It won't help them now. They're gone!"

"Grandfather wouldn't quit me!" I replied. "Never!" I got clear of them and ran before the surf pounded up again, thinking not of my peril as a mutineer, nor of my debt to Germanicus for rescuing Orlando the Black and Wild Drumrul, thinking only of *Black Crane* and what she represented—my family. I had no plan. I wanted her. Orlando the Black and Lazarus pursued me. And up ahead, coming down the beach to intercept me, were Germanicus and Motherwell.

I got into the water. Germanicus had his pistol out, shouted, "Grim Fiddle, don't make me! I order you to get back!"

All their imploring was then drowned out by a new barrage of fireballs that walked across the water toward the beach. Iceberg nipped at my leg. I fought the waves with my being. I saw *Black Crane* before me, twenty yards, less; I did not see the Volunteers in her at the helm and oars. Rather, I beheld a vision: I saw Peregrine and Israel and Cleopatra; I saw Grandfather standing up and pointing at me. I saw him thunder, "Damn all men who have eyes and ears and hearts but will not see and hear and turn to understand Lord God's judgment on the sins of the unbelievers!"

I stopped. I turned. I heard Germanicus cry, "Divil take ye!" I saw Orlando the Black throw out his arms in a dive. Iceberg took me down by the neck into a breaker. A fireball plunged directly atop *Black Crane*.

I remember coming up, choking, watching *Black Crane* yanked out of the water in two pieces and flung in fragments toward the cliffs. I remember the blast of heat. I remember bodies floating in the surf. I remember Germanicus and Motherwell hauling me out of the burning water. I remember Christmas Muir declaring that I was no mutineer, that I was trying to save the boat, that the "copper head" was badly hurt, that the "nig" was cut up, and the wolf was broken. I remember Wild Drumrul squatting over me, saying, "Fire, be cool to my brother." I remember feeling my face hot and tight, my beard gone, same for my hair, and a tear on my throat that I could put a finger into. I remember Germanicus telling me he would have shot me. And I remember telling him, "There is no God of Love. It is a lie. No God who loves would do this, make us fight and die because we want to get home. Take everything from us. Abandon us. Kill us. There is no God of Love. Peregrine fought his whole life, just to get home. God broke him, left him to sin and die alone. Sent Charity Bentham to torment him, then took her from him, took what little he had of his own. And when we tried to help him, it made it worse. Peregrine and Israel and Guy and Earle are left to die. Killed by what? There is no God of Love. God is a monster. He's a God of Hate. I denounce him as no better than Satan, whom he sent down from heaven for pride. What a lie! What is more arrogant than to dangle Charity before Peregrine, to dangle *Black Crane* before us, then to take it back? It is cruel and hateful and senseless. It is pride and stupidity. I hate Lord God. That is what he understands. Hate and murder and torture. I hate him!"

After that, Grim Fiddle does not remember. There was a black fantasy, a gruesome nightmare, and I was the face inside it, but I cannot recall it keenly enough to record it here. I write flatly that I do not remember what I did. It is a darkness for me. I have been told my conduct. I can record that. I refused evacuation as wounded. I took a weapon and returned to the Presbyterian church. I murdered beasties all night, took one of the heavy automatic weapons and held the graveyard. I led the Irregulars against a firepost and murdered Patties and beasties with my hands.

No one told me how I got from the Presbyterian church to the last barricades on the concrete wharves the next day, because none of the men I fought with in that graveyard survived to tell. I was said to have cursed any man who told me to fall back. I swung at Longfaeroe when he tried to sing psalms over my foul words at the enemy, the sea, at the "God of Hate." When the last boat was ready and Germanicus begged me to follow him, it was said I grabbed ordnance and charged the quay road again, alone. Germanicus and Motherwell pursued me. We were cut off by beasties. I charged their position, which by accident took me back to the wharves. It was said that I desecrated the corpses with a knife, that Germanicus shot me with a pistol to stop me. I was said to have torn at the dead and dying. I was said to have eaten the dead. Motherwell and half a dozen others finally clubbed me down by trickery after I turned on the Volunteers. They thought me dead, and the reason I was taken off East Falkland was that Germanicus would not leave what he thought was my corpse for the Pattie wheels. And it was said that Longfaeroe prayed over my body in the longboat as we cleared the breakers, asking his Jehovah to forgive me for "the blackest words ever said, a serpent's mouth."

All this I learned much later, and incompletely; there are some things done by me there that no one would ever tell me. It is not for me now to declare what was true, what was sealer's talk. It is for me to declare that the weight of my shameful, wicked conduct was something I bore hard in the years of remorse that followed. I became afraid of myself. I came to understand that there was a part of me that was fury without sense of proportion or limits. At Port Stanley's finish, I learned that I was that most reviled of men by Christian Norse, that most revered of men by pagan Norse, a shape-changer. In this peculiar way, Mother's magic had passed to me. I cannot now say how much of my nature was also derived from the anger in Peregrine that was revealed when he murdered Cesare Furore, nor how much was the cruelty in Grandfather that was revealed when he vouchsafed the razing of the North. I now declare this: Grim Fiddle met abandonment with pitiless abandon. The simple truth was that Grim Fiddle was no simple Christian soul. In battle, in deepest distress, in exile without hope, Grim Fiddle was cursed with the strength of a dozen dozen men, with the relentlessness and ravenousness of a wolfpack, with the fact that he cannot be killed by ordinary and mortal means. Grim Fiddle was a berserker. I am a berserker.

CHAPTER THE THIRD

THE KINGDOM
OF ICE

Shepherds and Their Calls and Mine

- Exodus ▪ My Albatross ▪

My Grandfather ▪ My Queen

- Christmas A.D. 2037

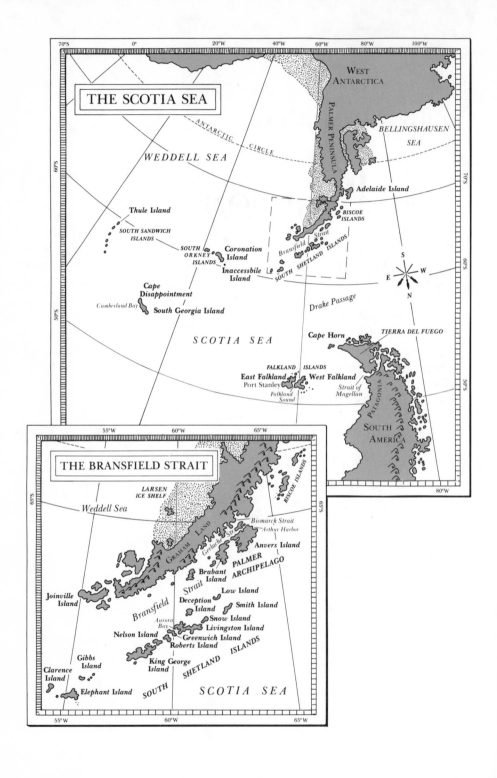

Shepherds and Their Calls and Mine

The God of Love is fine talk. I was not rational when I denied him at Port Stanley. It is a rational theme. I feel compelled here to respond to the Grim Fiddle who boasted of, as he cursed, a "God of Hate." Pagan Grim Fiddle welled up to drown out Christian Grim Fiddle, had to lie to cover his shame for doubt and murder. I feel that shame now for what he—I—said and must show that I understand now that the dark was in my mouth, I was wrong, wrong.

The God of Love is the Christian God. He was Jesus' Father. As I read the Fiddle Bible, Jesus spoke of a Father who provided in famine, weakness, doubt, who welcomed the repentant and especially the meek into the Kingdom of Heaven. Jesus' Father was kind, patient, fair-minded, sweet, forgiving. He negotiated more than he judged. He loved his children so much that he permitted a profoundly costly deal, that the unjust should arrest his son, persecute him, execute him, so that by this example, and by believing in the wisdom of Jesus, the mortal son of a loving father, the children of the earth could come to revelation and redemption. This is a sublime tale, full of tricks and mysteries, which have been made that much more confounding by later apologists whose motives seem to me suspect—creeds for power, heresy trials for aggrandizement, orthodoxy for contrived unanimity. I cannot comprehend much of Christian theology because of sloth of mind and ill education. The idea of the Holy Trinity eludes me. What I do get from Jesus' story is joy, for as Molly once told me, "the good guys win, sort of." It is wonderful to consider that into the breach the God of Love sent his son to save not the strong but the weak, not the pious but the most impious. It is also grand to think that Jesus scoffed at the notion of his being a warlord king, took a crown of thorns rather than of gold, and suffered his humiliation without thought of vengeance. He was a brave man; his courage was forgiveness. I also find in the Gospel tale a nagging tableau: that somehow, through hunger or lust or doubt (the very temptations that Jesus took courage against in the wilderness), God's children had fallen from the salvation they enjoyed by the grace of God, who brought them out of Egypt and into the promised land of milk and honey, and that it was required for the God of Love to sacrifice a human being to preserve and advance his plan. What nags at me is this: What happens once, reign to ruin, happens easier and worse when it occurs again—fall, salvation, exodus, fall.

Why have I opened this? I do not mean this question rhetorically. I demand it of myself. I know I say that my blasphemy at Port Stanley obliges me to demonstrate my reading and understanding of the God of Love, the true God, who was Jesus' Father. I sense now there is more to my introduction. I feel arrested in my narrative by a presentiment of something sinister that has haunted me many years. I feel I am compelled here to declare my understanding of Jesus in order to show that I am certain that Grim Fiddle was not a savior.

This declaration reaches ahead again, too far ahead to make sense of my frustration here. I must first relate my six years on South Georgia before I can begin to speak of the lost and the saved. Nevertheless I am crushed with a need to interrupt the continuity in my story to pronounce that I know Grim Fiddle's God of Hate was a lie, that I know that the talk of Grim Fiddle as a savior was a lie. When they talked of me at my trial as a Jesus-like champion of the fallen, lost, exiled, unrepentant, they talked self-serving distortion and the politics of falsehood.

What trial? I realize I hint at matters that I have not prepared. This bewilders me. I must be deeply upset by the recounting of the loss of *Black Crane,* of the abandonment of *Angel of Death,* and of my darkness. I must wait, and specify, and explore the meaning of the events of my life, before I can speak of my trial. Let it be sufficient here to say that certain men who did not know me, who were from the enemy camp, who said they were speaking in my defense, whom I cannot know whereof, they made much of my so-called virgin birth, my so-called invasion of a temple, my so-called assembly of disciples at Anvers Island. What distortions and nonsense they heaped, and for their own purposes, not in my defense at all, sneakily confusing the dark story of Grim Fiddle—bastard, fugitive, warlord—with the compassionate story of Jesus, son of the God of Love, disputatious preacher, king of the meek. Those distorters used a timeworn trick that has been used by many apologists for many outlaws who have fallen to crime, yet then enjoyed undue reward in myth as revolutionary heroes. I shall not give those odd-tongues any more weight by speaking of the ruin caused by all those false messiahs. My trial was the same sort of falsehood. When I get to it, it will be clear that my time at Anvers Island was no saving work, was the vengeance of a furious, criminal, fallen, pagan fool. I have already recorded enough to give the lie to those first two twisted claims. I have confessed the facts of Grim Fiddle to bury what could have become another deceptive myth—Grim Fiddle was like Jesus. I write no, completely no. Lamba was a virgin; mine was not virgin birth; there was blood. My father was not a spirit, was Peregrine Ide, in a telephone booth, a weepy, drunken, angry man. I did get inside a king's palace at seventeen, not grandly and righteously, rather as a servant's servant, and not to dispute men and women of worldly learning, rather to aid my family. I shall not pursue this further. I am probably overdoing. I do have a foreboding of what the politics of falsehood might have done with the lie that Grim was messiah of the abandoned on the ice. It has been such a long time, lies can seem as fertile as truth, bring forth rotten harvest certainly—food for glib men with bad motives regardless. I cannot know what that sort might have done, have done, after my trial and imprisonment, and I cannot get this confession out to show they were false witnesses. It likely came to nothing. I deserve, infamy deserves, forgetting. I read the stories of the infamous in the Fiddle Bible however, and there seem other ends: what they did was long-remembered in poetic lamentations. No more of this. I have been foundered by the rage and loss at Port Stanley. I have drifted from my time line. I have grasped at woe, shall now withdraw my hand, let it pass, for fear that contrived worry might become self-fulfilling. There is magic in the world; the bad magic can work like that. I am nagged by so many voices, all dead, all urgent and worthy, that I shall take my own advice and keep going. I stress, though it seems pretension, necessary only because in my Norse way I see the worst possible as most probable, that I am a man, my *Hielistos* at Anvers were human, we erred and failed and came to ruin as prideful fools, as victims who fell to crime, as false disciples of false gods, as wretches elected by no one for nothing but murder.

On South Georgia, for six years, there was a more immediately troubling distortion for me than the much later savior talk. It was said that I was a new David. Longfaeroe said it. Longfaeroe claimed that I was a new David for his flock on South Georgia and for those lost to the Patties on the Falklands. Longfaeroe would visit me, as my pastor, in my shepherd's hut high in the wind-gouged pastures above the main settlement on Cumberland Bay. There I had been settled by the Frazers, who took pity on poor, mad, orphaned Grim Fiddle. Longfaeroe would come up to me, would sing psalms to me, would tell me that he knew me, had known me when I crawled from beneath the cart to his side during the massacre on East Falkland's heath, had known me when he watched me fight the Patties and beasties, and that what he knew was that I was sent by Jehovah to him as a "wee David."

Longfaeroe meant David the Hebrew, youngest son of Jesse of Bethlehem, who was called to King Saul as a harpist, who rose, by bravura and luck, to become himself King of Israel and Judah. Longfaeroe's prodigy requires brief explanation of the Reverend Learned Sharon Longfaeroe. He was born in the Highlands of Scotland, brought up in the Wee Kirk of Scotland, a literal-minded group of Calvinists, also hard-minded, high-minded, vigilant, hungry for inspiration. He was the youngest son of a sergeant major, eventually killed in an imperial debacle in Egypt, and of an orphaned Jewess raised by nuns in Palestine, where she converted to Christianity and where she married the sergeant major. She was a second wife, produced a second family as soon as she removed to the sergeant major's mother in Scotland. Longfaeroe's upbringing was as confession-laden as mine. As the "bairn" of an intractable clan and an independent Jewess, Longfaeroe made his way by contrary trial and error to university, where he took a degree in divinity. He would have needed high learning to sort out the feuding between his mother and grandmother. After, he answered a call not unlike his father's, to be a soldier, this time for Christ. As a missionary of the Wee Kirk, he endured refugee camps in Africa, the Middle East, and South Asia until he was invalided back to Scotland with malaria and what he said was "coldness of soul." He had married in the Middle East, a beauty, an Armenian Christian, and tried to settle her and his two infant daughters in a Highlands community with sour patience for outsiders. There was trouble; one daughter was drowned in an accident that Longfaeroe blamed on himself, as is the way with hard-set Calvinists—what goes wrong is their fault, what goes right is God's handiwork. Longfaeroe saw to it that he was called away, far away, to South Georgia, with the help of one of his father's comrades-in-arms, Sergeant Major Balthazar Frazer, Elephant Frazer's oldest brother. That was the early 1980s. Longfaeroe brought with him his wife and surviving daughter and a sense of mission that was farfetched: to bring the Scots-Irish and Norse of the Faikland Dependencies, rude fisherman, misanthropic shepherds and sealers, to Christ. First he had to gather them to church. The war in the Falklands elevated him from the butt of derision to one of the strengths of the resistance. I have mentioned his notion of himself as a strong tower. He lost his wife in a drowning in the early days of the war, another accident. I was told it did not touch him as had the loss of his daughter. He was a passionate man; there were many widows on South Georgia. And what they, and everyone, came to respond to was a man who was a book. Longfaeroe's mind was the Psalter. He was a fickle, aloof minister, a garbled and not very fetching preacher. His gift was that beautifully rugged singing voice. When he lifted his head above his bent body to sing a psalm, he was inspirational and sublime. The rush of the sea was his choir, he was the soloist. And Longfaeroe did not make the psalms sound as Grandfather did—full of dread, dark warnings, last screams. Longfaeroe made them seem thanksgivings, full of hope and promise. It was the promise of the psalms that seemed to have led him to a visionary conclusion. His psalms were said to have first been sung by King David. Longfaeroe came to believe that his flock on South Georgia, spread over half a million square miles of violent ocean in their vocation of killing whales and seals, would come to Christ and their redemption if they were brought together by a single inspired leader, as David had brought together Israel and Judah.

Longfaeroe had encouraged another as "wee David" since his arrival on South Georgia and the explosion of the hate in the

Dependencies that had brought the war. Longfaeroe had chosen Samson Frazer, eldest son of Elephant and Dolly Frazer, heir to the large Frazer holdings in sheep and sealing. Samson was said to have been the quickest eye and surest hand on South Georgia—the stuff of faultless heroes. He had been a hero in a large battle on West Falkland early in the war, and was made legend for his rescue of Luff Gaunt's crew after the senior commander of the Volunteers failed to break the Pattie blockade on Port Stanley and died for his cause. Samson must have been a good man, strong, fierce, bold. Samson had also been the husband of Longfaeroe's daughter, Abigail, and the father of Longfaeroe's dearest possessions after his Psalter, two grandsons.

I have told the story of Samson's death, presumed death. He was gone from Longfaeroe, and South Georgia, almost as I arrived. Longfaeroe said that he was reawakened by his grief for Samson, that he was more convinced of his vision than ever before. He said Samson had served to prepare the way for me, that Samson had found me, leading those four longboats across Falkland Sound. This sort of justification for accident and tragic turn can become heartless. It did hurt Abigail when she heard it. Longfaeroe persisted, told everyone who I was, told them he had known me when he first saw me. This was disingenous: he had questioned me at length before he settled on me as his new candidate. That was not an easy task; I was badly wounded when I was landed on South Georgia, babbled madly as I mended, and spent my first two years there either speechless or mumbling garbled nonsense to sheep and misty shadows. I was a long while recovering from my first episode of darkness, and looked dire—shrunken, hairless, unwashed, and barely fit for Iceberg's company. Longfaeroe's notion of me was reinforced by my appearance and woozy conduct, however; my repulsiveness attracted him, as harmony to harp.

Longfaeroe was not Grandfather, far short; not that cruel, or full of himself, or limitless, furious, inspired. Longfaeroe was weaker and, I suppose, stronger for it. It might help to think that Longfaeroe played the minor prophet to Grandfather's Jeremiah. He was a man who demonstrated peculiar and extravagant resolve nonetheless. He could bend a will, even a wandering one like mine. The craftiest trick he used on me—when I could barely talk in full sentences on my own—was to teach me long passages of the books of Samuel (which contain the David story), substituting rote for reason in my mind. I can still do much of it without consulting the Fiddle Bible, like the words of the Lord of Hosts reminding David of his call: "I took you from the pastures and from following the sheep to be the prince of Israel," said God to King David. "I have been with you wherever you have gone, and have destroyed all the enemies in your path. I shall make you a great name among the great ones of the earth." I recall now how David thought to reply to the Lord of Hosts, asking him in effect, "You do keep your promises?" David was concerned with guarantees between parties with unequal enfranchisement, and wisely so. It is my experience that the always dangerous relationship between master and subject usually goes wrong—makes one a tyrant and the other a slave—because there is no guarantee of reason and decency mutually exchanged that can survive natural disaster and human crime: Lazarus had his written constitution; I had my faith in Grandfather. Neither was enough guarantee, but more of this later.

Over three years, I regained most of my faculties, also regained my weight and strength and demeanor, though my hair never did grow back properly—I was mostly bald, with long locks over my eyes. Nature also returned to me my acuity, which joined with my Norse skepticism to resist Longfaeroe's hammering at my identity. I argued that me being Davidic made no sense, that such proceeded from something wild-eyed in Longfaeroe, some sad foolishness to retreat from the world by cramming it into a familiar illusion that seemingly had authority because it was based on the biblical canon. I did not say it that way, since I did not then have the wherewithal; that was what I thought, however inarticulately. Longfaeroe made the mistake of cultists, investing a found object with magical powers that seem tangible because they are actually the longing of the investor for recognizable truth. I do not mean to defame him. He was good to me, if he also confused me; in his way he trained my mind by attacking it. Longfaeroe was manipulative, fervent, long-winded, cunning, playful, pouty. I listened to him, because he was my friend and I wanted him to like me. I defended myself, because I had to spend most of my time alone and wanted to know whom I was with.

I objected to Longfaeroe that the one similarity I would admit between me and David was shepherding. I said that I was a shoddy shepherd. I suffered lapses, talked to the mountainsides when I should have been counting spring lambs, was inept at shearing despite Germanicus's patient lessons. If not for Iceberg (she was pregnant by one of Goldberg's pups when we landed, recovered from her wound to deliver five wolves) I would have lost my herds in the winter storms; she, the wolf, trained herself and her pups, and the litters of half-breed collie-wolves that followed, to go against nature and to tend the sheep, did so out of loyalty to and love for me, and I took it then and still do as a profound example of what faith and kindness can do—civilize the beast.

I further objected to Longfaeroe that I was not the youngest son of a shepherd of Bethlehem, was the only son, and bastard at that, of an exiled murderer who had been born in the Black Forest of Germany. Longfaeroe was not discouraged, applied his imagination. He reworked my life, twisting my tale of how I had been fetched by Cleopatra to Grandfather at Stockholm—which, Longfaeroe said, had deferred Grandfather from his despotism— to have been the same as how Saul, King of the Hebrews, fell into melancholy tempers while making war on the Philistines, and that only when David the harpist was ushered into Saul's tent to sing songs did Saul return to Jehovah's plan. This is typical of the liberty Longfaeroe was willing to take with truth in order to advance his plan.

I can review this matter more dispassionately than the savior talk, because it began and ended with Longfaeroe, and what trouble it caused I left behind on South Georgia. As I recall it, I see that the reason Longfaeroe's notion bothers me is that there might have been weight to his fixation on finding me a "wee David." It had its dark, wrongheaded side in that Longfaeroe pressed on me that David did not worship a God of Love, rather a heartier God, more appropriate to the travail of the Hebrews, a God of Fear and Trembling. Longfaeroe said this was the same I spoke of as a "God of Hate" at Port Stanley. He was wrong about that; I was pagan then, denying God more than refashioning his identity. At the time, I was not fully informed of my pagan self, and was confused by Longfaeroe's contrivance. Now, I can reject it as an example of the damage overeager visionaries can do to their students. Yet, Longfaeroe's obsession also introduced a telling thought to me, one that I carried with me afterward and can still be irked by because I take the point. Longfaeroe pressed on me that David's story was more compelling than any other in the Bible because David was an impaired hero, made many mistakes, was remorseful, guilt-wracked in old age, when he had to watch his sons undo his work with squabbling and treachery. Longfaeroe said that, like me, David rose from humble origins, excelled first in battle against the Philistines' champion, Goliath, as I had risen from the ranks of the Volunteers to slay Patagonians and beasties. (Perhaps the most unhappy coincidence between me and David—one that Longfaeroe never made because I concealed from him my longing—was that concerning the coveting of another man's woman: David had his Bathsheba, Grim had his Cleopatra.)

I am not saying that I was Davidic. I am saying that Longfaeroe provided me a story of a king that reveals most of the lessons and ruin of kingship. I have mentioned how I was ignorant of Lazarus's political science. Longfaeroe gave me a course in politics that I believe unequaled. It is all there, in the two books of Samuel, and as I read the Fiddle Bible I nod in sadness. I was a warlord king, like David, but not of a land of milk and honey, rather one of ice and wretchedness. The differences between us are profound and entire. David was artful, daring, boastful, faithful, sly, arrogant, sharp-minded, weak of flesh and strong of spirit, generous to his people and unmovable before his enemies, a wise statesman and patient judge, a visionary and builder, above all a man who worshiped his God, the true God, with humility and zeal. Grim Fiddle was not any of that. He might have been. He was not. Grim Fiddle lost and fought for vengeance and lost the more. Grim Fiddle betrayed, ran away, succumbed to every temptation, turned from every friend, coveted power, murdered multitudes, stands condemned as the darkest of black princes, a monster.

Then there is a final philosophical consideration, since I have haphazardly and unintentionally permitted this to become a discussion of my identity. It is my notion, was no one else's, though it was Abigail, Longfaeroe's daughter and Samson's heavyhearted widow, who introduced it to me in passing. It does not threaten me, as the savior talk does and the David talk did; indeed, it fetches me.

It was my third summer on South Georgia. It was about the time of the visit of the British man-o'-war—no, that was earlier. It was about the time of the foundered plague ship. It was certainly about the time Abigail and I became lovers. Abigail had been the one who supervised my nursing after I was landed on South Georgia and taken to the Frazer camp. I did not see her again for a year, saw her infrequently when I went down to the Frazer camp on shepherding matters. The first she spoke to me was about a lamb she wanted for a pet for one of her sons. I thought her curt, very sad, aloof, lean like her father and hard like the Frazers. Then, one day in early summer, with the sun breaking through to flash gold on the gray landscape of the high moors, she came up to my hut with her eldest son and three other of the Frazer brood. She said they were on a hike. I gave them the shelter of the hut while I roamed outside, self-conscious of my looks, shy of people other than Longfaeroe and Germanicus. I was afraid I would have one of my spells, start babbling or ranting. She came out to me to ask me why I was looking west, toward one of the stark passes through the surrounding mountains. I had not been aware that I was, and when I thought that looking west had become my routine stance, to where I had abandoned my family, I turned away from her to weep. I was pathetic, a huge, tearful, clumsy shepherd; perhaps that is what attracted her back the next day, alone.

The incident I am thinking of happened later that summer. Abigail was cooking for me at the time, on the hearth fire Germanicus had helped me build in my hut. She was a good cook, a better listener—a tall, limber woman, her hair cut as short as a boy's, small breasts and tight composure, her thin arms swinging over the pots. I recall mentioning that her father had visited the day before, that he had promised to return that day. I hinted at my difficulty with him and the David talk. I had been cautious not to complain to her about her father, unsure of her opinion, presuming she would not welcome my criticism, would see me as an ingrate. Abigail surprised me then, drew me out on my complaint, then lost her temper, "Not that again, Grim. That's Dad's sickness. Him and his holy visions on the cliffs. He killed mum with 'em. She went up to fetch him down and fell."

I said that it was me having those visions. I saw Grandfather searching for me endlessly. I saw Cleopatra in chains. I saw Peregrine dead.

"Mind me, Dad's using you to make himself swell up. Dad did that to dear Samson, and he believed him. The lot did. Don't you tell me the Frazers have their ways. The Frazers're weak minds, and are already swelled up. Them and their Volunteers. It was a fool's chance and stripped this island of its boys and left us women for what? I mark them, mark Dad special for it. He knows. I told him when they sailed, that if he didn't bring my Samson back, he was no father to me. That's why he don't come up when he knows me here. Fight him, with your mind. Samson was a good man, kind when he wanted, but Lordie, he was not clever. You be that, good and kind and clever. You have learning, enough, and you have that Israel friend of your dad's. Keep at it. Never give Dad a handhold. Don't ever let me see you with a harp. Ah, Grim, it ain't funny. Stay what you are, sweet and sad. Be more reluctant than Moses. Eat."

It was just an image to her, "more reluctant than Moses." She never mentioned Moses again. I have kept it in my heart, with memories of her. Abigail was as full of images as she was of passion, a gentle lover, no, that is not accurate, a ravenous woman. She chewed on me, that lithe body and those sharp teeth, all over me in my hut, in the wind, content with my dogs and melancholy. She said sexual intercourse might be the only softness people like us would ever enjoy, and it was ours to be as hard in calamity as it was to be "terrible hot" in love. I never saw her naked; it was the cold, and her temperament, for she said she wanted me to know there was a needful part of her that was for me alone to touch and smell and remember, but not for the sins of the eyes. That was her Presbyterian soul in conflict with a heated-up nature. She told me she wanted to love me clear of Germanicus and Longfaeroe; she said she did not want to keep me; she said she did not want to lose me. I see the paradox, so did she, and she kept at it. She said a man might not have time for killing himself if his woman kept his face to hers, kept him well fed and busy fixing the house, tending the flock, waiting for her to lift skirts. She believed in her father's Jehovah, not overridingly. There was something private in her that seemed to want to make even God an observer, not judge, not helpmate, to what she could do, her ways. She had her sons, her memories, and what she called "my high dreams." Yes, I can speculate now how much she came to use me as she claimed Longfaeroe and the Frazers used me, how much what came to be her need for me was part of her fight with the dead husband she faulted herself for not being able to hold, with her love, from self-destruction. This does not mean I am suspect of what she did to me, for me. I liked it much. She was my friend. I did love her. I did want to marry her. She would not let me talk of marriage, though, and so our love was constrained from deepening. Nevertheless, it was a strong love, as mutual and kind and worthy as my love for Cleopatra never was. What blocked it from completeness was her anger at fate and at her father. She would not say it that way, proposed it sadly, that a woman should have only one husband, and that she had had hers. Sadder, given more time, she might have relented.

It is Abigail's mention of Moses that touches me now (as I think of her touching me, and her bites—she tore flesh). This is the first time I have turned Moses over in my mind. It is entirely my rumination, long afterward, harmless, not meant for self-aggrandizement, more to complete my search here, in this pause in my narrative, for the meaning of what I have done.

There are no historical parallels between what Moses did and what I did. I declare I see none. I am attracted to Moses as a character. Reading the Fiddle Bible, I find several kinds of Moses: the first is reluctant, the others are miraculous, suffering, prophetic. It is the reluctant Moses I appreciate. He was of humble origins. His mother tossed him to his fate in that reed basket. His rise as a young aristocrat in the pharaoh's court was luck. Then he murdered for pride, also for frustration, because he had a bad temper, felt lost to his destiny. A fugitive, he fled into the wilderness, became a shepherd by chance and took a wife who loved him and taught him her father's religion, of the God who dwelled on a mountain. It was on that mountain one day that God, called Jehovah, appeared as a burning bush, a fire that scared Moses. Jehovah told Moses what was required of him. Moses resisted,

"Why? Who am I? I do not speak well, have no tricks, am no general."

It was a complaint that Moses repeated severally throughout his ordeal at the new pharaoh's court—there is always a new pharaoh, how well I know—in the desert, on Mount Sinai, at the rocky waters of Meribah where Moses did worse, spoke rashly to Jehovah. I think Moses' reluctance was the reason Jehovah did not permit Moses to enter the promised land. Moses remained his own man; Jehovah did not like it. Moses was rash, did talk back to Jehovah, accused Jehovah when things went bad, such as, "Was it me who did this, brought these people out of Egypt where they were miserable and into the desert where they are more miserable and also rebellious?" Moses no more wanted the job of commander of multitudes than I did. At least, this is true before I let the darkness take hold and I grabbed power at Anvers Island. Moses' attitude was in great contrast to how David schemed for kingship and how Jesus accepted his mantle without marked resistance. Would Moses have serenaded Saul for favors? Would Moses have baited the priests and faced down Satan without complaint? He would not. God commanded and Moses backed away; God saved and Moses felt sorry for himself.

I am not saying that Grim Fiddle was like Moses. God never talked to me; I never turned staffs into snakes, a river into blood, or vouchsafed the vengeance of the Angel of Death. I parted no seas, climbed no mountains. It is true that Lamba Time-Thief clobbered me with a staff, that Grandfather's League turned Stockholm harbor into a bloody river, that I took revenge at my loss of Grandfather's *Angel of Death,* that the ice did part before me because of the volcanos, that I did try to climb a volcano to confer with a delusion; but that is all off-the-point, contrived coincidence, and I mention it here to show that it is folly to pursue such fancy. Yet I realize now that I felt like Moses did in the desert when I struggled with my fate at Anvers Island. I did not think this then; I ponder it now. I did not want what was thrust upon me, what I took when I wore vengeance. In this way I will admit I was like Moses. My errors as warlord king derived from my pride and from my dereliction of duty when success was right before me. I shall show the truth of this later. For now, I am reaching for an apology for myself. That I am condemned as a criminal and monster is justice. I hate it; I do not turn it aside. I ask, however, could not one argue, with some slight changes, that Moses' reluctance and resistance and rashness and anger brought great suffering to the very people he led out of Egypt? Could not it be argued that Moses might today stand condemned by the sons of Aaron for his interference and cruelty if not that Jehovah tidied up Moses' excesses and continued to intervene in favor of the Hebrews?

I dispute silence. Perhaps I should not make apology. I did not want excuses from others at my trial, did not want it from Longfaeroe at my hut, should not now turn to speculation and vanity in a work I mean as self-accusation. Moses was not a criminal like me; he did not murder multitudes. That was my conduct, and it would be disingenuousness like Longfaeroe's to try to cover my shame with eccentric exegesis.

I think now this detour has been worthwhile. I see here something that escaped me before I recounted my reading and understanding of Jesus and David and Moses. Those were three kings to three very different peoples: oppressed Galileans, beleaguered Israelites, enslaved Hebrews. Grim Fiddle was a ruler of people who shared one sure thing with God's chosen people: they were outcasts, undone, unloved. Grim Fiddle was a bad ruler, and I do not want to obscure that fact by declaring here, in passing, that it might not be possible to take up kingship in any way in this world devoid of refuge, sanctuary, peace, without also taking up the curse of pride that will eventually usher a fall. This formula only seems to be avoidable if one heeds the lesson of Jesus and takes a crown of thorns as a suffering servant rather than a crown of iron as an insufferable master. I did not follow such wisdom. I was a tyrant's tyrant—capricious, secretive, gory, vain, corrupt. Yet I see now that even in the worst of earthly monarchs, like me, there are elements of Jesus, David, Moses, just as even in the worst of earthly peoples, like my *Hielistos* and the slaves in the camps, there are elements of the Galileans, Israelites, and Hebrews. This seems a quiet discovery. It may therefore be crucial. Perhaps this helps explain the genesis of all that false talk about my so-called virgin birth, and all Longfaeroe's bloated talk about my so-called slayings of Goliaths, and my own loose talk about myself as a reluctant shepherd; it springs from a deep yearning in men to prove heavenly and predetermined sponsorship of what men do mundanely and blasphemously. Perhaps this is why I should be more forgiving of the glib apologists at my trial, and of overeager Longfaeroe on South Georgia, and of myself as I reflect. It might be a long-felt need for authority, for certainty of one's actions in retrospect, for justification of what one is at the same time regretful for. I should be generous. I should not continue to protest the need of the seekers. It was a mark of their hunger for God's love. I apologize, then, to those odd-tongues at my trial, and to Longfaeroe, for my peevish suspicions. What can their distortions do to me now? I was only a transient and counterfeit discovery in their search for an earthly ruler who is blessed with heavenly authority. It came to silence then, shall continue to be nothing.

Grim Fiddle was also a bewitched Northman. I am Lamba's son, and she was a witch. It was Longfaeroe who first assembled the clues to argue that Lamba Fiddle was Lamba Time-Thief. I suppose that what drove him to such a cluttered deduction was his competition with Abigail. He could see, by my third summer and the beginning of my love for Abigail, that he was losing my attention, so he grabbed at ever wilder proofs of his vision. He gathered what I told him of Israel's story of the blond girl in the telephone booth, what I told him of Thord's story of how Anders Horshead had suspected that the midwife at my delivery, Astra, had been more than she appeared, and what I told him of the bald sibyl and the hag at Sly-Eyes's party, and fitted all this together until he had the obvious, and some mystery left over. I did try to conceal the whole of Lamba's portents from him. He did eventually trick it out of me, everything from Skallagrim Strider's name spoken in ecstasy at my conception to the legend of Skallagrim Strider, to Lamba's prophecy of Skallagrim Ice-Waster. Longfaeroe seized upon this as if Lamba's sibylhood was some sort of prophetic calling. There is great confusion in the Fiddle Bible's books of Samuel as to what constitutes a call to prophecy, yet not so much that Longfaeroe did not know then, as I know now, that for one to argue that Lamba had been called to her task was perverse. Still, Longfaeroe sidestepped reason, challenged me,

"She bore the bairn! She named him! She watched over him! She meant you to be a king!"

I do not recall any extravagant surprise at Longfaeroe's revelation that Lamba Time-Thief was my mother. I did think it unhappy that Lamba had been an opportunistic mother, that what had begun so bizarrely could only get worse. Longfaeroe was not sympathetic, said that many had endured peculiar mothers, as he had. He would only concede that I had enjoyed more than most orphans, in that my mother had taken steps, painful ones, to make clear to me what she expected. Longfaeroe strangled sense about all this, used my bewilderment to trick more dangerous material out of me, such as my dreams. I dreamed bizarrely in my shepherd's hut: massacres, drownings, flying dragons, rams' heads, fleets of white ships sailing over seas of blackened faces with shriveled tongues. I did not abide any of this as worthy then, fought off Longfaeroe's crude interpretations. He thought my dreams referred to his South Georgia and the Falklands. I was frightened that they meant my family was dead. Did I believe I heard the ghost of Skallagrim Strider whispering to me in my sleep? Did I believe there was any worth to what Lamba Time-Thief, my mother, had told me of Skallagrim Ice-Waster, King of the South? Did I believe Grandfather lost to me forever? I believed none of it, which I now understand is the same as believing all of it.

Abigail helped me fight off both Longfaeroe's twists and my own dream life. She told me it was natural to reject asleep what I had not yet been able to accept awake—that I was cheated, purposeless, abandoned. She said it was simple melancholy and I should not try to explain fantasies. "I whisper to you when we sleep," she said, smiling, "and that's not for you to hear now, sweet Grim. What you dream is yours. Don't be telling me it's some brute dead a thousand years. Don't give them to Dad. Spare your breath to cool your porridge. What of it if your mum was heartless and cold? My granny was a proper crag of feeling. My greatgranny would have been human for being a witch. Your mum was a wee girl when she had you. Take her side in it. She was scared of that father of hers and made up stories to hide her fright. A king of what, she said? Black and hurt half-men? Begod, she might have tried fairy princes and slimy ogres. What is that inside you? You keep mind of what's inside me. You're special to me, not to any dead Viking. I have my high dreams. You have yours. Keep shut about them."

My dreams came from the part of me that frightens me, the shape-changed berserker who cannot be vanquished, the relentless and vengeful murderer. I do not mean to suggest that I blame my paganism for my crimes, as I do not attribute what truth I have done to godliness. It was all never so clearly served up. What fed me also poisoned me. It was brewed together, the pot stirred by Lamba, Peregrine, Israel, Grandfather, and luck. Pagan luck, holy luck, who is to say and what would it matter? Grim Fiddle feasted, and was consumed. The metaphor gets it done as well as any: Spare my breath to cool my porridge indeed, Abigail, sweet Abigail.

I was lucky. It was luck that the Frazers took me into their family. Germanicus treated me like a lifelong friend, more, made me feel like his older brother, which I took as a kindness and a sadness as I watched him forget himself sometimes and call me Samson. Elephant Frazer, who assumed the governor-generalship of South Georgia in the absence of British colonialism and with the death of Luff Gaunt Senior, gave me his far-reaching protection and a job. Abigail Longfaeroe Frazer gave me everything except her secrets. The other Frazers—they were a large, marrying and breeding family of first, second, and third cousins—gave my brothers from *Black Crane* both help and ambition. It was luck that Lazarus, who was badly burned by the explosion of *Black Crane,* healed over time, was taken in by the Gaunts (Frazer in-laws), and was rewarded for his learning with a teaching post at the island's school and eventually with the hand of one of the widowed Gaunt daughters-in-law, Violante—who gave Lazarus a daughter, Cleo, soon enough. Christmas Muir and his best mate, Martin Peggs, watched over Wild Drumrul and Otter Ransom, taught them sealing and whale-poaching, sent me shark's teeth for my rune-carving, my hobby after my darkness lifted. Orlando the Black did the best of all of us, recovering from his wounds quickly, marrying one of the evacuated Spanish-English women from West Falkland, having three daughters in three years, being appointed an officer in the reorganized South Georgia Volunteers, being given responsibility for the small settlement on the northeast shore, Shagrock.

And it was certainly luck that in late spring of my fourth year on South Georgia (December 1999), Abigail bore me a son. There were very few hard words over this, considering that the child was a bastard and that Abigail had risked her authority on the island by refusing to marry me when everyone knew I was the father. Longfaeroe pondered what his response should be, delivered the news that since I had never been baptized, and since this child needed baptism, he would hold a joint ceremony, just after Christmas. It was the first time he got me into his church, and I realized then the deviousness of the man. Because of the possibility of scandal and scolding, he also got a full house that Sunday, everyone of any authority was present or well represented: Frazers, Gaunts, Roses, Brackenburys, even the Hospidar. Longfaeroe preached on the sins of the flesh, on the mysterious ways of the spirit, on the necessity for men to keep themselves ready for revelation and miracle. Then he baptized me Grim Fiddle, and my son Sam. Sam was also Longfaeroe's grandson; that was not sufficient for Longfaeroe to oblige Sam with a last name. Should he have been Fiddle? Longfaeroe? Frazer? It was left undecided, Sam for Samson, and that pleased most.

I sat in the first pew with Christmas Muir and Otter Ransom, while Abigail sat on the other side with her mother-in-law and two sons by Samson. It could have been testy, became difficult only once for me, when Longfaeroe looked down at me and said, "Jehovah watches over the way of the righteous, but the way of the wicked is endless stumbling." Abigail sat right up, called over the baby's whimpering, "That's more for some than him, Dad."

Afterward, Abigail pushed through the tongue-clatterers to me and said, weepy, still puffy from giving birth, "We have this day. We have a son. They'll not take it or him from us, ever." Then we went arm-in-arm to the party in the adjacent parsonage, a grand affair, Frazer-style, the men in their Volunteer uniforms, the women in control. There were signs of the feuding at the time, and I saw the Harrahs and Lindfirs maneuver with the Hospidar, and Trip Gaunt snub Longfaeroe; I shall speak of this soon. It was primarily a day for Abbie, and she gave it her joy. Orlando the Black sent a note congratulating me, Christmas Muir and Peggs gave Sam a miniature harpoon, and Lazarus made a speech, sentimental, hopeful, surprising me with his buoyant contentment:

"You have heard that I come from America, and that Grim Fiddle, now baptized Grim Fiddle, is mostly American. I want you to know that this is not a curse. Among you here, I have discovered there are just ways to love, and they come to any man who is hard enough to accept his place. I count myself happy to be your schoolmaster, and Grim Fiddle, he just counts Frazer sheep. It's a good life, while we have it, and if there are disagreements now and then, that is all to the good. Now with my Cleo, and Grim's Sam, America has landed on South Georgia to stay."

I remember the toasts, the men saying that Sam would become a champion like his father, since I had become legend to the Volunteers for what I had done at the Presbyterian church at Port Stanley. I remember Lazarus dancing with his tall wife, Violante, and then with Abigail, and with the young woman promised to Germanicus, Jane Gaunt. I remember Elephant Frazer gathering me around the waist, making the photographer stand back to get my head in the shot, and then Dolly Frazer pulling me aside to assure me in a quiet voice that she would not rest until she convinced Abigail to marry me. I remember the Volunteers gathered around a map of the Falkland Dependencies, tracing the route Germanicus was supposed to be following in his second reconnaissance of the Falklands. I remember Lazarus saying good night to me. "Do you miss them? I think of her. I thought naming my baby for her would make it better. It has, I guess. I want you to understand that I was wrong about you. You did what had to be done. There was nothing more you could have tried. Orlando and I talked about you last Christmas when he was down. You were still sick. They couldn't have made it. It happened, and I don't see what we could have done. We want you to know, whatever you decide, we're with you. Stay here now. These are good people. To hell with that world out there." And I remember crying that night, apart from Abigail while we cleaned up after the party, until she caught me, made me confess: "For the first time, I begin to see what has happened to me. It hurts."

I speak of my luck. The ancient Norse had wisdom that applied to me on South Georgia, and I make it suit here by paraphrasing: Both good and bad luck, and plenty of both, must be endured in a life time spent in this troubled world. My baptism seemed the line I crossed from good luck to bad once again, and at everyone's peril. Germanicus returned with dire news soon after. That was his second voyage around the Falklands. During my third summer, he had made his first, sailing the Frazer sealing schooner, *King James,* in a great arc across the southern Atlantic, bringing back sketchy news of a forbidding quiet on the mainland of South America and observed news that the beasties had taken over West Falkland from the Patties. After his return, in the early fall ending my third year on the island, a ship had foundered off the northeast shore, off Orlando the Black's Shagrock, and the wreckage that floated ashore hinted that it was from Africa and that it either had been fleeing plague or had been a plague ship blockaded out of a South African port. This threat was kept a secret by the leadership on South Georgia. Germanicus was ordered to make a more military reconnaissance in my fourth summer, which was why he was away for the baptism party. His mission was manifold: mostly to investigate the possibility of plague, since any such threat would likely come on us from the west; partly to assess the state of the Falklands; partly to search for news of or the remains of Samson; and partly to look over Mead's Kiss. This last he did not tell me about at the time, at Abigail's anxious request, because she feared it would cause me a relapse. Germanicus did make a reckless landing on West Falkland, and a march to *2 de Diciembre.* Otter Ransom, a mate on *King James* by then, and Wild Drumrul, a seaman, went along on that march, and the two of them visited me in my hut in the early fall.

"The Patties have divided the islands into zones," said Otter Ransom, nervous, distracted. He was thought a fine figure in town, and I had assumed him happy. He continued, "More beasties on the northern shores, and that's where they are sick. I've never seen it. I've heard of it. We found bodies in a ditch outside the village. Half buried, two or three. They were blue-black, chewed up by birds. I saw these boil things. I knew what it was. We took care coming back. Searched her top to bottom. None of us got it."

I asked him if he was sure it was plague; it could have been a dozen diseases, including plain infection.

"How can we know, unless we get it?" he said angrily.

I asked Wild Drumrul if Germanicus knew, or the leadership was guessing, where it came from.

"Die Ratten!" said Wild Drumrul, gesturing in a Moslem way, cursing the earth. That was his way of saying that plague came from everywhere. He had grown to a cautious, faithful man—beautifully bearded, catlike. He said he had seen the plague in Asia as a boy. He said it was always the same. The rats died. Then the people died. Everyone died, because those that did not perish from boils or fever or dehydration, turning blue-black and sinking flat from hopelessness, were then killed by outsiders afraid of contamination. We argued the matter and concluded miserably. It might be the plague. It might not be. And I note here that we were never to be sure. What was crucial then was that if it was out there, it was at the seaports where they—the beasties, the outcasts, the exiles, the self-named damned—crowded and scratched for food in competition with the chief predator of human detritus, the rat, the rat that carried the flea that carried the bacterium that was the plague. Bubonic to pneumonic or septicemic, I know the difference now and it does not signify, as it did not then; plague was plague, horrible and sure, the end result of a breakdown in civilization, what Grandfather called the darkness. If it was out there, it was Otter Ransom's bitter opinion, it would be only time and accident until it reached South Georgia.

The leadership could not keep Germanicus's discovery secret. Precaution and panic at the rumor of plague damaged the life of the island over the following year. The South Georgians had endured defeat, massacre, starvation, increasingly brutal winters as the ice pack seemed to creep north each year, even the cholera that drove the Volunteers from Port Stanley. The plague was profoundly different for them. It was an antediluvian foe, merciless, sudden. It was also a biblical curse. The South Georgians were a seafaring people, enjoying the bounty of and the crash of the weather and sea, a volatile mixture of God-fearing stoics and blasphemous doubters. They did know their Bible. They were at elemental extremes. The plague, the rumor of plague, was for them less to be explained by Lazarus's talk of the results of political tyranny in overcrowded lands torn apart by racial and religious and economic fears than it was to be explained simply and dreadfully as a judgment of Longfaeroe's Jehovah. Even the doubters like the sealers, like Christmas Muir, who said they had no time to be Christian, were touched by the shadow of plague. There was a terror and completeness to it that they could not block out with their hard-mindedness. The Patties they could fight with blood. The cholera they could fight with sanitation. The cold they could fight with expertise. The starvation they could fight with rationing and summer dashes to Africa for grain, vegetables, fruit. But the plague, the rumor of plague, it rocked them. They knew it could be fought, but it was in their minds long before it could have been in their bodies, and there it wrecked more havoc to reason than it might ever have done to their health, there it made the defiant feel doomed in their stand, there it made them abandon decency for cruel decisions. I am not saying they were the toughest people who ever gripped the earth or sailed the seas, but they were heirs of that lot, and it was not enough.

South Georgia is a one-hundred-and-forty-mile-long aquamarine rock, mountainous, heath-mantled, treeless, wind-scourged, battered by the stone-gray seas of what the sealers called the "filthy fifties." This might sound desolate. It is, but also astonishing, haunting—misty blue peaks capped year-long with snow, naked heath laced with green fingers of fresh water. It is never more than ten miles wide except at its fat southern end, Cape Disappointment. It lies in a sailing arc between Cape Horn, a thousand miles upwind, and the Cape of Good Hope, twenty-five hundred miles downwind. In summer, it is gale-tossed, drenched, humid, at once sun-touched and cloud-tipped. In winter, it is deadly cold, dark gray, usually several hundred miles beyond the limit of the pack ice. In spring and fall, it enjoys violent changes of weather, is scraped by the passing of bergy bits and, in the spring, an occasional passing of an enormous ice island calved from the Antarctic ice shelf. At least that was the case for my first five years there. South Georgia's weather is usually determined by the fact that it sits atop the Scotia Ridge that surrounds the Scotia Sea, a bottomless, ice-clogged cauldron suited for whales and storms and little else. As Christmas Muir said, it is the sort of sea one could understand God granting the Scots.

The spine of South Georgia is a sharp-peaked hornstone mountain range cut intermittently by craggy ravines pitted with caves through which the wind rushes year-long. That island could sing; it could also scream. The main settlement, Grytviken, was on the lee shore, on the vast Cumberland Bay, and consisted of stone and sod and imported wood-built houses tumbled atop each other, a smooth plateau that was the marketplace, several wharfs and many warehouses surrounding the sprawling whaling factory that was the primary industry of the island, and a half-built submarine pen down the bay left over from the Second World War.

Grytviken grew quickly and out of proportion after the defeat in the Falklands brought several thousand exiles to the island. The new town was renamed Gaunttown for the dead Luff Gaunt Senior, who had been the patriarch of the island. It was surrounded with gunposts and a series of watchtowers on the cliffsides. The Frazer camp was south of Gaunttown, and up. My shepherd's hut was a few miles farther along a trail, in a natural amphitheater opening to the buffeted mountains of the western shoreline. The other settlements were on the southern shore at Cape Disappointment, mostly sour fisherman and old whalers and sealers, and on the northeastern shore, Shagrock, where Orlando the Black commanded a small group of sealers and evacuees from the Falklands.

After the rumor of plague, the leadership divided the island into precincts, arranging them according to priority for defense and for carrying on fishing and shepherding. All able-bodied men and boys were conscripted Volunteers. After my baptism, I was presumed recovered from my malady, and I was made an officer in the Volunteers, as supposedly befitted my status as a Frazer orphan, as Longfaeroe's Davidic candidate, as Abigail's lover, and especially as what they called "the hero of the Presbyterian church." I was assigned responsibility for a part of the southwestern shore, an important area because if any plague ships were coming, they would likely ride the westerlies from South America. Again, I do not want this to sound like grand militarism. The Volunteers and Falkland Irregulars in exile never numbered more than several hundred men and boys, committed to defend an island of two thousand mostly uninhabitable square miles from all sides, from nature.

It should be without excuse that I report that the leadership determined to stop any group wanting to land on South Georgia henceforth. There are excuses, however, worthy of my attention. The most profound might be that survivors, as we all were on South Georgia, are forever condemned by the fate that has permitted them to survive. This seems abstract, needs detail.

I learned gradually, once I was out of my hut and down to mix with the South Georgians, what had happened out there in the Atlantic since I had fallen sick. The so-called fleet of the damned had grown apace for a few years; the beasties had come to South Georgia as they had to the Falklands, not in great numbers, because the Atlantic was vast and violent and the African ports were downwind. What beasties that had made it were either dead soon after or were taken into Gaunttown, some at Shagrock, a few at Cape Disappointment. Then, without explanation, the fleet had disappeared in our part of the ocean. The news we could get on the radio (a most unreliable machine that far at sea) mentioned a "refugee crisis," said that potent councils of nations were struggling to solve the dilemma. A British warship called at Gaunttown my second summer on the island. The captain explained little, said he was on a "fact-finding mission" for special commissions established in Europe to resolve the "refugee crisis." I am using his slang purposely, to demonstrate that whatever was going on out there was treated like a secret by the very people, in Europe and the Americas, who should have known most. We on South Georgia, without resources, seemed to know more than they did. The British captain had not challenged Elephant Frazer when he had introduced himself as governor-general of South Georgia (before the war there had been only one governor-general for the whole of the Dependencies, based in Port Stanley), and had introduced Simon Brackenbury, a fierce Pattie-hater, as the governor-general of the Falklands government-in-exile. The commander of the Volunteers, a hard, devious, and enigmatic man named Gordon Hospidar whom everyone called "the Hospidar," made demands on the captain's stores and armory, and was obliged without comment. The captain acted as if he despised his compassionless task, hated what his government had made him, an emissary to charnel houses. The captain said he could do nothing to help the Falklander evacuees, could promise neither foodstuffs nor a British squadron for South Georgia. The message was clear: South Georgia was on its own. The captain did make one angry remark that became the focus of bitter jesting on the island. The captain said, promising to return, which he did not, "There's been no war. There's been one bloody shuffle."

That is descriptive of what the leadership on South Georgia inaugurated after the rumor of plague, during my fifth winter there. From the defeat to the visit of the British captain, they had nursed thoughts of revenge on the Patties, plotted possible attacks on Port Stanley; from the captain's visit to the rumor of plague, they had transformed the island into a fortress against anarchy; after Germanicus's return, they again transformed the island, this time from fortress to bloody shuffle. They thought like losers, acted accordingly. Reason gave way to meanspiritedness and worse. There were vicious arguments, food-hoardings, suicides, a sharp increase in the death of the old and the very young. The corresponding increase in funerals moved Longfaeroe back to the fore of the community as psalm singer. There were several other pastors in Gaunttown, mostly Falklander evacuees; Longfaeroe was their master. They combined to preach sermons that supported a hardening of everyone's heart.

The chief controversy, what began the collapse of the nascent goodwill that had seen South Georgia through its deprivations, came not from the outside, not from plague or Patties or British suzerainty, but from inside. It concerned the thousand-odd beasties who had been given shelter before and after the defeat at Port Stanley, mostly as subsistence workers, as outright wards of the South Georgians. They were three quarters from South America, the remainder from Africa, the Falklands, a few families off a freighter that had originated in Italy. With the reorganization in fear of plague ships, the Volunteer command recommended to the governor-general, Elephant Frazer, that the beasties be corralled into a single camp, in a ravine just outside Gaunttown. The camp was built that fall; the beasties were moved into it over the winter, made to live communally in longhouses, were given a curfew, sharp rationing. The men and boys were conscripted into work gangs to help build watchposts along the western shore and to seal the passes that ran through the center of the island, west to east. The women and girls were forced to work in the whaling factory that supplied the island's lighting and heating needs. A few were allowed to sail with the small whaling fleet left to us. In all, it was slavery. Longfaeroe dared to call it "Christian communism." I should mention that no one on South Georgia was living much better than the beasties in the camp that winter; many of the Volunteer outriders and those at Shagrock suffered worse.

Still, it was abject cruelty toward those sad, helpless, lost people. I should explain that over the years since the defeat, there had been tentative and short-lived opposition to various maneuvers by the Volunteers, in concert with Elephant Frazer, as South Georgia had moved closer to a military dictatorship. What kept it from an oppressiveness was Elephant Frazer's evenhandedness and the fact that the homogeneity of the island—cousins upon cousins upon in-laws—disposed people toward cooperation. The detention and enslavement of the beasties was overmuch. Lazarus, who had by then become schoolmaster, and had often before criticized Elephant Frazer and the Volunteers for their tactics, led the opposition to the treatment of the beasties, what he called martial lawlessness. He recruited sympathy among his teachers, among people who had intermarried with beastie families, and from the best-educated people in the beastie camp, notably the Zulemas. Soon enough, Lazarus was denouncing Longfaeroe as a "hypocritical scold," the Volunteers as "secret police," and Elephant Frazer as "our despot."

Lazarus made his worst attacks in the Gaunttown Assembly, a powerless body that was meant mostly as a place to air grievances against neighbors and that had no authority to challenge or direct the governor-general. Lazarus was a good public speaker, played on jealousies between the families, got increasingly larger turnouts as he slandered Elephant Frazer and the Hospidar. Elephant Frazer took this hard, told the new patriarch of the Gaunts, Luff Gaunt III, called Trip Gaunt, that he should control his in-law, since Lazarus had married a Gaunt widow, Violante. Trip Gaunt had no sympathy with Lazarus, but coveted Elephant Frazer's position—which would have been Luff Gaunt's if he had lived—and so took advantage. The Gaunts appeared to break with the Frazers, which in South Georgia terms was as if the right hand had denounced the left hand. They jointly owned the sealing schooner *King James,* and there was talk that spring of a seizure of the ship by the Gaunts when Germanicus returned from fishing and a run to Africa for supplies. Gaunttown felt obliged to choose between Frazer authority and Gaunt pride. The Falklander exiles under Simon Brackenbury stood against all beasties and with those extremists who thought the camp was coddling the beasties. Lazarus attacked the more, made a speech at the Assembly Hall (the old Society of Friends' Meeting House) in which he accused the Volunteer officer corps of making up the plague talk in order to tyrannize South Georgia further.

"Where is this dread disease?" Lazarus asked. (I was not present, off in my precinct building watchtowers. Abigail, who told me about it later, stood beside Lazarus throughout, as did Germanicus's promised, Jane Gaunt.) He continued, "Has anyone proved it? Has there been a word on the radio? Is it true? The Volunteers send a ship to the Falklands, at the risk of it and its men, in order to placate the Brackenburys and their hatemongers, and then tell us there is plague. What proof do they offer? None! Friends, friends, there is a plague. I admit it. It is the disease in their lawlessness. They imprison innocent men and women and call it proper. They take children from their homes and make them fill sandbags. That is the sickness! Where is this disease? Not in us. In them! And what is it? Not plague out there in some port. A plague in their minds, and the plague is tyranny!"

Within the week, there was a knife fight on the quays below the High Street, between a Gaunt boy and one of the beastie children who, as an orphan like me, had been taken in by the Frazers. The Gaunt boy lost an eye, the Frazer child was badly wounded in the stomach. The Frazer child had been one of the best young students at the school, a prodigy at mathematics, and that he would get involved in violence was telling enough of the stress the island felt. It became much worse when one of Longfaeroe's presbyters, a sly crank named Fergus Moog, declared at Sunday service that the real knife-wielder was Lazarus, whom he called a "copper-headed snake."

Events tumbled after that. Jane Gaunt, one of Lazarus's teachers, was accused of poisoning the minds of the youngest children against the Volunteers. And when Jane called at the hospital to tutor the two wounded children, she was blocked at the door by old women and some of the wild children who lived under the whaling factory. She tried to force her entrance, and was stoned. Those blows left worse than physical scars. When Germanicus returned from Africa to find Jane still convalescing from her wounds, he lost his temper. He denounced Frazers and Gaunts alike. Out of character, he drank too much one night in the sealer tavern, NIGHT SUN, and challenged his father's reluctance to heed the counsel of the Gaunttown Assembly, said his father was afraid of Lazarus as he had never been afraid of the Patties. Germanicus's words flashed through the Volunteers, because he was considered the champion of the young officers, about forty of us altogether. It was recalled that Lazarus had once said that the Volunteers were no better than the Patties. The question was asked, did Germanicus now agree?

The next day, Germanicus was humiliated by what he had done, rashly, in revenge for Jane's stoning, and realized that he had invited on himself the dilemma of either weakening the Volunteers' chain of command or watching South Georgia break into factions like splinters. In trying to correct his error, he stumbled further, calling for an emergency meeting of the Assembly (scheduled previously only twice a season) to air the doubts. The meeting was blocked at the last moment by the Hospidar, commander of the Volunteers, who said it was an invitation to sedition. The Hospidar acted cleverly, knowing his intervention smeared Germanicus's patriotism. This was meant as an affront to all the young officers as well as to the Frazers and, through Jane Gaunt, to the Gaunts. There was talk of a duel, also talks of a court-martial, also mention of a more outrageous solution— posting Germanicus to Cape Disappointment to guard the hermits.

Germanicus was shamed, would not reach to cover himself, apologized to his father and to the Hospidar publicly, offered to resign his commission. The Hospidar saw his victory, was generous in conquest, said Germanicus's contrition was not sufficient but that Germanicus's arms were necessary, as were all the loyal arms of all the loyal people of South Georgia. Simon Brackenbury was there that day, and added that he could promise that none of his people would ever question Elephant Frazer and the Volunteers while the Falklands remained unavenged. The Hospidar and Brackenbury thus combined to satisfy no one, to advance their own cause. The factions were left bitter, and were well armed. They might have been moved right then to assassination if not for the shock of a real crime against the island.

In December—early summer—someone set fire to the school. I recall the incident clearly because I was at dinner with Abigail in my hut, had gone out for water, when I spied the glow over the ridge. Abigail had left Sam with the Frazer women to come up to celebrate my twenty-seventh birthday. She explained the sparks of the feud as we watched the fire grow quickly in the wind. It was pathetic; South Georgia had so little, and then it had no school.

I realize this has become much detail. I suppose I record it as a way of making myself remember that I did spend almost six years there—though I can recall only that last year with acuity— and also as a way of feeling close again to people whom I did love, who did love me. They were not the most generous people, quick to anger, unforgiving, hateful of outsiders, especially if their skin color or religion or ways were not theirs. I am sure Lazarus's words would have been considered wise if he had not looked like the Patties, and I do wonder if Lazarus would have been more patient if he had not concluded too easily that his enemies were bigots instead of frightened husbands and wives. Overall, however, the South Georgians were more fair-minded than not—they had taken me and mine and a thousand beasties in—and struggled to remain sanguine and good-natured, considering how cruel nature was to them. More, I have emphasized here their fears and weaknesses and feuding, have not done justice to their decency. I am writing of an island a thousand leagues of water from despair, just ten degrees north of the permanent ice shelf, where there is nothing but wracking work and savage sea. It is natural then that they moved toward savagery to settle their disputes. I also admit that I might have jumbled the details leading up to the school fire; and I have left out or forgotten much of consequence, such as the turns of the Lindfirs, the Harrahs, the Roses, the Moogs, the Johansens, and the beastie family who ruled the camp, the Zulemas. The enslavement, the stoning, the suicides, the stillbirths, a theft from the Volunteers' fort at the lighthouse on the inlet point that I have not noted, and the Hospidar's defamation of Germanicus are a sad chronology. But there were even drearier details that I only heard rumor of, and there was one more sadness (which I shall soon record) that reached back before the defeat to the root of the vulnerability of the South Georgians. They were poor people, whale-poachers, high-risk sealers, ill-equipped to continue in a world of electronic warships. I record in this work my disgust for what I call the Age of Exile, the late twentieth century and early twenty-first century; however, I register that the South Georgians were the result of an earlier age's willingness to degrade and drive out and abandon men and women. One cannot believe that the Scots and Irish and Norse people who made up the families on South Georgia had elected to risk the Atlantic Ocean and to scratch a life on hornstone crags. They had survived there without anyone's help, without even the sinister charity that I identify as the source of the so-called fleet of the damned. They asked no favors, gave no favors, fought and endured and fought. South Georgia was their home, and I think they knew it was not a refuge, nor sanctuary, nor peace. It was a chance, and they took it for that.

The women of South Georgia were far more crucial to the struggle I recount than I have acknowledged: Abigail and Jane Gaunt, Violante Furore and Santa Bianca Furore, Dolly Frazer and Frances Gaunt, and many more. They organized, fed, gave birth, made peace, stood as solid as the cliffs. It was the women who held up better than the men in those days. They seemed to know that the war, the British abandonment, the plague, were fleeting threats, yet the loss of the school was a profound emergency. They responded in unison, outraged at their men for posturing while the children were deprived. There were so many suspects for the arson, it was an easy conclusion that everyone was guilty. Dolly Frazer pulled Elephant Frazer's beard, told him to act, and soon, or he could govern everything without a bed to sleep in. The Gaunt women and Rose women, and the Hospidar's sister, Victoria, followed suit. The Volunteers were left to complain in their cups. It was not funny. The weapon was spite, and the women used it. A new opinion was advanced that the sort of government that could fight a war and block out beasties was not necessarily the sort of government that could tend its homes. In a subdued yet serious way, revolution was in the wind. The shock of the fire brought Germanicus to my hut soon after, Christmas week, and with him Jane Gaunt and Otter Ransom. Abigail and Wild Drumrul were already with me. It was a damp night, a big storm coming from the west, and we gathered around my hearth fire eating mutton, very sad, yet in our way young and hopeful.

"Lazarus says we should force an election for a president of the Assembly," said Abigail. "I agree. We have a part. We must have a say. Lazarus says there should be a constitution, and a popular vote."

"So Lazarus says," said Germanicus. "My dad cannot."

"It won't be for governor-general," said Abigail. "For a president to speak for us wee folk. Elephant Frazer speaks for the elders. My dad speaks for the parsons and those pious hens of his. The Hospidar speaks for the Volunteers. Brackenbury, he speaks for the Falklanders. And the beasties, Toro Zulema says their part. Who speaks for me and Jane and the like?"

"Begod no, woman," said Germanicus. "Beasties and Patties ain't the problem now. Volunteers! The Hospidar has our sworn loyalty. I'd follow him to Davy Jones. If Dad tried to form a government of presidents and the like, the Hospidar'd say 'rebellion' and take over. Yerr talk be daft."

"So now we're shy of the Hospidar?" said Jane Gaunt, a rosy, round woman of nineteen, plucky, sharp, competitive of Germanicus, proud.

"Not that, Janey," said Germanicus, who I thought had a good point. "Lazarus'd be sure to be elected president right soon. He'd speak for himself all right, and against the Hospidar and Brackenbury. Dad'd be caught like a hand in a vice."

Jane suggested that Germanicus was jealous of Lazarus's popularity among the young people. Germanicus puffed up, did not reply. It was true that he had come to distrust Lazarus as I had once, for his arrogance, his high-handed intellectualism. It was also accurate that if there was an election, Lazarus would win easily; the mothers would vote for him in a block. He was their schoolmaster, and charismatic, and smart, perhaps the only man on the island who cared to show that he loved children.

"What if Lazarus stepped aside?" said Otter Ransom to me in Swedish. He was hesitant to participate, not just because of his poor English, but also because Germanicus was his captain and he was an appreciative and loyal seaman. I encouraged him to talk in English, helped him with his words and idioms. He told them of Sweden, when the King's government had stepped aside in favor of churchmen who spoke for the common people. He inadvertently scrambled facts, made Grandfather's revolution seem more sensible than it had been. I was taken aback at how another man, fifteen years my senior, and at one time a hunted outlaw in Sweden, remembered the crisis there. He made it seem logical, just, saving.

Abigail listened and shook her head, said that Lazarus would not stand by quietly. "They burned his school," she added.

"Oh, aye, his school now? A pity he's quarrelsome in his inks and books," said Germanicus. "I done wrong to speak against Dad, but not the half of what Lazarus done to stir up the folk. He's full of himself for a stranger here among those that feed him. Burned his school, did we? Our school, I think, and what does Lazarus say to that? Ten years I was in that school, and it'd be there still but for Lazarus's tongue."

"Lazarus doesn't matter, does he, because he's no Frazer?" said Jane Gaunt. "Or is it because he's married a Gaunt?"

"He be no Frazer," said Germanicus. The two of them separated.

"Why would he step aside?" Abigail asked Otter Ransom.

"In the North," began Otter Ransom, "there is a story of an assembly that met once a year, the beginning of summer, where the clans met for their talk and grievances. It had priests, like churchmen, who spoke for the peace of the common people. Grim Fiddle knows."

I explained that what Otter Ransom was recalling was the Althing, the legislative and judicial assembly for medieval Iceland. I talked slowly, because it was my discovery, listening to my closest friends on South Georgia, that they were better at fighting than at thinking about their fight. I knew myself a weak intellectual in comparison to Lazarus, but I saw then that what little I had absorbed from listening to Israel and Peregrine argue politics, and reading Charity Bentham's works, and studying Longfaeroe's notions about kingship and just government in the books of Samuel, made me their master in terms of political science, of reasonable government. I did know the difference between authority and tyranny. Therefore I described the Althing carefully, telling them it was a once-a-year assembly meant to adjudicate feuds among families. Thirty-nine priests presided over the Althing, men drawn from the major families from early in Iceland's history and whose offices then became hereditary. The priests were considered to be above bribery and blood influence. It was as close to democracy as the medieval North ever came, and I think it fair to say that the Althing was no less broad-minded than the much celebrated Greek assemblies that were responsible for words like *democracy, despotism.* I told them the Althing was created because Iceland was a refuge for outcasts from the North Sea kingdoms, men who hated kingship yet had to agree on how to live in harmony. I concluded, "The decisions of the Althing were final. Any man who dissented was banished. And that was the Althing's worst punishment for a crime—exile. Since Iceland was already an outlaw haven, exile from Iceland was the same as a death sentence."

"That's your Skallagrim Strider, isn't it?" said Abigail.

"From what you say," said Jane, "Lazarus'd be wrong for the presidency, because he's married a Gaunt. We need someone from outside the big families, but who could please the families and the Volunteers and Reverend Longfaeroe and Lazarus, also the Zulemas, the beasties. The Hospidar wouldn't dare against such a president. He'd be free of all, including Elephant Frazer. A people's spokesman."

"Lazarus's tongue, that be," said Germanicus.

"It's fine learning. It'd do some no harm," said Jane.

"I have my ways," said Germanicus.

"The Frazers have their ways," said Jane. "No use to us if there's a plague coming, or more beasties. Lazarus says a tyranny has less chance than an oligarchy, and an oligarchy less chance than a democracy. We need a constitutional assembly."

"If Lazarus says my dad's a tyrant, he's a liar!" We all talked at once, trying to calm Germanicus, trying to make peace between those two stubborn lovers. Jane loved Germanicus—who did not?— yet she also loved learning and was also a Gaunt. She would not let Germanicus's temper distract her summary.

"If we can propose a candidate to unite the families, a union candidate," said Jane, "your dad would see the sense of an election. Then we can get us a constitution. Lazarus says a government of men is lawless, a government of law is a rock."

"What're you saying, girl?" said Abigail hesitantly.

"You'd be a fine candidate, Abbie," said Jane.

"I'm a Longfaeroe and a Frazer and mother of a bastard," said Abigail. For their own reasons, Jane and Abigail laughed.

"There be a man," said Germanicus heavily.

"No! Hold your tongue, you Germanicus Frazer," said Abigail.

"Grim Fiddle," said Jane.

I had not thought Wild Drumrul understood what was said, but he then stood up and said in English, "In the name of Allah the Compassionate, the Merciful, Grim Fiddle!" I knew it the preface to his Moslem prayers, a way of announcing the profound. He put his hands on my shoulders, met me eye to eye. It made me recall the promise I had made to his dead brother, Dede Gone, in Vexbeggar. How had I been my brothers' keeper? Goggle-Eye was dead at Port Praia. Little Dede Gone was dead trying to get *Black Crane* back to me. Wild Drumrul was on an island that was spiritually farther from his heritage than it was physically. And he was still game, a seaman on *King James,* a Volunteer for people he barely understood. What right did I have for further exemption from struggle because I was orphaned, was sad, was ashamed for my berserker nature? What did Wild Drumrul have, and yet he engaged fate. And now he asked for my help.

I made a rambling attempt to protest their scheme. I could hear myself talk—a sign, Israel once said, that a man does not believe himself. I was not wise; I was healthy. I was not well-spoken; I could speak my heart. I was not humble; I knew some of my limits. I was not a good Christian; I loved and knew love. I was unqualified for anyone's trust; I was a young, earnest man who respected the truth. And now they called me to be a problem-solver by being a truth-teller. It did please me, my vanity and my courage. I imagined that it would have pleased Peregrine, and Grandfather. I imagined that Skallagrim Strider too had felt shame for his life wasted on his own concerns yet had met the call of his men when they were banished from Iceland forever. I watched Abigail as I debated my qualifications with Germanicus and Jane. Abigail's eyes were wet; she did not smile, she did not frown. I gathered her face and their words and felt stronger. To them I was an idea.

They carried the idea of Grim Fiddle, peacemaker, union candidate, back to Gaunttown, to Elephant Frazer and the Hospidar, to Lazarus and the Zulemas, most importantly to Dolly Frazer, Violante Furore, Frances Gaunt, Amanda Rose, Beatrice Harrah, Victoria Hospidar, and Bonnie Moog. Longfaeroe took up the idea as if it were a gift from Jehovah. The debate was quick, too quick for it to have been constructive, more as if conciliation were desired, not compromise. On the first Sunday in the new year, 2001, the first Sunday in a new century and new millennium Longfaeroe was happy to proclaim, Longfaeroe preached and sang on the rise of David from the flocks of Bethlehem to the throne of the Hebrews, a sermon—I was told, because Lazarus advised me to stay clear of the campaigning—that left the women of Gaunttown in tears and the men scarlet and resolute. The rumor was spread by my supporters that the mutton supper in my hut had brought together the noblest spirits on South Georgia, a Frazer and Gaunt and Longfaeroe and beastie and outlaw, calling to Jehovah for Guidance. Jehovah had sent a message, in that storm that broke over my hut as we ate and talked: Grim Fiddle was South Georgia's found hope. Did they call me a savior? Some did. Others said, usurper.

The debate flowed and ebbed through the summer. The original issue of the beasties enslaved seemed forgotten. Lazarus said the issue became: devotion with or without representation? Concessions were required and made by all sides. The assumed verdict was that no popular vote for the president of the Gaunttown Assembly would be permitted; instead, the president would be chosen by a ballot of the elders of the families. Also, the president would be the convener of and spokesman for the Gaunttown Assembly, nothing more, and the Assembly's power would remain undefined pending further debate. The hopes for a constitution and popular democracy were, as Lazarus mused, left on the tables of the taverns.

The South Georgians were dominated by Scots Presbyterians, a people who suspect kingship but who are equally distrustful of permitting commoners—just everyman—a voice in matters of property and blood-kin authority. Lazarus counseled himself and the young people to remain patient. He explained to me that South Georgia fascinated him as a political phenomenon where, because of its isolation physically and now economically, time had seemingly stopped, or regressed, to something very close to what America had been at its birth as a nation. Liberty was the desire, to be fought for at any cost; however, and paradoxically, that liberty was seen to be as threatened by universal suffrage as it was by despotism. The South Georgians wanted to live free, yet knew they must have some government, and so they concluded the less government they had, the better they would be. Lazarus concluded they were immature, and smiled in that expectant, self-confident, secretive way of his. He accepted, in late summer, the proposition of the elders to permit a qualified election of a constrained president of an ambiguously defined Assembly. Then he immediately set about campaigning for what he called a true republic for South Georgia—written laws, universal suffrage, elected officials, coexistent executive, legislative, judicial branches of government—which he said he would "harvest" (he also used the word *forge*) as soon as he had me, as the president, to convene the Gaunttown Assembly not only as a "people's voice" but also as a "constitutional assembly."

Lazarus saw his challenge as I did not, and prepared himself, with book learning and rhetoric, for the battle ahead.

Abigail came by herself to tell me the results of the elders' vote. It was late summer, coolish, misty. The election was not unanimous. The Hospidar's candidate, Christian Rose, and the Gaunt's candidate, Kevin Gaunt, took more than half the vote together. I was president by plurality, not majority, a result that I did not then perceive as auguring contrariness. The immediate result was that I was free of one flock, woolly heads, and promised to another kind, woolly-headed, hardheaded; I was also relieved of my duties as a Volunteer, required to move into the upstairs rooms of the Assembly Hall.

Abigail was heartsick. She stayed by the door as she told me how her father had hugged her after the vote, had thanked her for helping me gain my "divine role." She said it was the first her father had touched her since childhood. That was not the cause of her melancholy. Lazarus had told her she should be careful with me for a while, lest the other factions use a charge of profligacy against me, and she exaggerated his advice. She said we must stop our affair, that she had come to say good-bye. I knew she was testing my devotion.

"You belong to them," she said. "Lazarus says you're changed. You're the only elected official on the island. You're no more the man I've loved, no more Sam's dad, my man. They did this to Samson. They made him their bloody captain, and he was changed too. Even if he'd come back to me, I'd lost him to them. Lord forgive me, I loved you before when you were a bonnie sad boy, and I love you still. I can't help you do this thing. I mark them. They've taken you from me. I can't save you no more. Save yourself."

"What can happen?" I protested. "Lazarus says I'm a figurehead."

"Like the bow of a ship, what they shoot at," she said.

"Abbie, I'm not Samson," I tried, softly, "not David either."

I meant it to lighten her heart. It was our joke. She smiled, but if ever there was a smile of unhappiness, that was it. She said, "Oh, it's daft we are, the pair of us. Darling Grim, trust me, save yourself." And then she came over and kissed me, and took me. I was theirs, she said; she took me as hers. I cannot sharply recall her scent, or her touch; I can still hear her cry in passion. She was loud. I liked that. Afterward, I tried to convince her our lives would improve, that as soon as the troubles passed, we could live together, could marry, give her sons and our Sam a proper home. I tried to persuade her with my wishes, and Lazarus's ideas, and Germanicus's strength. I tried to prove to her we were not changed, just wiser. She said she wanted to believe me, said she was afraid to marry another to lose. She put her head on my breast, did not weep. I realized then, embracing sweet, sturdy, haunted Abigail, that we were changed, that I was changed. In her eyes, I was a man to lose. I pushed it away, that shadow, and pulled her closer to protect her from her doubts. In the weeks that followed, I continued my seduction of Abigail even as my new status took me from her. As the fall closed on us, however, all my eager words, all our high dreams, all that we as free men and women could do, were undone by a natural catastrophe.

Exodus

I have mentioned the fury of the Scotia Sea, raked by the westerlies and churned by the Falkland Current, what the sealers said was the home of the mothers of freak waves, as massive as rolling mountains, frequently dwarfing even that behemoth that tossed *Angel of Death* mid-Atlantic and more frequently draped in a dense fog that smeared the boundary between sea and sky. The sealers told another story of the Scotia Sea, one that overshadowed the dread of those saltwater ranges. They told of the thirteen consecutive winters when the ice pack that spread each winter from the Antarctic actually pushed out to wrap South Georgia in a howling white desert. That was said to have been in the nineteenth century, when only whalers and sealers sailed farther south than the fifty-fifth parallel, when only crazed sealers dared cross the sixtieth parallel for the wealth of the rookeries on the South Orkneys and South Shetlands. It was a broad account, sealer talk, what Christmas Muir told me was "banker's bait," meaning it was likely more an excuse for poor catches—passed on to the banking houses that funded the sealing expedition—than it was reliable oceanology. The notion that the Weddell Sea, which cups Antarctica from Queen Maud Land to Graham Land, could extend its ice sheet more than seven hundred miles beyond the Antarctic circle is fantastic.

I watched it happen May and June of my sixth year on South Georgia. Each clear morning, one in four that time of year, I would leave my rooms in the Assembly Hall and climb to the high heath to stand transfixed as the southeastern horizon brightened with what is called an ice blink. The vanguard of the pack approached in a line across the face of the earth. It was a military operation. Tabular icebergs calved from Antarctica's permanent ice sheet preceded the pack like shock troops, some a mile long and a few hundred yards wide, turning over suddenly as the tide tossed them, others tens of miles long and wide, drifting ice islands several hundred feet high, craggy, multicolored. The sea was also laced with bergy bits broken from the ice islands and with brash ice, sheets of ice independent of the main pack. The pack itself advanced both under the glare of the ice blink and under the astounding optical phenomenon of mirages of ice islands projected upside down against the steel-blue sky. At times, it could look as if a monstrous gray mouth yawned toward South Georgia, jagged white teeth of ice islands below and above—shimmering, bloodred at sunset, angry.

Christmas Muir and Peggs and Wild Drumrul would climb up with me. Peggs, a man who, no braggart, could reminisce about the seven seas of the world and the ice of both poles, did describe for us the gathering of the pack. After all this time, I still take satisfaction in knowing the natural process that has entombed me and mine. Sea water freezes at twenty-eight and a half degrees Fahrenheit. He was not precise about the science, and from what I recall, the air temperature is independent of the temperature at sea level. First, frazil ice forms on the water, like slush with oily water atop. Then, as the temperature drops with the wind and current, the frazil ice transforms into a sludgy layer called grease ice. Finally, the temperature plunging, independent sheets, called pancake ice, congeal into new ice that, when it thickens to nine feet, loses its salt content and bobs free of the water. This new ice crumbles and stratifies as the sea beneath, or a storm above, throws one floe against another, a process called hummocking or, in the case of one floe thrusting over another, rafting. Hummocking and rafting combine new ice into ragged, heaving walls that can grow to barriers forty feet high, the forward redoubts of millions of square miles of a tireless crystal army.

I enjoy how placid the process can seem. To watch it the first time was awful. I felt as if the sea were dying, all life slowing to an omnipresent nothingness. As the pack gathers strength, cooling the air temperature before it, it sends out new ice like claws that bend back into the pack, then dart out again to grab new sea or to anchor onto the ice islands that serve as advance guard. The pack was ever moving, ever violent. It had no plan, rather it was a condition; yet because the pack grew hourly, it seemed sublimely alive. It was actually the antithesis of life.

Have I communicated the noise? South Georgia was wind and rain, the sea smashing the cliffs, seafoam arching over the crags, elemental chaos building to endless howls. That same ceaseless wind rushing across the ice pack was transformed into an omnipresent scream. The pack rippled with the tides, which, ever changing, sent crackling explosions across a line, the pack shivering as a wave ran beneath the mass. Pressure ridges formed when one gigantic floe crushed against another, huge pieces of ice, whole bergs, fired into the air like cannon salvos. The ice islands were continually disintegrating in the sun's heat, and they whined as they twisted against themselves, roaring as a crack ran lengthwise, sludgy rivers cascading from their faces. Whenever the open sea broke through the field, it would catch up brash ice and throw it against the ice fronts with rattling, knocking, scratching sounds. And the fast ice, that which attaches to land masses, would rub up against South Georgia and the outlying rocks, screeching when the pack heaved north, ever north, to replace the vanguard melted off in the warm currents of the horse latitudes.

The pack swept over South Georgia. I am not sure if it was more frightening to sit on the ridge with the sea covered in a fog and listen to the pack rumble and whine, or to stand on the ridge under clear gray skies and watch the pack grow, a hundred hundred tongues of ice licking the gray waves. The contrasts were hypnotizing, and I came to anticipate them: one noon, the sun pushing through in the low northeastern sky like torchlight, not warm but reassuringly there, the pack would be solid to the west, but to the east there would be open sea pocked with wave crests, dotted with brash ice, some giant bergs bashing one another. The next day the pack would be everywhere, flat, glistening, wind-scourged, ice islands in the sky; then again in several hours the floes would part to shape a seamlike channel, the sea breaking through to shape a lake in the ice, perhaps a storm rolling black clouds and fog over the field. For beneath the pack was the cauldron of the Scotia Sea, thrusting untold billions of tons of water up against the ice.

"It's beauty to me," said Christmas Muir. "I been icebound more'n once out there. Peggs, he walked the pack once, no place to no place, to launch a boat. Out there, man forgets things. Until she moves on ye, or she squeezes yerr ship to splinters. And them killers come sniffin', those pig eyes looks at ye for supper."

Wild Drumrul asked, what killers? Christmas Muir laughed,

pleased that he had scared us, and told of the killer whales, thirty feet long, really large dolphins, that preyed in packs upon anything living or dead above or beneath the ice pack; that was in the Antarctic Circle, he said, and need not worry us on South Georgia.

Wild Drumrul spoke my mind, asking, what was it like on the pack? Christmas Muir started to joke, let Peggs answer soberly, "It makes a man want to sit down and quit. Jes' quit."

The pack had the same effect on South Georgia. The people of Gaunttown withdrew inside themselves. The only warmth seemed one's own heart, but then, even the pulse rate slows in the ice and dark, as if frazil ice were forming in the blood. It had been dreary before; with the pack sealing us from open water, it became morbid. By the middle of July, winter upon us, the siege was complete, a white desert for at least one hundred miles to the northwest, perhaps fifty to the northeast. The ships in Cumberland Bay were in continual jeopardy from the ice islands that spun by. If one of them had turned with the current and loomed down on Gaunttown, it could have crushed everything afloat, perhaps more. One ice island, fifty miles long and five wide, did ram the windward shore about forty miles north of Gaunttown, sending rumbles through the ridge each time the current heaved it up against the underwater rocks. It was fanciful to imagine, though there were those that did, a fleet of those monsters closing on South Georgia, horn-tipped and ninety miles long, to gouge away our ark of hornstone.

The melancholy of being icebound wore easiest on the sealers, like Christmas Muir and Peggs, wore hardest on the families. Elephant Frazer ordered strict rationing, confiscated several private stockpiles, arrested and imprisoned some black marketeers, for fear that the pack would not fully recede with the next summer's heat, might return for the next twelve years as in the sealers' tale. That was not credible, neither were the black-ice islands that emerged from the pack in July.

"I knew'd it, I mostly did," said Christmas Muir. "It's that Satan's Seat. I told ye, matey. Ye can still hear it growlin' if ye got ears like mine, underwater like, them black giants, like pieces of Hell, I tell ye, and don't forget that ram's head. Him's got notions, bad 'uns."

I accompanied Germanicus on a march north soon after, to
inspect the fort that had been built to guard the main pass through
the island, thirty miles northwest of Gaunttown. Germanicus regretted the excessive precautions the Volunteers demanded against
the beasties, the plague, the unseen, and was unusually disconsolate about the future. We camped off a humpbacked ridge west
of the central mountain range, in a shepherd's hut, that, because
of the pass, gave us a good view to the southwest. On the first
clear morning, we took a work break to have a look at the black
ice, more soot-colored, really, streaked gray, black bergy bits broken off. We were too far from where they must have originated—
about one thousand miles—for them to have been starkly black
against the white.

"I don't make much of that gab about that volcano," said Germanicus. "The Southern Ocean be as full of wild talk as whales. I
grew up with it. I remember as a wee boy hearin' Dad tell Samson
where Antarctica comes from. Dad said, once upon a time, long
afore, before Jesus, there was a great kingdom at the South Pole.
No ice blanket then, jes' cold and grand. It was ruled by three
kings, Beach, Lunach, and Maleteur. It was filled with hairy elephants and black diamonds. The folk lived off the sea and worshiped Jehovah, like us. King Beach, loneliest of the three kings,
loved an albatross and had a daughter with her. This princess
weren't beautiful, nor clever, nor good. She wanted to live with
ice birds, and she hated men, mostly, except when they made love
to her. She called that 'flight.' She taunted every young man she
could because they couldn't fly. She taunted special King Lunach's
son and King Maleteur's son. Well, she also must have sported
with them, because she had this child, a boy, soon enough. Her
dad was shamed and sealed her up in a palace, a palace made of
black diamonds and whalebones. He didn't know who'd fathered
his heir. He thought on his spite and decided to hold a banquet.
He had the bairn cut up into meat for pies and fed them pies to
the men he figured had defiled his daughter and the honor of his
kingdom. They ate hearty and went out for a stroll along a glacier, as was their way with full guts. King Beach told them there
what he'd done. They were angry. It weren't because he'd made
them eat a bairn in pies. That was their custom in times of famine,

to eat the small and weak. They were angry because he suspected all of them when only one was guilty. They went on screamin' at him, 'Mod, mod, the bleddy mon be mod.' That weren't all of it. It happened that no one of them could admit to being the bairn's father, since they'd all been with the princess, flying and the like. They were disgusted with themselves. They got worked up and killed King Beach and offered themselves to the princess as her husband. They understood that the man she chose was the man guilty of causing all the fuss and must be killed. The princess cursed them for eatin' her bairn and killin' her dad. She thought on her spite and one day called them altogether and named them all as her husband to be. This was daft, and they laughed at her stupid revenge. The princess went back to her palace of black diamonds and white bones and called upon Jehovah to avenge her. Jehovah was angry at the misery these men had caused, and granted the princess's prayer, though she'd never prayed before. He destroyed all three kingdoms with fire and brimstone. With volcanoes, I expect. Jehovah covered the ruin with an ice sheet for eternity. Jehovah then thought on his judgment and what he'd done, made a cold and grand kingdom into a frozen ruin, and he was sorry. He promised he wouldn't ever again send the fire and the ice to punish wickedness. He turned the men that was left into seals, the womenfolk into birds, the children into penguins, and the hairy elephants into whales. And that's where Antarctica comes from. Dad said them elephant seals were the seafarin' men."

"What was the princess's name?" I asked.

Germanicus laughed, clapping his sides over and over, saying, "It be a sealer's tale, Grim. I tell ye to show ye what to take from them sealers. On the ice, a man sees things. He thinks uncommon. That tale of that volcano, Satan's Seat, it be a sealer passin' time."

"But the black ice," I said, "if there is a volcanic range, if it is melting the ice, that might explain the ice pack pushing out this far."

"Black ice, black plague, no bait to me. It be black hearts that wreck us. Them, they won't stop being feared of what happens. We must. Samson died, it happened. We lost the Falklands, it happened. The ice came, it happened. There be what the Almighty does. There be what we can do as men. We can no more know the Almighty's ways than figure them. What we can do be to know men's ways, and figure them, and keep them right."

"You mean the Volunteers?"

"All angry men—Brackenbury, the Hospidar, Christian Rose, and that Lazarus. Like in Dad's tale of Antarctica. Them act disgusted with themselves for what has happened. The parson, he tells 'em the Almighty be punishing us for quitting the Falklands. He says the ice is a judgment. I don't swallow it. Too much like a sealer's tale. The ice happened. Not that I know what might be comin'. It be wearin' on Dad. The Hospidar be a rough one."

"Lazarus says when we finish the constitution, no single man can threaten our welfare. South Georgia will be a republic."

"So Lazarus says. Janey talks like his echo. That great number for that great good, with charity for all wee folk. True?"

"It's his foster-mother's mind," I explained. "He says her memory demands his effort. Lazarus is ashamed of what he has done. He killed a priest, I told you, and he regrets it. He says he wants to take the knife from the assassin, and the best way to do that is to make everyone become at the same time both the assassin and the assassinated. It's a complicated business, about Sweden and America."

"Rich lands and warm ways," said Germanicus. "This republic Lazarus promises, it'll last as long as a man in that water, if ten bad men, aye, one weak man, takes charge. My dad be what's between what meanness we got and killin'. Lazarus has learning, I say, learning for rich lands, not here. One God, one land, one man, one way."

"I respect what you say," I said.

"The Bible's way," said Germanicus.

"Abbie hates that. She says her father twists things."

"She has cause," said Germanicus. "My brother was a good man. He would've been a great one. She loved part of him. She loves part of ye. I don't mark her for it."

I started to protest the confusion between me and Samson.

"Ye're yerrself. Ye're stronger than you let on, and good, and hard. I saw ye when ye wanted yerr folk and when ye wanted revenge. I see ye now when my folk want ye to lead them through this trouble. Dad needs Grim Fiddle. He won't say it. I say it, he needs ye."

"What can I do?" I did not say I was a figurehead; it would have been an insult to Germanicus, who loved me as a brother.

"Trust my dad," said Germanicus. "Bide yerr time."

"I don't like the size of what you're saying. My father's friend, Israel, he told me stories too. In America there was a soldier named Nixon. He was a good man, from California, born poor, who struggled his way to university. He came back from the Second World War with high dreams, wanting to serve his people. Do you know Nixon? It doesn't matter. He was elected to the American assembly, and then, because he was young and bold, was chosen by a great American general to be president of the assembly and second-in-command of the American Republic. Nixon trusted the general and bided his time. When he tried for the general's job years later, he was defeated, but just barely, by another soldier from the other side of the country. Nixon was bitter for his loss. He was also angry about things in America—a war in Asia, discrimination against the Negroes, their beasties, and other matters about money. Nixon said America was losing its greatness. The Americans laughed at him, told him he was old and tired. For reasons I don't understand, Nixon waited many more years and was then elected president of America. By then he really was old and tired, and didn't believe in anything but himself. He tried to make America into what he had wanted it to be when he was young. He ignored the laws of the Republic and degraded the politics of democracy, like majority rule. He wrecked the young people who wanted to serve America with their high dreams in their time in their way. Nixon chased men like my father and Israel into exile. Nixon was hard, and full of vengeance. It made him weak. If he had trusted his own people, and trusted the laws of the Republic, I might not be here right now."

"Ye don't trust my dad?" said Germanicus, who did not evidence to me that he cared much for my story of Nixon the tyrant. Telling it had made me sad, thinking of Israel.

I sighed. "I owe your dad everything. It's not trust. Lazarus says I am the people's servant, not their master, and neither is your father."

"And what are ye if we ask ye to be our master?"

"That would be more for you than me, Germanicus."

"Nay, nay, I have my ways. Out there, on the sea, that's for me. You have the learning, and the strength, and they love ye."

I was not turned by his charm. I teased him that he was the Frazer heir, and it was his destiny to rule South Georgia if it was any man's. Germanicus stood firm. I did not want an argument, added, "We disagree. I need your help to get Lazarus's constitution accepted. That way every man, and woman, can speak for their own ways. Trust law, like Lazarus says, not men."

Germanicus pointed at the black-ice islands and spoke the last word that day. "I trust what I can see and hear. I can't see that volcano. And I can't hear the law. I'll trust a man, and a man I know at that, and my advice to ye be to do the same. Trust yerr master. Talk be ice, it melts in anger."

I brooded on Germanicus's words. He had as little faith in republicanism as did the Hospidar. They all believed in what Lazerus's books called absolutism, "one God, one land, one man, one way," what is really kingship without the onus of primogeniture. The crucial disagreement among South Georgia's patriots was not over form of government; it was over who should succeed Elephant Frazer. Germanicus had as much told me that he and his young comrades wanted me as their next master. The Hospidar wanted himself. This was not sophisticated political science. It was crude, antiquated, vulnerable, defeatist in its way. I was sympathetic. It proceeded from their disillusionment and stoutheartedness. The South Georgians saw themselves caught between the failure of modern republican states to maintain enlightenment in the face of man-made catastrophes (famine, war, rebellion) and their own imminent failure to maintain a marginal existence as an abandoned colony in the face of natural catastrophes. How could they reasonably be expected to embrace yet another republican scheme when the British Parliament had failed them completely? Their desire for absolutism was an anachronism, an insult to reason. Yet for them republicanism was ungainly, untrustworthy, an insult to their commonsensical instinct for survival. The young patriots were willing to accommodate their desire by reaching for a new master who was from outside the community and who was endowed with what they thought were extraordinary powers—

Grim Fiddle. I felt trapped by my discernment; I was puzzled as to whether Germanicus and his comrades were pragmatic or simpleminded.

One night that winter I asked Lazarus for help understanding the South Georgians. It was just after we had adjourned another poorly attended, acrimonious Assembly debating the articles in Lazarus's constitutional draft. We sat side by side behind the podium in a dimly lit and empty chamber, the wind outside like a woeful chorus.

"Slaves are stubborn," said Lazarus, tapping his pen, splattering squid ink. Lazarus had aged, grown heavier, with deep lines on the unscarred part of his copper face that made him appear less rusted than weathered, like iron at sea. Marriage and fatherhood had tempered him, had also made him mordantly earnest. He was thirty years old, proud, cool-hearted, able, fast. "The condition of slavery makes one intrinsically conservative. Don't change, you think, it will make it worse. These people have inherited the remains of the ruinous British imperial system that kept them slaves for generations—absentee landlordism, mercantile exploitation, like what Ireland, the Americas, India, Africa, and Australia threw off in the twentieth century. Because they're alive, they think that system was stable. They try to mimic it with despotic rule and oligarchical secrecy. We know better. What they have now is entropic and doomed. The beasties in the camp aside, old Frazer is a benevolent despot. He's well-meaning, blunders on, his authority weakened every time he must judge between factions. His major weakness is that he can make no sensible provision for succession. They don't see it. They expect another hero will emerge magically to lead them. That's what they think you are. It doesn't happen that way. The history of despotism is clear: The legacy of a strong ruler is a weak one. The weak despot will leave behind a strong one, but the transition will be chaotic and bloody. The best way to break the cycle—tyranny, anarchy, tyranny—is to provide the people with a means to determine their own destiny. That's what we're doing, Grim, leveling the highs of benevolent despotism, raising the lows of draconian burglary, while people like you and Germanicus develop confidence to rule by democracy, assembly, committee, debate, consensus."

I told Lazarus I liked how scientific he made it sound. I also asked him why what he said had not worked in Sweden and America; I added that Israel had told me that republicanism in the hands of bullies—Germanicus's ten bad men—becomes mediocre subsistence for the common people and unbounded luxury for the ruling class, and that whenever a dissident group challenged the rulers, it was isolated and corrupted, or if not corrupted, destroyed.

"It can look that way," said Lazarus. "Your Israel had a sharp wit. It misled him. What he said is true only if the people participate in their own degradation. Sweden and the United States are gigantic models. They might distort what I can say. I'll try. Plato, I've read him to you, he thought a good state had limits of size. South Georgia approximates his ideal new state, Magnesia, in that it is intimate, modest, moralistic, nonpoetic, cut off—meaning it's free from accidental invasion. We have problems, they're solvable. Virtue is possible here. It might have once been possible in America. No longer. America's Republic failed not because the philosophy of republicanism is flawed, rather because the white men who wrote the constitution were flawed and afraid of the will of the people their work enfranchised. They created a new man, free, ambitious, scientific, then came to see him as a monster. They released a truth—that all people are created equal—and then saw they could not contain it. The truth has no master. Over the following two hundred years the Republic thrived because of that masterless truth. Yet, yet, the continual yearning for universal suffrage, when combined with the fact that the population of the nation became increasingly nonwhite, led the white masters to conclude they were cursed by their own ancestors' accidental, philosophical genius. They wanted to remain more than equal in a country in which they had become a distinct minority. So the white masters, Israel's ruling class, alienated people from the power to assemble and vote. It's easily done—intimidation of a free press, telling people they are powerless to change their fate, confusing the opposition with the circus of party politics. America became a republic in name only. Actually, it was, is, a despotism, the president elected with less than a majority of those that vote, which number was itself always less than a majority of those eligible to vote. The president spoke for himself and his gang, and then eccentrically. He didn't have a majority mandate and he knew it, so he acted the sly prince, appeals to the godhead, manifest destiny, dreams, the Red aggressor. That was your Nixon. He was not much more than what we have in old Frazer, an appointed despot."

I paused, saw something, then spoke more to please Lazarus than myself. "Then America failed as a republic because it could not trust the beasties it attracted and enfranchised. Enfranchised?"

"A simplification, it will do," said Lazarus, no smiles. Lazarus had stopped changing expressions; the face of an angry young man was gone, replaced with a mask of inhibition, placidity, and a stare that seemed faraway. The burn scars covered the right side of his body but only a third of his face, dark purpie skin like fingers up from his neck and onto his cheek. He was self-conscious of the twisted part of his face, knew that smiling or frowning made his scars look worse. He had a habit of tapping his scar, doing so as he continued, "It's the people who are strong, Grim, and the strongest people are what you call beasties. By simple size of number, the beasties are strongest. They have more chances to get the future right. I know, I'm a beastie. Grim Fiddle is a beastie."

"Not strong enough, I think," I said. "What else explains what we found, that fleet of the damned?"

"A transient event. A function of anarchy. A product of a state wherein law and morality have broken down temporarily and yet the idea of national sovereignty has prevented the lawful nations from intervening. The idea of law can momentarily protect lawlessness. The fleet of the damned—really a superstitious name, misleading—that refugee exodus, then, it was also an example of the chaos that occurs between successive tyrannies in the cycle of despotism. It can be stopped with rigor and, yes, strong stomachs. We can stop it here, dismantle that camp, get Toro Zulema elected as a spokesman for his people, and all with a republic. A people's republic."

"What keeps majority rule—this people's republic—from becoming a mob?" I asked. "Or becoming a tyranny, like America in Vietnam? And isn't it true that a majority can cast out a minority? Wouldn't that be the will of the people, too? Isn't that what happened out there, and in Sweden, and in America with my father? What prevents frightened people from acting without decency? I read Charity Bentham's books. She said charity is a function of self-interest. She never explained to my satisfaction how to stop a group of nations—and not tyrannies, all of them republics—from each acting in their supposed best interest like murderers."

"One answer to your problem is to reformulate your question," said Lazarus. "Exile is one result of slaves being stubborn, like Germanicus. Factions such as the one your father represented, Vietnam war protesters, were not republicans. In their way, dissenters like your father were absolutists, and crazed, and self-destructive, typical romantic misanthropes, white men complaining that the world is not white enough. They said, peace or nothing. They got what they asked for."

"I don't think Peregrine and Israel asked for exile, nor did Guy and Earle ask for Saigon," I said. "And I don't think the beasties asked for Ascension Island. Sometimes, Lazarus, you and Plato sound more dangerous than the despots."

"It is not possible or desirable to rule innocently," said Lazarus, a hypothesis he often recited to me afterward, one that I have seen the truth of, and the ruin of. "Learn that. The people have a will. They must be shown how to use it. Forced, if it comes to that. Trust me. We can make them see we're the future here, and right, and their last chance. What we need is time and will."

"And luck?" I tried, ending our debate that night with what I meant as levity. I was trying then to love Lazarus, as he was trying to love the people of South Georgia. He was smarter than anyone on the island (he and Orlando the Black and Longfaeroe were our only university graduates), and his arrogance should be excused by his struggle to translate what he thought into what he thought we could understand. On South Georgia, his mind was somewhere between dogma and praxis. He was not yet ready to act as violently as he could talk. There was more to him than radical-republican-without-a-country, of course; for example, though he loved Violante and his little girl, Cleo, he did not conceal his sorrow about Cleopatra. He encouraged me to talk about Cleopatra, drew me out on my lingering fascination for her, as a way, I believe, of testing his own devotion to her memory. We shared an icon. We did not share a mind. He believed that revised Benthamism on South Georgia would protect South Georgia from what I now see as a ghastly distortion of Benthamism evidenced in the Atlantic Ocean. I remained reluctant to commit myself to him, as I also resisted Germanicus. Lazarus kept at me, for he was long-winded, detail-conscious, rhetorically adept, without humility or patience. He did have regrets.

I have mentioned his regret for the murder of Father Saint Stephen. He talked to me only once about it, though he referred to it often, obliquely, metaphorically. It was a long talk, what I understand now was a confession to the only man he thought then was still alive who had witnessed what he had done. He said he did not know who his natural father was, only that he was from the West Indies, an islander, probably dead. He knew his mother had been in a Cuban monastery, as either a student or servant. Either she had died, or run away, or become a nun. Lazarus, as an infant, had been placed in an orphanage in Cuba and then transported by mysterious means to another orphanage in the American state of Florida. Through Roman Catholic Church auspices, he had been adopted at the age of four by the Furores, along with Orlando the Black and Babe, who had been resident in the same orphanage. Lazarus was schooled by Dominican priests in Chicago, a private school, exclusive, almost entirely white except for him and his new brothers. There, he said, he learned disgust for the Roman Catholic Church, what Lazarus called "holy chains." He said that only once; it was atypical of his sense of humor. Did Lazarus have a sense of humor? Yes, he was readily amused by hypocrisy, his own and everyone else's.

Lazarus concluded his confession by saying that, when he had attacked Father Saint Stephen, he had been out of his mind with revulsion for what he said was the pious gangsterism of the Church that had crushed his mother, and very likely shamed her to give up her bastard to strangers.

Then he seemed to reformulate, clarify, that mind of his, pounding, forging: "I killed him because I felt like it. It was stupid, an intellectual waste. What's the point of silencing a madman? It hurt me more than him. He was out of his mind, and I let him pull me out of mine. It was sickening, to lose control like that. What you talk about, when you went crazy at Stanley, that sounds a lot like what I felt. I was angry! And I acted in a manner I absolutely revile and reject. It was like the beast in me, or . . .

awful, Grim, awful to remember. Did I know what I was doing? Yes, I did. And what's the difference between a murderer who knows why he kills and one who doesn't? None. I had cause to kill and I did. It was still stupid. I think about my father. Did he know what killed him, or why, or why he abandoned my mother and me? I know why. That is important. What I have, by accident, is the means to act on my cognition. I have an excellent education, despite all the claptrap about the mysteries of the spirit, and I have a sense of history that is completely modern. What Longfaeroe would say was a vision of history. It isn't magic, like your mother's. It isn't xenophobic, like your Grandfather's. It is logical and informed, and just. And I have a place to apply my gifts, here, now. It is mine to do or to fail. I must succeed. I think of an American revolutionary, John Adams—a white master, yes, but a republican all the same, swept along by the truth of egalitarian justice—and how he felt when he was elected to the outlawed Continental Congress, which marked him for hanging by the tyrants. He wrote, 'I wander alone, and ponder. I muse, I mope, I ruminate. We have not men fit for the times. We are deficient in Genius, in Education, in Gravel, in Fortune, in every Thing. I feel unutterable anxiety.' That is how it always feels in a struggle against tyranny and for justice. That is why you feel inadequate, spun around. We must be fit for our times, Grim. When I killed that madman, I was not fit. When you killed at Stanley, you were not fit. Now, we are. I say so. We must build. Any *campesino* can kill. We must succeed. If not? There is no *if not*. Death in any form would be less terrible."

I did not think to tell Lazarus at the time that he had explained his crime in almost the same words that Peregrine used to explain his murder of Cesare Furore, "because I wanted to" and "because I felt like it." I wonder now if Lazarus knew. There seems to me a profound difference between killing a number of human beings and murdering one man intimately. I have done both, many times, and believe that while killing many—war—is often a consequence of events, a tactical decision, vicious, but often meant purposely, a murder of one man is an act of willful blasphemy. There are sophistic excuses for the mass killer; there is no balm for the murderer. A single murder, call it an assassination, corrodes the will that engenders it. It corrupts. **The Norse** had another way of saying this: "The dead man lives in the face of the slayer." This means that the conflict that moved one to assassinate is not resolved by physical death. Assassination did transform Lazarus, taint him, weigh him down with Father Saint Stephen's nature. The Norse would have said that Lazarus was haunted by Father Saint Stephen's ghost. Lazarus seemed driven to create a people's republic in order to prove to himself that a man who has freed himself of "holy chains" is right, and that one, like Father Saint Stephen, who celebrates human death as the most courageous human journey, is wrong. Lazarus had taken Grandfather's verdict on Father Saint Stephen to heart—the priest was not only mad but also wrong. This fetches me, that my grandfather should have colored Lazarus, too. I am not saying that I saw Grandfather or Father Saint Stephen in Lazarus's face, but then, I did.

I suggest that Lazarus, a man who dismissed orthodox religion as irrational, and even denounced art as antirational, was a deeply religious man in his devotion to the revolutionary theory that he took from the republican spirit of the Greeks, the Romans, the Italians, the French, the Germans, the Russians, even the white masters of early America. He spoke much of a man named Tom Paine, whom I have too little knowledge of to connect to what Lazarus did. Lazarus worshiped republicanism like a tireless pilgrim. He had dreams; he called them ideas. Was he a fanatic? Yes, but that seems an unfair word for a man like Lazarus, who acted so coolly, resolutely, clearheadedly. Israel taught me that there is no school absent of a little sleight-of-hand, mystical chicanery. So for Lazarus and his republican schools. I suggest that in Lazarus's confession to me, the moment he proved his vision with the statement "I say so," he was introducing a matter of faith-beyond-reason into the debate. Grandfather and Father Saint Stephen, clearly zealous men, believed in the coming Kingdom of Heaven. Lazarus believed in the coming revolution. What made Lazarus qualitatively distinct from Grandfather and Father Saint Stephen was that his utopianism, his millenarianism (at the birth of a new millennium), was informed by his specific, earthly, demonstrable belief in the idea of the Republic of South Georgia.

Lazarus was a dreamer and a builder. I pause to marvel that in saying this I describe an orphan, bastard, beastie, revolutionary, who was almost a theoretical combination of his foster-mother the dreamer and his foster-father the builder. Father Saint Stephen had wanted to enrich the future through mass suicide. Lazarus wanted to enrich the future through mass enfranchisement. I have shown that they both used history—what Lazarus sometimes called "the agenda of history"—to justify their conduct. Father Saint Stephen had failed because he was wrong. Lazarus might not have failed on South Georgia. What he needed was time and will and men fit for the times. We were that, in the very end, I and Lazarus, men fit for our times. God help me, the truth of it, Grim Fiddle was fit for his times. There was never enough time on South Georgia.

Our fate was fixed by the time Germanicus and Lazarus and I had our separate conversations on the future of South Georgia. The events that undid us seem now sadly trivial, a protracted blood feud, and yet the situation revealed the shadow that could not be enlightened. Lazarus and I, for all our learning and magic, were beasties to the South Georgians, and anyone who stood with us, loved us, became a beastie too.

It began with the stoning of Jane Gaunt, when she tried to visit the two wounded children in the hospital. The stone-throwers were wild children and hags, mostly old sealers' widows. The Gaunts sought justice. Kevin Gaunt, Jane's older brother, a hot-tempered man, sought blood justice. Elephant Frazer could not give it, for the ringleaders of the assailants were pathetically old, beyond punishment, their motives clouded by hysteria. After her recovery, Jane Gaunt spoke at church, forgiving her trespassers. Most were proud of her for it, and all assumed the wounds were healed. This is not to forget the trouble it caused Germanicus, and how the incident led indirectly to my election as president of the Assembly. It lingered in the hearts of the guilty also.

The following year, midwinter, the ice freezing our hearts, one of the meekest among us, Lena Rose, a younger half-sister of the Hospidar's favorite, Christian Rose, was attacked on the high heath as she was walking up to feed her pet birds, albatross chicks. The attack was deranged, a knifing and possible ravishment, and

the girl lost her senses. She might have been tortured. She was
unable to name the criminal.

It was sadder still, because Lena had been born simpleminded and deformed. She was also a great favorite of the old
wives of Gaunttown, some of whom were the hags who had attacked Jane Gaunt. More, Lena was often seen in the company of
the other simpleton in Gaunttown, Robby Oldmizzen. The old
wives had never liked this; the hags among them called Robby
unclean and "demon-plagued." Robby Oldmizzen was the very
same young boy whom Germanicus had rescued at *2 de Diciembre*.
Through his great-grandmother (that old woman I carried to the
longboats, who had died in Port Stanley), he was related to the
Frazers. Robby had been tortured by the Patties and had lost his
senses when he was forced to watch the Patties break his uncle on
one of those wheels of theirs. This was significant, since it was
believed by the old wives, and others who should have known
better, that Robby was not simpleminded, that he was actually a
mad dog, and dangerous. He had screaming fits, similar to the
ones I experienced my first year on South Georgia; unfortunately,
Robby had his in Gaunttown, not protected as I was by Longfaeroe and the Frazers, and Robby's worsened as he got older. It
was also believed that Robby was the one who, in my third year
on the island, had lashed a ewe to a wheel and tortured it with a
harpoon.

Lena had been born with an overlarge head, crooked limbs,
and a severe limp. Robby's limp was from paralysis brought on by
torture. They limped about together. They shared weak minds.
There had been vulgar talk of a romance between them. That was
ridiculous. Lena seemed as innocent a creature as I have ever
known, a lamb. Robby seemed too absorbed by his nightmares to
have been able to concentrate erotically. Nevertheless, the suspicion was there, and I cannot deny that Robby loved Lena in his
way, and she him. They were a delight to many of us, to me, and
I often regretted that I did not find more time for them when, as
a shepherd, I had visited the market square where they played.
Robby and Lena were also usually among the few who attended
the assemblies Lazarus and I called to draft the constitution. And
Robby was one of Iceberg's favorite playmates; with his one good

hand, he once carved her profile in stone, and I named one of her grandchildren for him.

Longfaeroe called a prayer service to sing for Lena's recovery. Fergus Moog, the old crank who had accused Lazarus of being responsible for the original knife fight, stood up to say that no sane man would have "hacked up" poor Lena. His inference was clear, and he was not alone in his leap to vigilante justice. Some of the young Rose boys had already dragged Robby to Lena's bedside in hospital. She was said to have been shaken awake, to have looked at Robby and screamed. Robby screamed back and tried to run. Christian Rose was summoned and took Robby to the Rose camp, as he said, "in the name of the Volunteers." Elephant Frazer heard about this through Jane Gaunt, and sent a message to the Hospidar, commander of the Volunteers, to intervene. The Hospidar would not reply. Elephant Frazer took several Volunteers the next morning to the Rose camp and arrested Robby "in the name of the governor-general." Motherwell accompanied Elephant Frazer, had to wrestle one of the Roses to the ground. There were hard words before Christian Rose relented. By the next day, the whole of Gaunttown knew several versions of the confrontation. The Roses, to save face, demanded blood vengeance.

Elephant Frazer ordered me to call an Assembly. Nature then tried to help us calm tempers by serving up a raging storm that delayed the affair several days. It was not until a week after the attack that the Assembly met. By then, factions and counterfactions had formed. The meeting was chaos, all the anxieties of defeat, plague, the ice pack, and the rationing washing together to spill on this one concrete tragedy—Lena's desecration. Elephant Frazer refused to come inside the hall until I gained order. In the meantime, that night, he had Motherwell remove Robby from the governor-general's office above THE KELPER pub, where he had been kept for fear the hospital was too vulnerable to mischief, to the Frazer camp. It is my memory that no man of sense at that Assembly thought Robby guilty. It did not seem to pertain. Reason was in eclipse. The meeting became a mob, and a motion was moved to force Elephant Frazer to present Robby to answer accusations. Lazarus decried this as a "rape of civil rights," a terrible choice of words. Lazarus and I were hooted from the podium; a fight broke out between the Rose boys and the Gaunts, who were divided between Christian Rose and Elephant Frazer. Worse, one of the hags, the very one, Jane told me, who had stood over her and kicked her in the stomach, burst into the hall to announce, falsely, that Lena was dead, that the Frazers had hidden her body, and that Lena's ghost had appeared to her to demand "an eye for an eye." Jane and Abigail then took the podium and denounced the Assembly as a "Pattie disgrace."

"Shame!" said Jane, in a rage. "Lena be alive. I left her to-night. Shame! Poor Robby fought for us, a brave Volunteer. Ye have no proof again' him. Ye care more for yerr low ways than for poor Lena. Robby lays up there, terrible grieved, thinkin' his Lena dyin'. It ain't so! Shame! Get ye home and pray forgiveness, as I'll be doin', prayin' for poor Lena and for the man, whoever he be, what did this black deed."

Abigail was angrier than Jane. She reminded them that Robby had been beaten by the Roses; she used the word *torture*. She said Robby was in her care until this matter was settled to her satisfaction, and it had better be peacefully, and that any bullies that might come along would find her a harder adversary than a lame simpleton. She added, too tendentiously, "I won't be the one to name Lena's persecutor. I can name Robby's. He's bad sick now, his face all swollen and ripped, though it's been a week. Let Christian Rose and his brave brothers answer for Robby."

Over the following weeks, the people of Gaunttown, stirred up by the shamed Roses and the conniving Hospidar, turned against Elephant Frazer. Where before they had blamed the Patties, the beasties, the British, the "Divil cold," they came to fault Elephant Frazer, and for great and small things, what can go wrong in periods of long siege—bad water, lost sheep, miscarriages, and an outbreak of pneumonia in the beastie camp that spread to Gaunttown. Most of the time, the dissension was too mixed with heartfelt calls for justice for Lena for one to be sure who was seditious and who was outraged. Elephant Frazer had no resources with which to do detective work. It was hoped that the real criminal would confess, or that Lena would name her attacker.

Meanwhile, Robby Oldmizzen remained at the Frazer camp, where he became sullen and timid, heavily dependent upon Abi-

gail. She mothered him, made him like one of her children, so
that he played with Samson's two sons, Gabe and Adam, and
rocked my Sam to sleep. I visited when I could, though I was not
good about my time. Lazarus drove the both of us to finish the
constitutional draft for the spring; he directed me to visit the families with drafts, like an itinerant evangelist. I was not usually welcome and spent much of my visits in the kitchens arguing with
the women and old men about the beasties, the Frazers and Gaunts
and Roses and, above all, Robby. No one would dare to say openly
that Robby was guilty. They were angry and suspicious, because
Elephant Frazer continued to protect Robby from questions. One
old man, a Lindfir, surprised me when he used Lazarus's vocabulary, saying it was "the bloody will of the people" that Robby be
brought up on charges.

Winter ebbed, the ice did loosen. Lena recovered enough to
leave hospital and was taken in to continue her convalescence by
her great-aunt, who was, significantly, one of the old wives living
in a common house on the market square.

"They poison her, those witches," Jane told me soon after.
"The poor dear, she don't know what happened to her. They tease
her about a bairn. She's no pregnant, I can tell ye, Abbie and me
made sure. They won't let me or Abbie close, threw mud at Abbie
when she called. They make that child feel like she'd done wrong.
Those witches. You must do something."

I balked, asking, what could I do about old women and gossip?

"Take hold," said Jane, her sense of republicanism melting
like the ice, "ye, Mr. President, take hold and make right."

I told her Elephant Frazer had made more concessions to the
Hospidar, among them sending the Frazer's adopted beasties to
live with the Zulemas in the beastie camp.

"And we'll see Saint Peter himself on the High Street afore
those two sort out their minds. Ye, and Germanicus, take hold
now."

Elephant Frazer did confer increasingly with me and Germanicus, and even Lazarus, since he was pushed away by the elders of Gaunttown, who were bitter about Robby. These meetings,
between father and son and adopted son, made Germanicus uneasy. He felt it was coming to look like Frazer rule. For all his

instinctive sympathy for absolutism—rule by strong men—Germanicus was not insensitive to the peril of what Lazarus called "crypto-royalty." And more worrisome to Germanicus than this hint of Frazer dictatorship was that Lazarus's solution to the Robby dilemma was to begin advocating the formation of a "revolutionary court" to settle disputes while we waited for the constitution to be accepted and to set in place a judiciary. It was not a bad idea. It was too much for the Frazers, especially since the Hospidar seized on the rumor of Lazarus's notion to agitate for his obvious goal: a Volunteer state, military rule.

We did find what we hoped was a wise course, during one of our late night talks at THE KELPER. Germanicus, just back in *King James* from exploring the breakup of the ice and from taking several whales, admitted to us that he had delayed his marriage too long, for good reasons: war, weather, catastrophe. He offered not to wait for summer, rather to marry Jane in the spring. Lazarus toasted the idea, and we took it upstairs to Elephant Frazer, working that night with the whaling factory foreman on rationing. He was delighted. None of us thought it was polite to mention aloud that the major reason it was such a good idea was that it would go a long way to repairing the rift between the Frazers and the Gaunts, and with that, all the major families might come to peace at the ceremony. Jane was informed belatedly. She stopped by the Assembly Hall a few days later to confront me and Lazarus. She said she would agree to the ploy; she also said she thought it contrived.

"There's not flour for a proper cake," she said. "That's yerr real threat, not Roses and that Simon Brackenbury neither. Ye men get us flour and let us heal ourselves. No finery will have done like cargoes of fruit and wheat."

The day of the wedding was wet and anxious. There were sooty icebergs on the northwestern horizon. The people of Gaunttown turned out in their gray best. The bride, at twenty, wore white, Abigail's gown, which had been her great-grandmother's, with a veil provided by Frances Gaunt, Luff Gaunt Senior's voluble widow who had recently been caught up by spring love and had declared her intention to marry Simon Brackenbury come summer. I was the best man. Abigail was the matron of honor. There were Gaunt and Frazer flower girls, though we had no flowers, used heath grass and candles instead. Trip Gaunt, Jane's uncle, stood up for her. The Hospidar, Christian Rose, Simon Brackenbury, and Kevin Gaunt stood at the last pew for the Volunteers and Falkland Irregulars. Roses, McHughs, Lindfirs, Harrahs, Moogs, Oateses, Macklemurrays, and more filled the chapel, family by family, the young intermingling as they would, for the years since the war had seen a new generation of taciturn patriots push into the ranks. The Zulemas sat on the Frazer side of the chapel with the adopted beasties; Lazarus and Violante sat on either side of the young beastie prodigy who had originally been knifed. Longfaeroe preached a long, sentimental sermon beforehand, impromptu, on the spring of hope, and he closed it with a psalm that made Abigail cry. I was nervous, but collected enough to be bursting proud of my fellow South Georgians, who were strong to admit that their weaknesses needed heavenly intercession, and a little fun. By the time of the exchange of rings, I had relaxed, took note of the little Gaunt and Frazer girls, and that there seemed a missing place in the flower children, six on the right, and five on the left. The groom kissed the bride, and she him back, warm and lingering, and we paraded over to the Assembly Hall, decorated for dancing and feasting. There I got my first opportunity to talk with Orlando the Black, who had come down from Shagrock with his men for supplies and had stayed on for the ceremony.

My memory is that Orlando the Black and Lazarus and I were reminiscing about *Angel of Death,* awkwardly, painfully—it was one week shy of six years since we had set sail from Stockholm—when someone dropped a platter of haggis. It was not an extraordinary ruckus, barely discernible over the piper standing outside the door, bleating good cheer through Gaunttown. I did look up, to find Abigail's face across the room. She tightened, darkened, walked directly to me, drew me aside, saying, "It's Lena, Grim, oh, Grim, go and see. Dear sweet Jesus, why, why?" She wrapped her arms around me, would not sob. "I'm up to home. Come as soon as you can."

The dancing and piping continued. Motherwell and I got down to the High Street, were met by Wild Drumrul. He led us down to the near quay, backing on the church. There we found Christmas Muir and Peggs and several old sealers using poles to pull a body out of the water. We ran when we saw, cold inside, and by the time we got there, Christmas Muir was wrapping a flower girl in a shroud.

"Drowned herself, she did," said Christmas Muir. "Petey saw'd it and couldn't get to her in time. Two feet of water. Might've been shock, water's hellish cold, maybe." He spat. "Divil cold did it."

Why did she do it? People do not make consistent sense, and are not obliged to; it might then be superfluous for me to exaggerate my inquiry. Ascribe that day, all of that day, to the power of the irrational, the mystery of the spirit. It does now come to me that there is something telling to what Dolly Frazer later told me and Motherwell. We had carried Lena's corpse up to the undertaker. Dolly crowded in with some of the other matrons, intending to wash Lena and put her in a good black frock. She told me to get along, then took my arm, paused, said, "It was Janey's weddin'. She died for that. Whyn't ye men ken wee folk? Struttin' and scratchin' ye go. It were love, want of it, that killed the lamb."

I insist now it was a futile act of flight. I insist it was not the Devil's work, no, Grandfather, whatever your idea of Satan means, I declare the darkness cannot touch minds as gentle as Lena's. I declare that it was men who did it, in this case those hags who teased Lena to the point she believed she was as unclean as they said Robby was, and all of the elders in the community who used the crime and Robby's fear to advance their plans, forgetting, or not caring, that Lena and Robby were children incapable of knowing the difference between what they did and what was said they did. And I declare that if it was the wedding, it might have been anything else too that made Lena feel lost forever to her high dreams of love and family. The birth of the spring lambs, a christening, even a public kiss, might have triggered Lena's yearning for release from her degradation. Does this seem as if I am excusing Germanicus and Lazarus and me from contriving our solution to the feud—the wedding—rather than facing openly the fact that it was, on South Georgia, people with the very best motives who can do the very worst deeds? I am not. I know what we did. I will take the blame for it, not alone, my share.

□

Grief swept Gaunttown that day, like fire, fed madly by the longing that had hours before rejoiced at the seeming conciliation of the Frazers and Gaunts. Our hearts were open. The finality of what had happened tormented us. Elephant Frazer was dumbstruck; I know because I was the first to tell him of Lena. I watched him pull the frozen hair from her face. He could not talk, and would not wipe the tears from his face. The wedding party was consumed by the same grief, celebrants fleeing to their homes. I walked Germanicus and Jane to their bridal rooms at the inn behind THE KELPER. In the pub, the drinking was silent. By early evening a gang of Roses and their cousins had taken over THE KELPER, joining in a drunken wake for Lena. I was told that a wilder bout began at the sealer's pub, NIGHT SUN, where the men made terrible curses against the one living thing they truly believed had cursed Lena and, through her, themselves and South Georgia—Robby Oldmizzen.

I remember the skies cleared at sunset, a rosy gray over the peaks with towering clouds above the hornstone ridge, a usually happy vista from the balcony off my rooms at the Assembly Hall. I had gone home exhausted from running from the undertaker's to the church to THE KELPER, trying to get a sense of the gloom. I can remember not eating supper because I had a notion that I would get up to the Frazer camp later and eat with Abigail. The evening passed quickly, and very late I was still in my rooms, with Motherwell. Wild Drumrul, Otter Ransom, and Peggs had joined us. I do not recall Christmas Muir being there. We discussed small things, the ice, Iceberg's pups. My clock needed winding, and I fussed with it. We smoked Peggs's tobacco, which had been a wedding present, a great treasure, black and African. What was I doing at the very moment? I think I was winding the clock with a bent key, with difficulty, for I could not get my fingers to work correctly. I had the shakes. How delicate I was.

Lazarus came through the door. I turned and sensed trouble. He should not have been there so late. It was not his way. He asked me to sit down beside him. I noticed Orlando the Black and Violante in the vestibule outside the door. He pulled me down to my chair, began deliberately.

"Elephant Frazer has been killed," said Lazarus.

"I knew'd it, I knew'd it," said Peggs.

"Elephant Frazer, about a half hour ago, walked into the NIGHT SUN and put a harpoon into Christian Rose," said Lazarus. "Saul Rose took it out of him and put it through old Frazer's heart. He stood there and took it. They've dragged Germanicus out of his bed and put him in chains. The Hospidar has declared himself governor-general. Hear me out. Kevin Gaunt and Toddy McHugh are downstairs with ten Volunteers. You and I are under arrest for haboring a suspected murderer."

"Easy, laddie, give it again," said Motherwell, on his feet, reaching for the harpoon over the fireplace.

"Elephant Frazer is dead? Elephant Frazer killed Christian Rose?" I said.

"No, old Rose isn't dead," said Lazarus. "Frazer struck to unman him, they said. Davey Gaunt came for me at the school and told Vi that Frazer never missed a throw. Kevin Gaunt's asked that you and I surrender without a fight. They want you, too, Sergeant Motherwell, and you and you." He nodded at Wild Drumrul and Otter Ransom. "They won't say about Orlando, afraid of his men, I guess. Gaunt doesn't want more killing. I agree, this time, I do."

"Lazarus, why did he do it?" I said. I was numb. I put my hands over my ears, but could not muffle my mind's voice. I knew, as Lazarus said, "It's Abbie, oh, Mary and Joseph, forgive, forgive."

I screamed then, threw my body back and screamed off the chair. I might have done more if not for Motherwell, who then expertly knocked me senseless with the butt of the harpoon. He struck to kill. He later told me he wanted me dead but could not use the spear tip, it was rusted and would have shattered. He had seen me take Germanicus's bullet at Stanley and did not really believe he could kill me. He tried, partly because of what I might do, berserker among the panicked, partly because he was a hunter and knew mercy for the mortally wounded. He meant to spare me.

They had burned the Frazer camp. I am talking about a mob of a dozen boys bloated with drink and the black thoughts of their elders. They had stormed up to the Frazer camp's main house, a two-story stone-and-pine-built manse amid cottages and barns, and hammered down the door. Robby, as the only man at the camp, faced them. In some peculiar twist, he momentarily found his bravura long lost on the Falklands; but when they grabbed at him, demanding he account for his whereabouts that day, telling him as they did that Lena was dead, Robby was overwhelmed. He fled within the house, waking those upstairs. Abigail and Meg and Dorothy, Germanicus's two sisters, were already awake from the barking of the dogs. Dolly Frazer was still with Lena's corpse and the old wives in town. Abigail took charge and came down. She must have comforted Robby and taken him with her back to the front hall to rebuff the threat. The reports were sketchy hereon. An argument followed, Abigail commanding, "Get out, and fast with you, before our men come." The boys were ready to run. Robby started his screaming at them and went for a harpoon. There was a struggle on the front steps, and Robby was thrown down. The dogs sent up a howl. The claim later was that Abigail shot first, with a sealer's double-barrel shotgun loaded with buckshot, ripping away the face of Ian Brackenbury, wounding two of the other boys, a Rose and a Lindfir. The boys shot back as they fled, one salvo, aimed blindly, that struck Abigail. She was not dead, perhaps mortally wounded, perhaps just stunned.

Someone threw a torch, or perhaps a torch had been dropped in the scramble. In that wind, fire is sudden in the dry timbers of a house. Meg and Dorothy (Meg very pregnant by her husband away in the north) got the youngest babies out, one of them my Sam. They were all hurt by the smoke, and there must have been hysteria for the rescue work to have been so inept. There was no explanation as to why the boys who had not been wounded did not go back to help.

The toll was unbearable, eight of the Frazer household dead, including five children under twelve years of age: Gabe, Adam, Michael, Louise, Augustina, the cook, the servant girl, and Abigail. My Sam did not die; he was put in hospital, where Jane Gaunt did not leave him, breathing for him when he could not work his smoke-clogged lungs. The dead, including Meg Frazer the next morning, were buried two days hence in a mass ceremony, along with Elephant Frazer, Ian Brackenbury, and Lena Rose.

□

We, the arrested, were not permitted the funeral, a precaution by the Hospidar that was bald cruelty. Germanicus, Lazarus, and I were kept in separate cells. Otter Ransom, Wild Drumrul, and Motherwell were in the same cell, at the Volunteers' fort surrounding the lighthouse on Cumberland Bay. We could converse across the floor of our dungeon, did not at first. Longfaeroe came out to us the night after the funeral in order to sing psalms. I was still weak from Motherwell's clubbing and my grief, and listened disinterestedly until he stood right before my cell and sang Psalm 19, "The heavens tell out the glory of Jehovah, the vault of heaven reveals his handiwork. One day speaks to another, night with night shares its knowledge, and this without speech or language, or sound of any voice—"

I resented Longfaeroe's presence. He did not seem grieved by the loss of his daughter and two of his grandsons. His face was undecipherable, his words were not. He sang with cunning. I might have been wrong at the time, but I heard in his psalm a call for a hero, for me, to rise up and take hold of South Georgia: "Their music goes out through all the world, their words reach to the end of the earth. In them a tent is fixed for the sun, him!, who comes out like a bridegroom from his wedding canopy, rejoicing like a strong man to run his race. His rising is at one end of the heavens, his circuit touches their farthest ends; and nothing is hidden from his heat—"

I also thought at the time that he might have been calling on Germanicus. I had no patience for Longfaeroe, regarded him as much at fault as others I could name. He visited us several more times in the next week, to sing and to pass on messages from Orlando the Black and Dolly Frazer, not a word from Jane. Germanicus would not talk with Longfaeroe, a shunning that was the single sign he showed of his fury. Germanicus told me that his father would want us to keep calm, to gather our strength for our time. Germanicus seemed the same as before to me—hard, fatalistic, resourceful, the qualities that had first attracted me at 2 *de Diciembre*. There was nothing different. What was new was that he was focused, on revenge. I could not, would not, speak against it. Lazarus would not counsel against violent retribution; he did make it clear that he thought the Hospidar would have to put us on trial, and that we should not act beforehand.

If I am vague about the course of events immediately after Lena's suicide, it is because I was never told the complete story, and also because I do not want to try to remember too acutely, afraid of what I have forgotten. I remember this: I did not forgive them their trespasses, and they did not forgive mine. I know I should now, so long after, all of them broken and gone; I cannot. No, that is wrong.

I see now that the reason I could not forgive them was that I could not forgive myself. There was shame and disgrace for everyone. I am not sure now what could have been done to stop the feud, as I have not been sure what could have been done to save Peregrine's feud. I have endeavored to explain the depths of the fears, why those poor people on South Georgia could have fallen to such a wicked, wicked extreme. I have no heart to repeat the excuses for them. I know that one must be taught to hate. They were taught by expert brutes operating under every flag on the Atlantic, especially the Union Jack. And those bold gangsters who broke into the Frazer home, who were also pathetic children, were taught by their parents and elders to hate what they could not understand, such as the beasties in the camp, such as Robby Oldmizzen's damaged mind in his twisted body. Fear, hatred, revenge, deceit, whatever the resentments built up among the families on South Georgia, there can be and should be no final excuse for what we did to each other without mercy. Lena Rose was dead of shame. Elephant Frazer was dead of revenge. Ian Brackenbury was dead of hatred. Abigail was dead of deceiving herself she could stand up to the darkness. Christian Rose lingered a week, tormented by his castration, and then took his own life one night with a knife provided by his brother, Saul Rose, with his two sons looking on, agreeing. Dolly Frazer descended into a mourning that was a tomb. Gaunttown staggered with dread. Davey Gaunt, Jane's younger brother, who worshiped Germanicus and Lazarus at the same time, challenged Horace Oates, a Rose cousin, to a knife fight over a point of honor, cut him badly, was jailed with us for attempted murder.

"Them'll give us no trial," said Davey as we circled the fort's yard for our daily exercise. He provided reports from Gaunttown's factions that worried both Germanicus and Lazarus. "Them can't let us free. We be less'n beasties now."

"You and me and Motherwell be Volunteers, they owe us a hearing," said Germanicus.

"Them Volunteers stand with the Hospidar," said Motherwell.

"You might be right," said Lazarus. "If Christian Rose had lived, he and Trip Gaunt might have been able to stand up to the Hospidar. Now all three of the major families involved are splintered. If we had law! But there isn't law now other than the Hospidar. Even Brackenbury, for what good he could have done, is reduced for his son's crime. I thought I could talk us out of this. I don't see how I can get you people to stop this eye-for-an-eye nonsense you prefer; like, well, not even beasts fight like this."

"There's truth," I tried. It sounded a tinny plea, affected. "I'm the president of the Assembly."

"There was an Assembly, and you were its president, as long as Elephant Frazer said so," said Lazarus.

"There be justice," said Germanicus. "What's right. What's our'n to take for what's taken. What I say, when I say it."

"When will you understand?" said Lazarus. "Without law on paper, truth is what they say, justice is what they do! My constitution is the only thing that could have saved the Frazers, that could have saved us and this island."

"Isn't it the will of the people that we're here?" I asked.

"No, Grim," said Lazarus. "Sheep follow fools, and wolves in masquerade, and sometimes even wolves. We have a small chance. The Hospidar might not be able to untangle this mess. He can't just seal us up, and he can't shoot us without a trial. He might slip and give us a chance to speak in our own defense."

"We'll have our time," said Germanicus, "and not for talk."

There was a trial. It was for Robby Oldmizzen. The Hospidar outwitted all of us, even Lazarus, who had seen the end but not the means. The people, Lazarus's mystical insurance, were not invited. The panel of judges, jurors, and prosecutors were one and the same, the Hospidar careful to sit by without voice. Robby was made to stand throughout, in his Volunteer uniform, an honor that was cruelty because he had never been able to balance well with his crippled side, and because he had not healed from either the gunshot wound he had received at the Frazer camp or the beating he had received when they hunted him down in the high heath after the fire. Longfaeroe acted as Robby's defense counsel, and it was from him we learned the details. Longfaeroe urged Robby to tell the truth, to obey his commanding officers, and to trust in the Almighty. Robby admitted to nothing about the original attack on Lena, the knifing and ravishment. He could not recall that she had been attacked, said he did know something bad had happened to her, and that was why he was kept apart from her. The crucial turn was when they asked him to recount his whereabouts the day of the wedding. They did not tell him where Lena had died. Robby wept at the thought of Lena dead, said, "I was at God's house." He would not say he had been at the quay. No one had seen him there. They did not call the old sealer, Petey, who Christmas Muir had told me had seen Lena go into the water. Robby could not recall how he had gotten down to the church—if that was what he meant by "God's house"—or where he had gone afterward. When they asked him why he had fled the Frazer camp if he was innocent, he said he thought he would be blamed for the fire. They asked him if he had started the fire. Robby said, "Divil did it."

Therefore, Robby Oldmizzen was found guilty of ravishing Lena Rose and of drowning Lena Rose. He was also found guilty of setting the fire at the Frazer camp, killing nine more. He was sentenced to death, by firing squad since he was still a Volunteer.

"Brilliant in their determinist way," said Lazarus after Longfaeroe had come to us to report. He seemed admiring of the Hospidar. I faulted him for it then, still do.

"They have no shame," I said. "I'm partial to Germanicus. The time is past for talk."

"It's the will of the Almighty. Let it be," said Longfaeroe. Lazarus snorted, and sighed. Longfaeroe continued, "Heed the words of captive Zion, Grim. 'The memory of my distress and my wanderings is wormwood and gall. Remember, oh remember, and stoop down to me. All this I take to heart and therefore I will wait patiently: the Lord Jehovah's true love is not spent, nor has his compassion failed, they are new every morning, so great is his constancy.' And hear me, Grim. 'The Lord Jehovah may punish cruelly, yet he will have compassion in the fullness of his love; he does not willingly afflict or punish any mortal man.' You, Grim, know what I say. This is the time of the afflicted and the patient. It's your time."

"You want me to do what?" I said, exasperated. I thought Longfaeroe's words gorgeous and compelling. The Bible's words (and also Beowulf's) are the only art I have had in my life. They give me great comfort, yet they also bewilder me. That was my predicament standing there before Longfaeroe's quotation from what I now know was the book of Lamentations—Zion in exile and woe. I was frustrated by the power of poetry to take me out of my self, to make me feel reconciled to history, even when it was outrage. I collected my grief, and then I challenged Long-faeroe with the specifics of crime devoid of metaphor. "No David, now, Reverend, we're in the lion's den. And Abigail is dead! Murdered with Adam and Gabe! Robby wasn't at the church. Never! They have no proof! Do you really believe it's God's will that a lie should bury Abigail? Do you really believe—you! not God, not anyone else, you!—do you believe Robby killed Lena? And set the fire?"

"Abigail is gone to a sublime father," said Longfaeroe, trying to be the cold man he was not; for his coldness was a masking of his fear to face the inexplicable accidents that had taken from him his wife, two daughters, two grandsons, and were about to take his dignity if he persisted to vouchsafe the slaughter of innocent Robby. I pity him now, did not then as he continued, "Abigail was a willful child, sinned to take up that rod. I believe the Almighty has a purpose for what wee Robby has done. You are the purpose, Grim Fiddle."

"You do hear him, Grim? Sublime, he says," said Lazarus.

"Grim stands with me," said Germanicus.

"Fight the Hospidar," said Motherwell.

"Kill Roses," said Davey Gaunt.

Wild Drumrul and Otter Ransom nodded their agreement.

"You are pulling at me!" I exploded. I looked at them, looked at myself, said, "Grim Fiddle stands with Grim Fiddle!"

Robby Oldmizzen was brought down to our dungeon the next day. We were given our Volunteer uniforms, except for Lazarus.

We expected the worst. We tried to comfort Robby at mealtimes, were dragged down by his alternate hysteria and torpor. Robby had lucid moments. He begged me to forgive him for Abigail. I did not want to hear it, hoped he would forget the subject. But then, at dinner the night before the scheduled execution, he tried to give me his food. He said, yes, he had killed Abigail, he had killed Lena. I told him to stop. Germanicus and Lazarus watched us, no pity in their eyes. I told Robby that he was innocent. He replied by asking why he had run from the fire if he was innocent. They had wrapped him in their lies, and it was the only comfort he had, so he pulled it close. Robby fell down before me, grabbing at my boots; I tried to get him up. Through his tears he said, "She tol' Rob to get the bairns, Mister. She did. She say, poo' Rob, get the bairns and tell Grim. I's afeared, Mister. I couldn't, Mister. The Divil was there. He scared Rob away. The flames was Hell. And that pitchfork proddin' me, here, see, holes from that pitchfork."

"What did she say to tell me?" I asked.

He said he could not remember. He said the "Divil" killed Abigail and the babies.

The execution was delayed three more days. I see now it was the Hospidar's will that we be worn down by Robby's plight. It did seem to work that way. The gloom that had descended on Germanicus also fell on me. It was not the darkness of the berserker, however, more a tightness in the chest, bad breathing. Abigail's death became worse for me as it receded into history. And to have to watch Robby's fantasies was hard test. There were no lessons in it; more of the nothing of endings. Germanicus, Lazarus, and I drew apart. When they marched us out that raw November morning, we condemned were divided by anger and fear. Still, our enemies had underestimated what men might do when up against the darkness with scores to settle. I did not expect a better world after death, nor Longfaeroe's "sublime father." I did expect Peregrine and Grandfather, and Abigail, and I would have some high dreams to report, how their Grim had trampled on the wisdom pronounced by his grandfather at his birth: "My son, fear Lord God and grow rich in spirit, but have nothing to do with men of rank!"

The president of the Gaunttown Assembly stood across the

yard from the governor-general of South Georgia. The Hospidar was broad, blue-eyed, gray-maned, a short boulder with carnivorous eyes and a sharp tongue. I towered over him; he stared me down. Robby was taken to the wall of the courtyard. Saul Rose, now colonel commanding the Volunteers, read the charges and sentence of the court-martial. I turned away. I could hear Longfaeroe's prayers, the orders to set, the blast. I thought then, what had Germanicus and Samson, and I, saved Robby for at *2 de Diciembre?* For this, another blast, this time from his own people? I thought then, what a terrible dare it is to intervene in another's fate, how twisted the results could be. I think now, curious penitent, that decency is always worth a dare, no matter the results.

Saul Rose approached me, offered me his pistol, handle first, ordered me to administer the coup de grace. I did not respond. He asked Germanicus.

"No' for Rob I'd shoot," said Germanicus.

"And who'll offer a gun to shoot you in the head when it comes to that?" said Lazarus. Saul Rose smiled, offered the pistol to Motherwell, Otter Ransom, and Wild Drumrul, none of whom responded. Burl Lindfir did the job.

"Ye men are guilty of insubordination in time of war," said Saul Rose, and then he turned to look at Germanicus and said with viciousness, "and also of cowardice," to the man whose father he had harpooned. The Hospidar had finally managed to avoid the tradition of a trial; we could now be shot on the spot. Saul Rose continued, "I commend yerr fate to my governor-general."

The Hospidar came to us, surveying our faces, I studied him as well, as he walked before us, small steps. He did not seem resolute. It came to me that he might not have known what he was going to do with us. I saw the weight of his office, the strain of his long-pursued ambition, and that it was as wearying to him as our fracturing was to us. I took that as a lesson; as Lazarus preached, it was not possible, or desirable, to rule innocently. In the month since our arrest, and his elevation to despot, the Hospidar had tired, wavered. I know this might seem simple, but I saw then and still do believe that we were more fearsome to him than he to us. And for all Lazarus's conviction that there was no law or justice on South Georgia other than the Hospidar's, I declare now that there was a truth to what had happened, to what

Germanicus and Lazarus and I represented, and that it slowed the Hospidar's hand: truth can be smeared, can be interred, yet perhaps it cannot be erased.

"Think me the famous serpent, so laddies?" he began. "Ask away, what could be done? That daft boy took the risk, took the penalty. This island be damned if I let him free, Lena's killer not named. I take the risk now, me and mine, and aye, schoolmaster, we'll take the penalty if it comes. Who can say what comes now the ice be gone? Say ye, Germanicus Frazer? Did yerr dad? Aye, he were a bold one. I'm not scratchin' that. Mark him now! Left us, forgot us, took to feud as man and not governor-general. I don't say I would've done different. Happened to him. I must be bolder, and must judge the weak, as Frazer did not. I must hear my charges, as Frazer did not. So with ye, laddies. Would ye be free, ye would kill me, or perish for tryin'. Ye, Germanicus Frazer, now first of yerr clan, would cut out my innards, and Saul Rose's afore me. Ye, schoolmaster, would spread yerr lies at the womenfolk again, taking man from wife, son from lassie. Where on this island could ye be free? At Shagrock with the nigs, or at the Cape? Nay, for them don't want ye there. In the beastie's stew? Nay, for them don't want ye as we don't want them. And ye, Grim Fiddle, the hardest man I ever saw'd in a fight, no ten of my men could match ye. How could we turn our backs on ye, the more with yerr lot at yerr side? Begod, Grim Fiddle, ye're the one I mark most, for ye have claim to my post. Are ye able to it, then? Did ye give right when they called for Lena's ravisher? Did ye give right when ye were ordered to finish the daft boy? That he was, daft and a killer. Ye would not! Ye thought of yerr own ways, and not of this island's. Ye're not man for this office. I'm keener than ye, for I'm for what has to be done to keep here, give right when they ask for right. I say, I'm right for bein' bold, and ye're wrong for ye've not been bold."

I tried to talk, a hesitant contrition, for I took his words hard, not truth, but then again, not lies.

"Keep yerr tongue," he shouted. "I'd dun ye for no less than ye dare to judge me. I won't do it now. It'd do no right. Ye're guilty of withholdin' this island its right. I was aimin' to give ye a choice. That wall or get out. There be no choice. Yerr black hearts'll rot what ye have touched, dead or livin'! It be my say so

that ye and yerrs, and what man or woman who won't speak
against ye, be sent from South Georgia. My last words. Damn ye!"

What do I take most from this? I permit myself now, this long
afterward, to answer drolly: the human comedy of it. Two by two
they marched us into *King James,* my friends and my dogs, and
more, including the Zulemas and other beasties representing threat
to the Hospidar. I suppose that we were granted *King James* could
seem merciful; it was not, for no man on South Georgia would
have dared risk superstition to sail the Frazer schooner. The Hospidar had accused Lazarus of dividing families; he outdid him:
son from father, daughter from mother. The Frazers and their
cousins were divided with a knife; those that would not speak
openly against Elephant Frazer and Germanicus were sentenced
to exile. The old sealers were put to the test as well, Christmas
Muir and Peggs marked along with many of their recalcitrant
mates, like Ugly Leghorn and Ensign Ewart. Also, the misfits and
delinquents in Gaunttown who had no familial bonds were
grouped with us—thieves, hoarders, drunkards, sheep-poachers,
even the slothful and covetous. We got some of the hags, and we
got two of the wild boys who had been in the mob at the Frazer
camp. Most surprising—not to me but to the Hospidar—were those
who volunteered to come with us though they were not put to the
test of allegiance: Longfaeroe, without a bitter word, saying he
meant to follow Grim Fiddle to "glory"; and Annabel Donne and
her brother, she a midwife and Falklander widow who was in love
with Longfaeroe; and Jane Gaunt's brother, Davey, saying he
would serve death itself rather than Robby's executioners; and
Meg Frazer's morose second husband, Half-Red Harrah (a loss to
the Volunteers because he was one of the best whalers on the
island). *King James* was filled until it spilled over, and a second
sealer ship, *Candlemas Packet,* was crammed with beasties and in-
digents, captained by Sean Malody, a half-breed Falklander who
had a blood feud with the Brackenburys. In all, South Georgia
cleansed itself, South Georgia sullied itself.

The worst of it for me was Orlando the Black. He came to
me and Lazarus in our cells to confess that he had spoken against
me and the Frazers, that he had begged the Hospidar he be per-

mitted to continue as commander of Shagrock. He said he had humiliated himself before the Hospidar for a purpose: to protect his family. He said he hoped we understood and would forgive him, but if not, he would not alter his course. He did not weep before Lazarus, his brother, and Lazarus sat blank-faced. Then we spoke of my Sam, who could never have survived a sea voyage. It hurt me, perhaps not as much as it should have. We decided quickly. Was I wrong? I cannot pause here. Orlando the Black took my hand. He was a quiet, sober, undramatic man. It was his nature to take what he was given and make the best with it; his grasp was his reach. He gripped my hand and said, "One of us is here. None of them will outlive me. They're rid of the Frazers. Now they have Roses and Lindfirs. Don't forget me. Go with God. I'll have Sam. He'll know. He'll live and he'll know. I swear it."

Why do I insist on the human comedy of it? It was the poetry. There we were, men and women who had been abandoned by the twentieth century, and who, because of the slaughter of the meek, were condemned as some of the first victims of the twenty-first century; and yet we were struggling with problems set by the Greeks twenty-five centuries before on islands washed by a profoundly different sort of cauldron than the Scotia Sea. The problems have names: tyranny and democracy, despotism and draconism, tragedy and comedy. Those are Greek words. I repeat what Israel told me, that the Greeks thought comedy more profound than tragedy. Aristotle said it. Mankind proved it. Tragedy was history. Comedy was art. Comedy could humble the gods. I have been told that the Greeks laughed at plays about tyrants, thought it hilarious when a beggar called out for justice and was slapped down for his impudence. Those Greeks must have had strong minds, and stronger stomachs. I have laughed at chaos, have smiled at murder; it is not the sort of humor that fills me with joy.

I once shared Israel's opinion with Longfaeroe; he nodded, then shook his head, not in disagreement, more to turn over the thought in his mind. Later, Jane told me that Longfaeroe had preached the strangest sermon, using as his text the third book of Genesis, the temptation and fall of Adam and Eve. Longfaeroe had told his congregation that when Jehovah punished man for his pride by banishing Adam and Eve from their garden island to

slave and to perish in exile, he had created the first comedy out
of tragic history. Longfaeroe added that Jehovah had under-
scored his artful judgment by constraining and cursing Adam and
Eve with the knowledge of all opposites—man and woman, love
and hate, good and evil, comedy and tragedy. Jane had said that
she had no idea what had gotten into Longfaeroe, did I make
sense of it? I sighed then, I do now. If Israel was right about the
Greeks, if Longfaeroe was right about Eden, where is progress?

The most difficult part of the comedy for me came the day
of departure. I stood upon the quarterdeck of *King James* watching the wrenching scenes on the quays, families in torment, the
flavor of civil war never stronger, the smell of brine and insoluble
melancholy in the air. I did not laugh. Young Grim Fiddle did
not have the stomach he had later, has now. There was no humor
that day, if there was comedy. There was also revelation. Standing
there, watching Jane Gaunt kiss her mother good-bye, no tears,
anger in her eyes, hatred mixed with impossible remorse, I came
to understand at long last what it was that we on board *Angel of
Death* had discovered in the Baltic, the North Sea, the Atlantic. I
came to understand that this was how the outrage had begun in
every port, on every archipelago, on every continent. Catastrophe
and fear and feud had delivered up peoples who could no longer
live together. The solution, the sophists might say, is to learn to
live together. That is fancy optimism, I say, worthy but not rigorous, because there are times and places when and where it cannot be. On South Georgia that day, I saw that the Hospidar was
keen and bold and correct. He could not permit me and mine to
remain on South Georgia. We had to be sent away. I saw the
nakedness of it. I saw what it is to be right and wrong all at once.
I saw the risk and the penalty, for, while I and mine were free to
try not to be consumed with hatred, the Hospidar and his people
would forever bear the burden of their cruelty toward us. To us,
the Hospidar was a monster, but was not he also a dupe? To his
people, the Hospidar was a savior, but was not he also a liar? We
might disappear from their sight, but would not the memory of
us, our ghosts, visit curses upon them generation upon generation? We weighed anchor and set our course northeast for Africa.
Who could ever lift the weight of us from them on that shore?
And one more thing I saw that day. I saw what it was to become

what we were, sails full, bows pointed toward the sunrise: new members of the fleet of the damned.

My Albatross

I must pause for my Sam. He would be well over thirty, older than I was when I left him. I cannot know if he survived the fire and his abandonment. It pleases me to suppose that he did. He had red hair at birth, and chestnut eyes, same as Abigail's. What I could know of what was Grim Fiddle in him I determined by comparing him to Gabe and Adam, Abigail's two sons by Samson. My Sam was longer-limbed, not lean, more barrel-like, with heart-shaped ears. Those were Peregrine's ears. And that bushy red hair—my guess was that Sam had reached back to Peregrine's mother, Jane. Sam was nearly two years old when I last saw him, the day before Germanicus's wedding. He was large, aggressive, ran as much as walked, had a passing peculiar vocabulary, Scots-English, Swedish, a few Hebrew words Longfaeroe slipped in when he had visited the Frazer camp knowing Abigail was in town visiting me. I should have more detail of him, and that I do not should indicate what an inattentive father I was—much away at the Assembly Hall, or fretting with Germanicus, or hiking the high heath with Christmas Muir and Wild Drumrul. At the time, I justified my absences by thinking they were caused by the strained affairs between me and Abigail; I told myself I would be a better father as soon as Abigail married me. That was delusion. Of consequence, it is not credible that Sam, if he lived, could have much memory of me. He would have the stories of Dolly Frazer, if she lived; about Abigail and Frazers; and he would have the stories of Orlando the Black, if he lived; about America, Sweden, the Falklands. At most, he would have pieces of the puzzle of his father, not enough to understand why I left him to his fate. I did abandon him, no fancy argument shall remove my shame. If I could talk with him, I might be able to explain. That is impossible. There is this work of confession; if I could get it to him—but then, not even I can know its end. There is one hope. It is nonrational. I record it for comfort. As I inherited some of Lamba's magic, perhaps Sam also inherited an extraordinary sense. Perhaps my ghost, when it comes to that, can seek him out and whisper to him. Or perhaps he can see into the past, can separate history from myth, and know what I was and what he should be. And one more thing, though I should hesitate to mention it because it seems wild and desperate. I shall not balk, because that same thing became crucial to my own story as *King James* and *Candlemas Packet* rode the westerlies toward the Cape of Good Hope. My Sam, if you ever read this confession, which is more for you than any human being I can name, is it possible that once upon a time you too chatted with a pale albatross who can dance on icy gray gusts?

We were running slow under topsail through bergy bits, *Candlemas Packet* well away to our stern, our second or third day out of Gaunttown. Germanicus was an able captain, struggled to organize the crew and passengers straightaway (with Motherwell commanding our Volunteers) in order to keep the conditions belowdecks tolerable, the rationing sensible. We calculated we had food and water to make the Pacific Ocean. We supposed we could scout Africa for landfall, and if turned away could make a run for Australia. If that too failed, we had no better plan. We commended our fate to the wind and current. *King James* was a sturdy ice schooner built for a crew of twenty-four; we had more than one hundred and fifty people onboard, including children.

The weather came up threatening from the northwest, the ocean turning from green to slate gray, signals back and forth with *Candlemas Packet* to close up for heavy seas. We had ship-to-ship radios; we carried one receiver for international radio traffic. The looming storm worried us daylong, seemed to hold back. Germanicus came to me on the quarterdeck to report all was ready. He seemed resolved, and very, very tired; our imprisonment, and his failure to avenge his father, had worn down his pride. Germanicus was not a complicated man; he acknowledged one direction, ahead, and did not welcome irony. He surprised me then, standing arms crossed, for he spoke defeatedly, harshly: "We won't last that blow. I want ye to know it. Janey, she been on me for makin' square between us, ye and me. I've been no good friend. Ye've been as true a brother as a man can have."

I did not know what bothered him, offered sympathy and apology for my self-concern since Robby's execution.

"Hear me out. That'd be the day I faulted a man for keepin' his own way. Begod, we'll likely all be drowned afore midnight. I want ye to have my apology. I've kept a hard thing from ye. I had call. I were afeared ye'd leave us, when we could not've stood it. Mark me, t'were not mine to hold back from ye. It be plain. When I landed on the Falklands two years back, I came through the Sound and touched on yerr Mead's Kiss."

"Were there any graves?" I said.

"No man nor beast nor grave. T'were a marker, a great stone marker. Words on it. Said 'Fiddle,' with a date. Summer of ninety-eight."

I turned from Germanicus and went to the rail. I remained there through the night, old Iceberg my stalwart nursemaid, as that storm did break over us, huge seas and howling winds. I had seen it before, on *Angel of Death,* and was not moved. Germanicus and Half-Red Harrah yelled, climbed, and dared, did everything men can do in the face of unbounded nature; and I knew then it would not have mattered had not God spared us. That storm was an encore for me, a tempest heralding another time in the wilderness, and when it weakened two full days later, I realized that the tempest in me for six years was what made me indifferent to that blow. Grim Fiddle himself was a whirlwind. Why was I unable to set a course? Why did I wait for men and catastrophe to direct me? I was the unchallenged commander of that flotilla of discarded ships. I knew that those people would obey me, by right and by choice. I had acknowledged that the Hospidar was correct, that he had taken control and then concerned himself with right conduct. Why could not I do the same? What more charge would I require than that Grandfather had fixed a marker for me four years before, two years after I had left him on Mead's Kiss?

The storm broke. Violante brought me food on the quarter-deck. She said Lazarus was badly seasick below, as were many. She asked me what chance we had to make Africa or Australia if a storm days out of Gaunttown had nearly finished us. I would not answer her. She demanded attention, a quick woman with heavily accented English, full of challenge. She said, "If you are afraid, keep it to yourself. There are too many afraid. You are not allowed fear or anger, or, like Lazarus, apologies. Be brave, for us, not for yourself. If I were a man, I would take your place. I would be brave."

I remained at the rail. Violante had hailed me there. I was afraid and furious and apologetic. And it did not seem to matter that I admitted to it. It still kept me from taking charge. I had seen nothing but reversal, failure, hope abandoned, human out-rage—and what had it mattered whether men or women were brave or cowardly or indifferent? Do nothing and perish; fight like a wolf pack and perish. Once I had wondered when I should stand and fight. Then I had stood and fought, and it had come to this, another defeat, more ambiguity. I could blame it on my luck, or on the darkness, or on my own darkness—those first blank years on South Georgia—yet no finding of fault could release me. If I had been born to purpose, I was as ignorant of it as I was frightened of it. Voices! Did I hear voices when I slept? I heard them continually, and there was no single sense to them. I needed an interpreter.

Germanicus and his crew kept clear of me. Longfaeroe tried to approach me, and Iceberg growled him away. I stood there for several days after the storm, talking to myself, cursing the sky and Grandfather's Lord God, taunting the storm clouds that trailed us. I cannot provide a moment by moment account of what hap-pened in my mind. I do have this memory. I record it expecting it to fall short as an explanation of my future conduct. It is what I have.

Out of that swirling gray sky, out of the flocks of storm pe-trels and diving petrels and wandering albatrosses, there emerged a single pale albatross that caught my attention. I knew what Ge-manicus had told me of the wandering albatross, when we had spied their breeding nests on our marches on South Georgia. For sealers, they are laden with superstitition, and I think Germanicus told me the science of them as another way to exemplify the dif-ference between sealer talk and plain talk. The albatross makes landfall once a year, to breed; the rest of its life is devoted to circling the Southern Ocean alone or in flocks. It seems an animal designed by God for one thing, magnificent flight in all weathers, now skimming the waves, now swinging high and around, rarely needing to flap its wings as it banks this way and that to catch a gust and soar. It appears a lord of the ocean of air. The narrow bill is pink, the stubby torso is white, the long wings are black with gray feathers, the webbed feet are kept tucked except when it lands in the water to fish. More, the wandering albatross seems not of this world, either a refugee of another sort of creation or else a truly free creature who should pity us stumbling and graceless men.

This particular pale albatross swooped down over *Candlemas Packet*—running close to our beam after the ravages of the storm—and then followed a sinking straight line across the wave caps toward me at the rail, veering up with one tuck of a wing to circle and come down again below me, hovering, sailing. The bird repeated this neat maneuver several times, adding innovations, such as a spin over the wavelets. I watched the performance unfold and was gradually and haphazardly reminded of another sort of performance—also a dance—that I had watched from a distance long before. Keeping apace, twirling and gliding, the albatross seemed magic. Iceberg cocked her ears, did not go to the alert, was complacent. I laughed, started, laughed again, then called down to the bird as it came even with me, perhaps ten feet below eye level.

"Who are you?" I said.

"You know who I am," said the albatross, a woman's voice. I do not apologize for this. That bird talked to me.

"You remind me of the sibyl," I said.

"I am what you make of me," she said.

"If you are the sibyl, I figured it out. I guessed. Reverend Longfaeroe helped, but I did it. I guessed a long time ago. I tried to tell Israel. Grandfather wouldn't talk about you. He said you were a witch. Abigail believed me. She said you were cold and heartless, and afraid of Grandfather. Am I right? You did club me at Sly-Eyes's party. I know. You are Lamba Fiddle. You're my mother."

"A very disappointed mother," she said.

"Peregrine's dead. Grandfather's probably dead too. And Cleopatra and Abigail, do you know about them, and Sam?"

"Who are you?" she said.

"I'm your son, Grim Fiddle."

"No son of mine. My son had a true name," she said.

"You mean that talk about Skallagrim Ice-Waster?"

"Do I? Ice-Waster, Rune-Carver, Wolfman, King of the South. Do I?"

"The closest I got was president on South Georgia. Thrown me out. I am bald, mostly. You should be disappointed."

"A king is first king to himself," she said.

"I don't know what I want to be, if that's what you mean. You talk a lot like Israel. He said he was motherly. They want me to save them. I don't care."

"Is there anything you care about?" she said.

"No. Why should I? Who cares about me now?"

"Your mother cares about you. Nothing you care about?"

"Yes, there is. Grandfather. Your father," I said.

"He is a trial for both of us," she said.

"Is he alive? You must know he is!"

"I know more than that. What do you know?" she said.

"I suppose that I know that you are my mother, and that Peregrine is dead, and that if I could have my heart's desire, I'd want Grandfather back."

"Then you know what to do," she said.

"Wait!" I called, for the pale albatross then pirouetted on a wave cap and swooped up above *King James*'s mainmast, circumnavigated *Candlemas Packet,* and veered away, to the west, until it was a dash in the gray sky, was one with the curvature of earth. I took special note, because that albatross had flown into the wind.

Some time must have passed between my confrontation with the albatross and my conference with Germanicus, Motherwell, Lazarus, Longfaeroe, Wild Drumrul, Half-Red Harrah, Otter Ransom, Jane and Violante and Annabel Donne and Toro Zulema, leader of the beasties on board. My memory is that it was hours; it might have been days. They came to me as men at arms might have come to their lord and master. They seemed cautious, anticipatory, looked at me as if intimidated, expecting the worst, defenseless before my temperament. I had seen that look before, addressed not to me but rather to Grandfather, Elephant Frazer, the Hospidar. It was the look of discipleship. They hung back, hung on my nuance. I no longer was required to explain or justify myself to them. They wanted something more perilous. They wanted kingship.

Germanicus, their spokesman, explained to me in a strong, contrite voice that he had spoken rashly about *King James.* His panic had been exhaustion. It would not happen again. Sean Malody had reported low morale but no major problems on board *Candlemas Packet.* Germanicus said he had solved his staffing problems, that *King James* was overcrowded but sure, and that he and Sean Malody had crews who would continue able. He said we could ride out a dozen blows like that one, if not one tempest a dozen times harder. I told him there was no tempest that powerful, that nature had limits, same as men. He smiled, moving in a way new for him toward me—deference. He was not afraid of me. He was a proud man, gave me his pride while keeping enough for himself. It was the same for the others; together they stood there on the quarterdeck as my court, each with a posture turned to me. Lazarus was the least formal, the most manipulative. He was still queasy, did not look around, approached me in conversation with gasps and sighs. He managed to ask me what I was doing up here, alone, wailing like a dog. Was I discomfited? He phrased himself carefully, and it was a crucial change, as if my health were their well-being; I could be uneasy, could not be ill. Lazarus said people were despondent and anguished. Motherwell and Half-Red Harrah (a round, sturdy man, fat fingers, good hands) said Lazarus talked like a woman. Toro Zulema called me *padrone* and said his men were not afraid, took their strength from mine. They chattered among themselves about how confident they were, awaited my approval. Longfaeroe finally waved them to silence and became somber. He seemed the most certain of what he had to do, and of me. He asked me what decisions I had reached in my solitude, for surely I had been talking with the Almighty.

"Not that, you wouldn't understand," I said curtly, in a voice more Grandfather's than mine. I tested it again. "No burning bush, no Angel of the Lord either."

"The Almighty came into David's heart," he said.

"So he did. That was David. I have my own ways," I said,

then added slowly, "There will be a change of course. Into the wind."

"Where away, Grim?" said Germanicus.

"Signal Malody," I said. "Bring us about for the Falklands."

I am aware now that my conversion from shepherd boy to shepherd, from follower to master, cannot be explained by this Norse fairy tale of a shape-changed sibyl, a talking albatross. I did not trouble my men and women—for that is what they had become, my people—with the scene, and it is not without hesitation that I relate it here. It is a secret long kept, once broken, never again until here. If it appears contrived, this is not intentional. I am not concealing, evading, beguiling. I believe wholeheartedly that albatross was Lamba Time-Thief. I continued shaken by the fact of it afterward, still am. I cannot now prove that she, it, that bird, was my mother. There is much about that self-consciously mysterious female who was my mother that I have already recorded that I cannot demonstrate as verified fact—that is, verified by other observers. For example, I have said that Lamba first spied me in her magic hand-mirror late in the evening of the spring equinox of 1973. This is not another's opinion. It is my conjecture, based upon circumstantial evidence. She did have a magic hand-mirror. I saw it on her belt that night at Sly-Eyes's party; Israel said he saw it on her belt the night she confronted Peregrine. I also know that Norse sibyls used such mirrors like the crystal balls of other pagan traditions, in order to see the future. Also, I do not know why she was moved to call out Skallagrim Strider's name at my conception, nor why she persisted with his legend twenty-two years later at Sly-Eyes's party. There was no significant connection between the Norse Fiddles and the Norse outlaws on Iceland. They appear as far apart as an elephant seal and a Norse wolf. Why, then, was Lamba moved to burden me with such an arcane, fantastic portent? There does not seem to be an answer—unless, of course, one accepts witches and ghosts and curses and magic as what they could all be: in history. In other words, Lamba really was a sibyl, she was able to thieve time, she did tell me the truth.

And while I am asking such unanswerable questions, why did Lamba choose Peregrine? (I pause to muse at this, and now see something I have never seen before: Did Lamba then have prescience that she had a bird's shape inside her, and did Lamba see something avian and predatory in Peregrine? He was a man in desperate, angry flight. Or could it be, the joke of it, that Lamba heard Peregrine's name called out at THE MICKEY MOUSE CLUB by Israel, and just pounced, albatross on falcon? If this speculation seems to mock Lamba, so be it; she mocked me in her selfish, spooky, presumptive way, never said she loved me, as I never said I loved her, still cannot.)

More seriously, most seriously, why did Lamba curse herself with the role of witchcraft? Abigail said it was her fear of Grandfather. Wise men might suggest that it had to do with the desertion of Zoe, Lamba's twisted way of both emulating and defying her scold of a father. All credible, I admit. I declare now simply that Lamba elected herself, regardless of why. She said, I am this, I know this, what else either will follow or will not. Such conduct is arrogant, is dangerous, is also as rich a way as I can think of to plunge oneself into history.

This might be the deeper explanation of my transformation into despot for those aboard *King James* and *Candlemas Packet.* I knew who I was, and where I was from, and the faces of the people who had raised me healthy and good-natured. I had sufficient learning to judge this man just, that man less just. I trusted my own heart, and my heart's desires. Yes, I could have known more, much more; I was deficient in Education, Genius, Gravel, Fortune, in every Thing, like the men who Lazarus had told me dared to lead early America into rebellion and republicanism. Still, there was a moment, on *King James*'s quarterdeck, when I said to myself: now, Grim Fiddle, now, you have what you have, take hold, assume, ascend, lead. I felt charged. I felt magical. I elected myself. And it so happened that I believed that this moment was coincident with the coming of the albatross. I stepped onto the small stage of my destiny and spoke my first truly humorous lines in the comedy. Mother talked back, quip to quip, to quest.

More grandly, perhaps it did not signify what election I chose for myself; I could have voted for fisherman, pilgrim, hermit. I elected to lead. I chose to lead as a king. Or it was chosen for me, or it happened and let another say that it did not. I declare: As Lamba said she was a sibyl, as Lamba committed her being and her only son, Grim Fiddle, to a quest for that portentous fancy of hers, Skallagrim Strider, so Grim Fiddle said he was master of those exiles, so Grim Fiddle committed himself and his charges to a quest for Grandfather, and whatever else that would follow. I laid claim; I gathered my due; I plunged into history, in pursuit of, and in obedience to, my albatross.

My Grandfather

I have read over my account of my self-election and see that it wants clarity. It was not that as a despot with a tangible goal— my grandfather—I was without doubts. Mother might be able to change shape; however, there was no magic on earth, or in Longfaeroe's Heaven, or in the halls of the Norse gods, that could sweep my mind of worry. Like that American revolutionary Lazarus told me about, I was filled with unutterable anxiety. And so I kept it that way, unspoken, to myself. From then on, I concealed my lapses in confidence, my quixotic ambivalences. As the Norse would say, I guarded my word-hoard.

This was not the same as imperial aloofness. It was that I strove to lead as if I did not waver. It was not an inhuman policy, instead most human. It is human nature, as I have witnessed it, that a people much in distress—I mean life-threatening panic, at elemental extremes—not only will follow a relentless, keen, bold, and, yes, cruel man, but also will demand that this man rule them absolutely, increasingly as if he were God's prophet. The Presbyterianism that Longfaeroe preached, and that the South Georgians followed unquestioningly, interpreted the practice of this sort of despotism as if it were ordained before time; they called it predestination. This is not a reasonable theory, contains elements that must be regarded as defeatism. Yet, though it indicates a mind nearly overwhelmed by chaos, it also can be seen as a try for order. It is folly and it is bravery; such a contradiction always means high risk.

My experiment in despotism contained risk for me as well, for it is also my experience that a people in final peril will try to take control of their leader, not with sedition and insurrection, rather with feelings more insidious—by obliging their leader to assert a system of government that is plain tyranny. This exchange, of inexcusable cruelty by one man for obedience to a single-minded absolutism by the mass, becomes a dynamo of flesh. All else seems to flow with it and to fuel it. It is a false system of government—Israel had taught me that, and Lazarus had been quick to remind me—for it has within it the terms of its own failure: Man is not God, cannot know God's plan; Prophecy is a fleeting pridefulness; Freedom surrendered is reason scorned. But while it works, or seems to, it is a wonder, to be celebrated as it celebrates the will of man to overcome the violence of nature. When it stops working, it is impossible to separate man's brutality from man. It becomes then what it always was, no poetic image of a dynamo of flesh, rather a degradation of civilization, a blasphemy, a deceitful bargain with darkness.

I overstate the case, and I apologize, a result of my rune-carving, too quick to pretty words, too slow to philosophize rigorously. I see now my purpose. I am looking for an explanation of my grandfather, even as I was then directing *King James* and *Candlemas Packet* in a search for Grandfather. He was the man I was becoming. I knew that vaguely then, know it completely now. He was no modest Presbyterian determinist. He was a vengeful, scornful, autonomous man of an ineffable Lord God. It was my belief then that there was a solution to my plight. I did not know what it was. However, I did believe that finding Grandfather, perhaps just the effort to find Grandfather, would provide me revelation toward my end of solving the fate of me and mine. In my mind, in my word-hoard, Grandfather was enormous and mysterious and potent; he provided me with the closest analogy I possessed for the most awesome image in the Fiddle Bible, that of God the Father Almighty, Maker of Heaven and Earth.

Was my quest a search for justification, then, or was it a flight for release? Is it necessary to choose between redemption or escape? I still am not sure. It was why I did what I did. Measuring my life on *King James*'s quarterdeck, I saw that since losing *Black Crane*, I had been pitiable, wandering, selfish, pointless, contrary. The bad turn of being trapped with the Volunteers in Port Stanley, the good turn of being adopted by the Frazers, the bad turn of being damned by the Hospidar, the good turn of learning Germanicus's discovery on Mead's Kiss, all these inexplicable accidents, all of this luck, good and bad, all moved me toward a summary desire. I told the albatross it was my heart's desire. Grandfather was that and more. He was my treasure. Beowulf, King of the Weather-Geats, slayer of Grendel and mother, finally slain as he slew the unnamed dragon guarding another sort of treasure, he would have understood my face. Grim Fiddle did not feel destitute, damned, or lost as long as it was possible his grandfather might be found.

I did not tell those on board *King James* that Grandfather was the only reason we were making into the wind, with difficulty, veering into the horse latitudes to approach the Falklands from the north-northeast. I let them presume I had a plan for resettlement on West Falkland. Toro Zulema thought that the Falklands must be ripe for colonization after six years of Pattie misrule; Half-Red Harrah and the sealers harbored a need for revenge on the Hospidar, boasted they would sail anywhere in the Southern Ocean to establish a base for an invasion of South Georgia; Jane and Violante and Annabel Donne nurtured the women with tales of a new start at Port Stanley. I overheard them and remained removed. I did not think that Germanicus was fooled by my silence; he knew of Grandfather's marker, appeared ashamed for his deception of me, was willing to leave my will unchallenged. I had followed his father to the end. Germanicus owed me as much faith.

Two days out of the Falklands, the sea was pocked with ships in distress. There were many signs of a deliberate and ominous exodus. We had sighted lone craft more seaward. The ships in the sea-lane were closed up, ran in concert, as if with purpose. I made sure everyone of authority on board had as good a look as possible in the dirty weather. I wanted the fear to take hold in their hearts, and I wanted that fear tangible. I recognized the fleet of the damned. I was no longer reluctant to call it that. We were one with it.

A sudden blow that night cleared away the smaller craft, covered the nearby sea with wreckage. The next morning, we came about, having turned into the wind to ride the blow, and marked several large freighters well away to starboard as especially puzzling, neither flags nor radio traffic from them. The fleet continued that day to appear and fade in the fogbanks without a pattern, the wind tossing it up then pulling it apart. I no more understood the final reason for the fleet than I had six years before—where it had come from, where it was going—but I did know to keep my wits and not to permit the outrage to confound me. The fleet was an event that made war in one's mind, and the prudent captain denied the resultant despair, kept on regardless. I had Germanicus signal Malody to close up for slow running as night closed on us, had Germanicus turn out ordnance and gun crews. I let them believe that I anticipated all. I did not figure on *Candlemas Packet* breaking formation before dawn, so that she was well away to our stern and running sluggishly in contrary winds at daybreak—no match for a slim cutter breaking through the fog from the southwest. We were half a day out of Port Stanley. I knew that cutter was a pirate, feasting on the best-trimmed ships. Germanicus's seamanship saved Malody, getting *King James* up wind and in line to cut off the pirate's retreat, so that it made north for other game. I had Germanicus break radio silence (that close in it had seemed best to appear helpless) to inquire why Malody had fallen behind. I put my glass on *Candlemas Packet*'s deck, had the answer and a verdict before Germanicus confirmed the worst. Sean Malody had chanced upon refugees adrift in an open boat during the night, had accidentally rammed them, and rather than keep on as ordered had paused at their cries to rescue. The fleet of the damned had breached his good sense.

I did not hesitate, saying, "Signal Malody to put them over."

Germanicus did hesitate. I explained; he conceded. But we were not obeyed, or if so, it was too late. By the time we spied East Falkland's shore at dusk—a dark horizon of a hundred hundred hundred campfires—the signal from Malody included a report of a child sick with fever. There were medicines. There was no defense.

Our council that night was vitriolic. I put my court to the test, making sure the women spoke their minds at length, because I had seen on South Georgia how vital they were to morale and common sense. Germanicus spoke for me, another technique I had learned from Grandfather and the Hospidar, to have one's senior subordinate hold forth until the factions can present a consensus. It was also a notion I had from the ancient Norse, those protracted arguments in the halls of Asgard: Thor of Thunder versus Loki the Sly-One versus Frigg the Queen, terrible Odin standing silent and acute. Our wrestling was appropriately tumultuous. Germanicus asserted that *Candlemas Packet* was finished unless a quarantine was organized on board and the sick were put over in a boat; he also told them that Sean Malody had made a mistake, there was nothing we could do to repair it. Lazarus and Jane challenged Germanicus. I took note that Lazarus's power was lessened while we were at sea; his wordy learning could not overwhelm Germanicus's quiet militance. Jane said I was rash. Lazarus used the word *monstrous,* but he did not join in Jane's demand that I prove the fever. Our chief medical attendant, Annabel Donne, and Magda Zulema said they would never agree to a similar quarantine on *King James.* Toro Zulema wavered, an important detail, since most on board *Candlemas Packet* were from his camp. The council closed without agreement. I did not speak. Next morning, Malody reported another case of fever, despite a quarantine.

Baffling winds and a heavy fog closed on us. I had Germanicus pass very careful instructions by radio to Malody, also a sailing course well seaward of Adventure Sound that would permit us a rendezvous with him along a fifty-mile track. Then *King James* stood in for Mead's Kiss on a choppy sea, another blow coming. Several times we came upon freighters twice the size of *King James,* making on a course south. Germanicus had no explanation for the obvious increase in activity south of the Falklands, saying that on his raid two years before he had seen many beastie boats, all small, scattered. Now there seemed a pack, and a purpose, and urgency. There also was incessant gunfire, or thunder, or deep foghorns. We lived on alert. Our immediate enemies were hysteria and superstition. Sailing into such a murky vista did not shake me. The fear on board *King James* might have. I fought it with Norse magic, demanding from myself what I was not sure I could do, to show myself, as the Norse would say, girded by elves.

This introduces an important development for me on *King James;* I found myself turning more and more to my sense of how my Norse ancestors might have faced such peril. My choice of imagery changed accordingly. It shifted from the poetry of Long-faeroe's Psalter to the poetry of Norse myth. Bluntly, Beowulf replaced the Bible, not completely, just enough for me to take comfort in a challenge that would have come easier to seafaring warriors than to men standing guard on the watchtowers of Jerusalem. As the Norse would say, I ate a diet of certainty. I stood watch as long as I could bear the fatigue and hunger, as a Norseman would have done; I rested only briefly on a mat I had set up under the inboard steering, leaving Iceberg at my place on the quarterdeck, my icon, as a Norseman would have done; I concerned myself with posture, right-thinking, clear-thinking, high-handed and firm rule, as a Norseman would have done. With Norse fatalism I told myself that events would either bear out my presumptions or would not, and thrashing about beforehand was contrariness and weakness. In all, I tried to be as I thought Beowulf might have been on the deck of his wave-cutter. I also tried to be someone more familiar, of course, on the deck of his *Angel of Death:* impossibly removed, intractable, visionary, surefooted, iron-fisted, larger than life, and—when it was time to command—thunderous.

We broke through the dirty weather at dusk, found an empty sea, poor visibility. We rode out the high sea through the night, launched a longboat before dawn, Motherwell leading my landing party. At Mead's Kiss's waterline there was wreckage and a battered trawler, still seaworthy, no guards, bullet holes in the wheelhouse. There were remains of dozens of craft, stripped for firewood. Motherwell challenged a small figure that emerged from a rusted shell, and it faded into the shadows. We moved up toward the weather station. I knew what gray stone marker Germanicus meant, and knew the way. Davey Gaunt and Wild

Drumrul scouted ahead, told us there was a camp there, many bodies sleeping under lean-tos. Motherwell directed a weapon's check, though we were less anxious about combat with them than contamination by them.

(I write *them*. That is inexact. I have called them refugees without refuge. Peregrine called himself an exile. They called themselves damned. The South Georgians called them beasties. And yet I resist. None of these words are adequate for those hollow faces, swollen bellies, filthy complexions, terrified eyes, open sores, narrow and bent figures squatting in dust and mud, silent, past weeping, though it was true they cried out when they died. I feel now I have not been rigorous in my characterization of them. It is important to get it right here, at the beginning of my time among them. I am in conflict between calling them people or continuing to name them for what they appeared: broken, discarded, starving, diseased, deranged, half-men. I see something, a new thought. The Norse had a word for the North American Indians they discovered in their voyages beyond Greenland; they called them *Skrælings*, which means wretches. In the Fiddle Bible there is much talk of the wretched; Jesus came not for the blessed but for the wretched; Moses led the Hebrews out of Egypt, and from what Israel once told me, the word *Hebrew* might have meant wretches to the pharaoh. Also I recall that at some point during our exodus on *King James*, I began to think of the people out there on the ocean as wretches. This might seem a small point, but it occurs to me that on *King James* I was struggling to describe to myself how I and mine differed from the people we found on the sea, on Mead's Kiss, and after. That was false discrimination. I understand now that I was one with them, and I should now have the will to call myself whatever I want. I call myself wretched. I call them wretched, not hopeless, not beaten, not damned—wretched.)

My encounter with those wretches at the ruined weather station on Mead's Kiss was grisly revelation. They had set no pickets. There were more than forty of them, in clumps, a few women, no children. We surrounded them. Motherwell barked an order.

"No, no!" a tall man shouted in broken English. He urged his compatriots in Portuguese to remain still; the women bunched to the side. He said, "No gold! No guns! Over there, guns and gold, yes?"

The tall man with the red face kept babbling as we searched; they did have rifles, pistols, ammunition. Motherwell had the men lie face down in the mud. Wild Drumrul motioned me toward him; he pointed down an incline behind the wall of the weather station. The smell told what the shadows did not show. I asked if it was a graveyard. Wild Drumrul said no, a massacre, children too. Motherwell reported that the tall man said he was a French physician, an apparent lie, and that he thought we were Englishmen because we were so large. There was another Frenchman, at least in part, who said he was a priest, another likely lie. A third man, a leathery Negro, said he was first mate on the trawler. We got these three apart from the rest. Otter Ransom came out of the weather station, spitting, angry, shaken, said they had cut up some women in there.

"Pirates, murdering pirates," said Motherwell.

I ordered him to deploy scouts up the hill to check on the other side, told Indigo Zulema to get the three ringleaders over to the wall for interrogation.

They said they had been at sea more than six weeks, embarking from the Greater Antilles, from Haiti, or, in another version, from the Lesser Antilles. We struggled with our talk, because we had no French or Portuguese, they had bad English, so we used crude Spanish. The Frenchman, who called himself *Monsieur le Docteur,* said their party had been twice this size; bad weather and pirates had forced them to land repeatedly on the continental coast, where some had run away, others had died of wounds. He emphasized they were free of disease, that they had lost no one to *le choléra.* He said there was a war in northern Brazil, with airplanes. *Monsieur le Docteur* was partly educated, no university doctor, more likely a half-breed who had worked at a clinic. He was guileful, seemed well-fed, wore good boots and filthy clothes, had a woozy laugh. He asked, were we South Africans?

The fake priest, Raul, most likely a runaway from a monastery, said that he and some parishioners had been chased out of Fort-de-France by pirates, had purchased their way onto a boat only to have the captain desert them. He later said he had fled an epidemic. He was about to admit that it was plague, was jarred by *Monsieur le Docteur,* added they had seen plague in Brazil, had stayed clear. When they saw we balked at this, *Monsieur le Docteur* elaborated, telling of blockades, quarantines, mass deaths, warships sweeping through refugee ships sinking any boat with sickness. Of note, Raul was frightened of Wild Drumrul unusually, called him *le Maure,* and when questioned about this said that he had heard Moslems were slaughtering Christians off Africa. Neither of them mentioned America. When we asked, they hung their heads, said the Americans were a great people, were we Americans?

In sum, the two Frenchmen were full of lies, and when they did not deliberately lie, they confused what they had seen with what they thought we wanted to hear. They had advanced faculties to say and to do whatever it took to stay alive. They were wretched, probably killers, but they fought. They wanted us to take them along with us. We asked, all of them? *Monsieur le Docteur* said no, only those strong enough to make it through. This was our first hint that they had a destination.

"Where bound?" said Indigo Zulema in Spanish.

Monsieur le Docteur tensed, spoke French, then English. "The relief camps."

"Camps of the church," said Raul in Spanish.

The Negro asked for another smoke, spoke Portuguese, pointing. Motherwell gave it to him, told him to speak plain.

"South," he said in Spanish, pointing.

We recoiled, looked at each other. At that, *Monsieur le Docteur* and Raul opened up and rambled, as if our incredulity threatened their shaky but bright hope and they had to convert us immediately and totally to their fantasy. They overlapped each other in French, Portuguese, Spanish, broken English. What emerged was irrational and compelling: relief camps, church camps, food, clothing, Americans, Europeans, relocation centers, mercy ships, resettlement to Australia, America, Alaska. They stressed repeatedly that they did not mean the *arctique,* instead islands off the coast of Antarctica.

"Them're lyin', plain," said Motherwell.

"Where'd them hear it?" asked Davey Gaunt.

"Shoot one, them'll tell," said Motherwell.

Indigo Zulema said that the fat one, Raul, said that the priests knew about the camps, and that the fathers at Fort-de-France had known, and that the church would save those that got through the pirates and the plague.

"It is a lie," I said.

"Them'll say Hell's froze to save their skins," said Motherwell.

"They're not lying," I said. I had Indigo Zulema interrogate them again, from their embarkation—this time it was Brazil—to their landfalls on the continent, the pirates, the sweeps, the storms, their landing on Mead's Kiss after they were turned away from East Falkland by gunboats. They said they knew nothing of the bodies in the ravine or the corpses in the weather station. We listened again to their vision of the relief camps, "*les camps de secours.*" Raul repeated, "*les camps catholiques*"; he added also "*les camps glacés*" or the ice camps. They portrayed an ever more fetching scene: dormitories, clinics, transportation to new countries welcoming refugees. They believed by then that we were ignorant of the camps and that we wanted to join the exodus, so they tried to make it as attractive as possible, hoping we would take them with us. Thus, as we asked more questions, they got farther from what they knew, pathetic as it was, and we got farther from discovering where they could have heard such stories. What they said sounded fabulous. However, in their mouths and eyes, it seemed available, a genuine release. They proselytized a heaven on earth.

I walked away. It was their fear that made them convincing. I took in the stench of bodies, corpses, mud. I turned toward the wind. I regained my balance and purpose. I found Grandfather's marker, that same weathered, convex gray boulder he had stood me up against just before I had left him almost six years before. It backed on the weather station. A small female crouched there, fell down trying to flee me. I reached out to help, thought better, shooed her away. Grandfather's rock was his temperament, a giant stone tablet. I remembered it clean of markings; now it was covered with pitiable graffiti: names, initials, curses, dates scratched in many languages, scratched with knives, stones, hearts—all that was left to tell the tale of the thousands who had passed there.

Across the center, at what was my line of sight, were thick, well-cut letters. The message, "FIDDLE FEBRUARI 98."

I touched the letters, felt nothing. No, I felt very tired. Looking up, I noted smaller letters above, not obvious at first, something one would only note by accident, or luck. I reached as high as I could, brushed away black dust—fallout from the volcanoes—and found "M FIDDLE 11/96 60w."

It was lighting up by then. There were shots from the hillside above me. In the surprise, one of the pirates got a pistol and shot one of my men. Indigo Zulema fired wildly in defense. *Monsieur le Docteur* and Raul, sure we would kill them, tried to control their men, were shot down for it. There was more fire from the ridge, an attack from another encampment. We were off at a run. The Negro ran with us. At the waterline, while Davey Gaunt set fire to the trawler and Motherwell set our perimeter, the Negro became crazed, crawling, begging in Spanish, "Save me! I know the way!"

In the dawn mist the skirmish was a draw. We might have been trapped; the absence of an enemy commander spared us, since the pirates were required to fight to save their ship rather than to pursue us. As we got our boat into the surf I looked at the pleading Negro and made a decision. I was later glad for it. From what the Negro told Indigo Zulema on the beach, and, after we took him along, from what he told Lazarus and one of our Portuguese-speaking couples back on board *King James,* I learned much of the plight of the fleet of wretches, the wretched, in the Southern Ocean.

His name was Xique. He had been a seaman on a coastal freighter that had been scuttled in northern Brazil, at Recife, a year before. He said he had escaped overland, fought as a guerrilla, worked for the army as a gravedigger, then led a band of deserters down a large river until he was captured by the army, escaped, got on a frigate that worked first as a troop transport, later as a raider on the coast, and once as a mercenary blockade-runner to evacuate soldiers from Africa's Gold Coast. This ship was sunk by a gunboat at Rio de Janeiro, and he escaped again in an open boat with a group of seamen who soon forced their way aboard a trawler from the Caribbean—the same trawler Davey Gaunt had burned. That was where he met the two Frenchmen. They were killers, had murdered their captain and been chained as mutineers, and only the intervention of Xique and his mates saved them. The trawler then theirs, they had put in at various small ports down the coast, selling passage to refugees. Once at sea, they threw their victims overboard and put into port again.

His fantasies and deceptions aside, what he said that was most important to me was of the time he had spent on the coastal freighter before it was scuttled at Recife. His ship had been hired several times to run in convoys south to relief camps on islands off the coast of Antarctica. He described what sounded to my sealers to be the South Shetland Islands. When we challenged him for details, he said he did remember one island called "Elephant." That had been four years before. Also, the two Frenchmen had sold passage to a Brazilian man and his family, whom they had then drowned, but not before the Brazilian had told Xique that the relief camps were relocating refugees, had told Xique that he had been there as a seaman and seen such the year before.

At that point, Xique utterly contradicted and degraded his story, claiming he had been at the camps the year before, claiming he had been a soldier and not a pirate. Xique said the sea was covered with pirates and plague ships and warships, that we should be particularly afraid of raiding ships from Africa, because that was where the sickness was worst.

Xique said he could take us to the relief camps. In Portuguese he called them ice camps. He said a ship as good as ours was sure to be welcomed by the priests and the soldiers there. The oddest, saddest detail was that he kept talking about "English nurses."

My memory is that the very next day was Sunday. That may be off, a few days might have passed, since it took us time and seamanship to find *Candlemas Packet,* where conditions had continued to deteriorate. At Longfaeroe's service that morning, it was announced that I had forbidden anyone from voluntarily going over to *Candlemas Packet.* Longfaeroe's sermon was furious and blunt about the sternness and stoutheartedness of David of Jerusalem; he added a scripture lesson from the Gospel of Luke, Jesus' words to the effect that "He who is not with me is against me, and he who does not gather with me scatters."

I ruled a house divided. I had Germanicus announce our sailing course, which I had arrived at without counsel. The reaction was not pronounced—they were tough and pragmatic—rather it was skeptical, cautious. Longfaeroe's service ended and the debate began.

"More of the same!" said Lazarus. "The face of the bully!" What relief camps? What proof? A killer's lies? And show me the plague! Cholera, yes, typhus, yes, but where is this plague that chases us? Show me that we can't get ashore on Patagonia. Show me we can't run for America. Let Grim Fiddle answer me. He is using us, and all to look for a man, a monster, his grandfather, who is dead, dead! I know you, Grim Fiddle. I know your mind!"

"What've we become?" said Jane. "What sets us other than the Hospidar, to let those poor folk on *Candlemas Packet* die? And what if the sickness starts here? Throw bairns over? We have medicine. We can fight it!"

"My people are afraid," said Toro Zulema. "We are not sailors. I cannot know if that man is truthful. We fear the sickness and pirates. We want to go home. I cannot know if these camps, or the priests, will help us. I do not want to speak against Grim Fiddle. My people need help."

"Me, I seen the Shetlands, and ye that have too know," said Christmas Muir. "Ice and more. I ain't sayin' couldn't be camps. I ain't sayin' I won't go. I ain't sayin' I ain't scared of that Satan's Seat. I ain't sayin' I got answers. It be ice there, and more ice."

The talk did not sway the Volunteers under Motherwell, or the crew under Germanicus; it did not leave them untouched, either. There is much more I could write of the dissent. I push that aside now. My mind was set, perhaps from a point I cannot find, and it is misleading to detail the controversy, the more so because Lazarus was right.

The truth is that I did not care about the reasons to go south or not to. I was trusting my luck. I figured loosely: that if Grandfather had gone ashore on East or West Falkland, he was dead; that if he had gone ashore on the continent, he was lost; that if he had foundered, there was no hope. Yet he had gone somewhere between November of 1996 and February of 1998, somewhere that permitted him to get back to Mead's Kiss. In my mind, there was one chance. The relief camps might have been a fantasy. My quest for Grandfather might have been a fantasy. I married them, a union that I could not reveal to my people because it could not have withstood light.

Was I right to plunge them into the ice? Was I right to pursue Grandfather at the sacrifice of decency? I intend to be as harsh on myself now as I was on those people then. I was wrong. I have come up against this puzzle many times in my mind; I have told myself that I knew we were doomed, that I knew I could have given Germanicus sailing directions for any point on the compass and the end would have been the same, or worse. I remain unconvinced by this rationalization, because it is based upon an event and a decision that lacked reason. I put my desire before the high dreams left those one hundred and fifty on board *King James* and one hundred on board *Candlemas Packet*. I made a rash decision for the most good for the least number. I was no Beowulf, and knew it then—what vain romanticism—nor was I a David of Jerusalem, though I let Longfaeroe preach that imagery to reinforce my rule. I might have been doomed; I condemned those people. I might have been fated to hear the whispers of a thousand-year-dead outlaw, to converse with a pale albatross, to lose heart in a ruthless scramble for justification. That gives me no cause now, nor did it then, to drag, not plunge, to drag my people into my crimes. I was wrong.

I took my stand on the quarterdeck, and it meant that I turned my back on my people. The pride and anger in me matched that tumultuous sky of black and gray clouds above the most violent sea on earth, a steady westerly swell with thirty-foot rollers coming at us in groups of five, so that only when *King James* rose atop the last crest was it possible to study the horizon. The weather seemed to change hourly, a calm followed by a squall of icy rain, so that Germanicus would have to turn us to the wind to clear our lines of ice, followed by a sunburst that transformed the color of the sea from gray to ultramarine with red streaks, almost purple toward sunset. And around me, thousands of whalebirds, ice birds, shearwaters, and albatrosses, feeding off the flotsam, searching for more sizable detritus. We were not alone out there. There were large ships to the east, small ships to the west, some running under sail and alone, others under power and listing badly in the swells—either poor seamanship or badly loaded.

The wretched threw themselves into the Scotia Sea. Open

boats and wreckage were indistinguishable from bergy bits and small ice floes tossed like balls by the hills of water moving in diverse direction to form momentary mountain ranges. A sudden blow at evening of one of the first few days south of Cape Horn scattered the small ships, drove us east toward the big ships. We kept Malody in sight as long as possible, then radioed rendezvous points along our sailing course, south on the sixtieth meridian. The next morning, we were all eyes for *Candlemas Packet,* did not find her until we passed what is called the Antarctic convergence, what the sealers called "can't-no-more," meaning the weather becomes dominated by the wind off Antarctica and one can no longer predict the next day's sail. The wind stiffened, from the steady thirty knots of the "filthy fifties" to well over forty knots. We ran with topsails, were most concerned with keeping our bow up to the sea and our masts free of ice. A thick, sudden snowstorm covered us with large dirty flakes, kept the crew busy clearing the deck; it continued the next day, slackening to a driving sleet.

At least, that is my memory, though I cannot be sure now of the exact order of squalls, gales, calms, ice floes, and snowstorms. We experienced no murderous blow, a possibility that is remote but not impossible in early summer. Importantly, there were more calm days than bad ones, sometimes even a glassy sea, sun-kissed and magenta. I recall we spent Christmas Day fighting fifty-foot crests and contrary winds, so that Longfaeroe had to hold his service in parts belowdecks, most too seasick to sing. We were another week in the crossing, because we had to double back to find Malody, and because Germanicus and I grew increasingly wary of the large ships that passed to the east. We listened to their radio traffic, heard many languages, bizarre codes, little substance. They seemed cargo ships; at least one of them was a warship.

I sense I am making that voyage sound sensible. It was elemental terror. Germanicus was not intimidated by the weather; he and the sealers had crossed the Scotia Sea length and breadth their whole adult lives. However, the icy blows combined with the scattered ships of wretches were too much. We surrendered to our worst expectations, for good cause.

"There, hears it?" said Christmas Muir, an incident I recall because it was my first experience with the ice continent. We could hear a rumbling, just distinguishable from the howling wind and the heavy wash of the sea. "Tol' ye like, my ears, me and them whales, hears it. See there, the sky, lordie!"

The sky did darken, wet weather, ravaging raw cold, and a canopy of ashen clouds mixed into the fogbanks. We lost the sun. The rumblings strengthened to a low thumping. We were rolling into an oily sea of brash ice flecked with black cinders. On the morning it cleared, I was prepared to strain my eyes to the south. That was unnecessary. To port, fifty miles distant, loomed the giant mountains of Elephant Island, shrouded at their base by a thick mist that pushed miles to sea. Shafts of sunlight reflected off the glacier that wrapped the center of the island and atop it all a steady thin and black plume of smoke poured from the lip of an active volcano. As a result, the ice and snow were dirty, gray, black in patches. The volcano seemed to have a twin—unless it was a separate crater of the same—up and behind it, smaller but smokier, the two of them like black pyramids in that mist-shrouded range.

Neither of them was Satan's Seat; rather, that chain of islands before us, the South Shetlands, was a volcanic chain, part of the volatile Scotia Arc that curls from the Antarctica peninsula (Graham Land) northeast through the Palmer archipelago, the South Shetland, South Orkney, and South Sandwich islands, then curls back northwest through South Georgia and the Falklands to the tail of the Andean mountain chain in Tierra del Fuego. It was our discovery that the sealer tales of Satan's Seat (it did exist) had overlooked a whole chain of eruptions. The South Shetlands' volcanoes were awakened anew. Every one of the major mountains and some of their satellites seemed in various stages of eruption; tremors, seaquakes, steam venting, banks of ash and sulfurous poisons, lava bubbling up through fissures in the craters. It was not a cataclysm of fire on ice, instead a slow rupture of the earth, shaking, pounding, crumbling. I cannot now say how complete the rupture was, whether what appeared a general salvo was in fact only two or three volcanoes pouring steam and ash through seams in the mountains, like burrowing by a fantastic being. More, I have no science to report why it had happened, how long it had been happening. I can only report what I saw then and over the next twenty years.

That first day under that thunderous gloom—the stench of

sulfur, the lash of ashen waves—was filled with surprises. The major revelation was not the volcanoes, instead that the sea was pocked with ships arriving from the northeast, northwest. I took careful stock, helped by the fact that visibility in the Antarctic can alter suddenly from nothing to stunning clarity—what is one hundred miles can appear at hand. In between the banks of ash and steam, I watched the small flotillas of the wretched being intercepted by small white cutters. One such white cutter made for us. It signaled in international code. It wanted us to heave to for boarding. It did not threaten warfare. I put my glass on its side, did not hesitate; I ordered Germanicus to signal Malody, to bring us about to the west. The white cutter pursued but eventually veered off for a single frigate with a broken mainmast. We put to sea for the cover of a fogbank. The next day, we eluded another white cutter by heading into the steam canopy that ringed King George, the largest and most foreboding island in the South Shetlands. I ordered Germanicus to keep on slow for the sixtieth meridian.

I do not intend this narrative to become confused with mystery. I made a good guess of some of what we found those first two days, and with Xique's answers I realized more, far from the truth. The white cutters, marked with the red cross of international relief, were part of the fleet of what was called, what I called, the Ice Cross. They were dispatched to corral into sheltered anchorages the wretched arriving pell mell and battered. There were relief camps at those anchorages. Xique could only confirm for me then that there was one large camp on the lee shore of Elephant Island. He provided some details of the camp, but that information was four years out-of-date. More, I recognized that the large freighters were part of the relief effort, bringing in food and goods even as more wretches arrived. I only sketch here. Those camps were no relief; those mercy ships were no mercy. All this I would learn later. Then, off King George and heading for Roberts Island, I assumed that my magic had worked, my luck had held. I assumed that I had pursued a fantasy to discover a world of ice and ash and, yes, charity.

There is more that I do not want to become confusion—the portents by Lamba of Skallagrim Strider and me. Was he with me, that outlaw's ghost? It is a distortion to say yes, he stood at my ear as *King James* ran from Mead's Kiss to Elephant Island. Yet I did experience the phenomenon of seen-twice. I am aware that seen-twice might be an inappropriate explanation, for it can imply some form of reincarnation, as if one has lived the experience before in a previous life. I make no such claim, make a strange point nonetheless, consistent with Norse ways. The ghost of Skallagrim Strider seemed to whisper to me, seemed to give me the feeling that I had seen those hundred-foot crests and that purple sea and those thousand screaming petrels before. I was not Skallagrim Strider come again. I was Grim Fiddle come for the first time, somehow with the memory of a man who had been there. I too blink at the antirational nature of my talk. But how else was I to explain to myself that when *King James* was swamped by fog or snow, I knew what I would see when we emerged? It was an exact power: I could look at my hands stiff on the rail in the damp, could smell the brine and taste the weather, and believe that I had known what it was like to be there. I was not a timeless soul. That is not Norse. In philosophical talk, I was precognitive. The forbidding pinnacles of Elephant Island were awful, but as I studied them I realized that I was afraid of something with which I was profoundly familiar. I also had a sense of direction that should not have been mine, knew before Germanicus told me the proportions of King George, the sailing course toward Greenwich Island, the perils of the sound between Roberts and Greenwich islands. And most bizarre to me on board *King James,* I believed I could feel what it was like to be ashore on those islands, knew where the sea leopards and elephant seals gathered, where the penguins and cormorants flocked, knew how Germanicus had to keep close watch for the venting fin whales that crisscrossed our path.

This power, my ghostly familiarity, was not as helpful as one might suppose. It dulled my sense of self-defense, gave me a false sense of omniscience. It also made me at once keen for physical detail and careless about interpreting the meaning of the wretched. And because I felt that I was informed, as if I had been there before, and because I felt that Lamba's portents might have merit beyond precognition to some form of personal invulnerability, I set myself apart from the very people to whom I was most responsible. I had turned my back on them; now I dismissed them

completely. As I had elected myself to the extraordinary, I con-
descended to rule their ordinariness. As I challenged myself, I
spited others. Grim Fiddle was becoming a stranger to reason and
decency.

The fourth night off the South Shetlands we held an exhausted counsel. We were standing off Greenwich, an island of
three precipices, one venting steam, wedged between the smaller
Roberts and the large, W-shaped Livingston Island. Significantly,
Greenwich was cut by the sixtieth meridian. We gathered in the
surgery. Lazarus was edgy, not as disturbed as the rest; he made
a long speech of no consequence, then added, "I won't judge this.
Did we have to come to this place? Was there no other way than
this?"

Jane and Violante reported on our rations, Annabel Donne
on the health of the passengers, all done in voices cracked with
anxiety. They wept. I realized then how beaten down they were.
The sealers said they were not for the South Shetlands but would
go there if ordered. They said they had hunted there in their time,
and that Ugly Leghorn and some others had wintered there. They
were obsessed with the volcanoes, talked out of turn. Germanicus
was subdued about the ship and crew, said Malody's reports made
it imperative he be permitted to get his people ashore immediately.

"For his sake, Grim," said Germanicus, "we should let those
cutters take us in." It was generally understood that the relief
camps would help us, and that my resistance to such a course was
either misinformed or deranged.

I told them I wanted to reconnoiter one more day, perhaps
two, before I decided about the camps. I did not mention Grandfather or *Angel of Death*. They did not agree, they did not rebel.
We came about, *Candlemas Packet* lumbering in our wake, and
moved slowly into the mist filling the sound between Roberts and
Greenwich islands. I studied the shorelines as best I could—seals,
penguins, thousands of birds nesting and circling; their cries
overwhelmed our conversations. The lower slopes of both islands
were ice-free, matted with lichens and moss, which Peggs told me
was not unusual in summer. Other than the lack of heath grass,

those islands looked the same as South Georgia: cliffs, crags, pla-
teaus, unearthly solitude. The sealers pointed to the slick gray
cliffs above, worried that the volcanoes were melting the ice.
Christmas Muir blamed every little problem that day on Satan's
Seat, which he said was way to the southwest, on the peninsula of
Antarctica.

We were attacked late in the day, as we cleared the tidal rip
past Roberts Island and came about into the Bransfield Strait,
turning to starboard along the lee shore of Greenwich. I was on
deck, distracted. Two small cutters, single masts, rushed from the
mist and opened fire with heavy automatic firearms. I did not
witness the entire action, kept down by bursts, so my account must
be general. We were blasted. Our helmsman was shot down first.
Davey Gaunt crawled to the wheel and held our course until his
wounds overcame him, and then Ferraro, a young Falklander, took
his place until he was shattered by flying splinters. Our return fire
was ineffectual. We clung to the deck and waited to die. The sea
helped us at first, running up heavy, and strong gusts kept us
ahead of the attackers, heaved us toward rocks that might have
ripped us apart, did not, but kept the attackers back. There was
no help for *Candlemas Packet;* it came under cross fire, lost its foremast, was set afire. I do not know how long we took it. At some
point the firing ebbed, and there were boarders on deck. Motherwell and the Volunteers fought hand to hand. Germanicus, Otter Ransom, Wild Drumrul, and I held the quarterdeck with
Indigo Zulema and five Falklanders. We killed small, dark-faced
creatures, filthy and animal-quick, without self-regard or sensible
tactics. They were dressed in sealskins, smelled rancid and smoky
like burned wood, were armed with harpoons, knives, clubs, no
firearms. We shot and shot and they kept coming on. I saw one
try to bite Indigo Zulema's leg, as would a wolf. A fire was set on
our portside that we could not control. There were screams from
below as the boarders got into the hold. Germanicus and I fought
side by side through them; they fell easily, would not stay down.

We were rescued. That is the simple fact of it, and regardless
of the outrages I would later discover done by the Ice Cross, I do
not want to take from it the credit for the lives of me and mine
that day. A large white cutter came out of the mist and opened
fire on our attackers. It passed us on our starboard quarter, hard

on for *Candlemas Packet,* launched boats, rammed the smaller attacking boat. I cannot say what else was done, because I was too occupied on *King James*'s deck. The white cutter withered the enemy. The undamaged attacker broke off and escaped into a fogbank to the south. By then *Candlemas Packet* was sinking. The white cutter took off survivors; however, Malody's people were kept in longboats rather than taken on board the cutter. After we had cleared our decks (and I note how perplexed I was to find the dark-faced creatures seemed hardly to bleed), I ordered Germanicus to try to clear one of our boats to help the rescue of Malody's people. We were signaled by the white cutter to do nothing, then signaled to follow. Another white cutter appeared. Germanicus reported our radio was cluttered with orders in Spanish back and forth between the two rescuers. We had drifted well into the Bransfield Strait. Across, one hundred miles to the south, was the blue-black landscape of the Antarctica peninsula, now and again visible through dancing fogbanks. That was my first glimpse of the continent. I was in shock, covered with blood, and it did not signify. What did was our casualty report: at least a dozen dead, including brave Ferraro and our greatest loss, Toro Zulema. There were so many wounded, we did not count. And belowdecks there seemed carnage, for the attackers had gotten down there and cut their way through women and children. Motherwell assembled the Volunteers at the mainmast and then reported the missing-in-action, including Peggs, Ensign Ewart, the little harpoonist Khartoo, and, worst of all for me, Wild Drumrul.

King James's steering was wrecked. We were afire, but with muscle and plain courage Germanicus and Half-Red Harrah got us about, controlled the smoldering, and followed the white cutters into the mist along Greenwich's coast. Sometime that evening (there is no sundown in Antarctica's summer), we dropped anchor in Aurora Bay, off the lee shore of Livingston Island, before the wharves and outbuildings of an ice camp.

What did I see first? Aside from the other ships, and a small steamship off-loading goods, there were long, low-built structures on the shoreline, tucked cleverly into the ravines in the rockbed; there were the two white cutters we had followed in; but the most striking feature was the sheer wall of gray-white stone that shot up from the interior of the bay to disappear in the mist above.

That wall of rock shuddered with each rumble from the volcanoes; it would come to represent a gigantic clock, new cracks for new eruptions, seams growing ice-crystal arrays whenever the wind poured a gale from the Scotia Sea.

I was wounded, splinters and burns, was bandaged below. The Ice Cross men were waiting for me on deck. There were more than two dozen of them, well-armed, in dirty white parkas, bearded, weathered, the confidence of veterans and the posture of the forever tired. Their leader was a German named Dietjagger, or something like that. He asked my name and our port of origin. Germanicus did not want me to talk with him. I understood that I must. I answered his bad English in my poor German. That surprised him and, I think, explains why he was as forthcoming as he was, something I know was not procedural. He had an impossible, defeated, vile job and knew it. He was to judge us, asking for details that centered on our health. That was the crucial issue, what determined our fate. Dietjagger insisted his men inspect belowdecks. This took time, and meanwhile Dietjagger hinted at affairs. He used much obscure language, and preferred jargon and half-sentences. It was from Dietjagger that I first heard of the Ice Cross. There were other clues about the situation in Antarctica, most of which were no help then. Now I know, better than any man alive, and can translate Dietjagger's obtuseness. The Ice Cross was a colloquialism for the International Committee of the Red Cross Antarctica Relief Collective. That was mother mercy on the South Shetlands; it was sponsored by many sorts of patriarchs, such as the Antarctique International de Paris, the same in Rome and Munich and many more: Europe, Africa, the Americas. The Ice Cross men knew their sponsors by their myriad acronyms and by nicknames, such as the one Dietjagger used about his masters in Munich, *Der Eisvater*. Altogether there was no real international community involved, only haphazard confederacy, funds from here, goods from there, food from governments and private industrial consortiums, and most especially from the Roman Catholic Church. Altogether they were charity. The Ice Cross was the enforcer of this charity. It should not have functioned as well as it did, staffed with volunteers, convicts, pilgrims, true patriots, truer saints, and what came to be an elite of the world's cruelest and most rugged mercenaries—soldiers of fortune, though I would prefer to name them soldiers of charity.

All that, I would learn later; then Dietjagger explained matters to me in a ritualistic, high-handed manner. He said the camp before us on Aurora Bay was administered by a Roman Catholic order, the Brothers of Perpetual Witness at Golgotha. He said that once we were ashore, he had neither jurisdiction nor concern. His advice was to keep my people together. He said the Brothers were better than most, that they had spiritual concerns, that the food was said to be regular. He pointed to the off-loading freighter as proof of our welfare. He added, flatly, not as if he believed it, that as soon as possible I should seek out a representative of a treaty organization for petition for resettlement—I forget the acronym he used, probably SATORE, at that time the relief network with jurisdiction over offshore African islands. He did not explain how it was I could seek out this patron.

I looked at Lazarus as Dietjagger concluded, and he shook his head no. Now near shore again, Lazarus resumed his authority for me. I challenged Dietjagger's glibness.

"I have done what I can," he said, disgusted. His men returned to report we were disease-free. There was no mention of plague. I asked about *Candlemas Packet*. Dietjagger would not answer. I understood then that Malody's people were lost to us, would be committed to another camp receiving the infected. Dietjagger began to recite dogma again, saying this camp, Livingston Southeast I, was our assignment. He made a slip, used the jargon for the camp, Livingston Southeast I. He called it "Golgotha."

Dietjagger had kept his most threatening requirement to last. We were ordered to surrender our firearms; we were told that we could keep our knives, harpoons, blades. He anticipated resistance, told me we had no choice, that his captain would not hesitate to enforce Dietjagger's duty.

"You are holed along the waterline. Your rigging is rubbish," said Dietjagger. "You have many dead and dozens wounded. The Strait is death here to Anvers Island, friend. This is the end of your struggle. Surrender. Accept the future."

I saw what I must do. I paused to tell my council. They argued the obvious. Oddly, it was Longfaeroe who was most dark-minded, came as close as he ever did to turning from my lead. He did not want us to disembark there, said, "Golgotha is no place for Grim Fiddle's people. The place of skulls."

After we had obliged Dietjagggger's orders, concealing as many weapons as possible, Dietjagger's men, an international lot, mostly Spanish-speaking, organized our ferrying ashore. Dietjagger peronally wanted to withdraw. I sensed he was afraid of more questions. He was not accustomed to being challenged, was used to corralling people too hungry and wasted to care what was next for them. His task was more servile than it first seemed. My defiance made him think about what he was doing, and that made him despondent, bitter, weak, also made him philosophical. I went up to him at the rail, not to thank him, more to get the measure of his mind. He must have thought I was going to revile him, because he turned defensively, said, "You will find life here is not different from what you have left. Nor from what I left. You are from the North? A Scandinavian, yes? I, too, from Prussia, East Germany, yes? My people are socialists. I am a nothing. We are the same. You will find death is different here. But we are not dead, and what does that matter? These islands are claimed by many nations. There is food, and some hope. It is much worse elsewhere, in the Pacific. Much worse. And I have heard that in the Caribbean the camps have revolted, and they are letting the epidemics do the police work."

"There has been no war," I said, repeating the English captain's curse of Gaunttown, "just a bloody shuffle."

"My friend," he said quietly, "if we are lucky, we will both be dead before it finishes. Good-bye."

Dietjagger climbed down into his boat, kept looking up at me as he was rowed back to the white cutter. He called to me in an angry voice. He recited what I took to be a German aphorism; I repeated it later to Lazarus, who translated it correctly. "That's Nietzsche, son of a Lutheran preacher. It means, 'Madness is rare in individuals, habitual to groups, parties, nations and ages.'" I did not like that aphorism then, think even less of it now. The Norse would have said it was the work of a bard-clatterer and an odd-tongue. It rolls out with self-conceit, says nothing neatly, craftily. It is sophistry. It speaks of the same misanthropic pridefulness as New Benthamism, pretending to describe mankind's

nature while actually it dismisses mankind with ornamental cynicism and calculated half-truth.

I have done a poor job narrating those four days from our
arrival off Elephant Island to our surrender at Aurora Bay. It
comes to me now not like a nightmare, rather like scenes too cluttered with pain and ignorance to recall with resonance. We were
deprived of security, food, *Candlemas Packet,* Toro Zulema, Wild
Drumrul, many more; and most of all, of information. All those
ships of wretches, where had they come from, what did they hope
for, what was their end? It is too easy to say, and yet it is all I
have to say, that they came from the Americas or Africa, that they
hoped for sanctuary, that they were imprisoned in those camps,
where they died, or escaped, or waited. And waited for what?
Their high dreams? Abigail's notion fetches me. I believe that every
man and woman, no matter what their station or luck, is granted
a right to high dreams. If one exercises such a right, it costs. One
pays with heart. That is not a bottomless account. It can be re-
plenished after depletion—the sun, some good food, a human
kindness—but it can also be exhausted, and after that sort of despair, death has no meaning I can think of. And I insist these high
dreams speak every language, come to the very old, the very criminal, the very young. High dreams are what linked *King James* with
Candlemas Packet's survivors, with the wretched we watched founder in the Scotia Sea, with those dark-faced creatures that killed
Toro Zulema, with Dietjagger and his brutal men, with the very
smallest of the wretches at Golgotha. And, yes, with the Brothers
themselves, who in their sorrowful, pious, otherworldly, and ineffectual ways not only had high dreams but also did their best,
all they knew, to convey their peculiar high dreams to us wretches.

There was one incident that stands out in my memory that
should help illustrate both my meaning of high dreams and the
anxiety I and mine suffered leaving *King James* and entering Golgotha. Lazarus and Violante's daughter, Cleo, then four years old,
had a doll, a stuffed sheep dog, made for her by Charmane Gaunt.
Cleo named the doll Goldie, for her own reasons. Because Cleo
slept with Goldie, it regularly flattened and lumped, so for stuff-
ing I would give her hair that I combed out of Iceberg. Cleo

learned to sew, made Goldie outfits, including a greatcoat like the sealskin ones we wore. As we proceeded across the Scotia Sea, she clothed Goldie in ever bulkier outfits. She also insisted Goldie share her rations, which Violante obliged in theory. Cleo once asked me to tell Goldie what our new home would be like. I told of a sheep ranch on a green plain, with a huge kitchen where Cleo could bake bread to feed all the hungry people, with a large sheep herd for Goldie to tend. Perhaps one can understand how it was harder to lie to Cleo than it was to commit *King James* to those seas, much more so in retrospect, because she believed me totally, believed that if Goldie was happy with her future, so was she.

The night after the attack, while we ferried ashore, I saw Cleo on deck. She had wrapped a discarded bandage around Goldie's flanks, carried the doll in a sling the way we transported our wounded. Cleo was crying, was talking to Goldie like a good nurse. She went ashore before me, and afterward I heard of her confrontation with the Brothers. They were small, strange men, fasted two of three days, maintained vows of silence. Lazarus thought them dumb fanatics, said that if they had talked, it would have been to deny life itself. I disagreed, not the least because when Cleo moved through the reception hut with her mother, she asked that Goldie be given an identification tag like hers, to wear around the neck. One of the Brothers—and we did not know then how to distinguish between them and their auxiliaries, the Little Brothers, a troublesome lot of convicts—obliged Cleo. This caused difficulty in the barracks. We were grouped in arbitrary units called families. There were no beds, just blankets, and the families were centered around stoves for heating and cooking. Each stove was allotted so many families, which meant so many adults, male and female, and so many children. Because Goldie had an identification tag, a number, he had a child's place and a child's ration. It was not until my people were transferred, from the barracks that were temporary quarters for the newly arrived, back into the main camp's longhouses, that the error was discovered and corrected. The Brothers were not rigidly scrupulous keepers, but space was a crucial problem. Goldie lost his tag. Cleo was undone by this, lost her courage, fell into mourning, said she would die along with Goldie. This was not entirely her invention, since Cleo had observed that when an internee died, his or her tag was removed.

That was how the Brothers kept what count they could for rations. Violante panicked at Cleo's mood, because the earliest indication of death in Golgotha was when a person stopped trying: the pulse rate plunged, the eyes glassed over, the movements became sluggish. Cleo did seem inconsolable, took Goldie to the altars in the longhouses (built crudely, yet in general much the same as those in the cathedral in Stockholm) to bless him before he died. Cleo told Violante she never felt warm as she slept, because Goldie was too cold to sleep with. And no matter how much Violante fed her (our diet was fish paste, rice, beans, sea weed pulp, supplemented with bird, whale, and seal meat), Cleo kept losing weight, musculature, alertness.

As January ended, and the weather worsened, Violante was sure Cleo was dying. We sang to her, argued with her, pretended to feed Goldie, held Goldie up close to the stoves; nothing worked. Otter Ransom saved Cleo. He explained to her in the singsong English he had developed that Goldie was ill because he was out of place. Goldie, he said, should not be with us in the longhouses, rather with the dogs in the service huts, where Iceberg and Beow and the rest of the brood would take better care of Goldie than we could. Cleo thought upon this, wept the more; but then, with small ceremony, she presented Goldie to Lazarus to take to Grim Fiddle to take to Iceberg and Beow. She gave instructions about Goldie's wounds, diet, personality. After that, Cleo slept without shudders, because, I argue, she had regained her high dreams for herself and Goldie.

Golgotha was not a place of skulls. It was deprived and badly built, bathed in fumes and continually trembling, but it was not a grave. The Norse would have called it a beggarly fen and made do with a camp of stones baked hot with huge bonfires. We lacked such luxuries, made do nonetheless, terrified of what winter would make of man-made caves. We learned as we burrowed. Because of the Brothers' vows of silence, we gathered Golgotha's history from the Little Brothers, the custodians of the camp. They were liars and thieves, all convicts transported to the South Shetlands for this duty. The most senior of them, Mosquite, had been there two years. What seemed reliable was that Golgotha was five years

old, built on the remains of a weather station, and that the first
wretches had arrived there in a derelict driven by storm and madness across the Scotia Sea. I now regard that tale as apocryphal,
because it was one I heard repeatedly from other camps, probably
only applying to the first of the camps.

The flood of wretches, however they arrived, overwhelmed
the weather station. The Little Brothers could not explain how
the Ice Cross had come to the South Shetlands, did not think the
Ice Cross required explanation: they were slaves, we were slaves,
what slave cares where his master comes from, or why? They could
also not explain why the Brothers of Perpetual Witness at Golgotha, another of the rogue orders that flourished in the Age of
Exile, had come to choose Livingston Island for their mission. I
note that the Brothers did differ profoundly from Father Saint
Stephen and *The Free Gift of God;* they were kind, muddled, long-
suffering servants of Jesus, mostly Europeans, and at that mostly
northern Europeans, Latvians and Poles. It is credible that the
original wretches were landed at Golgotha by a ship, or ships, not
unlike what *The Free Gift of God* had been before Father Saint
Stephen and his men were overwhelmed by the perversity of their
charity and collapsed to their worst nightmares. There was much
that was not credible about what the Little Brothers said: that the
Church was dispatching thousands of priests to convert the camps;
that some of the Little Brothers had been soldiers captured in a
war in the Caribbean (like Xique); that the camps were now being
stuffed with wretches deliberately transported to the South Shetlands by governments gripped by civil wars. There were whole
areas left blank then: how dependable the supply ships were; who
had provided the earth-moving and construction equipment in
the service huts; where we were to be resettled if and when someone arrived to hear our pleas.

For the year I was there, Golgotha never contained more than
five thousand internees. We were housed in several dozen crudely
linked longhouses carved into the bedrock. Someone had done
that earthmoving, and with powerful, sophisticated equipment; we
would never learn specifically who. The death rate at Golgotha
was hard to measure; my guess is that it was less than ten a day.
The perilously damp cold, caused by the excessive humidity offshore of Antarctica, did not kill outright. It weakened the strong,

ravaged the indigent. There were at least fifty Brothers, aping anonymity; and twice that many Little Brothers of all sorts: brutes, lechers, *campesinos*. Together they were not our jailers, needed our cooperation as much as we needed their access to the Ice Cross's haphazard authority.

Inside the camp, the society of mankind showed its commonplace vices, as Dietjagger meant when he said it was not different from what either of us had left behind. Food, heat, and space were the needs. Selfishness, despair, and accident were the threats. The Little Brothers were the chief transgressors, pathetic sneaks. They bought women, hoarded food, had firearms, which they brandished oafishly. There were beatings, hangings, persecutions, lawlessness. Barter was the currency. The Little Brothers, many internees, and my people, indulged usury. Rations were always inadequate, because one had to work or keep moving to fend off the damp, yet this caused one to need more food. The heating was makeshift. Those of us from colder climes, like my people, knew how to insulate, how to bear the rawness, and did what we could to teach those from equatorial climes how to survive. A few learned, most did not. We burned the coal we were given, also burned blubber we got by hunting, both of which filled the longhouses with thick smoke that blackened our skins. There are many tricks on the ice: bathing in urine, keeping one's extremities dry; it is a hard game, and can be won, if not indefinitely.

A significant mystery for us at first was that the barracks had an internal heat source. We determined that the heat must come from the mountain, that the camp must have been sited there because of the eruptions. I think this sort of heat is called geothermal. We called it godsend. Also there was hot steam in the cracks outside, along the ravine, on the glacier; and in two of the longhouses there was a pool of boiling hot water that proved a curse, for many had bathed in it, shedding their body oils, becoming defenseless to pneumonia. From what I know of science, and from what I later learned, it is probable that the eruptions had opened up heat seams throughout the South Shetlands; one of those seams, on Elephant Island, proved to contain very hard coal, which was mined by slaves for slaves.

My people came to flourish in Golgotha, if that word flourish is sufferable. We were homogeneous, tough-minded, and our

learning brought us to the fore of the community. Community! I
do not intend irony; my words fail to portray the extremes there,
make it seem as if Golgotha was like human culture everywhere.
That is a lie. I strain to get it right. We South Georgians took over
the work battalion, divided our labor between shoring up our space
and hunting outside, on the slopes of Livingston and in longboats.
This soon involved us in the camp's security. The Little Brothers
were morbid about the dark-faced creatures they called the *Hie-*
listos. There had been an attack every summer, they said; we
guessed that meant there had been a massacre every summer, the
Little Brothers quitting the defenses to hide within. We had the
few firearms we had secreted from the Ice Cross; the Little Brothers were armed, would not give up their guns to us. It was obvious
to us that what protected us was chance. I assumed that either the
Ice Cross kept those dark-faced creatures away, or nothing would.
Closer to the truth was that we were a small camp, unworthy of
regular raids, and that the *Hielistos* were crudely organized, that
they were us one step removed—condemned, inept, ice-cursed.
Lazarus solved that puzzle, saying *Hielistos* meant, figuratively, ice
brothers.

I have cause for presenting Golgotha as tolerable, fair-minded.
It was our shelter in the darkness. It was never as bad as it could
have been, as I know other camps were. There was more continuity than my people had enjoyed since leaving South Georgia.
Our wounded either died or lived; we starved and scratched—not
other than would have happened at sea. We were situated badly,
but arguably better than might have been ours on a strange coastline against chauvinists like the Patties, or against disease. The
Brothers tried to divide the supplies equitably, mercy to those more
in need, such as children or disabled. The Little Brothers cheated,
could be bribed. The quaking was incessant, with occasional cave-
ins, yet that was not worse than those huge seas. After the first
two months, my people had adapted ably, had mixed with the
internees guilefully. The other wretches thought Golgotha more
than a shelter; they held it dear, like a miracle. They were victims
of untold wars, catastrophes, outrages, had sunk to complete des-
titution. Lazarus, tattered and sharp-eyed, regarded them
shrewdly, at first seemed to proselytize among their leaders in
Spanish and Portuguese. He was actually propagandizing, and not

for what I supposed, a more subtle strategy. His health had returned to him—though not his equanimity, which none of us would ever find again—and with it a purpose as sure as the wind. I watched him come and go, a shadowy missionary in shadowy halls, and waited for an explanation, which came late summer.

"This is paradise for the beggars. They lay down and whimper like whipped beasts," he said, waving his hands in the direction of the corridor that led from our barracks to the axis of the camp. By then, we had bargained for the best available—the greatest good for the least number—and dispensed from our largesse for our own gain and for no other reason, assuredly not for decency.

I was in a low mood. It might have had to do with some rationing problems, but then, I was ever in bad temper at Golgotha. I looked at Lazarus and said as rudely as possible, "I should think this a fit place for your Plato."

"You mock me. You have changed. I have changed. For cause—time is a thing. It does bite, like the cold. Listen carefully. There is no need to panic here. We have a postrevolutionary society. We are caught in the stage between anarchy and tyranny. The Brothers are Mensheviks, not bad, whimpering fools, blind and dumb. They cooperate ignorantly with our antisocialist hooligans, Mosquite and his lot, and the imperialists, the Ice Cross. Would you understand me if I said that our call is to assume the idiom of the Bolsheviks? In France, it was the Directory that had to be crushed by Bonaparte."

"You are babbling. Don't give me any history lessons," I said.

"I suppose not," continued Lazarus, black eyes focused again on something very distant, suggestively supernatural. "You do see that Silva and the Brothers think they have established a society of the Sermon on the Mount? The Brothers look to mysticism, to the afterlife in their Heaven, for proof of their conduct. They tell the beggars to wait for Jesus, and they do, simpleminded millenarianists. See it, Grim, crumbs of bread and oceans of promises. There are elements of dissent. The conditions overwhelm. There are the *Hielistos*. I wonder if they have government—probably more tribal confederacy. These are the worst of man, subrational. Beasts, Grim, whipped and whipped. I wonder if the Ice Cross knows there is a point, a discernible moment, when you can't whip a beast any longer. He attacks, instinct to survive gone. That beast needs a master who loves him, frightens him, can use him."

I told Lazarus to stop condescending to me. He seemed to me almost hallucinatory—rambling, moving his hands in the air. That was a sign of hypothermia. I should have comforted him, did not. He was pitiless, I returned the same. I told him that I did not require his high learning to know that Golgotha was possible because all those fine republics of his had become mobs without consciences, let alone justice.

"Justice is what one argues it to be," he said. I relaxed. Lazarus was hysterical. He continued, "The law is human. It has limits and needs continual amendment. I know you, Grim Fiddle. You have absorbed that antirationalism preached by Mord Fiddle. Lutherans! You and your grandfather! Fantastic architects, dividing what is into the Kingdom of Heaven and the Kingdom of Earth, and then applying your double truths, man's law and God's law. You Lutherans continue the worst excesses of the Roman church you rejected. You turn your face from the Age of Reason that you helped birth. You do believe that reason is, what, 'the Devil's whore'? And your heroic stubbornness, your delirious pigheadedness, leads you to denounce law because it is not infallible, because it can be broken by the men who made it. You crave absolute certainty. Not finding it, you declare yourselves absolute judges. And how do you rationalize—excuse the word—justify your crudity and mistakes and crimes? You reach for the so-called mystery of divine forgiveness of sins, like some alchemist's trick. Whoosh! The just man is redeemed! And the unjust man? Why, he has always been damned, from before time! And that faith of yours, unshakable, since you declare it is a faith in God Most High, Lord God Almighty, that is beyond demonstration. It is, in fact, faith in your own pigheadedness. You Lutherans are born tyrants. But useful ones, constrained miraculously by your sense of dignity. Not a king of kings, but a tyrant of tyrants. Not even the Gospels you Protestants make a fetish of will make you balk. Admit it! That is why you, Grim, cannot abide the Brothers. You denounce the Sermon on the Mount as inappropriate law for this world, as defeatist, because it gets between you and your idea of your great judge, Lord God. Denounce, and condemn, and decry, and pound, that is your nature. And underneath that martial piety, still the

Viking, slashing at civilization because it is not certain enough for you. And if I come to you to ask for a government, a system to preserve justice without need of a tyrant, you sulk, or accuse, or bully. What would you have for us weak children? What would you not scowl at? What is enough for you, Grim?"

"Not this place, and not your republicanism. Lies," I said.

"Grim, Grim, my virtuous brother Grim," he said, his voice hoarse from the damp and his diatribe, "you know what you are? Grim Fiddle is a good man. Paradox does not shake him, not even the problem of evil. It does not move him. Grim Fiddle speaks the truth he sees and names the lies he sees, and then stands straight and proud. He is not a hypocrite. He is good."

"None of your tricks, speak plain," I said.

"I mean what I say. Remember what I say. Grim Fiddle is a good man who is becoming an angry one. You believe in justice, absolute justice—what you call righteousness, or godliness, or truthfulness. And you will enforce that belief, and your faith in yourself, enforce it absolutely. You might understand this: There is no more dangerous animal alive than a human being who is good, who knows what defeat is, and who determines to fight for dignity and then gets angry. Such a man is possessed, a moral monster, and limitless." Lazarus sighed at his own argument, waved his hands toward the corridors again, added, "This might be a paradise for them. I shall give them a god to fear."

"Lazarus," I said, "I am tired of you."

He did not smile, rubbed his scar, coughed deeply, stood up, and bowed. He bowed. As he did, I could see how badly his clothes hung. He was starving, and shaking from the damp, and beaten, and exhausted, yet he preferred philosophy to melancholy, unless those are the same on the ice.

The first of the great fall storms heaved ice floes up against Aurora Bay. The Ice Cross paid its last visit until spring in order to bring a freighter of goods and three small boats of wretches from Africa, dehydrated beings with cavernous mouths. The Brothers prayed over them, sang those rich hymns—not as dark as disengaged, they prostrate before their giant crucifixes. The Africans knew they were done, still begged charity. Decisions were permitted that were not Christian, were not just, however it is argued. There must be no excuse for our conduct, not even the winter that closed on Golgotha in screams. The winds off the continent can reach immeasurable, unimaginable strength, with the temperatures plunging well below zero, however calibrated, Centigrade or Fahrenheit. There are said to be worse places in the North, long settled by gritty Northmen. The peninsula of Antarctica and the offshore islands are not anathema to man; the temperature in the summer is above freezing, and the worst temperatures midwinter are far short of those in Finland, or the Yukon, or those of Russia north of the Arctic Circle, to give examples I have been given. I declare that the measurement of the severity of offshore Antarctica, the South Shetlands, does not signify; it is what such conditions do to the nature of a trapped and imprisoned human being. The howls get in the mind, the damp makes the heart feel like a lump of ice; and then there is the black of April.

What is the use of detailing that winter at Golgotha? We were daunted by natural and supernatural foes. Hard work and stern character kept the South Georgians sane, even as their rations were cut. My people had more than others; we knew what we were doing, stole shamelessly. We flopped about in the longhouses, told stories, sang with Longfaeroe, withered, began again, waiting, remembering. We also died. I thought I had emptied of tears. Now that I write of Golgotha, am again at Golgotha, I find I can still weep. I resist sentimentality; it encloses me. It was so sad. No matter how many plans we made, about repairing *King James* in the spring, about training more of the wretches as hunters, another meaningless death dragged us down. I doubt that I can communicate what the blackness of the Antarctic winter does to the will. We South Georgians knew what only a glimpse of the sun winter-long does to resolve, and the sealers had experienced the ice continent itself. None of our experiences were enough. We were always tired, always hungry, always afraid. We did not want to die. We each in our own way, and as God-fearing folk, held to what we most desired. I have spoken of high dreams. There is another phenomenon that comes with the long night of the south. One remembers everything one has ever done, seen, heard, dreamed of, tasted, recalls it all with what seems exactitude. The memories come tumbling up while one works, idles, or dozes. One can be conversing with another, and just as one tries to make a point, a memory of a conversation from long before wells up and overwhelms, and one drifts. For me, my memories of Abigail were bliss and torment, the same of Peregrine, Israel—all my confusions, all my failures, tumbled right before me. On the ice, everyone hears ghosts, everyone meets the dead, and to see a man or woman talking to nothingness is not to see madness. That can be a purgative; it can also be extreme peril. We had to tie lines to those displaying excessive perceptual difficulties, in order to keep them from wandering away; had to keep knives and even stones from those who started talking about homicide or suicide. And those who refused to get up, became lethargic and glassy-eyed, we had to pull to alert, shake them, push and shout, make them care. There is one weapon against such despondency that works as long as one has it to give. One must love. One must hold the afflicted, sing to them, tell them they are needed and blessed. That is what mankind has to fight the ice, to fight abandonment and cruelty and defeat. My mother first said it, and I saw the truth of it. "As long as you are loved," she said that night of Sly-Eyes's party, "you are safe from their shame."

It was awful to live, is awful to relate. I had intended to tell of Jane and Violante and Magda, how they kept the children alert with stories from the Bible and the Apocrypha, especially Daniel, Ruth, and David. I cannot. It hurts to think of their fight, one less child each week, and how we almost lost Jane to her nightmares when one of the smallest children succumbed and she could not believe it. Longfaeroe sang and loved; we all did. How many times must I say that whatever we were or did or hoped for, nothing was enough.

And hatred: it came to that for me, and for many more. There is a point when love seems to fail, and one turns to the shame of hatred. We knew our need of God, could not abide that Heaven was all that was left us; we were sorrowful, found no consolation in grains of rice and frostbite; we tried to be gentle, had only frozen earth to die upon, and were obliged to steal from the weak to survive; we were hungry, could not fill our bellies with hope; we tried to show mercy to those more wretched, knew no mercy for ourselves; we struggled to keep our hearts pure, yet saw nothing but ghosts and corpses and the icicles on the walls; we tried to keep peace among the internees and in our own hearts, had to confront suicide and murder, hangings and strangulations commonplace; we were condemned and persecuted because we had stood for right on South Georgia, and what was the use of knowing the Kingdom of Heaven would be ours when the Kingdom of Ice tortured us because we would not quit?

We stood and fought with human love for eleven months. I am angry now for the remembering of it; I feel as I write that I am reexperiencing the same generation of fury that I suffered then. I should recount more of the courage of my South Georgians and the Brothers, and even the Little Brothers, at Golgotha. I shall not. What would it serve to say that they were brave, that they were good and humble and weak and bitter? Would it give them peace? Would it ease my frustration with my failure to find worth in what happened there? Lazarus meant to mock me when he said that I decried the Sermon on the Mount as inappropriate for this world. Perhaps I did, and do; perhaps he did know my heart, and his own. I confess my blindness to such wisdom then, have not paraphrased it idly. Yes, I know that there is no justification for making war on others; and yes, I know that vengeance is not mine to take or vouchsafe; and yes, I know that the yearning for freedom is common to all men and women, regardless of station, and no specific warrant, no detailed petition for redress, can usurp the majesty of those who preach love, forgiveness, and patience for divine justice. I do not balk, nevertheless, for what I and mine wanted were some food, some warmth, some release. We were slaves. We were less than slaves, rewarded for our perseverance by slow death. No one man, no one group of the nations of men, was murdering us. We died for no reason. Does that have meaning, to say that needful, sorrowful, gentle, hungry, merciful, pure-at-heart, persecuted, righteous, faithful and godly human beings can perish for no reason at all? I will not accept that, will not accept on this earth or in Heaven or in Hell that I was born, my loved ones were born, those wretches were born, to be murdered and buried so that we could find happiness in afterlife. I will also not accept that we should have been content to swallow charity. They, all the unnamable theys, took our decency and hope and forced on us the gruel of charity. In my time, I have learned that a man or woman upon whom such an exchange is forced will fall, and fall most savagely, to revenge.

Longfaeroe did sing, "O praise Jehovah!" If he had been with us at Golgotha, Wild Drumrul would have sung, "Allah is merciful and compassionate!" I believed it, for God created a world where men can know the renaissance of the return of the sun. And with the sun, my remnant at Golgotha was out again on the ice, hunting and planning. Germanicus and Half-Red Harrah threw themselves onto *King James*, finding her battered but not wrecked by the winter's ice. The sealers showed us how to shed the winter's weariness, and but for the shaking of the volcanoes I think Christmas Muir and his mates would have been joyous with the spring. The first supply ship arrived in convoy with Ice Cross cutters near my twenty-ninth birthday. There was green on the slopes; and Germanicus took a whale that was so disoriented by the quaking that it did not run on him. By then, my people had moved to the leadership of Golgotha, not without the jealousy of the Little Brothers, a rift that required Lazarus's dialectical skills. Lazarus did manage to secure a document from Brother Silva that permitted me to speak for the camp alongside of the Little Brothers' gang-leaders, Mosquite and Hardava. I was not elaborate to the Ice Cross commander, telling him through my translator so much: "Hosannah!"—save us. The Ice Cross officer was a shrewd, French-speaking African, mixed blood, a black marketeer certainly, named Ariadne, whose replies were always prefaced by *"Quel cauchemar!"* ("What a nightmare!"). In bad Spanish, Ariadne said that we best save ourselves, and not only from hunger but also from the *capitanes de los Hielistos*. That was the first I heard of the infamous Jaguaquara, and more, learning enough to guess that the Ice Cross was in jeopardy. So far from a persecutor, the Ice Cross thought itself condemned to combat against the omnipresent outlaw wretches. Ariadne whined, said that the mountains above us were alive with *Hielistos*, that the white cutters were being overwhelmed in the early battles of the thaw. I have much to say on this, and more accurately; it must suffice here to say that I realized our work on *King James* could be short-lived. Our ark was an invitation to plunder. Ariadne recommended we burn her.

I shared Ariadne's fears with Lazarus and Germanicus, and two tough-minded internees we had taken into our confidence, the Brazilian whaler Cavalobranco and a Russian refugee befriended by Otter Ransom, from eastern Africa—a giant called Gleb the Hewer. Lazarus counseled me to order the work on *King James* continued, and that I should have my sealers formulate a plan to take over one of the supply ships for escape. Germanicus and the other military men were incredulous at the thought of revolt, said it would be suicide: we were mostly unarmed, were starved to where we only had energy to hunt, could not match the Ice Cross's guns. Yet I was persuaded, and so Lazarus prevailed, to surprising ends. As Lazarus intended, the fantasy of escape did hearten my people and the other wretches at Golgotha who had come to depend upon us. The rumors became wild and ebullient; however, with them, perversely, came conflict over who would go, who would be left behind. Lazarus assured me that it was worth the trouble, that we had to make them stronger than they were. There were fights, suspicious hangings, a sudden conversion of hundreds to the Brothers' otherworldly futility. This is human nature, I understand now. As contrived and misconceived as our ambitions were, they were hopeful; as with bread, we gorged on them. Also as with bread, some hoarded, others gave away what was not truly theirs, and then succumbed.

My wolves determined my work at Golgotha. I was the best informed at how to handle sled teams, and so organized a transportation system over the glacier to the rookeries where my hunters ventured. It is also true that my wolves determined my fate. This sort of causality is very Norse. It reaches back to that burning cold night at the King's castle, when Earle Littlejohn placed two pups in my arms, and, in that, seems to present an uninterrupted line over twelve years, leading me from the discovery of my father's heart's desire to the discovery of my grandfather's heart's desire, and mine.

I had not given up Grandfather. It was that I no longer felt free to desert my people as I would have at Mead's Kiss. That dynamo of flesh had enclosed me. They gave me power and I feasted on their obedience, and more, since Lazarus saw to it that the whole of Golgotha knew the magical reach of Grim Fiddle. I was doubly captured, believed I could not turn my back on them. I did covet a secret program. My guess was that Grandfather, whom I wholeheartedly believed alive, as the albatross had implied, was in one of the camps on Greenwich Island. I had made investigation of the possibility with Mosquite, and challenged Ariadne if there were lists of the camp's internees. He did not laugh at me, *"Quel cauchemar!"* He said that he had come to the South Shetlands in search of his brother's family, had found them, dead. He also astounded me by saying that there actually was a resettlement effort, that Golgotha was scheduled that summer for assessment and transportation. He said that his new commander-in-chief had ordered the resettlement program reinitiated in order to keep the camps in line. I asked him if there was rebellion in the camps. Ariadne shook his head. He said there was the warlord of the *Hielistos,* Jaguaquara. That was left mysterious. And yes, yes, there was one more revelation. It comes to me now as I think of myself on the quay before that monolithic wall of rock, Ariadne and his men ferrying new wretches ashore. Ariadne was trying to explain in bad Spanish why it was that the resettlement program could be delayed. He gave me the name of the new Ice Cross commander-in-chief; he said, "Lykantropovin first means to bend the *Hielistos,* and only then turn to the camps."

(The Norse said, all names are names. I do not challenge the epigram, only addend that some names are warnings: Lykantropovin, the face of the wolf.)

Golgotha had a dozen huskies from the original supply by the Ice Cross. I added Iceberg and her large brood, took on apprentice dog-handlers, notably Gleb the Hewer, who had run dogs in the Ukraine as a boy. We built sleds from ship's wreckage, fashioned cargo runs up the glacier, north and southwest, to the best rookeries.

It was on one of those sled runs, after the new year, that I should have discovered a clue to my heart's desire, did not. There had been odd happenstance the day before on the route to the sea leopards on the southern shore. One of our men was missing. I told Germanicus to increase sentries on the near shore of Aurora Bay. Gleb the Hewer went up, sent back word that I should come for a look. I mistakenly let Mosquite know I was going out.

He had come both to despise and rely upon my authority over the internees, and insisted one of his thugs accompany me as bodyguard. He sent the little one we called Pistole, a murderer and suspected torturer, who was frightened of me and did not concern me. I took one sled and four men, and after some delays due to slides, located Gleb the Hewer, sent his team back, and continued toward the rookery, where there was a gang of my sealers under Ugly Leghorn scrambling the beach of a nearly-played-out hunting ground.

It was a turbulent, ashen day, the sunlight turning the sea fog orange, the wind offshore, white caps covering the Bransfield Strait. My lead dog kept veering from the track, disturbed by the quaking. Iceberg stayed ahead with her huge son, Beow, as scouts. The mountain above us was ice-barren from the slides to about three hundred feet, was also dotted with blue-eyed cormorants and Cape pigeons, an occasional fulamar, nesting there out of the wind. Ahead of us and up were circling skuas—the vultures of Antarctica, for they are predatory hawks, will attack men, in my experience are associated with battles on the ice. The Ice Cross said when one saw a skua, one saw the eyes of the *Hielistos*.

We were just a mile short of the beach, at the edge of the glacier, when we heard Iceberg let out a howl. We had poor visibility, went to the defensive. My men were armed with harpoons and knives. Pistole had an automatic weapon. Gleb the Hewer and I ran up, Pistole followed at a distance. We found Iceberg and Beow standing legs firm in the gravel, heads back, yapping like talking, eyes searching the face of the mountain. Before them, nearly buried in a small crevasse of an ice formation, were two corpses—or what was left, arms and legs hacked off. I shall explain later, but that was the way *Hielistos*—some *Hielistos*—killed. The dead were not from our camp. Pistole panicked, "Mother of God! They come! Mother of God!" And then he fled.

"*Ya nee guveroo, comrade, no ploka, ochen ploka,*" said Gleb the Hewer, meaning that he knew this was bad. Beow started up the mountain; Iceberg barked him to halt, then snapped at me purposefully. I stood in the direction of a shelf overhead, took my harpoon and drove it into the ice. I had some notion I could bargain with them. I listened, heard the wind, the sea, the squawking skuas, and nothing else. Gleb the Hewer breathed hard. It is true that one can smell men in the Antarctica; one's own smell is impossible, but a gang of men is a wrenching odor. He shook his head, pointed down to the rookery, meaning we had to get our men in. I waved him to wait, squinted as hard as I could up the pass. The Ice Cross also said if you can see them, they are not *Hielistos.*

Iceberg growled at me. I was wrong not to obey her. I had followed less tangible premonitions. I knew my error when I got back to the team and Pistole commanded us at gunpoint to return to the camps. We left the hunters to their ends.

That evening, Golgotha was awash with the frenzy of doom. Pistole had told Mosquite he had seen *Hielistos,* a lie that sent the Little Brothers into their nightmares. They clattered on the radio for the Ice Cross. I held my own council, and decided for caution. We pleaded with Mosquite for firearms. There was a riot in the most desperate part of the camp—the new arrivals and a party of Brazilians—and the Little Brothers fired into the barracks. Golgotha's population was reduced to less than three thousand after the winter's losses, and two thirds of these were children and the dying. At most, I had two hundred able-bodied men and women as fighters. Mosquite sent a message to me to get my best people away from the camp and not to return until after the attack. He said the *Hielistos* wanted food, weapons, recruits, and would not pursue us once they got what they wanted from the camp. Then he and his brethren retreated within the camp, to caves where I presumed they had always retreated when the *Hielistos* came. Germanicus and Motherwell, with Cavalobranco's men, did what they could to set our defenses. There were so many approaches, we decided to defend the axis of the camp and risk sorties on our flanks. Germanicus took care to hide Jane and the children within as best he could. We pulled in our sentries from *King James.* It was a long night of defeated decisions. I remained aloof from the particulars, felt increasingly that I was making, had made, a profound miscalculation—that out there on the glacier I had missed my opportunity. I believed myself responsible for our peril. When I had looked up the face of the mountain, I had felt eyes on me, my own eyes.

The Ice Cross did not answer our pleas; but then, this was not of itself significant, because radio transmission in the Antarctic is haphazard. The weather worsened as the sun moved toward the horizon, long blue shadows across Aurora Bay. We prayed for a gusting snowstorm to pick up the sea and provide us a natural redoubt. The wind did increase, not enough, and as I made my rounds along the trench, I heard the sealers giving instructions to each other like eulogies. There was one rumor about the *Hielistos* that racked even them: that they ate the dead.

The waiting was of course the worst of it. I did not want to talk with Lazarus, or Longfaeroe, and felt too black to try to bolster Germanicus in his vigilance. I walked away from all of them, my two bodyguards trailing me, and made my way down through the tunnels to the service hut. I wanted to be with my friends, my wolves.

I meant to sit with Iceberg and her brood until the alarm was sounded. The kennel was a long, low-slung structure, with no more than a four-foot clearance, located a quarter mile down the peninsula from the camp entrance. There were wretches hiding even there, and I had my bodyguards clear the place, told them to wait outside for me. Grim Fiddle was absolute at Golgotha. He showed no mercy. He gave no charity except for self-interest. My face was fit for my audience, wolves with their blood up, howling and snapping. They were arranged in crisscrossing lines, tethered on short ropes to stakes in order to keep them from each other. I moved in a crouch along the empty stakes. I waved my harpoon at them, inciting them to wilder fits. I yelled nonsense at them. Grim Fiddle preached fury to his wolves. Then I tired of my taunting sport and turned to Iceberg, demanded to know if she remembered her sister. I did ask, was Goldberg on the ice? Was Goldberg with Mord Fiddle? She snapped, yanked at her chain, unsentimental. I thought, the last living thing to link me with my childhood, my blood kin, and it was an animal slipped to the beast. She wanted release; they all did, maddened at being chained from their instinct to run. We men might be confounded by threat, might grasp at vainglory. My wolves knew murder was at the door.

The alarm came in course, with distant cannon-fire. A runner came down to me, and my guards alerted me that Germanicus needed me up top, that *King James* was cut adrift and afire. In my disgust I shouted at them, "There is no ark, no ark either, no ark! Grandfather, hear me now, no ark to be had!" It is difficult to recreate the inanity of my self-pity. One might think that after so many instances of danger in twelve years in darkness, Grim Fiddle would have been girded before such catastrophe, would have achieved some tolerance of the comedy. He was, in fact, flat weary with bitterness, pressed flat by the weight of his pretension to rule, not serve, to rule the wretched. I looked at those three men, wasted, bent, taking their power from mine. I thought, I despise you hopeless creatures. I realize now my feeling was worse, self-hatred. I told them to get on, that I would follow. I turned to issue some pompous last testimony to my wolves, thought again. I pried open the outside hatch with my harpoon, moved down the lines with my knife, and cut them free. They sprinted for the ice. When I came to Iceberg, I thought upon killing her—all the sort of mercy there seemed left to me—instead cut her line and said good-bye.

Iceberg had more heart than Grim Fiddle—part beast, yes, but also part of my luck. It so happened that her instinct to survive was in league with her desire to regain her own blood kin; and it so happened that her high dreams were coincident with mine. She went to the hatch with Beow, halted, came back at me, snapping and pleading. That was a Norse wolf with purpose. She commanded me. I studied the hatch, also the tunnel back to Germanicus. It is truth that my bloodlust was up with hers, so was my self-serving fear, and that when I should have most held to my responsibility to my people, I quit them, and reason, for inspiration, or portent, or plain egotism. Grim Fiddle was cursed at Port Stanley; Grim Fiddle was reluctant on South Georgia; Grim Fiddle was rash on *King James;* Grim Fiddle was cowed at Golgotha.

And what use is there to explore my cowardice? I ran with the pack. I fled to my destiny in my own way. Did I hear Goldberg? I did not. Did I have a plan to get to Greenwich Island and find Grandfather? I did not. I was a low-minded coward, and nothing more. I got outside on the escarpment and fled down to the windward shore of the peninsula. The wind from the north off the Scotia Sea was whipping ice into the air; it was like a snowstorm with overlarge flakes swirling into the crevasses and into my eyes. The wolves had scattered right and left, some silhouetted atop high ground. The barking and screams told me the *Hielistos* were discovered, though I could not see them. I made my way deliberately up the closest ridgeback to look down upon the waterline on the Bransfield Strait. There were several small cutters beached in concert, fires lit before them, small figures scampering in concert. This gave me cause to reconsider the assumption that the *Hielistos* were disorganized pirates without tactics or discipline. Out in the Strait there was an imminent sea battle. Two white cutters were running through the fogbank, coming about to avoid a jade-colored berg. Our rescuers had come after all, and what awaited them was a squadron of open boats filled with *Hielistos,* the sunrise and snow-gale at their backs. Golgotha had been bait. This was the jaw closing. Was there rebellion? There was Jaguaquara.

I wanted to see the face of my enemy. I screamed down at them, taunted them in all my languages—polylingual blasphemer. I pranced along the ridgeback, cursing the wretched of the earth. I found a suiting hollow, my back against a boulder formation, the ground slick with lichens and bird droppings. The ground mist made my landscape seem a cloud. I thundered and howled, and when my voice cracked with strain, I leaned back and waited. I did not want to die. Why had I come out here? The answer was sad—because I thought myself special and was rewarded for my election with meaninglessness. I was undone by my own pride, had little strength to lift my harpoon. I thought—how queer it is that one thinks one sees clearly when in such hysteria—that it was fitting judgment upon Grim Fiddle that he would not end as either hero or berserker, instead as weakling, weeper, deserter, betrayer. They started throwing rocks, tumbled from their holes, filthy creatures without firearms, come to stone a deceived man. I saw the humor, did not laugh. Nothing was to be left me, not even the boast that I had freed slavish beasts, for then a wolf flung itself off an incline and bounded to my side. It was Beow, the tip of a spear in his flank—brave Beow come to stand with a shirker. And when they finally closed, from all sides, Beow fought herowell and died for it, and I fought miserably and did not. I lost my harpoon in one, my knife in another, my dignity with my terror. I have the memory that before I went down, I had one before me, and ripped at its face, to find the eyes of a child, or woman. I saw my enemy and was shamed as I was pummeled still.

I did not lose my wits, or perhaps I did and only have the

delusion of being dragged down to the beach, helpless, not unlike the sensation I had the night at the King's castle. I believed that I deserved whatever end imaginable. I believed Golgotha overrun. I was thrown facedown in a heap before one of the bonfires. They did not bind me, kept me down by holding harpoons against my back, at the nape of my neck. I could taste my blood, was restrained from wiping clear my vision. There were *Hielistos* very close by, excited muttering either in celebration or anticipation. I vomited soon after, could not breathe well with cracked ribs. The fire baked one arm, the wind threw icy spray up to numb my legs. What I try to convey is that I felt adrift in a sea of endings, in shock certainly, also in pity. I pitied Grim Fiddle, not because he had dishonored himself, but because he was stupid. The harpoon was pushed farther into my nape, and the pain cleared my thoughts. I could not recall a single prayer of forgiveness. I heard men and authority. It felt endless waiting, might have only been moments since I was captured. There was a command in Spanish, and another in German. The circle about me opened. From the end of the earth I heard that voice, like far thunder, much reduced, wavering. He told them to get me up. They could not, only rolled me over. I could not see him clearly. I said, "Is it true, Grandfather?" At least, that is my memory. I might have thought this, and I am not sure now what I meant by it. He made no reply, though there was one, the yelping of a white wolf and a gold wolf spinning in aged play amid attendants and beside an elaborately fashioned sled, upon which, in the splendor of a Norse outlaw, lay Mord Fiddle, white beard, too white face, blue eyes.

My Queen

The *Hielistos* called Grandfather *Barbablanca*—White-beard. They spoke in fear. Grandfather was not in command of the *Hielistos'* attack at Golgotha, was nevertheless a powerful supernumerary. The *capitan de los Hielistos* was a South American named Iacovella, an able soldier despite his reputation as the Butcher of Deception Island, a man I would later enlist in my leap to warlord at Anvers Island, and would still later abandon to his enemies among the *Hielistos*. That day at Golgothá, Iacovella spared me and my South Georgians. He had come this time neither for food nor recruits, rather to slaughter the Ice Cross, and once that was accomplished—two white cutters in flames, their crews cut up for skuas, fish, men—Iacovella withdrew his forces under the cover of a big storm from the north. Grandfather remained at Golgotha with his four-dozen bodyguards, and with a surprise—Wild Drumrul (several toes and fingers gone, but sound for his year in captivity), now promoted to second officer on the rebuilt and heavily armed *Angel of Death,* Grandfather's stout wavecutter on the ice.

There was no peace for me in the delivery of Golgotha. Grandfather was dying. We carried him inside the camp, laid him out in one of the barracks. The Little Brothers were no more threat; with the *Hielistos'* help I had them disarmed and chained. Grandfather's *Hielistos* were eager to obey me. They regarded me with an awe that derived from their veneration of Grandfather; also, they were very afraid for the life of their protector, *Barbablanca*. Their first officer, a Russian whaler who called himself Kuressaare, begged us to save Grandfather. He explained in exaggerated detail what peril awaited *Angel of Death* if it were to return without *Barbablanca* to the *Hielistos'* fortress at Anvers Island, which I knew roughly to be in the Palmer archipelago, several days sail across the Bransfield Strait. His men echoed his woes to my sealers, groaned of Jaguaquara and figures unknown to me such as Fives O'Birne, Hector the Fat.

Grandfather spoke briefly before he collapsed from exhaustion. He assured me there would be time later for that worry. He said Lord God had returned me to him, and he must pray his thanksgiving in solitude. He said it was his time to die: I was not to leave him; I was not to disagree; I was not to let them keep him alive with medicines. He was very reduced, a waste of a man, bones broken and badly healed, lips, ears, nose, and eyelids all scar tissue. He could not walk, and we were never able to feed him more than broth. Annabel Donne studied him as he slept and said he was a miracle. Kuressaare stood guard with Goldberg; he told me *Barbablanca*'s appearance should not fool us: *Barbablanca* always got up to take his revenge.

That first night, I sat by Grandfather as he slept, held his hand, knew that Kuressaare was wrong: Mord Fiddle would never get up. Germanicus and some of the other senior sealers came in, more to get a close look at Grandfather than to consult with me. The whole camp soon learned that a legend was among us—Lazarus's doing, probably, though Grandfather's *Hielistos* were quick to boast. Later, Longfaeroe approached, asking if he might offer his thanks for our survival. As he sang his psalms, Grandfather appeared to smile in his sleep. With his eyes closed, he was a corpse. By morning, however, almost as Kuressaare had said, Grandfather was awake, and if not sanguine, certainly returned to an extraordinary measure of resolve. He waited for my lead. I took it, asking one question, "Are they all dead?"

At that, he began to talk, of Heaven and Hell, of the war of shadows and the "whore of Babylon," and most completely of Satan's Seat and "Satan's Own." He was half a month talking and dying. In that time, Grandfather's metaphors fell upon me, and I suffered their burden, first the confusion of them and finally the revelation in them. In pursuit of Grim Fiddle, Grandfather had walked through the darkness, and he survived just long enough to tell the tale.

And yet, if I were to report straight out what Grandfather told me at Golgotha—and I remember it as acutely as the cold— it would undermine my purpose. I do not want this account to become so heaped with mystery that the truth is lost. I must first speak clearly of the ice camps. And so I defer briefly from Grandfather's tale. Grim Fiddle has his own mind.

□

I cannot conceive how, at this late date, any decent man or woman cannot know something of the ice camps. I also worry that such selective ignorance might still be possible, even fashionable, as I was told was the case of crimes against humanity in both my father's and grandfather's times. Israel once told me that the larger the crime, the more likely it is to be argued to have been an inevitability, the more readily it is to be recalled and recorded not as outrage but as fate. I remember how Israel said it, speaking of his people, the Jews, "Kill ten, it's murder. Make ten thousand vanish in the night, it's a phenomenon. Obliterate a million, it's the Devil's work. Remind them of what's been done, you're called a conspirator, or worse, a storyteller."

Grim Fiddle is prepared to be disregarded as a conspirator, alone here in his conceit, the last whisperer of Lazarus's shattered republic of ice. More, Grim Fiddle is prepared to be dismissed as a storyteller, an odd-tongue clatterer, like the priests who copied and recopied the saving history of the Hebrews, changing a gang of forty outlaws into an army of hosts doing the Lord's work. I have not exaggerated the ice camps. My error is more troublesome than hyperbole; in order not to degrade the truth, I am underestimating the horror of the camps, reluctant to speculate about the politics and catastrophes that delivered up the wretched to the South Shetlands. It seems fair to say that the camps were not a cause, only a product of untold crimes committed by people on every continent. It is my presumption that my experiences in Sweden, on the Atlantic, on the Falklands and South Georgia, illustrate the whole that I cannot know whereof. This is my testament, and I leave it to others to re-create theirs that carried them, like me and mine, into the Antarctic Circle.

At this point, what I have to say of the South must intersect with facts and testimonies that should be, must be, available in the modern world about the camps, their generation, their administration, their conclusion. When I mention Elephant Island and Anvers Island, it cannot be the first time they are portrayed in writing, nor can my passing reference to the pit of Clarence West and the hell of Anvers be novel. And yet, I cannot assume, and I certainly cannot be sure, how much detail has been arranged to someone else's needs. I believe it is imperative, then, that I characterize the camps in my own way, for my own purposes. I choose not to begin with how many hundreds of thousands drowned, starved, disappeared, because I know such a report is not credible on the page, and because it is off my point: I want to explain how the camps were for us inside them, and why it was possible for me and mine to do as we did. Therefore, I choose to begin with an explanation of how I have come to understand the camps. I have been helped by my Norse learning, and must pause to render quickly Norse cosmology in order to explicate my mind's picture of the ice camps. If this is mythologizing, then at least it is confessed, and it is mine. It comforts me.

The ancient Norse spoke of all that existed divided into three realms: Asgard, Midgard, and Niflheim. One should think of them arranged like cartwheels, atop each other, spinning beneath and overshadowed by the timeless ash tree, Yggdrasil. This is the guardian tree, the tree of life, with roots reaching into the three realms. Yggdrasil is indestructible, is said will survive the final cataclysm, Ragnarok. This notion did not make sense to me until one day, when I was twelve years old, I was daydreaming beneath a great old ash tree at Vexbeggar as a thundercloud hurtled from the Baltic. I watched the limbs bend in the gusts, listened to the dance of the leaves and the first big drops popping against the canopy, realized there were many birds and insects above me sheltering like me from the blow. I understood the majesty of Yggdrasil; of course it would survive me, and of course its roots held all that existed together.

Asgard was the home of the gods. It contained subdivisions, such as Valhalla, the hall of the slain heroes; Vanaheim, home of the fertility goddesses like Frigg the Queen; and Alfheim, home of the light elves who were magical goldsmiths. Asgard's first citizens were the warrior gods, like Odin the Terrible-One, or Thor the Dim-Witted and Righteous. The Norse celebrated more than worshiped Asgard, for it was regarded as a place of epic folly: starvation and death were unknown, though pain and melancholy possible. I have always thought Asgard simpleminded and too often trivial, but that is Grim Fiddle's mean way.

More significant for me is Midgard, the middle earth, home of mortal mankind. Here also lived the giants at Jotunheim, and the dark elves and dwarfs in caves and burrows. One traveled from Asgard to Midgard over Bifrost, the trembling road. Midgard was surrounded by a vast, forbidding ocean containing the monster Jormungand, who was so long he could encircle the realm to bite his own tail. Midgard was the paramount battleground, where man struggled against nature. The Norse were as sentimental as they were superstitious, and studied the tales of Midgard to find a balance between their mysticism and their fatalism. In Midgard, one discovered answers: What is brave? What is defeat? What is truth? Disease and death were commonplace, fearlessness was regarded better than a faint heart for any man who put his nose out of doors, and not even the gods could change fate there, or guarantee happiness, kindness, decency.

Niflheim was the home of the dead. It was a place of bitterness, unending night, untellable cold. The Norse made only a slight distinction between the honorable dead and the wicked dead. The Norse said, "Dead is dead." Niflheim was ruled by a pathetically hideous female, half black and half white, named Hel, daughter of treacherous Loki the Shape-Changer; she lived in a mansion, Eljundir, near the rock Drop to Destruction.

I repeat: I have paused to explain Norse cosmology because my knowledge of such has helped me to solve what I believe was the largest mystery of the camps: What was their place and meaning in the world? I am a poor thinker. I cannot sustain a philosophical discourse. I need pictures of the world to help me remember it. My intention here is to present a model that I can hold in my mind's eye as to how all that existed in the Age of Exile came to act upon me and mine at Golgotha and afterward. I did not see it this way at the time. I was blinded by fear and vengeance. I see now it was how all that existed weighed upon me. This is Grim Fiddle's cosmology of those days. And if I borrow too heavily, and distort too broadly, so be it. It feels natural for me to have come to think of Antarctica in terms of my Norse ways: The North interprets the South.

□

At the beginning of the twenty-first century, all that existed still divided into three realms. The proportions had altered radically since first my Norse ancestors daydreamed beneath the grand ash tree of life, Yggdrasil. Asgard, still the home of the gods, had grown to encompass all the shimmering towers of Babel ruled by latter-day magic, called logical positivism. The gods had faces and voices: American, European, Asian, African, the masters and mistresses of a bountiful harvest. Their politics did not signify, capitalist to socialist to nihilism; their religion did not signify, humanism to mysticism to atheism. There was no single Odin, instead a thousand thousand of terrible ones, fickle, compassionless, one eye for more of the same. There was no single Frigg, instead millions of well-fed, well-loved, and enriched queens. Charity Bentham and Cleopatra had been such Friggs, as Cesare Furore had been such an Odin, and all three had descended from Asgard to tamper with and then destroy my family. This modern Asgard was not simpleminded, was, rather, boundlessly avaricious, profoundly charitable. Few died violently. Starvation and disease were obsolete. The gods followed the sun. It was the realm of the New Benthamites, measuring their pleasure and pain units to determine which hall of gods should be most pleased, where the feast should be held next. The halls were heaped with largesse, which the gods dispensed with sly intent. The hedonic calculus was cunning. Asgard practiced a benevolence that the New Benthamites called the Charity Factor. The scales were weighed meanly. In order to safeguard their feasts, the gods dispatched armies of charity to minister to those shunned from the hearthtable by birth, by chance, and by murder. It was at such a charitable moment that Asgard dispatched the Ice Cross, over the trembling roadway of the Atlantic. When *Angel of Death* crossed Bifrost, there was no returning.

Midgard, still the realm of mortal mankind, had shrunk to the fens and ditches and backwaters of desperation. There, clinging to rocks like South Georgia, mankind suffered and died, caught between the charitable whims of the gods and the violence of nature. And when man was backed up against the uncrossable barrier of the sea, he struck out ineptly against the sea monster Jormungand, now made of steel and spitting fire. The continent upon which the fen was located did not signify, a hovel is a hovel, whether Asian or African or American. The skin-colors and regrets did not signify, lost is lost. There were still monsters and giants. There were still dark elves and dwarfs cowering in the damp caves of places like the South Shetlands.

In this way the ice camps were the very edge of Midgard, the last chance of the last remnant. We were dark elves in the camps— our skins turned black from burning seal and whale oil; and it was generally so that only the smallest, most dwarflike, survived the conditions. Cast out of Asgard, or in flight from giants doing the bidding of the gods, or simply deprived of sense by accident, most of the wretches of Midgard were eaten by metallic Jormungand. The few who escaped were swept across, or sent across, the Southern Ocean to crash against the ice.

Israel always joked that the gods keep several sets of books. I understand the sharpness of his wit more completely here, because this must explain why it is impossible for me, without resources, to provide details of how many wretches arrived in the camps each week, how many died each day, how much was required to feed them, or starve them. I suppose, though, that it is probably impossible for anyone, even back in Asgard, to reconstruct a wholly accurate scheme of the camps. I have mentioned some of the Ice Cross's patrons. I caution that the variety of the camps could be misleading. They tended to be either those administered directly by the Ice Cross or those administered by religious societies, such as Golgotha. Because the Ice Cross was international, there were European camps, five huge camps run by South Americans, at least one run by South Africans, perhaps a half dozen overlorded by North Americans. Also, there were small camps administered by international treaty organizations, and several with ties to socialist blocs. Then there were the Roman Catholic Church's camps, from the extremes of Father Saint Stephen to the Brothers of Perpetual Witness at Golgotha. It is instructive to suppose what one political philosophy might have linked such diverse sacrifice. I have already suggested my solution: the Charity Factor of the New Benthamites, generalized benevolence on a world scale to assure stability among the pleasured while doing little to comfort the dilemma of the pained. This explanation must fall short, of course, because it presumes that the ice camps were conceived with vision and maintained with precision.

The truth was the ice was an impartial executioner; there was no one in charge; the Ice Cross and religionists suffered with the wretched. The bulk of the work for the camps was done by convicts like the Little Brothers who had been transported to the South Shetlands. This permitted the Ice Cross no real assistance. Even the elite of the South Shetlands, Ice Cross officers like Dietjagger and Ariadne, were not exempt, were sad itinerants who had plunged themselves across Bifrost for money but no gain. The Ice Cross did a ruinous job, committed atrocities that should never be forgotten; however, it is also true that it never stopped struggling to the limit of its mandate for charity, until Grim Fiddle stopped it.

Consider the difficulty of establishing order on the ice: an international brigade of adventurers, renegades, and the not rare saintly man, provided with warships and the absolute power of life and death, let loose upon a sea of ice and refugees. Who can be surprised that the Ice Cross came to be mind-crippled? What the Ice Cross was asked to do was absurd. Nothing good could be done. The only release for the Ice Cross was betrayal, either of humanity or of themselves. This alone should explain why the best of the *capitanes de los Hielistos* were Ice Cross turncoats.

Consider the task assumed by the mandate of charity: uncountable multitudes worldwide scrambling for a place under the sun, some several hundred thousand of them crushed into the ice camps, who must be disarmed, sheltered, fed, nursed, and only then, if they survived the winter, the quakes, the hopelessness, relocated to lands already awash with refugees. The resettlement program did exist. It collapsed from abuse and contradiction, drowned by the flood of flesh. And even if it had worked as designed, where to put them? What utopia then? That is the answer in the question; no place. The promise of resettlement became a whip with which the Ice Cross controlled the camps. I have explained how I was at first persuaded by the hope of resettlement. For the less lucky the thought of a new land, a new Eden, justified any disgrace. Worse, the resettlement program was soon made into another kind of trap: many nations, especially republics in Africa and South America, used the false promise of resettlement

to persuade unwanted populations to submit to roundups, depor-
tation, and final imprisonment on the ice.

Nevertheless, I do not mean to portray the South Shetlands
as if they were a chain of death camps. That would be wrong.
Yes, the camps were a result of Brave New Benthamism or old
and familiar totalitarianism, in all, the apologetics of the politics
of falsehood. And yet, yes also, the camps did become the focus
of a colossal relief effort, one that required genius and compassion to bridge Bifrost in order to get goods into the Antarctic.
Modern Asgard—those grand republics—was neither deaf nor
heartless. For every Odin, there were Thors and Balders, well-
meaning guardians of men, people capable of decency. They must
have sacrificed a great deal in order to get that food to us. They
must have sent up a roar that shook the pillars of Odin's halls. No
banquet could have been without a woe-singer reminding the gods
of our depravity. There must have been heroes and heroines in
every nation who deserved credit, not the persecution they likely
suffered. And I can suppose their frustration, gathering funds,
hiring transports and transporters, fending off competing chauvinists, reaching across Bifrost to save the ice camps, only to watch
the situation at the edge of Midgard worsen, descend.

For there was one aspect of the South that no god, no hero,
no machinery of shimmering Asgard could overcome. I could explain it glibly by rendering it with Israel's cynical remark that the
only difference between a man and a dog is that the dog will not
bite the hand that feeds it. I shall not, because it pertains completely to my conduct on Anvers. I confess forthrightly.

The wretched in the South, we wretches, we were not all innocent victims of some fabulous conspiracy to disenfranchise
lambs. It is this point that shows me that my fantastic model of
twenty-first-century Asgard and Midgard has distorted the truth.
For we wretches were the worst possible remnant. The genuine
meek, the genuinely wronged, they had been left far behind, dead
in their hovels, on the beaches, in the sea. We in the ice camps
had come through our ordeals because we were tougher, wilder,
crueler than our brethren. We were the lucky remnant. We were
the most violent wretched: pirates, killers, thieves, madmen, lost
to reason and utterly embittered. As we suffered atrocities, we

were atrocious. We did have high dreams, but they had come to be twisted by hatred. Those of us who survived, we came to believe that only the most murderous could endure the ice camps. What was the face of our enemy? It was not only the mind-corrupt Odins, or the self-deceived Thors, or the miserable Ice Cross. The enemy was also the reflection in the ice. How to say this and convince in a blow? We did drink the blood. We did eat the dead.

I read over Grim Fiddle's cosmology, and I perceive that I have overstated; in so doing, I have reached too far ahead, anticipating events that I have not explicated. This seems an inherent trouble with models and model-makers. I saw this with Charity Bentham's works. My cosmology has separated the world of men too severely, has contrived rather than described the meaning of the camps.

The truth was that the South was ever covered by a pervasive gloom, like the wafting fogs of the Antarctic convergence. I correct my excess in the same way one confronted that climate, by plunging into it. I shall set aside my mythology of the Antarctic for the moment and try to penetrate the lost history of the South with specificity. It too may fail to gain the whole. It is all I can do. It is my hope that somewhere between the universal above and what I know of the specific outrages below, there is the same revelation I once experienced—and some understanding of what we did there.

My hope also is that this, the last testament of my family, will convey my lasting fury for their murder. I have already told how *King James* came to the ice. Our exodus was late. I shall now return to the saga Grandfather related to me that fortnight he lay dying at Golgotha. I shall translate as best I can Mord Fiddle's cosmology. It would be contrary, however, if I were to narrate only Mord Fiddle's story, and so I shall weave in what I know now of the genesis of the ice camps and of the travail of my family. Grandfather's story spanned the seven years he waited and searched for me. It began with his reply to my question, "Are they all dead?"

Grandfather said, "No."

□   □   □

Elephant Island

Grandfather blamed Israel when I failed to return in *Black Crane*. He shouted down my family's protests and chose for them, they would winter on Mead's Kiss. They had sufficient supplies; this overlooks their fears. The major event that winter was that Molly Rogers gave birth, a son, named Solomon for Israel's dead father. By late spring (November 1996), the increase in refugee traffic, the dissension among my family, the threat of the Pattie gunboats, all obliged Grandfather to declare himself. He carved his name in the rock, then put to sea, south on the sixtieth meridian.

Grandfather kept to his sailing course for over a month, back and forth between the Falklands and the Antarctic convergence looking for *Black Crane*. The cumulative stress of the blows finally shattered *Angel of Death*'s foremast. They were driven east toward the South Orkneys. Somewhere just off the edge of the retreating ice pack, they were rescued by a European warship—Russian, I think, perhaps an escort for a whaling fleet—a forerunner of the as-of-yet-unborn Ice Cross. They were taken to the first landfall, the well-built British naval station on the southwestern shore of Elephant Island, then serving as a staging point for the several northern European republics asserting their claim over West Antarctica. There was no network of camps then, probably not more than a few thousand wretches scattered from the South Orkneys across the Scotia Sea. The refugees were not then the major concern; instead, several republics of the North were in the early stages of a confrontation with republics of the South over territory—sea, land, and ice.

The volcanic eruptions were worse then than when I wintered at Golgotha. These ruptures blocked an attempt that summer to evacuate the wretches. It would seem that the panic had set in among the authorities, as it did at Stockholm, Port Praia, Port Stanley. I also speculate that the darker aspects of the Charity Factor had taken hold: no nation state, no treaty organization, would accept relocated refugees prematurely without an international agreement, for fear that such benevolence might make them host to an alien, dissident population. In brief, desperation made policy: mercy to a point, no voluntarism. Charity Bentham had described a system, New Benthamism, that came to regard the complete salvation of the wretched to be without utility, not the greatest good for the greatest number, and so the Charity Factor was applied in full.

The winter closed on my family on Elephant Island. Their situation was severe, if not as bad as what we found at Golgotha. But then, terror is relative. My family were some of the earliest prisoners of the ice. Grandfather would not quit. Neither would Cleopatra. Those two seemed to have conjoined in will and desire the first winter on Mead's Kiss. Grandfather did not expand on their negotiations; Cleopatra would later say only that she did what had to be done. The two of them struck a fateful bargain. Cleopatra promised Grandfather that she would help him get what he wanted, into a position where he could continue his search for Grim Fiddle. Grandfather promised Cleopatra that he would help her do what she had to do to save herself, and also, her mother. The very same mother whom Cleopatra had tried to despise as a betrayer of Cesare Furore, Cleopatra transformed into the motive for Cleopatra's complete sacrifice of her blessings. I shall have much more to say of this perverse turn later, for it hardened the heart of a woman already disposed to imperial coldness. For now, it suffices to say that it was a martyrdom fit for the comedy, to say that the daughter so loved the mother that she gave her only true treasure, her pride, to protect that mother's only true treasure, her daughter.

Cleopatra became the mistress of one of the ablest officers at the Elephant Island naval station, an African colonial named Peter Grootgibeon. She thereby secured the welfare of her mother and my family through that winter. She might well have gotten them out the next summer: Charity Bentham was a Nobel Laureate, even given that she had forfeited what currency she had in the world in order to regain Peregrine. Their good luck did not hold. A man-made catastrophe intervened. Grandfather said it was a war of shadows. This is descriptive of what must have been a running skirmish fought by warships of republics of the North and South. The war zone stretched from Tierra del Fuego to the

South Orkneys to the Antarctic itself. I have been told the antagonists gave the killing a name: the Inaccessible Affair, for the island on the South Orkneys where, it was said, they opened fire.

The Birth of the Ice Cross

And what was at issue in the Inaccessible Affair? I suppose the New Benthamites would hold bald-facedly that the republics of the North and South dispatched warships to secure the pleasure of overlordship of several million square miles of ice and volcanic ash, where nothing of consequence can grow, but where there is a bountiful sea, and where there might be a bountiful cave of minerals. The New Benthamites would hold that the pain of not holding the ice exceeds the pain of holding it. More ludicrously, the New Benthamites would hold that the republics of the North and South fought the Inaccessible Affair for the greater good of ruling what the Church fathers once named *terra australis incognita.* If one deciphers this New Benthamism, one is left with amazement that men went to war for their chauvinist claims over *incognita.* That war of shadows, that Inaccessible Affair, was a blood feud, without reason. Israel told me the truth of this, and I have seen it: Men will go to war for nothing. In the South, they did go to war for nothing. They feuded for feud alone, and nothing more.

Yes, there must have been claims that the rescue of wretches then pouring into the South Atlantic and Southern Ocean was also at issue: the republics of the North might have said they dispatched warships to administer charity; the republics of the South might have said they dispatched warships to determine if it was charity or imperialism. This was a sham. The victims of their crimes became an excuse for their crimes. My guess now is that the battles in the Scotia Sea were a spillover from larger blood feuds in both South America and Africa. The size of the area of conflict required more bluffing than combat, however, especially in the Antarctic. More, the wild weather in the Scotia Sea probably daunted all antagonists, and when that danger was combined with the threat of the fleet of the damned, the warring nations must have realized that they had to turn from confrontation to subterfuge. That is how the Norse conducted blood feuds—if there was a standoff, retire and wait for night. In the South the darkness was almost complete.

Before the end of the Antarctic summer (March 1998), the antagonists had arranged a cease-fire; the Inaccessible Affair was said to be done. A settlement was negotiated, outside of Cape Town, South Africa; hence it was called the Treaty of Good Hope. That was about the time of the British warship at South Georgia, and I assume that when the captain said there had been no war, he was being both disingenuous and defeatist.

I also assume that when the captain said there was just a bloody shuffle, he was thinking of one aspect of the Treaty of Good Hope, which established an international peace-keeping force to manage the flood of wretches into the South. I cannot be certain whether that peace-keeping force and the International Committee of the Red Cross Antarctica Relief Collective were one and the same, or separate units of a larger, world-scale construction. I have no library to certify any of my speculations. What I do know of those days, however, tells me that the New Benthamites—caught unprepared for the size of the war of shadows and its victims—amended their ways and once again applied the Charity Factor, this time to the whole of the Antarctic. What had been the British Falkland Islands Dependencies' Antarctic claim (the South Orkneys, the South Shetlands, the Palmer archipelago, Graham Land), was reconstituted into a de-militarized zone, to be administered by volunteers of charity. The Ice Cross was born.

It cannot be accident that the Treaty of Good Hope, which was signed as I spent my third winter on South Georgia, heralded order among republican masters and chaos among the wretches. The camps on the South Shetlands were organized. The round-ups, deportations, and transportations in the following summer were orchestrated. I swear it. There was a plan. I cannot prove it, but again, I have never learned anything to contradict my charge. And yet, after all these years, I recoil before the monstrousness of what was done. Could the ice camps actually have been a policy of men? Who could have given such an order? Could they have thought it the solution? There must be records. I have no proof.

I am certain that the British naval station at Elephant Island was transferred to the Ice Cross. It was quickly expanded into a huge warehouse of goods, and into a series of connecting camps that were then filled with wretches gathered from across the South Atlantic, the Scotia Sea, the Southern Ocean. The Ice Cross was mother mercy, and Elephant Island was her hearth.

Peter Grootgibeon

On Elephant Island, Cleopatra's efforts at this point again seemed to have secured berths for my family on a relocation ship, to leave as soon as the ice broke up in late spring and sufficient transport was arranged for incoming and outgoing refugees. Something ruinous upset this plan. Peter Grootgibeon's good offices failed. Grandfather said it was a Satan jest played on the Jew. I suppose from this that Israel lost his temper, did something vainglorious to compromise Grootgibeon. As a result, my family was punished. Also, Grootgibeon either resigned from or was transferred out of the British Navy. In either case, he was soon an officer in the Ice Cross.

Grootgibeon might have volunteered. He was a tall, quiet, mercurial man, born in Southwest Africa, raised in the merchant marine, a homeless soldier of fortune. It would seem that he did love Cleopatra, with passionate foolishness, and knew that she did not love him, or would not. Grandfather said he was like Saint Andrew. That was a compliment, and sharp judgment: Andrew, the simplest and most muscular disciple, crucified by the Romans on a cross in the shape of an X, the patron saint of Rusland and Scotland, therefore a Norse saint. Grootgibeon might have been a plain hero, bold, guileless, obedient; or he might have been a clumsy follower, thickheaded, impressionable, spontaneous. He does seem to represent the contradiction of those who aspired to sainthood in the South. There were many like him, quick to fight, slow to think. Lazarus might have described Grootgibeon's nature best when he said that a good man who determines to fight for dignity and then gets angry will become a moral monster, possessed. And was Grootgibeon limitless? That was determined by his luck.

Grootgibeon was assigned to Ice Cross sea duty, the command of a white cutter. Cleopatra honored her bargain with

Grandfather and persuaded Grootgibeon to include Grandfather, Gizur Sail-Maker, Skyeless, and Tall Troll in his crew. This is a clue that Israel's rashness had tainted Guy, Earle, and Peregrine, along with Thord and Orri. Grootgibeon was assigned a patrol east of the Drake Passage. He ran the Scotia Sea several times that summer, into the fall, once to the Falklands in the aftermath of a battle on Tierra del Fuego. It was then that Grandfather got ashore on Mead's Kiss to carve his second message. It was all he could do, because of the plague ships.

I have not emphasized the seaport plague to this point, because I never saw it. It did exist. I have heard too many reports from too many different sources, over too long a time, for it to have been a rumor. I do believe that the threat of the plague is what moved so many wretches to dare the Scotia Sea. The plague, more than the volcanoes, would explain the panic on Elephant Island the first summer my family spent there, would explain the growth of the camps throughout the South Shetlands the second summer they spent there, trapped by Israel's rebellion, separated from Grootgibeon and Grandfather by war. The wretches must have been told, or learned by rumor, that the ice camps were plague-free, that the camps offered health care and food for the broken and malnourished. More, there was the attraction that the ice camps were said to be administered by the Church. Grandfather told one gruesome anecdote about the Church and the plague. He said that he saw that summer a thousand-mile-long coastline under quarantine, and that he also saw several ships commanded by priests like Father Saint Stephen that ran the blockade into the infected areas. They knew there was no return, and yet they had to be shot out of the water.

Grootgibeon was ordered to winter his ship at one of the new camps on King George Island, thus prevented from getting back to help Cleopatra and my family. Grandfather emphasized to me that he convinced Grootgibeon to winter instead on Greenwich Island, cut by the sixtieth meridian, because Grandfather was certain that one day Grim Fiddle would come south on that heading. Grandfather had by then become Grootgibeon's confessor; he used his familiarity with Cleopatra in order to bend him. Grandfather would not elaborate on his relationship with Grootgibeon; he preferred to speak of their deeds. I speculate that Grandfather gave

Grootgibeon the strength of mind he lacked, and that Grootgibeon gave Grandfather the strength of arm he lacked. As Grandfather bartered with Cleopatra, he came to barter with whomever
was necessary. I write with pity. Grandfather's weapons were his
will and his magical voice. He was prepared to, and did, forge a
pact with violent nature, violent man, deranged politics, anything
that would help him achieve his heart's desire. He said he did not
bargain with Satan, however; repeated this to me like a chant.
Would he have? He did not.

The Birth of the *Hielistos*

The Bransfield Strait was filled with the first of the black-ice islands that winter, because of the volcanoes. The eruptions could
kill then, a toxin in the fumes that I would witness much later.
This poison augured another kind: Privateers came to the South.

The privateers originated because the republics of the South
who had signed the Treaty of Good Hope did not genuinely trust
New Benthamite diplomacy but could not hope to match the might
of the warships from the North. Therefore they in effect hired
the pirates who were already preying upon the fleet of the
damned, provided them with sophisticated stores and logistics, and
dispatched them across the South Atlantic in order to promote
their chauvinist interests. Of course, it was folly for the republics
of the South to believe—and perhaps they did not—that pirates
would do anything but continue to pillage and murder, even with
clandestine support by nation states. In the Antarctic, this soon
meant that the privateers turned to attacking the Ice Cross and
raiding the ice camps. And why? For food and goods, yes, and
also for the serpentine strategy of the republican masters; but there
was also treasure. Many wretches did carry gold and gems. I know;
I have filled caves with the stuff in my time, as useless to me as it
was to those privateers.

The threat of the privateers probably explains why Grootgibeon wintered away from Elephant Island—to defend the perimeter from raiders. It also explains the gradual transformation of
the Ice Cross in 1998 and 1999 into a war fleet. The privateers
were said to be responsible for the first massacres on the ice.

(Grandfather said that Golgotha was built on the ashes of an American Quaker camp.) And significantly, the privateers had many bases across the Southern Ocean, from Bouvet Island to Thule in the South Sandwich group to Cape Adare in the Ross Sea, yet there was one group of privateers from South America, and with South American republics' sponsorship, whose ships were larger, whose reach was farther, and whose commanders were fiercer than all the rest in the South. Their main base was on the remains of a weather station in the Palmer archipelago at the southern end of the Bransfield Strait, at Arthur Harbor on the infamous Anvers Island.

The following spring (October 1999), Grootgibeon was appointed one of the senior field commanders in an Ice Cross campaign launched against the privateers. The Ice Cross's orders were to exterminate the enemy, and the cruelty on both sides was unbounded from the Falklands to the Ross Ice Shelf.

At that same time, the secret employment of the privateers by some signatories of the Treaty of Good Hope—which had begun as a harassing and reconnaissance tactic—became a general strategy by New Benthamites North and South. Many of the sponsors of the Ice Cross also became sponsors of the privateers. They hired pirates to represent their interests over and against the Ice Cross they also sponsored. They sent a war fleet against their own war fleet.

Again, there is no proof. Grandfather said that Grootgibeon believed it, as did many of the Ice Cross commanders. This treachery prevented the Ice Cross from accomplishing its main task that summer, rescuing and relocating the wretches. More were said to have perished in one season than in all the years previously. This would explain why the fleet of the damned disappeared in the waters around South Georgia. The privateers sank it in order to delay the Ice Cross assault. Grandfather said, "Satan cut the waves."

By summer (January 2000), Grootgibeon had joined in an Ice Cross siege of the privateer fortress at Anvers Island. They fought on the sea, on the Mount Français glacier, in the caves. Grootgibeon and his subordinate commanders trapped the privateer squadron in a pincer from the Joubin Islands and the Bismarck Strait, so they could not run for the fogbanks in the Bransfield

Strait or onto Graham Land. Ice Cross victory was imminent. Grandfather was inexact about the next turn: either Grootgibeon was captured, or he surrendered himself and his flotilla, or he was persuaded by the privateers to negotiate, or he deserted the Ice Cross and went over to the privateers. From what I have learned of the man, and from the feel of him, the last is most likely. He must have had a fast sense of his own dignity. The treachery of the signatories of the Treaty of Good Hope was too much for him. It is also my experience that when a simple and obedient disciple believes himself betrayed by a master whom he has trusted, then that disciple, if he can, will commit himself to that master's destruction with equal fervor. As Lazarus said, there is a tangible moment when the whip no longer cows the beast. For Grootgibeon, that moment must have come when, deprived of Cleopatra, deprived of the protection of the very ideals he had sworn to, he could no longer kill men who were endowed by the same paymaster as he. Could the privateers have purchased his defection? Yes, but not unless he had already made his decision to betray. Thirty pieces of silver will not buy a saint; the saint will fall down, then scoop it up, then laugh.

Grootgibeon's defection at Anvers might also be explained by the fact that he was under Grandfather's spell. The depth of the corruption at Anvers, its Babylonian pall, might have fascinated Grandfather. It might have called forth his Norse paganism, that outlaw temperament that once propelled him in the North. If Grandfather saw at Anvers Island that the privateers were more useful than the Ice Cross, were more available to his power and for his ends, then he would not have hesitated to go over, and to take Grootgibeon with him. Grandfather had never had any faith in the greatest good for the greatest number, or even in the greatest good for the least number. He said, in his way, that he believed in one good for one man, Grim Fiddle for Mord Fiddle.

There is also evidence that there were many defections by the Ice Cross that summer, and that the privateers welcomed as much, because they had been abandoned by their sponsors. It would seem that the original sponsors of the privateers—South American republics—had developed reservations about the murder they had engendered. In theory, they had wanted to show their flag. In fact, the master had created what he could not continue to control, and not only in the South but also across the South Atlantic, murder raids from Havana to Buenos Aires, from Tangier to Cape Town, pillaging as far north as the Mediterranean, and warlord conclaves from the Caribbean to the Indian Ocean. That South Georgia was spared a murder raid by privateers can only be explained by luck.

My guess is that the signatories of the Treaty of Good Hope recognized the threat of the privateers that summer, began negotiations that would culminate at Cádiz in another New Benthamite treaty called The Peace of the Frontier. I am piecing this together from many informants I had long after Grandfather's version, and I am aware I could be distorting the history. This is what I have, and I support it with my assumption that the secret war of the privateers must have been a large drain on resources also taxed to feed the wretches. The Peace of the Frontier is said to have worked eventually in warmer climes. It did not in the South. The situation in the Antarctic deteriorated over the next year to the point that when the New Benthamites finally did withdraw their monies from the privateers, the privateers did not necessarily withdraw. No longer bothered by orders and strategies from republican masters, they shed their disguise to become the obvious: pirates. Yes, most of the original pirates had been slain by ice and men, and yes, some of the pirates struck out for the Pacific to find new sponsors. Yet many in the South, and many different kinds of pirates, chose to remain.

It interests me to suggest why. Perhaps, like Grootgibeon, they had accounts to settle. And perhaps the darkness had become so broad that there were no more reasons and no more ends; the means were all. I have explained this thought in Grandfather's metaphor: that there was no peace, no sanctuary, no refuge, nor even an ark. I want to restate this more suitably here. I declare that the pirates in the South, their ranks first filled from renegades and then swelled by wretches they conscripted as well as preyed upon, were moved to realize that when there is no refuge under the sun, what one calls one's own place is worth all the will and cruelty one can give it. The South is a white desert, a nothingness. Nothing was all that was left to the pirates, and they would come to fight for it as if it were paradise. It has always been so with New Worlds, and with the desperadoes, outcasts, and exiles

that take them for their own. As in the North, so it would be in
the South.

There is a still darker way of saying this. The Treaty of Good
Hope had established the ice camps to give charity to the masses
of wretches who would not quit, and it had also endowed the
strongest of the wretched with weapons and a battleground, the
Southern Ocean, to exist upon. Men turned pirate had been moved
to taste human blood and had not been reviled. The Norse said,
when the wolf tastes your flesh, consume it or be consumed by it.
At Anvers Island, the abandoned privateers become bloodlustful
pirates, the betrayed Ice Cross disciples, the enslaved conscripts
from the exodus, all joined in their hatred for each other and for
everyman. They were the wolf pack. They were the antithesis.
Their minds were as wasted as the ice. They cursed themselves
and the immediate representative of their fall to beastliness—the
Ice Cross. What sense of the comedy could have moved the *capitanes* at Anvers Island the following summer (January 2001), as
the Peace of the Frontier was signed at Cádiz, to convene themselves as what they called the Brotherhood of the Ice. In Spanish
tongue, the *Hielistos* were born.

The Death of My Family

I must write of Peregrine's death. I have known that it was coming these long years I have been making this confession. Now that
I am here, it seems the work of a Norse riddle-master. It does not
feel believable. I know this means that I have not accepted it, and
I also know that setting it down is a move toward understanding
what has happened to me. I must kill my father and my family
again.

Without Grootgibeon's protection, and because of Israel's
rashness, Cleopatra lost power to keep my family and hers from
the severe changes at Elephant Island. They remained in the oldest section of the base, Elephant Main, and were spared the deprivations suffered by the wretches in the new camps that grew
around them. Through that winter, the rations were cut, the discipline disintegrated, medicine and sanitation collapsed. Cleopatra
was approached by, or approached, several Ice Cross officers, and

did barter herself for privileges. The most powerful of the lot was a Chilean, Fives O'Birne. I knew the man. I killed the man. He was dishonor itself, and small.

Something happened at winter's end (September 1999) that took Fives O'Birne away, or moved him to desert Cleopatra. He might have sold her to the officer's brothel at Elephant Main. Cleopatra was pregnant then, very advanced, by Grootgibeon. At least, it is my belief that it was Grootgibeon's child, and it was his belief. Cleopatra never denied it, and that was ever her way of saying yes. Cleopatra does not seem to have been bothered by her pregnancy at first, and neither were the Ice Cross officers. A peculiarity of life in the camps was that birth was considered the epitome of eroticism. But then, at the end of her term, Cleopatra suffered a breakdown. She might have tried to kill herself. More likely some internal change gave her clarity and permitted her to see her fate. Her joy was canceled absolutely, became rage, and she turned it on herself. She stopped caring, lost weight, became glassy-eyed. The tolerable conditions in the brothel did not help. Soon after, Cleopatra was either returned to her mother, or returned herself.

Cleopatra was dying. To keep her alive, Charity Bentham and Peregrine Ide roused themselves in what was a suicide pact. I have few of the facts, because the only survivor I had to ask other than Cleopatra was Babe, mute witness; Grandfather only heard the details secondhand from Orri before he died. Cleopatra told me, "They fed me." I suppose that Charity and Peregrine starved themselves, forcing their rations on Cleopatra. Still, that would not have been enough if Cleopatra had determined to die, and I must also suppose that Charity used some motherly power over her daughter. Grandfather said that Thord, Orri, Guy, and Earle also tried to share their food but were prevented by Charity from sacrificing to the extreme. In the end, the magnificent ambition of Charity Bentham raised itself up and directed her own consumption and that of her beloved Peregrine. Theirs was not a quick finish, for they had to keep themselves alive long enough to get Cleopatra and her baby, a boy, through the spring and the deprivations exacerbated by privateer raids against the Ice Cross. Peregrine died first, sometime around my twenty-sixth birthday. He was fifty-one years old.

Charity Bentham lingered into early summer. She was the last restraint on Israel. He had to watch not only Peregrine die but also Molly and his son, Solomon, wither to paralysis. Charity and Molly died in the same week. The camp continued to decay. There was a rebellion about the time of the new year. Orri told Grandfather that Israel was involved peripherally. Cleopatra told Lazarus that Israel was a ringleader.

I do not know what happened. Nor do I know why Israel would have been so foolish to rebel against the Ice Cross. There was said to have been a massacre inside one of the satellite camps. Other than that, the record is silent. Orri could never tell Grandfather more than that Israel and Earle were sent away to the "plague camp." That was the wretches' way of saying Clarence West. When did Guy die, and where? And what happened to Thord? Orri loved Thord more than life. He did not speak of him. Cleopatra did not know what happened to the men, because she was separated from them when Fives O'Birne returned to Elephant Main in early summer (January 2000). She was returned to the brothel, or returned herself, soon after Charity's death, taking with her Israel's son, Solomon, and her own, Cesare, making their welfare a condition of her obedience. She was also permitted a protector, Babe, who buried his mother and then transferred his heroic allegiance to his sister. Orri survived the rebellion by accident, was transferred to the male aspect of the brothel.

I cannot reach any farther into the darkness and locate the circumstances of my family's murder. I cannot even suppose. Peregrine and Israel were alive. Then they were dead. I have no more to say. I want to bash something, some source, and force it to tell me Peregrine's last thoughts, Israel's reason for rebellion, Guy's and Thord's last words—and Earle, how could he be killed? I realize I am not the last to lose everyone he loves to a pit. I also realize that a search for cause can too easily become a justification for revenge. I know that there abound examples in history of when a people, a way of life, was swept from the earth in such a way that nothing was left. I am insufficient legacy. I want a marker raised, more, an arch of triumph built across the whole of Elephant Island, and on it I want recorded the accusations of the murdered, the defense of the murderers, the verdict of Grandfather's Lord God. I know hundreds of thousands died on the ice that year, mothers and fathers of children who were never granted the luck I have enjoyed. That is no comfort. I want my family remembered. Consider how pathetic it is to have left only what I have related: Peregrine and Charity starved themselves to death; Israel, Guy, Earle, and Thord were enslaved and made to disappear because they stood up against cruelty; Molly, cheery, poetic Molly, died despite everything Israel could do. This is all I have. Yes, I can wrap myself in Norse fatalism—dead is dead, mourn and keep on. I was not permitted mourning. There are no graves. There are no witnesses to tell the story. Peregrine was fifty-one years old. At that age, his own father, who was also my grandfather, was a well-pleased American, with three sons, my uncles, who were likely well-fed, regretful of the prodigal Peregrine. By accident, by bad luck, Peregrine's path took him into penury, crime, exile, and abandonment. I am not saying that Peregrine was special—though he was to me—or that he deserved better than the multitude of wretches born into a poverty and hopelessness that I have never known. I am saying that such a man, my father, was born as one of the most fortunate creatures on earth, an American eldest son, and yet it was possible that he came to vanish into a silent, cold nothing, and there is no marking of his passing. He was created in joy, yet consumed in hatred. And why? How was it possible? Who was responsible? Show him, them, it, to me, and I shall make them account. But there is no one to show me, and there is nothing to be shown. I pound at silence.

"The Whore of Babylon"

My family vanished. Cleopatra, Babe, Orri, and the two babies survived. Cleopatra took charge of their fate. Her transformation was far from complete. She was cautious, guarded, a result of her starvation and recovery, knowing that if she did not act effectively, she could lose her will again. She was beginning to build her resources: she understood that in order to survive, she had to become as ruthless as possible, without moral limits on what she could do. As a first step, she made herself the center of a resourceful group of women and men in the brothel, including Orri. Babe made Cleopatra special, her armed might. What gave this clique added authority was that the brothel at Elephant Island was less a slave chamber than a temple of hope—in it, desire was possible, and it came to represent a mystical power to the Ice Cross and the wretches.

I do not understand how Cleopatra managed Fives O'Birne. He was a low, sly, ugly little man who might have been a double agent for one of the South American republics. I puzzle if Cleopatra was his mistress at all, instead a weapon he found and used. He permitted her unusual license in the brothel. He sent her to other Ice Cross officers as a gift. And yet he coveted Cleopatra's strength, probably assassinated several Ice Cross officers who abused her, unless that was Babe at Fives O'Birne's direction. Sometime in early 2000, Cleopatra became the consort of one of the new senior commanders at Elephant Island, Jaguaquara, a cagey, able, well-blooded Chilean. I cannot ignore my suspicion that Fives O'Birne directed this turn also. Jaguaquara, who called himself *Islas Desolación,* was then thought a brilliant butcher, veteran of several campaigns against the pirates in the Atlantic and Pacific. He was also thought one of the most merciful and competent Ice Crossmen, responsible for rebuilding camps destroyed by pirates and for improving conditions at Elephant Island.

Cleopatra's motives are lost to me, especially since she left Jaguaquara's quarters and moved back into the brothel that fall, while Grootgibeon and Grandfather were defecting at Anvers. This does not seem to have been a punishment.

Cleopatra only sketched this for Lazarus; knowing we were curious, she rationed her secrets. Cleopatra returned voluntarily to the brothel, because there she and Fives O'Birne had a network of spies, procurers, agents, that required her presence at the center of the web. Cleopatra also had several other Ice Crossmen, whose names are lost to me, and it would seem that from the brothel she was able to dispense herself like a poison, not to kill but to enslave the enslavers. She shaped the brothel consciously into an institution, with many births, many pregnancies, taking in children as servants, granting privileges to some and taking them away from others, including the leadership among the wretched in the camps. There was a powerful priest named Barracuedes who opposed her reach, who tried to turn the Ice Cross commanders against her. He was soon sent to Clarence West and disappeared into charity. I have heard many stories of her machinations, so many that I now understand that to her everything lascivious and voluptuous was attributed, as if she were a goddess. A goddess of what? Fertility, yes, but also dread. She groomed herself for purpose. She was beautiful, educated, merciless, and, I once believed, resolute. I once believed that she was maintaining as many portals as possible because one of them might be her way out. Now I puzzle if she did not waver, if the authority she gained at Elephant Island, the imperial corruption of her power, did not become her cause. Her portals were murderers. Her route was murder. But where did she think she was going? What was she reaching for? She enhanced herself as grandly, as fantastically, as mythologically as possible. She described herself as "the queen of slaves." Grandfather called her "the whore of Babylon."

I do not want to overstate her achievements. Cleopatra suffered her prostitution. If it is true that her father's murder buried her childhood and her faith in goodness, then it is also probably true that her mother's murder interred her heart. Cleopatra was not heartless. Her grief was frozen in Charity's grave. It was the loss of that very grave that scarred Cleopatra in some sinister way I could never understand. It happened about a year after Charity's death. Cleopatra had required Jaguaquara to bury Charity in the graveyard reserved for the Ice Crossmen. A series of eruptions opened a fissure that crawled along the shelf for weeks, then ripped through several barracks and swallowed the graveyard. Cleopatra did not think this an accident. She blamed the Ice Cross. It might have been why she sent a message to the newly constituted *Hielistos* base at Anvers Island, to Grootgibeon, whom Fives O'Birne had told her had defected. That may be apocryphal, because the timing is not precise. That fissure did seem to cut into Cleopatra's will. She lost her control for a moment, turning against Jaguaquara, who tried to appease her. The loss of her mother's grave also explains Cleopatra's obsessive fear of earthquakes on Anvers Island much later. It cost me dearly once, as she interrupted a campaign to move her household from my hall to one of her own, which she claimed was beyond the grasp of Satan's Seat. I know this is confusing detail. What is important here is that Cleopatra had a breakdown at Elephant Island when she was at the apex of her power, when she could have used her authority to get out of the South. If I could say that she became mad, then her conduct would be at once excusable and unanalyzable. Instead, she, "queen of slaves," "whore of Babylon," became logically and coldly crazed, shrewd in her capriciousness, deadly in her fits.

More crucial to her fate, she was tormented by her bastard son, Cesare; at least, I can suppose so by her conduct with regard to the father, Grootgibeon. It is possible that Grootgibeon did not know of his son when he went over to the *Hielistos*. It is also possible that Cleopatra's message (if it happened that way) did shake him, make him reckless. I do not choose to and have learned not to be quick to discount the incredible in the South. Cleopatra's power has appeared to me to be as unearthly as Antarctica. If anyone could have sent a message from the brothel at Elephant Island more than three hundred miles across ice and ash, it was she. The camps were sieves by then, wretches pouring in and leaking out, the Ice Cross battling the *Hielistos*, transport ships and merchantmen diverted, pirated, bartered between camps. Whole camps were exterminated by nature, only to be resurrected with new arrivals.

Finally, in the summer of the year 2001, Grootgibeon led a murder raid against the Ice Cross on Elephant Island. He actually captured Elephant Main for a few hours. Grandfather credited Grootgibeon with inventing the strategy then that I later perfected, if that is the word: combat by massacre. The victorious is as reduced as the defeated. However, if one commands filthy little creatures, half-men who fight for no gain at all, one can waste them in great number to gain a distinct goal. Grootgibeon's prize was Cleopatra.

Anvers Island

I must speak of the worst possible, of the third realm in Grim Fiddle's cosmology. As there was a new and aggrandized Asgard, home of silent gods, as there was a new and reduced Midgard, hovel of wailing wretches, so there was a new Niflheim, realm of the murderous dead. Grootgibeon stole Cleopatra from the edge of Midgard and carried her into the pit of the *Hielistos,* Anvers Island.

The Norse were inexact about Niflheim, which means Misty Hel, because their sense was that its forbiddenness should remain unspeakable. I emphasize that the Norse did not think of it as a punishment. It was not meant to be an equivalent of the Christian concept of Hell. There was no distinction made between the after-life of those who died justly and those who died as criminals. Dead was dead, and the corpse was thought to travel to dwell in Niflheim for eternity. Yes, it is true that dead heroes traveled to dwell in Valhalla for eternity; however, that was such a small and elite number that their fate was not meant to condemn those who died by accident, disease, old age, and who abided in Niflheim.

Niflheim was said to be nine days' ride downward from Midgard into a dessicated cold that extinguished joy. Anvers Island, a forty-mile-by-twenty-mile juggernaut of towering glaciers, thunderous peaks, fume-spitting cones, was four days' hard sail from Elephant Island, southwestward across the ice-streaked Bransfield Strait, through the ashen fog of the Gerlache Strait, to the fortress originally built by the privateers on the southwestern shore, at Arthur Harbor. Niflheim had a citadel, called Hel for the half-serpent half-woman, black and white, scaly and sad, who ruled there. Hel's mansion, Eljundir, was built beyond the rock Drop to Destruction. The fortress at Arthur Harbor was blasted into the rockface about the remains of the weather station, was sprawled before the tumultuous motherlode of the eruptions, Satan's Seat, set back on the peninsula of Graham Land several hundred miles farther southwest. The Norse said Hel's servants were a man, Ganglati, and a woman, Ganglot, who snaked about so slowly they did not seem to move. Anvers Island's lava carved steaming cracks in the blackened glaciers. The Norse called Hel's plate Hunger, and Hel's knife Famine, and her pallet Sickbed, hung with trappings called Glittering Misfortune. There were many dark names for the *Hielistos* at Anvers; and the reason so many of them were small was that there were as many women and children as men: the women ate less, weathered the cold as well, were as brutal as the males. And while Anvers Island's *Hielistos* had almost endless supplies—not only robbing the Ice Cross and the religious societies but also plundering the merchantmen and, at first, receiving large shipments from the southern republics that sponsored the privateers—it is not an exaggeration to say that the *Hielistos'* plate was hunger, their knife was famine, their dwelling in the caves was sickbed. The caves at Anvers Island were certainly hung with glimmering misfortune, the bounty from a hundred raids on the camps.

Grootgibeon was not the leader of the *Hielistos*. It seems to have been at first an oligarchical structure, what Lazarus called tribal confederalism. The Spanish-speaking predominated. Grootgibeon's well-armed cutter, and his flotilla's commanders, made him a leading *capitán*. His murder raid on Elephant Island propelled him to the fore of the ranks. Afterward he established himself and his men, along with Cleopatra and her courtlike brothel, in the best-built sections of the fortress. They had slaves as they were slaves. Grandfather said that the fortress then, before I rebuilt it, faced seaward, cut between the sheer rock walls vulnerable to bombardment from cutters laying off Bonaparte Point. It was thought to be impregnable. It was not. However, it seemed so for the Ice Cross that summer. Either the Ice Cross was completely on the defensive, or else the answer to why Grootgibeon and Cleopatra were able to establish themselves securely and to begin to gather the diverse warlords of the South into their control was that Anvers Island for the Ice Cross, like Niflheim for the Norse, was thought to be magical—bad magic, cursed magic, supernatural. It was a sulfurous waste. It was a realm of pirates. This combined with the madness there to transform it for the *Hielistos* and the Ice Cross into a place of depravity. They seemed monstrous, so they acted monstrously. This last should not shock now. I have prepared the way.

As the Norse spoke of the immortal dragon, Nidhogg, who dwelled in Fiflheim, gnawing the roots of the eternal tree Yggdrasil and sucking the blood from men and then eating their corpses, so at Anvers Island there was the spirit of Nidhogg: cannibalism. Grandfather said Grootgibeon tried to contain the worst of it, more by shifting command from the worst privateers to the Ice Cross defectors than by forbidding the *Hielistos* from eating the dead. This does not explain the phenomenon for me, for when I ruled, Nidhogg remained unkillable. I found that no amount of food, no guarantee of continued supplies through the black winters, could keep some men and women from cannibalism. It would seem to be part of the beastliness that remains in men from antediluvian times; when famine and hopelessness and rage take hold, slumbering Nidhogg awakens, hungry.

Barbablanca

In such a place, it was the cruel-minded and hardhearted who gained. I speak here of Mord Fiddle. Grandfather would interrupt his story with a defense of his conduct that was actually a self-serving justification. He said he believed since leaving Stockholm that Lord God was punishing him for his great sin of abandoning me at birth, was testing his resolve to make amends. He believed that when he lost me at Mead's Kiss, Lord God tested him by casting him among "Satan's Own." Grandfather believed that no matter what he encountered, it was a test of his will not to abandon me again to suffer the evil in order to find me and release me from the darkness. His righteousness in seeking me was what he believed was his armor against his Satan.

I think it telling that Grandfather would not actually join in the butchery. He would stand by; he would countenance anything; he would not actually kill. The *capitanes de los Hielistos* did not resent Grandfather's passivity, regarded him with awe. His manner was ghostly. He thought he was in Hell and moved like it, with the aura of the damned. Grootgibeon would defer to him, and none of the others dared challenge him. More importantly, Cleopatra continued to honor her bargain and gave Grandfather the protection of her corruption. After the raid on Elephant Island, Grandfather refitted *Angel of Death,* captured in the attack, and entered into his mission. He became a seeker. The *Hielistos* thought of *Barbablanca* as a charm. From what he described to me of the battles, he would hang back in *Angel of Death* until the carnage was complete, and then he and his attendants would move over the landscape, praying and prying, looking "into their hearts." And what was he seeking? The obvious answer is Grim Fiddle. I think there was more to it. I suggest he was also looking for a sign, a message from his Lord God, that would confirm for him that what Mord Fiddle was doing, and seeing, was as wrong as the

Minister of Fire must have known it was. He permitted his search to blind him. How else to explain how a man who had seen the darkness long before any reasonable man had known what was coming could then have let himself become lost in that darkness?

The proof of what I say is that when Grandfather found me, the scales lifted from his eyes. His self-deceit began to kill him. Kuressaare said that *Barbablanca* had collapsed before. The profound distinction at Golgotha was that while telling me what he had done and seen those seven years in the darkness, he reconsidered his conduct, and it shriveled him. I suppose now that such wasting away had begun before our meeting on the beach, had begun when word of the capture of a man who was Wild Drumrul reached Grandfather at Anvers. When he finally got Wild Drumrul (captured in the attack of the *Hielistos* on *King James*) before him at Anvers Island, Wild Drumrul could only tell Grandfather that I was last seen offshore Greenwich Island, but this had been sufficient for Grandfather to press his reconnaissance in the camps. When his men had taken Ugly Leghorn on the glacier, Grandfather had known exactly where I was. I was not wholly right about that day on the glacier; he had not been up there, only skuas and his *Hielistos*. He was too reduced by then to climb, had lain offshore in *Angel of Death* while the *capitanes de los Hielistos* closed their trap on the Ice Cross. All had been for Grandfather's purpose: to blunt the Ice Cross in the neighborhood while he reached into Golgotha to find me. I was also not right about why there had been no *Hielistos* raids. From the moment Grandfather had heard I was in the South, Golgotha and several other camps on Roberts, Greenwich, and Livingston had been under the absolute protection of *Barbablanca*.

Cleopatra's Luck

Grootgibeon's murder raid on Elephant Island wrecked the infrastructure of the Ice Cross. Out of the carnage the *Hielistos* established bases on Deception, Smith, and Livingston islands. By March 2001, Jaguaquara was made acting commander-in-chief of the Ice Cross in the South Shetlands, more because he was the remnant than because of merit. He grew cautious, had the measure of the chaos, rebuilt Elephant Island as best he could, directed the Ice Cross to help the camps and to avoid the *Hielistos'* cutters. His masters, the signatories of the Treaty of Good Hope and the Peace of the Frontier, disapproved completely, ordered him to obliterate the fortress at Anvers. Jaguaquara knew this was futile, and not just because of the worsening fall weather. The *Hielistos* were all-powerful, and Jaguaquara urged his masters to negotiate with Grootgibeon and the *capitanes* at Anvers.

It was nature that called the next tune. In early fall (April 2001), the volcanoes erupted with colossal explosions, burying many camps, poisoning the Bransfield Strait, pinning both sides in their caves. So much ash was heaved into the sky that it was said to be black. This blocked off the sunlight preternaturally early, which seems to have increased the reach of the pack. That was the winter the pack enwrapped South Georgia. In Antarctica the pack leveled everything, especially the success of the *Hielistos*. Nature had done what the Ice Cross could not have; the *Hielistos* ate themselves.

The following spring (November 2001), as me and mine were sent from South Georgia, a new commander-in-chief superseded Jaguaquara at Elephant Island, K. H. Lykantropovin. No one knew his real name; I still do not: Lykantropovin was said to be his self-chosen nom de guerre. There were many *capitanes de los Hielistos* who venerated Lykantropovin, some even defected to him; it was his reputation of limitless cruelty, so much that he could seem more a curse than a man. He was said to be the grandson of a Russian general deported once by the Soviets for suspicion of loyalty to Russia and not the revolution, who had been resurrected to fight the German blasphemers, then again sent into exile, north of the Arctic Circle, to the mines at Vorkuta. This might be fanciful; it is true that Vorkuta means "the people of the underworld." The grandson, Lykantropovin, was no Russian devil, was no Russian saint. I think now he might have been the face of war. He certainly was a hired mass-murderer. I have learned that by the time he came to the South he was a veteran of murder campaigns against wretches in Africa and the Far East. He is best understood as an imperial errand boy, dutiful, ingenious, incorruptible though seemingly corrupted completely by envy and ambition. Also, I think Lykantropovin was a sincere and even tormented fanatic. No man could have served so faithfully in such abysmal conditions if he lacked self-conviction. His god seemed order. His fist was iron. His face was said to be awful—a wound of the cold. He was physically pale, willowy, a fish-eater and insomniac. I never heard him talk. He remained to his end an indomitable Northman with a ghastly name and simple quest, to subdue his enemy. If even I seem admiring here, it is because I was, and remain; I shall have much more to say in course, for between us we slaughtered multitudes. For now, I declare my sympathy because he is in my face, Lykantropovin, as all men are, said the Norse, whom one has murdered.

Lykantropovin realized that his opportunity lay in going to the attack immediately. He first launched a campaign against nature, renovating the largest camps for heat and supplies, blasting away the glaciers that threatened the deep-water harbors at Elephant, King George, and Livingston. Lykantropovin knew that he had to provide the wretches security, not because he pitied them, but because he had to turn their sympathies, their hearts, from the *Hielistos* and to the charity of the Ice Cross. He also rebuilt Elephant Island into a fortress that dwarfed the one at Anvers. He then launched an armada of new ice-cutters and retook the South Shetlands from Clarence Island to Deception Island. The East German Ice Cross officer Dietjagger must have been part of that sweep. And while we South Georgians huddled at Golgotha, Lykantropovin sent a fleet against Anvers Island.

It was Cleopatra's luck that now turned the hem side out, as the Norse said. It could not have been accident that Jaguaquara, relieved of his command and shunned as a lesser butcher, led the main assault at Anvers. Lykantropovin might not have known how crucial it is that a commander accompany his forces on the ice— loyalties can change as suddenly as the weather. His quick victories along the South Shetlands may have left him overconfident. From the fortress at Elephant Island, Lykantropovin directed Jaguaquara, by undependable courier and radio, against what he presumed to be the heart of the Brotherhood of the Ice, Grootgibeon and the Ice Cross defectors at Arthur Harbor.

Jaguaquara's bombardment was expert, ripped the cliff face of the caves, drove the *Hielistos* into the deep fells. The pirate fleet was also blasted, and Jaguaquara closed the net with beach landings. The *capitanes de los Hielistos,* led by one called Hector the Fat, were ready to quit and pleaded with Grootgibeon to ask for terms. Jaguaquara sent Fives O'Birne into the fortress under a truce flag with Lykantropovin's demand for unconditional surrender. Fives O'Birne told the *capitanes* they must accept chains, and insulted Grootgibeon, meaning to separate him from the pirates. At this, the *capitanes* recognized that Lykantropovin meant to slaughter them all. They also knew they could not break the siege. Grootgibeon made an honorable gesture, too late, too naive, and offered to travel to Elephant Island to negotiate a surrender. Fives O'Birne boasted that the only part of Grootgibeon he would take to Lykantropovin would be his head.

What was required to break the impasse was a heart that could tolerate any treachery. I suppose that Cleopatra's namesake might have clasped her lover and her asp to her breast and sunk into glorious defeat. A name is a name, true, but some names, say I, are warning. Surrender was not Cleopatra Furore's temperament. She rose to intervene in the *Hielistos'* counsel. She descended from the fortress with Fives O'Birne, Babe, and her hall-guard, and went aboard Jaguaquara's flagship.

Some said she stayed there a day, some said a gale blew from Graham Land and buried the siege in a tomb of ice. Nothing moved but the skuas in the sky and the tongues in the liars. Grandfather was not in the fortress, was trapped on Graham Land, and was not a reliable witness. He said that every *capitán* in the fortress knew that Cleopatra meant to sell everyone to everyone, the "whore of Babylon" forging a Babylonian treaty. Cleopatra was never helpful on the particulars. It was said that she directed Jaguaquara to inform Lykantropovin by radio that she would negotiate only with him, and not before he returned her mother's corpse. If this was so, she must have known it was a mad demand. And did she actually, as I was told later, kiss Grootgibeon when she rose from the counsel table?

The end was metamorphic, all were melted and thrashed. Cleopatra, daughter of Brave New Benthamism, revealed the pagan root of the Charity Factor; in Christian terms, it is called Judas-talk. Jaguaquara surrendered himself and his fleet to Cleopatra. Cleopatra made Jaguaquara the warlord of Anvers Island. And as a taunt to the impotence of the Ice Cross to best the self-named queen of slaves, Cleopatra was said to have ordered a cutter sent to Lykantropovin, manned by the Ice Cross officers who had originally defected with Grootgibeon, each with his fingers cut off. Peter Grootgibeon's corpse was nailed to the boom spar.

□   □   □

At Golgotha, the South Georgians shuddered before my translation of Grandfather's story. After all, it was not of some distant country Grandfather spoke, but our world—Grootgibeon was dead less than a year. And Lazarus was so outraged at Cleopatra's debasement that he tried to reject what he learned. He said Grandfather offered two distorted and farfetched portraits of Cleopatra: Either she was a conspirator rivaling a mythical empress, or else she was a pirate's treasure. He said it was the most obvious slander Grandfather could tell to paint Cleopatra a prostitute who had raised herself up by seduction to rule through the tempted. He said Grandfather lied. He said Grandfather was insane.

After two weeks of confession, Grandfather started to repeat himself, and to rant and babble. I do not think his mind was gone, more his concentration. I thought to put specific strategic questions to him about the *Hielistos,* for myself and my sealers. The answers made our plight look worse. My sealers grew resigned; they embraced their morbid fatalism. Our escape plans were set aside as folly. The sealers said the South was a tomb for those who would not fight and that whatever course was taken next, it must be decisive. Germanicus spoke forthrightly, said it would be better to die a pirate like the *Hielistos* than to wait for starvation or slaughter at Golgotha. I could not disagree, fell to silence as Grandfather retold his story with ever wilder images, heaped murder upon treachery, described the torture and slaughter and hopelessness of the camps, and in general fashioned the landscape of the South into a fantastic and fantastically black struggle between Lykantropovin and his Ice Cross and Jaguaquara, his *Hielistos,* and his dark-haired queen.

Longfaeroe recognized my burden, and worked to insert himself between me and the woes of my sealers. He must have

responded to a kindred heart in Grandfather, and seemed to enjoy his opportunity to solace the soul of a failed warrior of the
Word. This might be overmuch. Who can say what those minis-
ters of Christianity see when they confront each other? I do believe Longfaeroe found in Grandfather the extremes he had
pretended to on South Georgia, in Africa and Asia, and fallen
short of. They could not converse, lacking a common language,
and whenever I was present Longfaeroe avoided meeting Grandfather's gaze, moving gingerly around the room as I translated
Grandfather's words for him and whomever else was present. Yes,
there might have been envy there—the sort of longing those holy
men have for one who has faced their Satan, perhaps even beaten
their Satan for one moment. But also there was great respect.
Longfaeroe sang psalms that not only reinforced Grandfather's
illusionary architecture of the world, but also celebrated a victory
of the spirit over the flesh. Longfaeroe sang, "Even though I walk
through the valley as dark as death, I fear no evil, for thou art
with me . . ."

Longfaeroe also worked to contain my sorrow. He feared that
I would again wander from his vision of me. Longfaeroe realized
that what troubled me most deeply was not the world of darkness
but the world without Grandfather. He sang to me, "What is more
grievous than the passing of a good shepherd? Who among his
flock will not cry? Who will survive if he does not put his faith in
the shepherd's shepherd, O Jehovah?"

I was not comforted, sent Longfaeroe from me when he became too insistent. If I was shepherd to the South Georgians, then
Grandfather was my shepherd. And there was nothing that could
shield me from the fact that my grandfather, whom I thought a
beacon only slightly less brilliant than God, was dying.

Grandfather understood my face. He had lost me. He had
found me. He realized that it was Grim Fiddle who must now lose
Mord Fiddle, forever. And so he provided for my welfare. He
must have rehearsed himself for years. Yet he could not have been
certain until he had me before him if his Lord God would grant
him the time to cover me with the only defense that is impregnable. Grandfather dressed me in the cowl of fantasy, one that he
had stitched, one that he believed would protect me from the
darkness that had consumed him. This explains why, as he lay

dying, he told such a deliberately metaphorical tale of the struggles in Antarctica. He knew my heart, because it was his; he knew my strength, because it was his. He was not sure of my will, because he believed it could be weakened by doubt, as Peregrine's once had been.

Therefore, Mord Fiddle lavished his last might in order to paint a portrait of the South that was a compelling lie in its parts, as Lazarus had suspected. Grandfather presented the Ice Cross as exaggeratedly bad, the *Hielistos* as exaggeratedly just, and Cleopatra as exaggeratedly fallen and imperiled. He gave me a purpose beyond my quest for Grandfather that he hoped would usher me onto a path that might one day carry me free. Rather than tell me what to do, which might never have been enough, he created a fabulous landscape and cast me in the role of a champion. Such was an art Grandfather had worked upon his whole life, rendering mankind's murky history into Lord God's clear plan.

It could only have been Grandfather's plan that if his grandson was to survive in the three realms I have called my cosmology, then Grim Fiddle must descend into Niflheim and await Ragnarok—the Twilight of the Gods, or, to be partial to Grandfather's word-hoard, that Grim Fiddle must walk among the most wretched and await the second coming of Jesus, when Lord God would judge the quick and the dead, would welcome the righteous into the Kingdom of Heaven.

And how did Mord Fiddle, doomed seventy-four-year-old man, move to attain his triumph over history and also to color my fate? He merely set the stage and cast the characters in his fortnight of talk. Grandfather ignited the drama with a last spark, preaching a sermon that Grim Fiddle, abandoned twenty-nine-year-old man, could not turn from.

"You are not the first nor the last, Grim. I have told you, I have shown you, we have seen, there is no peace. Satan is in the world. There is no refuge. It is wrong to seek refuge, wrong to hide from the wickedness Satan has brought. Stand, move, attend! Cleave to righteousness. That is your sword. You see Satan's harvest. Fast, Grim. Grow mindful, Grim. Do not shy from the light of that mountain of evil. Look into it. Show Satan you are not afraid of him. Lord God braces your arm. Lord God girds your loins. Make war on Satan. Attend! It was my life. Make it yours. Strike! Go to her."

Such is my memory of the last testimony I heard from the Minister of Fire. I was away from him, inspecting *Angel of Death* with Kuressaare and Germanicus, when he died. Longfaeroe told me when I came in. They were afraid of me then, with cause. I tried to bring him back. I kissed him. His lips were cold, and hard. I touched him and there was none of the fire that made him, only a wasted old man, released.

Much is at issue in Grandfather's last cogent testimony to me. One of the most significant puzzles is, did Grandfather actually say, "Go to her"? I am certain he did not use a name. Whom did he mean? Could it have been Lamba? Could it have been Zoe? More worrisome to me, he might not have said, "Go to her." It might be that my memory, which has often failed me throughout this work, has here fooled me. Did I want him to say, "Go to her"? Did I imagine the whole testimony in order to preface "Go to her"?

I suggest the truth of it might be that Grandfather himself invested his last testimony with the mystery that was Cleopatra. Grandfather knew he owed Cleopatra a debt he could not himself pay. She had protected him at Elephant Island, and then again at Anvers, had permitted him to continue his search for me. Grandfather had promised in return to help Cleopatra save herself and Charity. Some might have said that the debt was canceled when Cleopatra chose to fall to the corruption at Anvers. My grandfather would not have agreed, did not. Yet as Grandfather increased his debt to her, he increased his revulsion toward her. She gave him her charity, and it enslaved him, and he reviled her for it. He did not call her "the whore of Babylon" idly. Nor did he cast her as the protector of fertility idly. I suppose now that Mord Fiddle was caught in the same paradoxical position that Cleopatra forced on all who loved her and despised her. Honor the mistress, defame the mistress, she remained the mistress. I did not then understand the depths of Grandfather's problem. Like Lazarus, I saw only artifice in Grandfather's portrait of Cleopatra. Now I have come to see that my cosmology of the South (Grim Fiddle's North interpreting Skallagrim Ice-Waster's South) can solve Cleopatra's role in the South. I realize it might not be any less artificial than Grandfather's creation, but it is what I have, and it does continue to comfort me. I suggest that Grandfather was confounded because he owed a debt he did not know how to pay to a human being who had become half a woman scorned by fate and half a serpent scorning fate. Cleopatra was both a monster and a protector. I shall not press this more than to say that Mord Fiddle commanded Grim Fiddle to attend a queen of slaves who was black and white, scaly and sad, her mansion Eljundir and her name, Hel.

Mord Fiddle was dead. I would like that this event could explain, or excuse, more of my conduct. I suppose that the reason I am unable to recall accurately Grandfather's last testimony is that death, which lifted the shadows from the face of a failed despot, dropped those same shadows on my mind's eye. The Norse would say: Grim Fiddle was death-darkened.

Germanicus tried to restrain me; Jane and Violante tried to nurse me; Longfaeroe tried to get me to mourn in a ceremonial fashion. Lazarus alone stood by silently. I am said at one moment to have collapsed dull-eyed and feverish, at another to have pushed aside their nurture, to have commanded that the wretches of the camp be led by Grandfather's chamber to bow before the corpse of a Norse hero. My hysteria is said to have lasted a week, while Grandfather's corpse blackened and putrefied. I am said to have heeded eventually their pleas for decency and to have orchestrated Grandfather's funeral, washing his body, trimming his beard, dressing him in robes I took from the Brothers, building his pyre above Aurora Bay. When Mosquite tried to betray Grandfather's *Hielistos* to the Ice Cross who came in search of their lost ships, I am said to have ordered him hanged the day of the immolation, and also to have ordered Kuressaare and his men to massacre the Little Brothers. Then I am said to have taken up the torch. I said my farewell to Grandfather's remains in a state of mind that looked to my people to be a dream.

It was a deep dream, a berserker's dreaming. I have mentioned that when I changed shape, I became a beastly killer, inflamed and dauntless. What I have withheld is that the change also acted upon both my mind and my mind's eye, so that not only Grim Fiddle changed shape, but also figures, events, and words appeared to Grim Fiddle to change shape. As I was bewitched, so I saw magically. I have kept this revelation, because it seems insupportable by the record; there was never anything I read in Norse myth or legend to explain what I experienced while in a berserker state. There is certainly no rational explanation for what I want to present. I should defer. I cannot.

It is true, I did not report my dreaming while a berserker at Port Stanley; it was lost to me while I screamed at the mountains on the high heath of South Georgia. I shed it deliberately; Abigail's love helped me shed it completely. My dreaming following Grandfather's death is carved in my mind. Though it is not a logical tale to record, I want to try. I have embarrassed myself so often in this confession, I am left without such philosophical delicacy. And also, I can rely on the fact that I learned after my dreaming lifted what actually happened in that year or so of Grim Fiddle's darkness. I shall relate in detail what Germanicus, Lazarus, Longfaeroe, Wild Drumrul, Kuressaare, and Cleopatra told me of my conduct. It was straightforward enough: Grim Fiddle abandoned his responsibility to his South Georgians; Grim Fiddle took *Angel of Death* and the best of his sealers and Grandfather's *Hielistos* to Anvers Island to slay and to rescue, and when seduced by murder, and by the dark-haired queen, Grim Fiddle remained to usurp and to avenge.

First, though, there is this berserker's vision of my crimes. Why? I want compassion. At least, I want understanding. I want some other human being to see as I saw in my dream, wherein Grim Fiddle transformed from death-darkened to vengeance-gorged, wherein Grim Fiddle wielded righteousness as his battle-shaft, and wherein Grim Fiddle, sea-wise and strife-eager, struck and attended and paid a debt, and one more thing, wasted the ice.

I have the head of a hero. My hearth-companions call me Bulwark of the South. I am sharp-witted and have the clue to war-success. I enjoy the weather of rainbows. I take the high seat in my ice-carved hall and share meat with my long-eared hounds. My retinue gathers at my drinking tables to hear my bards make hall-songs of my contests.

The bards sing of the season when the sea boiled with waves of flames, and war-creatures from western shadows stained beaches with the children of men. I was in my early manhood. I rode the salt-trails on a sound wood wave-cutter. My captain was a white-bearded giant, the blood of feuds in his breast. His name was Hard-Fisherman. He was gloomy entertainment. He coveted me as his own. I left the company of Hard-Fisherman to seek signs of safe passage through western shadows. I led a war-band. My eye drew us into the company of men captained by a black-bearded whale-killer. His name was Elephant Son. Our blades were dulled by ripping at bone joints. We fled to a keep where we were trapped in burning halls. My need was to return to Hard-Fisherman. My new-tarred boat was destroyed by no fault of mine. I waded into the war-creatures from western shadows. My battle-shirt was craving. My blood-price was a host. My wounds gave me sleep. Elephant Son carried my body to the east, to his home, the Land of the Whale-Killers.

The high-pitched bards, in my favor-rich hall, sing of my seasons among the Whale-Killers. I wore the dress of a keeper, and lived among the children. I wept for my need of Hard-Fisherman. He was the father of my mother. I longed for Dragon-Worrier. He was my father. My teacher was a bitter-tongued man. I matched his wits with tales of my youth, in the Land of the Fire-Scolds. I passed my happiest days in the company of slender-armed women. One, Poor-Patience, asked me to set aside my war-ways. We gave thanks to God for our child. The clearness of Heaven revealed no end to strife. The King of the Whale-Killers was fame-winning. He was not blameless. He was too much away from his halls, where drink gave men contempt for slaves. His name was Elephant Father. At his table, sly hall-fellows, who used their blades on their kin, spoke against Elephant Father. They claimed there was a new evil, born in the defeat in western shadows. They said that Elephant Father had lost his bright edge. The hall-fellows captured children and placed them in keeps. Elephant Father called the hall-fellows mischievous. Elephant Father called upon me, in my keeper's clothing, with the smell of a slender-armed woman on me, to take up again my battle-shaft and to give chase to the new evil. I turned to the counsel of my brother, Copper-Crowned, who had the secret to the beast in men. The slender-armed women bestowed on us their attention. We asked God for help, for without Everlasting Might there can be no victory. I stood before the hall-fellows and told them that the new evil was not born in defeat in western shadows. I told them that the new evil was an old evil that comes into men's hearts when famine covers their tables. I wrestled with the old evil that has no name, that feeds on faith. The old evil stalked the Land of the Whale-Killers, and broke the seal of the linden-wood halls, and tore the flesh of the children. I protected many, but not all. The hall-fellows blamed Elephant Father for my failure and murdered him in his grief. The screams of the slender-armed women slowed my reach. Poor-Patience was pulled down to her sad ending-day, and I was stilled. The hall-fellows feared my wrath. They captured me and my brothers. I cursed the hall-fellows as kinsmen who make nets of malice for harsh gain. I led my brethren and the children onto a deep-chested ship, where we gave our backs to the mischief of the Land of the Whale-Killers.

The sharp-tongued bards, in my well-wrought hall, sing of my season on the sorrow-laden sea. I guided my deep-chested ship into a storm tossed by sea-beasts. I met a shape-changer. Her name was Time-Thief. She was my mother. She recalled her charge to me in my youth to follow the ghostly leavings of a thousand-year-dead outlaw. She recalled her charge to me that I must rise to rule the black and hurt half-men of the wall of blizzards and behemoths. She shamed me for my wandering ways and for my time astray covered with the blood of other men's feuds. She gave me true terms to follow my heart. I commanded my company to begin my craved-voyage for Hard-Fisherman. We sailed into western shadows. Among ice islands and fire mountains we were set upon by creatures in dense escort. We were defeated. We accepted the guidance of men in tall white warships. They led us to shelter in a smoky fen on a stone beach covered with lost hopes. My war-band wavered before the bark of the fire mountains. I fed my company my patience. I dressed in endurance. My war-hound sounded a cry for her lost sister. I was pregnant with memory of ancient counsels, "When want is crime, I am outlaw." God gave me courage and then he gave me Hard-Fisherman. He was come to his ending-day. He took my eyes and made them his, took my ears and made them ours, took my sorrow and made it joy of promised triumph. He gave my soul a need for revenge against the murderers of my father and the eaters of my father's brothers. Hard-Fisherman chose his words with the cunning that was his warden. He left me with a quest-thirst for a dark-haired queen who was gripped by *the kindred of Cain. I laid my arms, thick as oak trees, across Hard-Fisherman's pyre and swore an oath. "No shades, no shadow creatures, no talon of the evil one, will keep me from wresting the dark-haired queen from her prison of affliction and setting her freedom as high as mine."*

The keen-eared bards, in my deep-dug halls, sing of my seasons with anger's billow against an alien brood. Hard-Fisherman's soul had departed this earth. My mourning burned my throat. I proclaimed to my company that they should commence prayers for my soul, for I was bound by oath and would not turn from my duty unless death broke my limbs. My brave shieldsmen walked to my side. Elephant Son said, "Your tracks, our steps." Copper-Crowned said, "The black-eyed fawn, that dark-haired queen, is my sister, and you are my brother." I welcomed my thanes onto Hard-Fisherman's curved-prow ship, where we joined with those who had followed the white-bearded seeker. We loosed the hawsers and pushed off from those stone beaches. We did not heed the cries of the slender-armed women left behind who were unconvinced of our promise to return to them in their smoky fen, who gave sour portent, "Those who feud break their promises like battle-shafts."

Elephant Son set our special sea-dress, and we swam through an ocean afire with hatred and covered with crackling ice islands. My ship was Glad-Hunter. I stood at the prow with my truth-cleated battle-shaft. No sea-beast bent our line. No fumes from Hell bent my head. My thanes said a wonder-smith had forged my reach. I slew the ice, and gave waste to ice-wasted shores.

Elephant Son's sea-wisdom brought Glad-Hunter beneath the gaze of the kindred of Cain, who Hard-Fisherman had told me held the dark-haired queen in chains for their pleasure. The kindred of Cain were behemoths grown swollen by feasting on the flesh of black and hurt half-men. They squatted in a cliff-keep built by long-dead giants. It was nameless. It was walled perfidy. I was not blocked from driving my curved prow wave-cutter onto the poisoned shore. I bolted on my honor-linked armor. I sprang to the ice-draped rocks. I was at the noon of my might. I was ripe of mind for my quest.

There was no morning or evening in the nameless cliff-keep. Murder slew time and falsehood made one day as long as a season. I led my thanes through the underground trail. The dark cast thickened. The stones ahead boomed beneath the step of an approaching behemoth. He dragged his loathsome body before me. He said his name was Brother Murder. He said he was first among the last in the nameless cliff-keep that was walled perfidy. He said that the dark-haired queen was his hard-won consort. He said he was pleasure for the dark-haired queen, whom he called Hard-Heart.

I met the treachery of the boastful behemoth. His breath was without cure. His eyes were pits. I kissed my memories of Hard-Fisherman. I was unafraid of his lust. I did not pity him. I commanded my thanes to stand in my reflection. I spoke out, son of Dragon-Worrier, "I am the Champion of the Land of Fire-Scolds."

He spoke out, First of the Last, "You are Hard-Fisherman's Sought-Treasure. Your coming has long been told. My queen, Hard-Heart, had entertained me with tales of your wasted days of longing. My queen, Hard-Heart, who gives me pleasure as I give her pleasure had ordered that you share our feasting table. I would have you slain before you sleep. My soft-armed consort commands that you must first suffer the sorrow that slays sleep."

I spoke, Champion of the Land of Fire-Scolds, "Your lies are as clear as my quest. No false contempt will deceive me, no rancid meat will sicken me, no sleep in this hall of monsters will tempt me, for I am come on a pyre-sworn oath to free the dark-haired queen from your embrace. I am Hard-Fisherman's Seed's Seed, and I wield a mind no less bright-edged than my battle-shaft. When I strike for my desire in this stinking fortress I shall gather to me the slaves whom you feed upon as I shall dispatch you and your Cain-brothers to your welcome in Hell."

Brother Murder fell into a silence that contained a foul learning. Brother Murder led, and I and my war-band followed, through the underground trail to the roasting hall where the kindred of Cain gathered for their feast.

The dozen behemoths who ruled there, joined by the first among the last, displayed themselves in treacherous entertainment at their long table. I and my quest-companions walked among them. I cast my eyes hard, for no light penetrated that smoky fen. I could not glimpse the dark-haired queen whose fair form I had come to wrest from the ice-mere, and I told my sea-warriors that the desire of my quest must be sealed within the nameless cliff-keep.

"Behold Hard-Fisherman's Heart's Heart," spoke Brother Murder to his eleven Cain-brothers. "He is no fool. He is a warrior deprived of the knowledge of who is a prisoner and who is a warden. He has spoken that he comes to set free our queen, Hard-Heart, chained here by our cruel direction."

I spoke with unblunted anger, son of Dragon-Worrier, "Hold your twisted words and show your murder-dulled battle-shafts. I shall cut your numbers one throat at a throw unless you deliver me the dark-haired queen, whom you torture for your pleasure!"

Brother Murder stood among the eleven other behemoths. They hissed and choked at my words, the mirth of shades and fiends. I would not await more false invitation. I waved my sure battle-shaft over my head, faster and faster, so that the dark air of the hall swirled in a wind that lifted the shadows. At the head of the feasting table sat that fettered fawn, Hard-Heart.

"I am here all the while, Hard-Fisherman's Oath-Taker," she spoke, the dark-haired queen.

Brother Murder spoke up, First of the Last, "Tell our queen, Hard-Heart, how you, mistaken warrior, have come to cut the binds that we have wrapped round her soft flesh." So great was his enjoyment of my doubt, he could not complete his taunting request.

I spoke to the dark-haired queen, "These stabbing thoughts cannot stain my mission. I am Hard-Fisherman's Tall-Hero. I was born to rule the black and hurt half-men of the wall of blizzards and behemoths. This assembly does not blunt my might forged by wonder-smiths. I am not moved to loose my strength on these shades until I keep my pyre-oath. I am come to rescue you, Copper-Crowned's sister, from your dolorous fate, lost child."

The dark-haired queen spoke, Brother Murder's Pleasure, "You have come to rescue? And how would you accomplish this tardy work? Can you rescue my life, that was glad-hearted and full of promise in golden king-doms, that has been taken from me and exchanged for a hag's end of regrets? What is it that you have come to rescue, slow-footed inheritor? My flesh that cannot be cleansed, my mind that cannot be emptied of fright, my heart that has become as hard as the land of ice? This is my home and this is my prison and this is my inheritance. What keeps me here is not these gluttons who give me pleasure as I give them pleasure. What chains me to my high-seat in this fen of despair is my loathing for those who have abandoned me and corrupted me. What holds me here, misguided thane, is that my pain is my purpose is my pleasure is my pain."

I looked into the words of the dark-haired queen, and a fresh sorrow came to me, victory-blest man. I saw that it was not full measure to swing my battle-shaft through the dozen behemoths. To free her, lost love, from the chains she pulled close in her pain, I must break the bonds of her thoughts tied to long-lost and long-remembered days. My compassionate war-band and I knelt before her and wept for her struggles in the ice-wasted land. Our true tears became a torrent that crashed against the walls so that a flood rose higher and higher, immersing the dark-haired queen's loathing for past wrongs, washing the hatred from her flesh.

I told the dark-haired queen, Hard-Fisherman's Heart's Heart, "Quest of my quest, Hard-Heart, rise from this table stained by faults of a wickedness alien to your true-ways, and stand free of your memories of long-lost and long-remembered days. Rise free, queen of my love, and accept your true name, Glad-Heart."

I have the head of a hero. My hearth-companions call me Bulwark of the South. I am sharp-witted and have the clue to war-success. I enjoy the weather of rainbows. I take the high-seat in my ice-carved hall and share meat with my long-eared hounds. My retinue gathers at my drinking tables to hear my bards make hall-songs of my contests.

My bards finish their song of my quest to free the dark-haired queen. My companions cheer for the hard-won victories that thrust me forward as king of ice-clogged salt-trails even as my love won a soft-victory over the dark-haired queen. I accept the hails of my strong and numerous war-band. I turn in my high-seat to touch the hem of the flashing gown of my queen, Glad-Heart. There is no pleasure on her face for the songs of my bards. I ask her if she is not made glad to hear again of the long past days when I came to rescue her as Hard-Fisherman's Ghost's Heeder. I ask her if she does not love me, proud-headed prince, as I love her, proud-headed princess.

My dark-haired queen, Glad-Heart, speaks thickly, "It is not I who am troubled. It is you who have the pallor of the sick and the fever of the dying. It is you who appears to have fought his last battle in your wave-skimming ship, Glad-Hunter. It is you who seems as a man come to his sad ending-day."

And it is true. Though I enjoy the weather of rainbows, gray clouds course across my vision, death-knells sound in my ears, and I taste my blood on my lips. I sink at the feet of the dark-haired queen. My brave shieldsmen rush to my side and weep at the sight of their bold king helpless on his hall floor. Elephant Son and Copper-Crowned lay their hands on my brow. I shout to them. I make no brave sound.

At last, my sight gone, my breath unable to stir a feather, I smell the love fragrance of my dark-haired queen, Glad-Heart, and I cry out like a child, Time-Thief's Portent-Carrier, "Forgive me, Glad-Heart, for not loving you as you merited at my side, and for permitting my thoughts to wander to Poor-Patience in her grave and the son we made in the Land of the Whale-Killers."

I feel my body fall from a craggy cliff and tumble end over fore into a rain that blows warm and soft. I hear Glad-Heart above me, and she is angry. I hear Glad-Heart call to me in a hard voice that does not suit the soft-armed consort that I thought gladdened by love, and this new voice that is an old voice tells me, "I shall come to Hell to get you back. Death's door cannot keep me out. I shall come, for your work at my vengeance is unfinished, and there is no other like Skallagrim Ice-Waster, Rune-Carver and Wolfman, King of the South."

Christmas A.D. 2037

I must interrupt this unhappy work. I have been ill for a long time, coughing some blood again. That is not my dilemma. My life is not in jeopardy, not that way. My purpose is threatened. My worst worries seem realized. There is a sudden spectre of manipulation, degradation, new lies where I had sought old truths. This is much to ask. I feel I should shout to God, "Test me, test me!" I cannot. I can only set these words down, and this does make me feel stronger. Confined like this, alone save for my wolf, all conversation with my keepers proscribed except once a month with the commandant, my writing has become my intimacy. I have been too long away from my paper and pen. I do feel firmer. I shall continue as long as my concentration at this sitting.

I see now how simpleminded I have been to believe that I could complete my work before my luck changed again, and these years of effort were strangled. Grim Fiddle is a lucky man. I should have anticipated that what began in contretemps, continued in serendipity, would come to failure. I intended years more of autobiography, greedy and lonely man. I had hope for a manuscript thrice this size, more, since I have had no need to finish before my own end. There is intervention. My work is arrested unfinished, and what I have managed to remember and to confess could be for nothing if I do not gain the time to explain completely.

I should not have kept my circumstances apart from my confession. Now I must confuse my undone work with details at odd angle to my narrative. I suppose that I thought when I began that anyone who read this might know some of Grim Fiddle, and those who did not would not care to be confused by the author's day-to-day endeavor. This supposition was itself complicated by the fact that there was no single point that began this work, no first page, first chapter, instead stories that tumbled in my mind, that required drafting and redrafting until I was able to teach myself what little I know of how to tell a story. I am embarrassed to admit that even these few hundred pages have taken all my strength, and how long? I cannot say accurately, twelve years, more, for I started, stopped, paused for years, began again.

I also suppose that I kept secret my place in this world because I was and am ashamed of what I am, did not want to taint the honest spirit of my work. I write as much for companionship as for other cause, like my Sam. This manuscript has been my dearest friend, filled with the voices of my loved ones, and what would it have served to cut it up with the diary voice of Grim Fiddle, author and convict.

The answer is that it would have served the truth: Grim Fiddle is a prisoner convicted of crimes against humanity. I stand condemned of conspiracy to make war, and of making war, against governments and peoples. They referred to me variously as "this remorseless mass-murderer" and "the twenty-first century's first unspeakable monster." Their verdict of guilty was less interesting than the justification not to execute me. My tribunal ruled that the best lesson to be achieved by the condemnation of a man like me was to refuse to take my life. My judges said, "Too many are dead. Let this mercy put all who murder to shame." More, my judges opined that the most fitting punishment they could conceive for me was not to release me from the weight of my guilt, rather to keep me imprisoned for the remainder of my life that I might consider what I had done. I am meant to live as long as humanly possible in infamy.

That is nearly three decades past. Now Grim Fiddle has grown old. That is what he is, an old man, sickly now and again, still extraordinarily game, with no evidence death will soon release him from his punishment. My judges are dust. Their just wrath lives on in this place, my prison. My guards call it the ice prison, over the objection of the new commandant, who has replaced Joannes Diomedes Nestoraxes, the old soldier. Diomedes was my jailer for nearly fourteen years. He regarded his work as seriously as his prayers and books. He obeyed the letter of the law's verdict on Grim Fiddle. Nevertheless he was my friend, granted me my she-wolf, Helen, a pup when the guards found her on the glacier. It was Diomedes who named this place the ice prison, and me the ice prisoner. It and I are man-made complexes, located above the quay, beneath the towering southern lip of the jade glacier. This is Elephant Island, the southeast shore. The Ice Cross's headquarters, where Lykantropovin ruled and died, was a mile to the west, under what is now a fresh mountain of volcanic rock. That is also where Peregrine and Charity and Molly are buried, somewhere under a mountain that was my ally in my victory over Lykantropovin nearly thirty years ago. I celebrated what would have been Charity's ninetieth birthday this past winter, and have looked forward to Peregrine's same next winter. Not that I would be permitted to get over there. I have not left this prison for nearly twenty-nine years.

My ice prison is administered by an organization that changes its acronym frequently. I think of how Diomedes would joke, when he read me my charge and sentence once a month as dictated by law, by scrambling the words of the sponsoring body into anagrams for me to decipher. The present commandant, a Canadian national named Gardiner, whom I think of as new though he has been here four years, does not care to keep me informed of affairs back in the place that four of the guards, Germans, call among themselves, so I overhear them, "planet Earth." They do not laugh when they say it. This post is no honor. Gardiner seems to believe he is banished here, for unexplained cause, and has brought with him a niggardliness that has worn on morale. He has none of the

poet's blood that made this an austere pleasure for Diomedes. To-
wards me, Gardiner is terse, stiff, moody. My guess is that Gardiner was a man of action who momentarily lost his self-confidence,
or his nerve. At first, Gardiner was hostile, suspicious of me, but
that has disappeared. My present person does not fit the legend I
suppose he has of me. After his caution passed, there was curiosity, prying, about how I pass my time. He would come in here
while I was up top exercising or taking the sunlight, and he would
handle my rune-carved blocks and stones, would turn through my
papers, and once went so far as to take parts of this manuscript
from me. I worried he might destroy it, or confiscate the whole
of it, or forbid me more paper. When he returned it and showed
no inclination either to take more or to make comment, I worried
about what he thought. My poverty includes a dearth of critics.
My readers and not my characters are imaginary. Gardiner has
never responded to my inquiries, though he must face me once a
month to read the text of my sentence. I try to interrupt him by
asking about my manuscript, "What do you make of Israel?" He
stiffens and reads on. I once knew that piece of paper he reads
so well that I could sing it. Oddly, I lost that trick, and the whole
of it. It dances in my mind, yet when I try to write it down, I lose
focus. Diomedes memorized it and came to dramatizing it in English, French, and, my favorite, in Greek Homeric couplets. Gardiner seems to have no need for burlesque. After four years, not
including the months he is granted leave (when he travels to Cape
Town), he has not changed a note, has made no casual remark
afterward, has always ended, "Is all in order?" My answer is my
cheeriest "All is in order!"

Perhaps now my shock this morning is more understandable,
when Gardiner appeared with the cook bringing me my Christmas dinner. I am granted extra fruit on my birthday, and on
Eastern and Western Christianity's Christmas, a legacy of
Diomedes's devoutness that Gardiner has not altered, though he
is cynic and not Christian. Helen does not like him, and growled
when he sat down on the bench. I have worried he would take
her from me also, and quieted her quickly. He had taken a seat, a
first in my presence. He had an envelope in his hand, a letter. He
seemed annoyed and anxious. He knew he should not have been
here, a week early, out of the ordinary, a break in regulation. I

was as flustered as he, flopped about to get him a chair. He told me to calm myself, to get back in bed, and to listen.

"Within the week," he said, "I have received a communication, by letter, from my predecessor, Lieutenant Commander Nestoraxes of the United Greek Republic Navy, and, after studying my position, and weighing the implications of this confidence in terms of your sentence, have come to tell you of the parts of Commander Nestoraxes's letter that concern you."

Diomedes has retired to the Aegean island of Naxos. He decided at the last not to enter the Church, instead to settle on his pension in the village at the foot of the monastery. I can see it all, the azure Aegean, the bright beige beach, the dusty white town arranged in geometric acuity, the green and brown ridges rising to the stone and wood monastery pirouetting above that meditative seascape. For me, the image is voluptuous. Diomedes described it so well in the notes he put in the margins of the books he lent me—our secret dialogue—that I feel I can smell the olives and taste the goat's cheese. I imagine Diomedes passes his days not too dissimilar to mine, excepting the profound differences of climate and food. He reads his philosophers, works he passed me from his library here, and he writes his memoirs—from a young recruit in battle against the Turk to a naval officer assigned to international treaty organizations charged with maintaining the law across the face of the earth. Diomedes called himself a professional truce-keeper, and only incidentally a warrior. I called him the old soldier. He was a student, and a poet, and a keeper, ever watchful with words and men. It was he who encouraged me to make a manuscript of my confession. I suppose his work is now as demanding as mine, for his adventures were no less sweeping and sad than mine; he was one of those who were ordered into the Pacific basin during those times we called, between us, the Age of Exile.

Diomedes believes that he, as a Greek, understands completely the ideas of banishment, redress, and revenge. He said that his ancestors invented exile. He said that God had granted the Greeks all those islands so that they might grasp, all at once, what it is to be surrounded by the unknown. Also, Diomedes said that the Greek thinkers could be as rash and antagonistic as they were because the island culture provided a way for despots to dispose of present dissent without disposing of dissent's uncanny quality to transform itself, as with magic, into future dogma. Diomedes said that a Greek was a heaven-sent keeper for problems such as Grim Fiddle. He thought of Elephant Island as a challenge worthy of his blood. I think he is more comfortable on rock surrounded by ocean. It matches his mind, a keeper surrounded by forgetfulness.

Diomedes writes me, through Gardiner, that he misses me, and our secret talk, and feels ill-used without the ice and wind to combat. He asks after Satan's Seat, which was silent all the while he was here, which he resented for depriving him of an experience approximating the great volcanoes that periodically tore apart and then reawakened the history of the Aegean. It was his favorite story of mine, the eruptions of Satan's Seat. I think he was envious of my memory, even jealous of my relationship with past catastrophes. Naxos, he writes, baked white waste of the Cyclades Islands, is in comparison to the Antarctic an infant's crib, or an old-age pen.

Most importantly, Diomedes writes that he set aside his own writing to investigate some of the history that I touch upon with ignorance in my work. He knows that the many holes I have left weaken my project, and it is a great kindness that he has determined to educate himself in my favor. I realize that he must have been planning to write at length to help me, and I can guess that the obstacle he saw he had to overcome was how to reach me. It is one of the cruelest terms of my sentence that I am not permitted to correspond, nor am I permitted mail. I suppose then that his delay in writing these last four years has involved his effort to discover some way to pry open Gardiner.

In the course of his researches, Diomedes has not only consulted records entombed in the vaults of whatever treaty organization that now represents the remains of the Ice Cross, but also has written letters of inquiry to Sweden and America. I do not believe he has contacted Cleopatra. He does not mention her. This may mean she is dead, most likely means nothing. He races over these matters to the crux of my crisis. Diomedes says his surprise was unbounded when he received word (not a letter, some sort of communique from a technology of which I am ignorant) from an American journalist who spoke of me, Grim Fiddle, as the center of a political controversy in the Americas and Europe—in the North.

It seems that a clique of uncertain persuasion has seized upon the history of the Age of Exile as an issue they can exploit for their own aggrandizement. I am supposing. I am intrinsically antagonistic. They call themselves the One World Reunion, also the One World Society, also the Reunionists. They have cells in every major northern city. Their platform is vast and monolithic, with a unifying theme that seems to be opposition to the political-science fashion of the last one hundred years, since the Second World War, which they say has been characterized by extremism, separatism, chauvinism, liberationism, and ever more divisive polemic supporting racial, geographic, and religious purity. The Reunionists are rabid heterogenes. They are savvy revisionists. They claim—and I translate this into my terms because I am not sure of their language—that politics is not a science but a curse of the Tower of Babylon, so much babble at cross-purposes. The Reunionists have launched themselves against the hypothesis that there are legitimate concepts such as the first world, second world, third world, nonaligned world, developed and underdeveloped world, Christian and Moslem world, the East, West, North, and South. They decry what I have called fantastic architecture. They call the assumption of separate self-authentication to be nonsense, claim that a house divided is no house at all, assert that there is no man or woman on earth today who belongs to just one country, ancestry, religion, or race, and therefore the idea that people of color, or people of a holy book, or people of industry should gather separately is folly. They claim that the fracturing of the world into a series of silent confederacies has silenced reason, and that the reunion of mankind is the call of the future. Their enemy is what they call liberationist separatism. Their aim is conflation, synthesis, and metamorphosis. They say they are the champions of the mongrel.

I reiterate that Diomedes has written in haste, promising another letter soon. This must mean that he has found the crack in Gardiner's heart's door. This outpost receives a delivery by ship roughly once a month during the summer, so I cannot hope for more until late January. In the meantime, I must suffer the implications of Diomedes's brief remarks about how the Reunionists have addressed themselves to the history of what I have called the wretched, what Diomedes and I call the Age of Exile, and in particular the politics of the ice camps, the Ice Cross, the rest of it, including the whole story I have yet to tell of the rise and fall of the Kingdom of Antarctica, the birth and measured infanticide of the People's Republic of Antarctica. It hurts me that I am obliged to introduce these last matters in this hasty, sloppy way. I have been so cautious. Now I must gloss. I have cause. Diomedes writes that the Reunionists are pressing American and European treaty organizations to reopen the arrest, indictment, trial, condemnation, and imprisonment of me, Grim Fiddle, fallen warlord of Antarctica.

The Reunionists say that I am a victim of lies and collusion, say I am unjustly condemned, made to bear the whole weight of a period that vouchsafed the murder of millions by starvation and hopelessness. I suppose that if the Reunionists knew my mind, they would say they have countercharged Brave New Benthamism and counterindicted the Charity Factor. The Reunionists declare my twenty-nine years of mute confinement to be far in excess of humane penance, inappropriate for any transgression I might have commited as an outlaw, guerrilla, terrible avenger, and warlord. In his letter Diomedes uses the phrase "long-wronged and forgotten hero of the long forgotten and wronged."

The sum is this: The One World Reunion is maneuvering for the resurrection of what they see as the aged scapegoat Grim Fiddle.

Gardiner finished his presentation without a sigh, abruptly, as if in midsentence. He would not show me the letter. I have hope that he might, for he seemed moved by my reaction. I wept and I shook. Gardiner presumed that I was rejoicing at the hope offered by such an aberration, and ended our exchange with contrived pity. He said that he had not told me of the letter immediately upon receipt, which he seems to have gotten on my birthday last week, because he said he was anxious that my age, my health, might make me too vulnerable to false promise. This was disingenuous, of course, since the chief reason for his delay was that he was assessing what he had to gain in contrast to what he might lose should he violate the letter of the law.

Despite his condescension, I was touched by Gardiner's pity

and defensiveness, am now puzzling what changes might be in the future for our relationship. In one sense, we are closer than lovers, jailer and jailed: he rules me, while I represent his reason for being. He folded Diomedes's letter, rose, shuffled. He might have been waiting to see if I might descend into a swoon, or worse. The medical officer here suspects my heart, says that it is too large for a healthy man. Gardiner's pause was appropriate, for my blood raced, I was pallid and sweaty. I got control of my breathing and tried to show him that I would endure by offering him some of my Christmas fruit. I understood then that his reading of the letter was Gardiner's Christmas present to me. I have his secret now. He is sentimental. We share a chink. The stern, disconsolate commandant of the ice prisoner's keep has a hidden compassion. Gardiner started to speak in English, mumbled what seemed a prayer, or epigram, in an odd tongue. Was that American Indian? Is this a deeper confidence? He is Canadian, a career naval officer, a professional truce-keeper like Diomedes, and has mentioned to one of the sergeants of the guard—I overheard them—that he likes to hunt on the ice because it reminds him of the Elizabeth Islands. My map, hidden in the Fiddle Bible, the one book I am permitted in my own library, shows me the Elizabeth Islands are part of Canada's Northwest Territories. Perhaps Gardiner is a half-breed like me, part Eskimo, or with blood of a remnant of the fabled Iroquois nations. Gardiner has become a new mind for me to explore. Gardiner cleared his rich face and said, "Is all in order?"

Gardiner misunderstands my upset. All is not in order. I am fractured as the faults ripped the South, as New Benthamism ripped God's children. I am in agony at the thought of a hope that is a curse. I find my strength has gone just now. I shall explain the more tomorrow. I wish myself and Helen a merry Christmas, and shall turn to reading from the Fiddle Bible—the Gospel of Matthew—to an old and patient she-wolf.

This new turn is more and worse than I could have supposed. My fever returned to pull me to bed five days ago, on Christmas night. This triggered nightmares that bathed me in sorrow. I have not mentioned before that it is a phenomenon of Antarctica that when conditions are physically worst, as they were in the ice camps, or on Anvers Island, as they can be for those unaccustomed to the six months of winter's howling blackness, one does not have nightmares. One dreams grandiosely. An extreme example of this might be the berserker dreaming I re-created this past winter to speak to my ascendancy to kingship, a passage that might represent the last thoughtful work I shall manage on my manuscript. It has been one of my punishments in this prison, where I am physically well cared for, that my nightmares here suffuse my memory—awful fogs that I cannot reproduce when rational. This new threat has called up hideous images of the sleights of the hand of fate. I feel my body pulled inside out, as if a wizard had reached inside my mouth and pulled my soul onto the outside, with handwriting wrapped around and around my being for all to read. Surely this must be some bizarre transformation of Diomedes's letter, my first letter in twenty-nine years of anathema, the first communication meant just for me since I found Grandfather's stone marker on Mead's Kiss thirty-six years ago. Diomedes's words have seared my thoughts and burned my flesh.

I have promised that I would explain my upset at the news of the Reunionists. It is straightforward. I fear them. I reject them. It is the same. I have buried so many of my loved ones as well as my enemies; all my love may be in the coldest ground. I held myself also safely done, in the frozen ground, buried. Now these strangers, who do not love me, whom I can never know, intend to disinter a corpse. Yes, my heart races and my mind makes this confession. Yet I am dead to all that apostasy on "planet Earth." I am exiled by law. I am condemned by mankind. A justly convened tribunal sent me into infamy. I accept my sentence by them as an act of genius. I deserve what has been done to me. I am guilty of crimes against humanity. I did make war, did murder countless numbers of God's children. I can see and hear them die again and again. This is my due penance. I have served my time here without once looking toward or praying for release. This is meant to be, must be, my end.

What right have these strangers, the One World Reunion, to scratch an ice grave and bring forth the decay of a man wracked by his own guilt and haunted by his own ghosts? What right have they to drag a tormented soul back into a world that had no place for him in 2009, might not even have had a place for him at his birth in 1973? What right can they possibly claim to increase my punishment? This seems manifold jeopardy. They are trying me again. Mankind has done of me. Let mankind's verdict stand. Let me be.

I do not want to mislead. I do not think the Reunionists do demon's work, or angel's work. They are men and women. What men have done wrong, men can do right. That is a certainty to embrace relentlessly, a vigilant philosophy. In this case, though, it would seem that what men have done—wrong or right—they in their overweening pride presume they can do again, wrong or right. Who are these Reunionists? Their philosophy, expanding from the scraps fed me by Diomedes, seems as smug and superficial as that of the New Benthamites. They seem opportunists more than revisionists. Grim Fiddle smells the stink of sanctimoniousness.

I exhaust myself. It feels fine, though, to sweat out my bile. And my fear. I have found the wherewithal for this outburst. Perhaps I have resources I have long underestimated. This does not mean that I do not trust my own measure. I have made a profound decision. Its finality gives me calm for now, though I know it will not last. I have paused to explain my contempt for the Reunionists, and their hollow campaign to resurrect Grim Fiddle, because I spy them clearly from the vantage of a set course. Such disgusts me, yet less so than the thought of being plucked from my grave to be carried on the shoulders of opportunism as a hero. I hate the lie as I love the truth. It is my torment that I am confronted now by two lies, neither more terrible than the other. I have chosen.

I shall take my own life. I cannot say when. Before, that is enough. Gardiner has not returned since Christmas morning. I do not expect him until the reading of my sentence after the new year. Then there is the onus of the next supply ship, which might, no, certainly will, bring another letter from Diomedes about the Reunionists. This gives me at least a fortnight to press my flesh smooth, to make peace in my mind, to get my heart's prison all in order. I shall make more specific arrangements then, how to do it, at what moment—sunrise and sunset being impossible in the land of the midnight sun. I am sure now of this one thing: I will not let them have me. I have nothing left but this, my life. I want to keep it. I do not want to die. Yet I shall not bargain with fate. It is my life my way or not whatsoever. I shall not surrender myself to my deathless enemy, the lies of tyrants, the politics of falsehood. It is a lie to take one's own life, I know, and suicide will undoubtedly prejudice my final judgment. That is understatement. I shall risk this prejudice rather than give comfort to my enemies. This smacks of self-sacrifice. That might be part of it. I am primarily thinking of myself. Either I take me, or they will.

I am in panic, I can feel that. I can also see that I might have transformed Diomedes's letter into a phantasm of persecution. Yet I have no time for patient reconsideration. I must anticipate. Diomedes has been gone four years. There is no knowing how long he delayed writing me about the Reunionists, or how long the Reunionists have been conspiring against me. It is good tactic in conflict to presume the very worst. Therefore, though I have just learned of my peril, I presume the Reunionists are poised as I write. There must be no delay. I learned long ago to trust my luck. As Peregrine said, without misfortune there is no fortune at all. I trust now that my twenty-nine years here in solitude and reflection have been good luck. I trust now that my luck will go bad unless I act decisively.

It does not interest me to defend my decision further. There is a maddening sidebar. I cannot and should not now expect that anyone will ever read this manuscript. I must prepare myself to destroy it before I destroy myself, for fear the Reunionists, deprived of a false scapegoat by me, can take my confession and twist it to hold up their pious robes. What bitterness, and yet perhaps such a comedy as this deserves the jest of remaining untold.

I can do what I will, then, a freed prisoner. I could choose fear and self-pity and sleep. I shall not. I shall rush to complete my story as well as I can. I shall write pell-mell. I have the time to Diomedes's next letter.

THE PEOPLE'S REPUBLIC OF ANTARCTICA

My Crimes ▪ My Fall From Satan's Seat
▪ My Sam

My Crimes

I ruled Anvers Island absolutely for six years. The length of my
reign over what I call the Kingdom of Ice is more in question.
In my construction as self-elected regent, the Kingdom of Ice
was seeded by the exodus of several hundred thousand wretches
into the Antarctic over the decade of epic ruin that closed the
twentieth century; was given life by me and my company one black
winter of corruption and murder on Anvers Island; was given
shape and strength over five years of piracy, murder-raiding, and
all-out war against the Ice Cross; was elevated to youthful grandeur over another black, hallucinatory winter marked by madness
in the camps, colossal eruptions through the South Shetlands chain,
and the collapse and capitulation of the Ice Cross; and was finally
cut down and dismembered at the close of its sixth year, early
summer, not by a blade wielded by its enemies but by the tongues
of its counselors, and particularly its queen.

I should give voice to my defamers, who were finally the tribunal that condemned me. Some said that the idea of my Kingdom of Ice, and the kingdom itself, was a ruse, said that I was
never a king, as my archipelago state was never sovereign. Instead, I was said to be a warlord, a guerrilla chieftain who gathered to himself the title of king in order to aggrandize his outlaw
horde and to chain to his throne the people of the ice camps. I
was said to be a sham king who deliberately promoted himself as
regent over a geography that was no land, rather an accident of
weather, and over masses that were no people, rather refugees en
route to new worlds. I was said to have stolen peace, to have murdered truth, to have buried decency beneath ice and chaos.

I have no heart to answer my defamers, which is why I list
their accusations bluntly. It is for others, safely in the future, to
ask, when is a state not a conceit? When is a king not a pretender?
When is war not a crime? I could point to the birth of so many
kingdoms in the North as models of the events acted out yet again
on the ice of the Bransfield Strait. A fortified tower becomes a

duchy; a duchy becomes an oligarchy of warriors; a gang of chieftains becomes a kingship born of necessity in battle against another oligarchy; and then the kingdom becomes a ruin after long struggle to justify itself by conquest and theft as empire. The evolution rolls along as easily as it rolls from my pen. What an old, tired, splendiferous tale. Yes, I simplify. I ask, however, is not there crude simplicity in whatever mankind does when it begins and ends in murder?

The Kingdom of Antarctica, then, my black kingdom on the black ice—whether one recognizes it as my illusion or as a genuine catastrophe—was ever a twice-told tale. I believe this profoundly true, because what I have called the Age of Exile does appear to me, abandoned here in my timeless ice prison to ponder and to muse, to be a cruel repetition of the Norse Age of Migration. That is what the book writers called the close of the first millennium *anno Domini,* without irony. All I ought to know of the Age of Migration, ten, eleven, twelve centuries back and half the circumference of the world to the north, ought to be fog, screams, and the transcendant language of the document that shines through that darkness: the holy book of the Age of Migration, *Beowulf,* King of the Weather-Geats, slayer of Grendel and mother, hero of heroes. Instead, I can convince myself that I have lived through that same darkness at the close of the second millennium *anno Domini.* The fleet of the damned has raised sails over the oceans of time.

The joy is gone for me now in the poetry of Beowulf's evil-battling days. And I believe it no coincidence that my berserker dreaming can resemble the book of Beowulf. As to why, I have two minds. Either one can argue some Norse virus was awakened in my blood, like an infection of ideas, when I thrust myself from Golgotha into the terror of Anvers Island, so that the language of Beowulf spilled up across a millennium to flood my mind with ghastly images; or else one can argue that the mind of Grim Fiddle was overwhelmed by the loss of his grandfather, father, family, and reason for being, and thereby Grim Fiddle was hurtled back into a language that he had studied more closely than his heartbeat when he was warm and secure with his loved ones.

I do not choose. Both are revealing. And my dreaming was not a fleeting nightmare. I lived it. Yes, Mother's portent, her theft of the future, was fulfilled in the most bizarre way—in my dream. But not only there. How shrewd of Lamba Time-Thief not to have mentioned that Skallagrim Ice-Waster, Wolfman and Rune-Carver, king of the black and hurt half-men of the wall of blizzards and behemoths, heeder of the ghost of a thousand-year-dead outlaw, would also, and at the same time, become the warlord of Antarctica. How humbling of my luck to discover that when a prophecy becomes a history it does not salve the sting of truth. Murder is still murder, crime is still crime, and no matter how fancifully one has envisioned it—the head of a hero, or the Bulwark of the South—there is no going back. It is a fate in a dream from which one awakens covered in genuine infamy.

My crimes were legion. The worst was pride. I pretended to be greater than those wretched people. In my vanity, I pretended to lead the meek to glory. I did not see at the time that when a fallible man takes upon himself the work that belongs only and finally to God, he must fail, and fail in the worst way possible. I did not try to be God. I tried to do his work. This is still prideful, and ruinous, and damning.

Grim Fiddle caused the death of Jane Gaunt, Violante Furore, Cleo Furore, Annabel Donne, Magda Zulema, who were innocent of murder, who were murdered by the Ice Cross; in revenge, Grim Fiddle murdered the Ice Cross, slaughtered it without mercy. Grim Fiddle put his blade to the officers and crew of the Ice Cross frigates *Repulse,* and *Coronation Mercy,* and *Good Hope,* and *Nightingale,* and *Ursula,* and *Cape Agassiz,* and more, many more. Grim Fiddle was also the murderer of Jaguaquara, who had murdered Grootgibeon, who had murdered Xavier Grumpa. Grim Fiddle was the murderer of Hector the Fat, who had murdered Lalo the Butcher of Port Stanley, who had murdered Iacovella the Butcher of Deception Island. Grim Fiddle was the murderer of Fives O'Birne, who had murdered Cuellar Alcanfores, who had murdered Gumic Blades the Liberator. And Grim Fiddle was the murderer of the Little Brothers at Golgotha, was the murderer of the Fathers in Agony, the Dominican Relief Mission to the South Orkneys, the Holy Father's Mercy Commission at Elephant Island. Grim Fiddle murdered the ice camps on

Livingston Island, King George Island, Smith Island, Elephant Island, Clarence Island.

Three generations of mankind were murdered by me, grandfathers and fathers and sons, grandmothers and mothers and daughters. Grim Fiddle murdered them with his own hand. Grim Fiddle murdered them with his rank. Grim Fiddle murdered by depriving them of food and permitting the ice to close over them. Grim Fiddle murdered them for revenge, for hatred, for conquest, for strategy, and for power—always for power, to increase his reach and to justify his reach and to gain grandeur from his reach. I did it. I gave the orders. I watched them die. I, me, Grim Fiddle, Butcher of Anvers Island, murdered Lykantropovin, Butcher of Elephant Island.

There are so many dark stories in just these crimes, and I am prevented by time from relating them properly. Each of my victims deserves my attention. I cannot give it. There is no room in my future now. There might not ever have been paper enough for me to explain what I did, and permitted, and am guilty of. Perhaps there is telling justice in this turn. Perhaps only my silence before what I remember can convey adequately the monstrosity of my crimes. So many dead, killed by me—not by starvation, or the ice, or the Charity Factor—by me. Cleo Furore. I loved her. I would not permit Germanicus to get back to her and the South Georgians my first winter on Anvers Island. I held him to my side. The Ice Cross killed her when they obliterated Golgotha in 2004 in revenge for my attack as the new warlord of Anvers Island, on their blockade at Arthur Harbor. I do not even know how she died, because Cleo was accidentally left behind when Jane and Violante led the remnant of my South Georgians out on the glacier, where Germanicus rescued them before the storms closed on them. Was it exposure, gunshot, drowning? Did they grab Cleo up and condemn her to Elephant Main or Clarence West? We looked for her there. We always looked for her. She disappeared as if she had never been, like my family, but with this distinction: I murdered her just as surely as if I cut her down.

This must not become false witness. I sense how confession has in it the hallucinogen of self-pity. I am revolted by the possibility that in my haste to denounce myself I could be distorting my guilt. My depravity was not total. That would be like none at all. My depravity was selective. I knew goodness and did the worst. I understood truth and lied. I had the power of mercy and more often than not withheld it. I knew in my heart what was right and wrong, even when my mind was drowned by the darkness. To this point I must clarify something about the berserker dreaming that swept me from Golgotha to Anvers Island. It is a fact that I was gripped by a madness, that I sailed *Angel of Death* into Arthur Harbor and then pushed into the fortress at Anvers in a fantasy. I was not Grim Fiddle, mourner; I was Grim Fiddle, Hard-Fisherman's Debt-Payer and avenger—a berserker who cannot be killed, with the strength of a dozen men, without the conscience or limits of any man. I was wrapped inside a bloody delusion, and continued that way for more than a year, in which time I ascended to the rule of the *Hielistos* at Anvers Island.

This berserker dreaming might suggest that I might not have been responsible for what I did. What nonsense. The lie that Grim Fiddle might not have been guilty by reason of momentary unreason. I recall that same sort of sly talk was used at Peregrine's trial for the murder of Cesare Furore. As broken and ill as Peregrine was, he scoffed before his tribunal. I did the same, do the same. I report that when my tribunal asked me why I had done it, all of it, war-making, mass-murdering, I spoke out more clearly than at any time in the proceedings. I quoted my father: "Because I wanted to."

That is correct witness. I testified against myself. If I was not of sound mind when I murdered Jaguaquara that first summer at Anvers and set the slaughter in motion that spun me like a fleshly whirlpool to *el capitán de los capitanes de los Hielistos,* the King of the South, I was still Grim Fiddle. Who else was Grim Fiddle but Grim Fiddle? If I was not of sound mind when I slew the *capitanes,* whom I call behemoths in my berserker dreaming, and gathered Cleopatra to me, and took her, physically took her, ravaged her, cut her body and violated her body and beat her body, I was still Grim Fiddle. Who else? I stole her from herself. She did not agree, she did not resist. I did not ask. I am not sure now of what she filled my berserker mind with in that long black winter on Anvers Island. I can guess, "Revenge us!" I concurred. Grim Fiddle said, yes, get back at them; mad as I was, I still did it. And the following summer (January 2004), after my first victory over the Ice Cross blockade at Anvers, and after the *Hielistos* celebrated me as their butcher of butchers—because I was angrier and crueler and beyond even their ghoulish sense of what was murder—after all that, when I collapsed at Cleopatra's side and emerged from my berserker dreaming as if I were dying, I was still Grim Fiddle. I awoke from that dreaming weakened, disoriented, sickly for a while, appalled at the news of what I had done, the dungeons, the decapitations, the flesh-eating, the scars on Cleopatra's flesh. But then, when I was certainly of sound mind, I did not run from my criminal authority. I enhanced it as I used my counselors, Lazarus, Germanicus, Cleopatra, to raise me up over the wretched. I did not then give a serious thought to quitting my vengeance. What I had begun in mad blood lust, I carried on in measured cruelty. And why did Grim Fiddle do it? Not because of that sleek epigram "When want is crime, I am outlaw." No, not that, no. I did it because I wanted to.

I must hurry. I have figured that I could abridge my year of treacherous assent and my years of bloody rule in this scratchy fashion so that I could have the pause to relate one totally revealing crime. This gives Grim Fiddle his terrible due. It took place three years after my berserker dreaming. I was in rough strategic command of the *Hielistos* from Adelaide Island to Joinville Island; Lazarus was my prime minister; Cleopatra was my queen; and Germanicus and the sealers were my hall-guard. I was acute and hard and locked in combat with Lykantropovin. There can be no possible claim that what I did was because I was not of right mind. Grandfather told me at our first meeting, "Make right by doing right. All their talk, it does not matter. You shall be judged swiftly and finally by Lord God." Here is proof that not only did Grim Fiddle make wrong by being wrong, but also that what I have done can only be forgiven by a God whose compassion is ineffable. For this alone, Grim Fiddle condemns himself.

It was late in the summer, the ice heaving onto the South Shetlands, the volcanoes pouring a sulfurous cloud that was so swollen in places there seemed new ice islands where there were only ash-heaped floes. The skuas screamed, and the sky and the sea were one wash of imminent oblivion. To sail into that thunderous and putrescent panorama was wild risk. It was also bright strategy. No ship, large or small, armed or crammed with filthy little creatures, was more able than another if the real adversary, Antarctica, was not battled effectively. That climate crushed the quick and the doomed. That climate was my ally, the reason why my small, ill-led, poorly armed guerrilla force could best the superior strength and discipline of Lykantropovin's Ice Cross. We did not care if we lived or died; we cared only for revenge.

I was escaping a sorry defeat off Gibbs Island, southwest of Elephant Island. My *capitanes de los Hielistos* had overreached themselves, been caught by Lykantropovin's in-home flotilla. My flagship went down under me. I got off in an open boat with Davey Gaunt and twenty others. We fell in with one of our small cutters. We came about in an effort to get free of the tide that ripped us seaward. The wind stripped our sail. The cutter, captained by Coquito Blades, brother of a man I had executed for betrayal, gave us a line. We made for the closest landfall, Clarence Island. By late in the day, the sun a small torch at the horizon, we were at anchor in the inlet, shaped by a glacier and a natural bulkhead of rock slabs. A huge ice island—green and blue, carved by the wind to contain deep caves where seals and penguins hid— had hooked on the underwater rocks and swung around to push against the beach, bashing the Ice Cross boats at anchor against the bulkhead. The sea shivered about us, a big blow coming from the west. A large freighter had foundered in the harbor and was slowly being capsized by the aground ice island. I ordered most everyone off both cutter and longboat; I chose the men who would stay aboard the cutter to ride out the storm. We thrashed ashore, using a grotto in the ice island as an entry ramp. There is no way to describe what it feels like inside an ice island. We were so tired and desperate there were men who wanted to stay in there rather than risk the beach. We expected to be overrun immediately by the Ice Cross detachment at the camp on the bluff above, the notorious Clarence West.

The attack did not come. A white flag was raised on the redoubt that fronted the camp's main entrance on the bluff. That was not a fortified position, more a large barn, half-crushed by a rockslide, situated at the mouth of the elaborate cavelike network that led into the camp's barracks. We were too cold to care about the possibility of a trap, or the other, infection. We hurried up the escarpment. Coquito Blades led the assault at the gate. It should have meant our massacre. Instead, the Ice Cross commandant surrendered, begged for mercy for himself and his men. By the time I got inside, my *Hielistos* had done their duty, leaving the commandant for my decision. I had him interrogated and then nailed up over the camp entrance. Within the hour, I was in command of the whole of the camp, with the auxiliary staff—more than two hundred of the Fathers in Agony—lined up for questioning. What I learned was not all that unusual. There had been a revolt four days prior to our arrival, triggered by the advance of my fleet, and the wretches were in control of the main part of the camp. The Ice Cross had surrendered to me rather than to the inmates and their diseases.

We cared only for ourselves, got on dry clothes, ate, and rested in preparation for departure as soon as the blow lifted. Davey Gaunt woke me to tell me that the barracks leaders had gathered in the tunnel, pleading to meet with me. It was not sane to go down there. I went because I felt that I had become invulnerable by the freak of our escape from the sea. The Fathers of Agony formed a cordon between me and the barracks leaders. The Fathers were another of those rogue orders I have mentioned, with the important difference that they took their initiates from the camps. We had real priests on Anvers Island, who denounced them as gravediggers. I grant them their worth, for no other order— not even the Dominicans—would go into Clarence West. Coquito Blades wanted to kill them. That would not have helped; they died harder than the *Hielistos*. I told the Fathers I did not intend to harm the inmates. In the dark of the tunnel I heard a man call out in Spanish, "We know! It is told! Great Grim has come for us!"

Portent ruled Clarence West. This should explain my reception, "It is told!" I was the focus of their high dreams. It was as Lazarus planned. He taught me that I could never fight Lykantropovin as effectively as my legend could. Lazarus maintained that the idea of me, unkillable warlord, not only helped frighten the Ice Cross but also helped win the loyalty of the wretches in the camps under Lykantropovin. The formula was simple. What the

wretches lacked was hope. Lazarus made me into their hope incarnate. It was often too successful, moving the wretches to premature revolts. In every camp, I was spoken of as immortal, with
the strength of a hundred Lykantropovins. They said I was everywhere at once, attacking by sea at Half Moon Island, attacking by
land on King George. Skallagrim Ice-Waster was my dreaming.
Theirs was called *Grim El Grande*—the Great Grim.

And no matter how many wretches my *Hielistos* slaughtered
while fighting the Ice Cross, no matter how little food my *Hielistos*
were able to provide to the camps that fell under my control, or
how much worse were the wretches under my protection than
they had been under the Ice Cross, there was ever hysterical at-
tendance and celebration of *Grim El Grande*. Lykantropovin offered them the Charity Factor and security. I offered them hope
for a better day. It was a fantastic hope, an impossible hope, a
false hope. They must have known that; on some level, they must
have understood that if the sponsors of the Ice Cross had cut off
our supplies, we all would have perished. This did not happen.
Lykantropovin never even threatened to let all the camps starve—
despite the fact they came to siding with me. He fed them food
and I fed them fantasy. And how does one explain their hatred
for the Ice Cross and their worship of me? Lazarus said it, and I
restate: The wretches wanted me to be more than their loving
Jesus or their militant David or their visionary Moses; they wanted
me to be an angry god.

That is why the wretches at Clarence West screamed for me,
all that night, into the next day, and the next, when the storm
finally weakened, and we had to get away before the Ice Cross
came looking. Davey Gaunt and Coquito Blades forbid me to go
down again into the tunnels. They were afraid of disease, yes, but
more, that the wretches might have torn me apart in celebration.
We listened to them, chanting, singing, in many languages, and
always refrains of "Great Grim!" and "Freedom!"

No more than a few thousand broke out to get to me. Somehow, as if they could hear through ice, they knew I was leaving.
There was a rush up the main tunnel that carried through the
cordon of Fathers and outside, before the redoubt. Some of the
leaders attempted to keep them out of the wind. The camp was

near riot, many more thousands below chanting and marching, waiting to hear how those up top fared. I was cut off from my ship by a mob who expected me to save them.

My memory is that it was late in the day. The storm was finished, and so were we unless we got off. More than the Ice Cross threatened us by then, for the mob inside was trying to force the gate to the redoubt. The Fathers told us they could not hold them. There were killings, many children were being trampled. The leaders begged me that I give their people ships, food, clothing, medicine. Davey Gaunt wanted to fight our way through. Coquito Blades said we could not make it. It was madness until one of the Fathers came up and provided me part of the answer, saying, "Go to them. They won't hurt you. Tell them they're free."

I did it, no one else. Grim Fiddle gave the lie to those people, though he had the truth. I went out on the beach and walked among them. I told them to settle down and to wait. I could have told them to go back inside and wait for another day. It might not have deceived them. I did not try it. I knew I was not mad. I knew I was wrong, just as Father Saint Stephen had been wrong. Three thousand wretches lay down before me like sheep. They listened to me as I got up on a beached berg and preached to them that I was in control, told them the story of how my ships were coming to save them, to carry them, well-fed and warm, away to the west and north, to new lands and bountiful lives. I had to scream over the wind as the sun melted to the horizon and the temperature plunged. I serenaded them with my corrupt pride. That is the sort of shepherd Grim Fiddle was. In my great seal-skin mantle, in my wolfskin cowl, holding my harpoon and my truth, I told those wretches to sleep, because when they awoke it would be a new day, and they would be under the protection of the invincible. I had fires built along the waterline, not for warmth but so they could see me silhouetted there against the glacier as they closed their eyes. I waited with them through the night that was no night, that was a long, howling shadow from the north. I refused shelter, moved back and forth among them huddled in clumps like rocks. And when they were all quiet—because they were dead, or if not that, dying—I left them.

That is the sort of black shepherd I was. I sneaked away in the ashen night, like a Norse murderer. My crime was done to people who loved me, was done in the shadows, by deception and betrayal. What could have been a more infamous crime? I murdered them in the worst way, violating any law ever conceived, pagan or Christian or New Benthamite.

No, it was worse. After that shadowy night, nothing done by Grootgibeon, or Jaguaquara, or Fives O'Birne, or Lykantropovin, was a match for my work. I see the truth of it now. I have denounced my enemies as heinous. After that night, I was the same. I committed the crime of the Charity Factor all over again, justifying my choice as the greatest good for the greatest number, that is, saving Grim Fiddle for his realm. I became that night the darkest criminal in the South, the avenger truly deserving of revenge. My war came back to me and obliterated my pretense of justification. I became an outlaw from my own heart. I confess now that I murdered those wretches as another had murdered my family. I was he. It was as if Grim Fiddle had taken Peregrine, Israel, Guy, Earle, Thord, Orri, Gizur, Molly, and Charity out onto the ice to die, and told them at the last, "There is no God of Love. There is a God of Hate. I am his servant. My crimes are my monument."

My Fall from Satan's Seat

For those six years at Anvers Island, Lazarus was my rock. Lazarus was also my traitor. While it is an exaggeration to say that I built my kingdom upon him, it is not overmuch to say that his temperament fashioned the idea of my kingdom. It is also accurate to say that his temperament led him to overturn me. He was kingmaker and regicide, and proud for both. "What we have done!" he would say as we went out onto the ice for another season's combat. And as often he would say, "What I have done!"

Lazarus did not interfere in my revenge on the *capitanes de los Hielistos*—that was all bloody and spontaneous. I stormed into their fortress, and they fell back in anticipation. I murdered their chief, Jaguaquara, and they celebrated me. I took their queen, and they bent their heads to my blade and to the blades of my sealers. Nor did Lazarus assert himself the following summer (January 2004), when, in order to dispatch a rescue mission to Golgotha, I led the attack that broke the Ice Cross blockade of Anvers Island—that was all berserker cunning and luck. Then I collapsed, weakened by my berserker fury to free the dark-haired queen, so that I lay insensate for months. I had leaped to the mastery of Anvers Island only to retreat to my hall and to lie down. It was at that moment that Lazarus stepped forward as my prime minister. He sealed my sick bed, set Germanicus and Kuressaare as my protectors, Cleopatra as my surrogate, and then ruled through her and thus through the legend he made of me. I did recover in a matter of months, but afterward I did nothing but conform to Lazarus's sense of my grandeur and power. I was the king Lazarus made of me.

And how was it that a man who spoke so eloquently of a republic founded upon universal suffrage and written law could become a tyrant's eyes and ears? How was it that Lazarus Furore was both conceiver and destroyer? The answer was the man; at least, that is all I have. Lazarus would say that he did what had to be done. I say that he pursued his heart as I had pursued my albatross and my heart's desire. I cannot display Lazarus's heart any more tellingly than the events allowed. I can say that Lazarus carried in his breast a profound contradiction that should not have worked, except that it did—that of the noble democrat and the terrible demagogue.

It was Lazarus the democratic teacher, as in Diomedes's stories of Aristotle the Athenian lecturing the masters of the Hellenistic world, who came to use the six black months of each winter, when the *Hielistos* were prisoners of the ice in the caves at Anvers Island, as an academy for, as he said, "the revenge of the just." The *Hielistos* mocked Lazarus at first, called him a mad priest, but as his reputation grew apace with mine those *capitanes* came to fear him. His program was grandiose. He told the *capitanes* that it was their duty to understand their historical significance. He pun-

ished any *capitán* who called himself a pirate. He made them recite in a singsong chant that they were crusaders, soldiers of the
revolution, and, most of all, servants of a historical certainty. He
said Lykantropovin was not merely our enemy, he was the enemy
of the future. Whenever we struck at Lykantropovin, he said, we
struck for the coming freedom of all just people, and so we must
fight fiercely because we were the champions of billions in slavery.
Lazarus said we were the future. Lazarus especially liked to tell us
we fought for "all just people." Whenever he used that phrase, I
knew he was leaving me and the death in the caves and breathing
the air of a faraway vision of what he believed the world would
become.

He was not, in those trances of his, forgetful of how he must
marshal the *Hielistos* and the wretches in the camps. Lazarus might
have preached of warm, well-nourished utopias, however he remained fixed on the marching order to that end. This represents
Lazarus the demagogic strategist. He commanded my council
meetings with those quick eyes. He was ever wary of rebellion
among the *capitanes* and mutiny among the *Hielistos,* was ever
attentive to intrigue at Anvers Island. He put to death many in
my name for disobedience, perhaps just for disaffection to Lazarus's idea of our crusade. He commanded his hall-guard of spies
like secret police, and they were everywhere: always second-in-
command on my warships, or second-in-command in my battal-
ions. Lazarus rarely interfered in the tactical planning of a murder raid. He would say that, as guerrillas fighting a long campaign,
we would gain victory as long as we never surrendered. He would
preach that as long as we, the *capitanes,* survived our raids, Lykantropovin would suffer defeat though he controlled the length of
the Bransfield Strait. Lazarus presented this dogma in an unchar-
acteristically colorful metaphor: Grim Fiddle was the head of an
unkillable beast with a thousand fists. And the Grim Fiddle that
was the head was not the human Grim Fiddle, was the man who
was the hope incarnate of the wretches. Lykantropovin could sever
a hundred fists, said Lazarus. He could never extinguish hope as
long as I lived in the legend of Great Grim, *Grim El Grande, Grim-
magne, Der Gross Grim.* More, as Lazarus gave the wretches Grim
Fiddle as hope he gave my *capitanes* Grim Fiddle as their purpose.
Lazarus preached that I was the way to victory because I was the

victory, and that serving me was serving the future. Once, Lazarus took me aside; I could see his eyes were afire, and that he was gripped by one of his faraway visions. He told me, "Hell can be organized. I have organized it. The Devil cannot be killed. You cannot be killed. No matter what else, don't leave me. I need you. Take your vengeance. Come back to me. What we have done. What I have done. What there is left to do!"

I have discussed Lazarus at length with Diomedes. Diomedes said that he too had struggled with men like Lazarus throughout his career. Diomedes thought Lazarus a man compelled by a bottomless ambition for power, yet at the same time a man who yearned to justify his greed by demonstrating intellectually that he was more worthy than the men he ruled and conquered. Diomedes said Lazarus was a usurper. Diomedes insisted there was no more to find. Lazarus usurped the Furore family after Cesare was murdered; Lazarus usurped South Georgia when it was cut off by the fleet of the damned; Lazarus usurped my office as president of the Assembly in order to aggrandize himself as the drafter of the constitution; Lazarus usurped Germanicus at Golgotha by preaching to the wretches that I was an angry god and that he had my ear; Lazarus usurped my authority at Anvers Island by sealing me in my sickbed and ruling through Cleopatra; Lazarus usurped my possession of Cleopatra in a way I shall soon relate; and Lazarus usurped my kingship once I had defeated Lykantropovin.

Some of this is true, some of it is not. I do not fault Diomedes, for his Greek learning did much to help me see Lazarus the better. It might be that I should ask, what did Lazarus think of himself? He called himself a revolutionary. I suppose he would not have, in the end, turned aside the applause that he was a hero of his revolution. There is merit to his heroism, and it would be a disgrace if I were not to emphasize the hero, the lover, the heroic lover that was Lazarus. He died for his selfless love. I do not have the details, or certainty, only a rumor that he was killed the year after my arrest, while helping to rescue an ice camp from an eruption; there was also a rumor that he was killed by panicked wretches escaping that same eruption. Either way, he died because he loved his ideas enough to act upon them.

And how did he love? Lazarus wanted to take mankind by

the hand, as a lover, and not only lead mankind to a document but also show mankind how to write its names at the bottom of that document—conceived by men, written by men, intended for men—which would secure freedom and justice and, yes, charity for all just people. This introduces the major departure between Lazarus Furore and Grim Fiddle, and I would rather speak to his love of the wretched.

No, perhaps this is wrong of me. Perhaps I should speak to Lazarus's sense of charity. Lazarus thought charity a form of love. Lazarus wanted to give men, unasked, his will and his law. He often said that if the wretched resisted, he would force them to accept his charity. He talked of how he would "forge" men. I heard this as a boast. I might now more completely regard it as also the bravura of a tyrant. He did not seem to believe that the wretched could build their own future. He believed that the future must be given, forced upon, rammed onto, the wretched. This might mean that Lazarus no more believed in the people's will than I did, and he might have had less faith in the wretched than I did. Lazarus sought to dictate that document of freedom, justice, and charity; he did dictate in the end. That is not the mark of a compassionate republican. That is the mark of an arrogant, sinister, murderous man. That is the mark of a puppet-master.

I cannot agree to this. Lazarus sacrificed much for me. His grief over the loss of Cleo at Golgotha was complete; he could not speak of her. His grief for Violante, who died in an Ice Cross murder raid on Anvers Island our fourth summer there, was less sad, more complex. She had deteriorated before us at Anvers, as did many of the South Georgian remnant, so his mourning was mixed with ours for ourselves. Lazarus told Cleopatra about Violante: "She was hard enough." By this I took that he did not think her death was a judgment on her resolve. She died for no reason. Lazarus often counseled me after another defeat on the ice, and especially after my murder of those wretches at Clarence West. He told me, "This was not useless, or meaningless, if we are not. Don't speak of what is. Speak of what must be!"

I can speak to the only thing that Lazarus favored more than his masks of pedagogue, demagogue, kingmaker, and lawgiver.

Lazarus Furore was in love with Cleopatra Furore. He loved her most humanly, and was perplexed by her most humanly, and hated her most humanly. It was she, not his "agenda of history," that gave Lazarus strength. It was she, not the ice or the rebellious *Hielistos* or the grueling Ice Cross, that could weaken Lazarus, disrupt his will.

I have mentioned—when I wrote of that day I met Germanicus at *2 de Diciembre*—how I believed Lazarus and Cleopatra were lovers when they arrived in Stockholm, and how I believe they continued their passion on board *Angel of Death*. Their union was a maze to me. So was their reunion on Anvers Island. I risk incoherence to report: Lazarus depended upon Cleopatra while she tolerated his attention; Lazarus ignored Cleopatra while she venerated his genius; Lazarus spoke against Cleopatra while she trusted his heart. He could denounce her in front of my council as a victim of self-delusion, mocking her claim as the "queen of slaves." He could also worship her openly before my council as the most durable and determined warrior in the fortress. He gave her no pity when she ranted and wept for Charity, or for Cesare; he was courtly to her when she drifted from us to care for the children.

There was the dark side of their reunion, and I puzzle if I have overlooked it purposely in my appraisal of Lazarus: Lazarus was jealous of me. If he was a usurper to me, so was I to him. I took his Cleopatra and made her my queen, and my slave. Lazarus could shudder into silence whenever Cleopatra announced that she would share my bed, which she did when she willed. And yet he could also come to me in somber measure and urge me to go to her because she needed comfort.

Were those two what the philosophers call a marriage of true minds? I cannot answer this. Was I their dupe, or was I their child, or was I their victim, or was I their battleground? I watched them for five years at Anvers Island—once I was relieved of my berserker dreaming—and they appeared to me closer than any two people I ever experienced, Peregrine and Charity, Earle and Guy notwithstanding. Is that what Grim Fiddle was to them, then, an interloper, an adulterer?

For all my talk about Lazarus the rock and traitor and Cleopatra the "queen of slaves", it might come to this, then—that they used me as I used them. There was a man, Lazarus, who thought he had vision of the future; and there was a woman, Cleopatra, who thought herself shackled to the past that she shackled to herself, and who found in Lazarus a liberator. And what happened? Grim Fiddle cut them apart and made one his right hand and one his left hand, made one his pain and the other his pleasure. This cannot be all there is to say. I must look to Cleopatra.

If Cleopatra did rule Lazarus as would a queen, then I indulge myself to say that Cleopatra, more than Lazarus, was the imperial seat of my corruption as a warlord king. It was of a piece, Cleopatra the queen, Cleopatra the victim of the vengeance, Cleopatra the engima. I turn from Lazarus, my rock and my traitor, to Cleopatra, my lust and my cipher. There seems pathetically little to say, as there is time left to say it. I tell the truth: Grim Fiddle did not love Cleopatra Furore. That is the tale, beginning and end.

And yet my loveless adoration of her, my possessive passion for her, seems a flood of woe-singing. I have tried to convince myself that I loved her from the first, on that ballroom floor, amid swirling privilege and indifferent learning, me the oafish lackey, she the sleek inheritor. Did I love her then? It is a lost notion to me now. If it was love, it did not grow. It lingered where it commenced, immature obsession with the unattainable and unknowable. Perhaps when I claimed I loved her, I was bluffing love, dimly aware that it was futile. There was false joy in it, purposeless abandon. I have written, in romantic hyperbole, that our love was from the first as unlucky as it was hopeless. I strike that thought now. It was delusion. If that was love—angry lust, fighting and hurting and twisted, fleshly, lurid coupling—then what was my unshakable love for Grandfather, my sweet love for Abigail, my enduring love for my Sam?

I confess my failure to love Cleopatra. Why pursue it? I am old. She is gone. There seems only misery to speculate how she regarded me. That it fetches me is a sign to me of how lewd was our intercourse. Back then, she was a hunger, yet now she is a stinking gluttony. What can I say of her nature now that could be more succinctly telling than how I envisioned her in my berserker dreaming? She was the dark-haired queen, Hard-Heart. When I changed shape, I saw what Cleopatra had become. Her pain was her purpose was her pleasure was her pain. I did not trust my insight, not even in hallucination, and wrongly believed her name changed to Glad-Heart. This was childish yearning. Cleopatra was Hard-Heart, and remained Hard-Heart. Cleopatra Furore was hard, and hard enough. Have I once in my record of her provided any cause to think of her as glad?

And why did God harden Cleopatra's heart? God has the answer. My guess seems self-serving; it is mine. Through Cesare Furore, Cleopatra was born to luxury. Through me, she inherited degradation. She must have hated many, wanted revenge on multitudes; however, she must have completely hated me and wanted total revenge upon me. I would like to write this as final. It may be. I recoil at the depth of her call to hate Grim Fiddle. How could I call myself her lover? I was her persecutor. I was the thrust of her torment. How did I ravish her? Most vilely. Look at it for what it was, Grim. Better that she could hate me rather than have to examine the cruelty of her fate. This must be why I confess that I did not love her. It is more of my promised debt to her. I pay and pay—no love, all darkness. No true love could be born of such unhappiness. Our fate was joint calamity. To the end, we reached for that ruin.

My memory of Cleopatra has hurt me. My hands feel as heavy as my heart. I have one more episode I must try to tell. I introduce it by mocking myself. I have rushed to explain the rise and fall of my kingship as if it were to be explained by the motives of the players. This is foolishness. I anticipate a criticism: does such a thing as effect follow from such a thing as cause, or is not every event an independent effect of nothing, a result of nothing? Be lucid, Grim. I ask myself what difference there would have been had Grootgibeon or Jaguaquara or Fives O'Birne gathered control of Anvers Island, and I and mine had bent to their will, or perished in hopelessness? I see none. Hundreds of thousands would still have died abandoned and forgotten. The home of the gods would still have feigned ignorance of our plight and enjoyed their stolen fruit. Black and hurt half-men might have made the camps what they were, but it was Antarctica, that wall of blizzards, that determined what happened in the camps, or perhaps determined nothing, lay absolute and unchanged by what we wretched suffered on its icy shores. More confusing to me still, there is the question: Does perceived history determine mankind's future; or does mankind have the authority to remake its own history any time mankind wants, and continually? Grim Fiddle here acknowledges his consternation before the paradox of predeterminism and free will. I translate to the tiny scale of me and my loved ones: What would it have signified for the ice camps and my ice kingdom if Cleopatra had not been corrupted by her loathing? or if I had been able to love her and set her free? or if Lazarus could have set aside his doubt about me, Cleopatra, himself, justice, and taken charge of our destiny?—ours, and not that of "all just people." I suggest a good reply is that it would not have signified. The wretches would still be dead. The gods would still be luxuriating.

I realize this is suspect, as if the New Benthamites have captured my mind, have convinced me that love, fear, decency, sacrifice, revenge, criminal responsibility, freedom do not signify, as if what pertains is just the hedonic calculus, and philosophy is a whine. This is not the case, yet I believe I lack the wisdom to set down my discrimination keenly. Men and women think that what they do and how they do it does signify. History is what they have done. Philosophy is how they have done it. Yet there are turns of such pervasive darkness that the will and the heart, the history and the philosophy, of men and women are lost in the turmoil.

My Kingdom of Ice seems a fit example. We wretches threw our high dreams and our weak flesh against Antarctica. The ice and the volcanoes continued as before. What is accusation against one's brother in the face of a black-ice island? What is massacre of tens of thousands in the face of the fumes pouring from Satan's Seat? What is food for a famine-bloated child in the face of that black winter that blots out compassion? And then, the scale of it, what is truth and falsehood in the face of that endless wind that hurtles off the Antarctic plateau to churn the rock and sea into an ice world that does not seem the planet Earth, that does seem a place and a time where and when no human being could ever venture? What fool Grim Fiddle is to ask. How pretentious

Grim Fiddle is to think that what he wrought in the South matters. The heart is the truth, I claim. Antarctica has no heart. It is five million square miles of near lifelessness, where only at the edges can anything that feels pain cling to misery to know it is still alive. Antarctica seems one step short of the cold, black, exploded universe that spills over my ice prison. The deepest mystery for me here in my ice prison, looking up to the sky whenever I can, is not, why does the universe exist, why does that aspect of the inhumane cosmos, Antarctica, exist? It is, rather, how strange of God to have made mankind, surely a mistake caught between the utter fire and the utter cold of creation, and to have made mankind in such a way that a sinner and penitent like Grim Fiddle can think that he ever counted for more than a germ. Grim Fiddle's history and philosophy, mankind's history and philosophy, is no sense. It is laughter.

I relate hurriedly my last days as King of Antarctica. It was early summer, six years after Grandfather's death and my murder of Jaguaquara, at the beginning of my seventh summer as warlord of Anvers Island. The Bransfield Strait was open with several lanes through the floes. Lykantropovin was dead seven months, not by my hand but by my office. Germanicus was dead two months, of wounds and despair. The past winter had ripped up the ice camps as one might gut an elephant seal. My *capitanes* in charge of the camps sent cutters to Anvers pleading for food, discipline, hope. Another cutter arrived from the Falklands bearing an envoy from the republican signatories of the Treaty of Good Hope and the Peace of the Frontier, who presented Lazarus with terms for a truce. My *capitanes* remained in their halls throughout the Palmer archipelago and the South Sheltlands, waiting to continue the war or to die. The Ice Cross was defeated by me; my army was defeated by Antarctica and by a blood lust that had finally ebbed, leaving melancholy, madness, starvation. I too stayed in my hall; I was recovered from my wounds from the battle at Elephant Main, yet still in the lingering grip of my own darkness. Grim Fiddle, the berserker warlord, had become increasingly only that. This was a fraud, however, for I had come to rely upon my rage to get me out of my hall, onto my flagship, into the blood-work. Now, summer come again, the disease that is murder had corrupted my limbs as well as my heart. I was sick of the blood. I had killed so many that I thought and felt and saw only killing. I presumed the worst in all, because I was the worst of myself.

I must be blunt, though my brevity beggars accuracy. My berserker dreaming of my rise to kingship had been replaced by a nightmare that was more mortal than that of a shape-changer. I had abandoned my sense of myself as Skallagrim Ice-Waster, Hard-Fisherman's Promise-Keeper, left in the ocean of hatred that had been my home for six years. Without Lykantropovin I thought there was no more purpose, and if there was, it was not for me. I saw myself in my dreams as a coward, a cheat, a lie, in all, damned. That was the overwhelming image. I convinced myself that I was the servant of the God of Hate. There was no one left to comfort me. Longfaeroe might have contained my ranting—he never emerged from a cave-in on Anvers; the sealers had disappeared one at a time in battle against either the Ice Cross or the whales; Otter Ransom and Wild Drumrul had obeyed my order at Elephant Main and drowned for it. I have no strength to continue the list. They were gone. I remained in my hall. I would give no orders. I refused to go out into the sun, preferred to wrap myself in the walls of my cave. I see what I was doing most clearly now. It was prescient of me, another misused gift from Mother. I sensed my guilt, put myself on trial, accused myself of slaughtering nearly everything I had ever loved and of having gained nothing from taking revenge. I judged myself a criminal without remorse, and stood condemned to a solitary prison. My mind was in premature retreat. I wanted no answers, no opportunities, no hope. I recall that I was able to go very far in my self-torment, for I betrayed my memory of Grandfather.

I convinced myself that Grandfather's service to his Lord God had been wrong, because there was no God of Love, rather there was a God of Hate who had made mankind wretched the more to toy with and torture the sinner. I cannot re-create my reasoning; it was not reasonable. Nonetheless, it felt more real to me than the cold. I screamed at myself, refusing food and sleep. I will not bother to reproduce here my blasphemy. The sum of it centered on my recurring delusion of the God of Hate. I claimed that I had defeated Lykantropovin and the Ice Cross as a servant of the God of Hate, claimed that I was as good a servant as was the Dark Prince, Satan. Grim Fiddle, the Black Prince of the black ice, filled himself as a well would fill with bad water and pretended even unto the power of Satan, Grandfather's Satan. I boasted I was in league with Satan, that he was my brother-at-arms. I vowed to give myself to my comrade, to open up the Southern Ocean as Satan had opened up the doldrums. I was mad. None of it makes sense. I was mad. I chanted to my own slaves, "Satan is my ally. We are slaves of the God of Hate."

Lazarus came to me, ministering to me as a father. He blamed himself for my condition. He said he had asked too much of me, said he was prepared to relieve me of my burden. He made long speeches, colored by Lazarus's mix of the mystical and pedagogical, yet concluded with his sense of the practical. He tried to draw me out of my hall with promises. He said the Ice Cross wanted to surrender to me at first opportunity, that the Ice Cross had guaranteed massive resupply of the camps and immediate resettlement of the camps, had also guaranteed amnesty and rehabilitation of the *Hielistos*. Lazarus also tried my vanity. He said that though I was a hero to the *Hielistos* and the camps now, soon I would be to the world, said that I had shown that the Treaty of Good Hope and the Peace of the Frontier were death warrants, and that now the disgrace of the fleet of the damned was done and I was a great man.

"This is what you fought for, Grim," he told me, and later, "You must act now, Grim, it all waits on you," and then in ever more desperate terms, "We can't let the summer pass, Grim, the camps won't make another winter," and, "We've won, you've won, this is the time!"

I countered Lazarus's pleas with descriptions of the plots against me, how the Ice Cross was attempting to defeat me with trickery, how I could no longer trust my *capitanes* or my councillors. I told Lazarus that he was a dupe of my enemies, told him that he was a defeatist, told him, yes, this was the time, the time to attack. There was also crazy talk that we must prepare for a summer campaign, must hide the women and children, especially my South Georgians (who were all dead), for I declared Lykantropovin was alive, my *capitanes* had brought me the wrong head.

"There is no refuge from my enemies!" I thundered to Lazarus and my councillors. "There can be no peace! Satan is our ally! The time to attack!"

Cleopatra came to me later, and along with her, her shadow, Babe. I expected more of Lazarus's persuasions, began again about the conspiracy against me, and thus her as well. She sat beside me. Babe stood vigilantly behind her. Cleopatra was no longer a beauty, her hair cropped off, her teeth rotten, her body weakened by starvation, the cold, the sunlessness, the sort of fatigue from which sleep is no relief. For some cause that I have forgotten—an accident that not even Babe could prevent—she was slightly paralyzed. She had to look and talk out of one side of her face, had to use one arm to lift the other. I did not pity her. I appealed to her hard heart. Her heart answered me.

"You have it right," she said.

"I am surrounded by enemies," I said.

"You must act," she said.

"Satan is my ally. My enemies are his enemies. I shall assemble my army and attack!"

"There is more than that. You must do more," she said.

"How do you know?" I said.

"She told me, your albatross," she said.

It fills me with wonder now, twenty-nine years later, to recall Cleopatra's wasted face when she spoke the lie that slew the Kingdom of Antarctica while in the same instant it gave birth to the People's Republic of Antarctica. One of her eyes was moist with tears because she had to keep opening and shutting it by hand. Her lips were cracked, her skin pitted with sores. She might have wanted to change her expression in order to give conviction to her deceit, could not, because of the paralysis perhaps, more likely because, in imitation of Lazarus, Cleopatra had forsaken smiles, grimaces, surprises. Her face was a single facade. It surely would have misled a saint into thinking he beheld a victim. I doubt if even a looking glass could have displayed Cleopatra accurately. Yes, there was misery, mourning, hatred there; but more tellingly there was a "queen of slaves" who was willing to do the last that was necessary to settle her fate. That face was resolution. I do not blame her. I suppose I am proud of her for her cleverness, can still feel my admiration. She possessed one confidence to use against me, for only once had I shared my secrets, and that was when I ravished Cleopatra after murdering Jaguaquara. I told her I had reached for her because it was my destiny, and then I told her of Grandfather, Skallagrim Strider, and Lamba Time-Thief, in specific, of that pale albatross.

I credit Lazarus's role as well, for he must have been behind Cleopatra's ruse. I guess that he had gone to her to debate what could be done either to enlist my aid in making truce with the republican masters or to conceive a plan to unseat me. My *capitanes* were caught between their self-interest and their loyalty to me, not out of love, out of fear of what I had done to all who wavered. I was their purpose; I was also their peril. They fought for me, or they fought me. Lazarus could not negotiate without their cooperation, which meant that he had to have my authority. I see his dilemma. I see the wisdom of his treachery. The king was mad. My victory over Lykantropovin was a defeat for hundreds of thousands unless the *Hielistos* accepted the Ice Cross's surrender and the offer by the republican masters to relieve the deprivation in the camps. What had to be done was clear. How to do it, and with what weapon, was not clear. Lazarus needed to get rid of me in such a way that he could sign the truce while not shattering my kingdom into dozens of conclaves of pirates. If he had assassinated me, he would have risked having my *capitanes* put forward a new warlord who owed nothing to Lazarus and his plans. Therefore, Lazarus had to keep me alive, and a threat to the *capitanes*, but also had to keep me out of the way until the truce was in effect. Cleopatra provided Lazarus with a weapon, a perfect blade, a lie she knew Grim Fiddle would believe. Cleopatra picked up my mother's power and thrust it into my heart.

I do not recall much of the convoluted debate that followed her lie. I must have knelt before her, thinking she could provide me with genuine counsel. That does not mean her task was easy. She had me, she had to maneuver me. Who introduced the idea of a new quest? Who first raised the possibility that a pilgrimage to Satan would give me new strength to carry on my war? Who began talk of a journey to Satan's Seat so that Grim Fiddle could confer with his ally? I recall dimly that I did most of the ranting, that Cleopatra did not raise points so much as confirm my hallucinatory logic.

There was another voice in our conference, a real thunderer.

As we talked in my ice cave, Satan's Seat rumbled way to the south. It made Cleopatra bend, from her fear of sudden fissures. It made me thunder back, a pathetic imitation of my birth, when I sang the upper part of that Fiddle duet. I convinced myself that as I had answered Grandfather, so now I should answer Satan's Seat, as I had condemned everyone on board *King James* and *Candlemas Packet* in pursuit of my heart's desire, so now I condemned myself in pursuit of my black heart's desire, Satan.

Cleopatra withdrew. Babe trailed behind her. He gave me a sad, hard, fertile look. There are no parting words with her to record. I have not seen Cleopatra since.

For his part, Lazarus did come to me, while I prepared my pilgrimage. He said he understood my decision was final. I suppose this means that even then, as he watched me ready my own regicide, he had his plans firm. I said that my decision was inspired. He said yes.

I can sympathize with his betrayal. I had fought for revenge as fury. Lazarus had fought for his idea of the future as duty. The truce with the Ice Cross was in his grasp. Also, I can suppose, he knew that within his reach was a profoundly more significant document, the declaration of a people's revolution that commenced the People's Republic of Antarctica.

I have not seen Lazarus's triumph. I have been told, by my tribunal, and by Diomedes. It is said to be a single sheet. It is said to be entitled "The Constitution for the People's Republic of Antarctica." It is said to indict a tyranny and to declare the tyrant, Grim Fiddle, overthrown. It is said to announce that henceforth the people in the South are citizens of a republic in which no man or woman is above another, in which there is neither black nor white, male nor female, first nor last.

It is said to be in Lazarus's hand. Did Cleopatra sign it? That is my fancy. There would have been no need for signatures. The republican masters would have accepted any scrap in order to conceal their crimes and put a new face on their war with Grim Fiddle. With that document, and with the power to interpret it as they wished, Grim Fiddle was made the transgressor, the ice camps were made Grim Fiddle's victims, the Ice Cross was made the beleaguered savior of the South.

Lazarus could not have been surprised when he, the traitor,

was soon betrayed by his enemies, the faceless benefactors who sponsored the Ice Cross. It pleases me to suppose that Lazarus had thought through his deed. He sacrificed me and the kingdom we had built out of revenge in order to give birth to a people's republic of mystical egalitarianism, in order to insure that this people's republic existed only to be dismantled immediately and its citizenry resettled a world away as soon as possible.

What else for him? The camps were doomed. The *Hielistos* were uncontrollable. The Ice Cross was broken by exhaustion. Only a bold stroke, a magnificent philosophical construction, could have saved anything. Lazarus took up his pen and made those marks, "The Constitution for the People's Republic of Antarctica." He called it a people's republic because that was his mind. For this alone I reward his genius.

Lazarus knew that the republics of the North and South that had signed the Treaty of Good Hope and the Peace of the Frontier would try to corrupt the government that represented the victorious *Hielistos* and the ice camps under their control. Lazarus knew that if he went to them representing a hierarchical government—a monarchy, or parliamentary monarchy, or congressional republic—then the republican masters would be able to manipulate the negotiations by promising amnesty and resettlement like bribes, to fall to the powerful in the conclaves of the *Hielistos* and the ice camps, while the wretches were abandoned again. It would have been the oldest, most trite manipulation: the victorious oppressed seduced to become the oppressors. Lazarus understood that only by making every human being in Antarctica an inviolable equal in my victory could he insure immediate and complete dismantling of the camps and relocation of the internees—the most wretched out first, the most wretched out last. And Lazarus knew that the only way to promote such a fabulous desire was to constitute the ice camps and the *Hielistos* in such a way that they represented a truly unworldly idea: All men and women are equal. I believe it no accident that the language I am told that appears in Lazarus's document resembles a description of another unworldly place, the garden of Eden.

Lazarus conceived the Kingdom of Antarctica to secure impossible liberty, then he conceived the People's Republic of Antarctica to secure impossible justice. I am aware that the record shows now that Lazarus's dare was a failure, that the dissolution of the ice camps that did follow his negotiations in Africa and the establishment of the ice state by "The Constitution for the People's Republic of Antarctica" was almost as ghastly as if it had been done by madmen. This does not mean to me that Lazarus's grasp and reach are forgotten or dismissable. To repeat his balm to me, do not speak of what is, speak of what must be. Lazarus stood firmly for the highest ideals conceivable by him, a perfect egalitarian state, an Edenic republic. He was a hero. If he failed to save hundreds of thousands, he did save tens of thousands, and he did so by making a deal with men he knew to be treacherous. They were what he had. And if they were soon overwhelmed by the scale of their task to relocate the wretched in the camps, this does not take from Lazarus. Lazarus knew himself, knew his enemies. He could have stood by reluctantly, could have made excuses and stalled. He chose instead to gather his reason and his inspiration and then to plunge.

And is it my excited mind, or is there not a lovely joke in Lazarus's triumph? Did he not overthrow me in order to construct what he believed as perfect a state as man will ever manage on the Kingdom of Earth? In Lazarus's People's Republic of Antarctica there was no time for factionalism, rebellion, cynicism, blood feuding, and degradation. There was only time for a smile at the grand conceit of an icebound Eden. And then it was gone, its loyal citizenry back to green and purple fields. Its birth was its death.

In my rush I have sung poorly of that great man, Lazarus Furore. I met him one wild day when I was almost twenty-two years old, and found him a copper-skinned ideologue, a sharp, fast, angry young man. I left him one wilder day when I was thirty-five, and left him a scarred, shrunken, weathered mourner, also a brilliant leader, a splendid hero who believed in freedom, a better day, the goodness in all just people. Most tribute of all, Lazarus Furore believed he was right and was willing to give all that he had—love, life, history, honor—in order to make right. Lazarus was his own monument.

He did betray me. I accuse him of that. He is guilty. I cannot believe that he also intended for me to be delivered into the vindictiveness of the republican masters. He could not have thought that I would return from my false quest for Satan, two hundred miles south into mountains never penetrated by man or animal, and after that up the ashen slopes of an active volcano. He must have thought that when we parted at the shore of Anvers Island, I was a dead man. We did not meet again. That was chance, for within the week he was gone to the South Orkneys and then to Africa to speechify for his high dreams, the People's Republic of Antarctica; and within the year he was gone to his Maker, where I imagine he continues to speechify to the angels themselves for his high dreams, and perhaps for a People's Republic of Heaven.

"Good luck, Grim," he said to me on the shore.

"I'll show them, you'll see," I said, some crazed sense of the coming Twilight of the Gods glazing my vision.

"You have done. I have done. We have done. What we have done!" he said, and that was the end for us, unless, I note, my memory is tricking me and he actually said, "What have we done?"

My flight to Satan's Seat did not take much longer than Lazarus's to the camps of our enemies. I loaded a thousand pounds of supplies atop my sled. It was the best I knew to build, hand-lashed, light, doubly strengthened ropes. I harnessed nine of the most rugged dogs I could risk, all huskies, part wolf, part everything else, from the stock the Ice Cross had brought in. Such a beast is not calm unless dead. My wheel dog was a massive veteran, nearly blind from fights, sure footed, reliable; my lead dog was one of Iceberg's great-grandchildren (Iceberg and Goldberg died weeks apart, in their sleep and, yes, peacefully), a gray heap of scar tissue and muscle who could sense crevasses like meat, could break trail without a man leading him, and was blessed with a fierce sense of loyalty: he would always turn the sled when I was pitched off, would bark murder to the team until I righted myself. My team was mongrel and mean, could live on blubber and pemmican, and when that was gone, would live on the promise of more, until hunger made them killers.

Once landed on the continent, I commanded, "Haw!" and we were off across the ice, weaving between the hummocks, over fields broken with jagged slabs, up onto the glacier that I chose as the first leg of my highway to Satan. My dogs did not sense my delusion. They ran heads down, best when wet and cold, their tails raised high behind them in the wind like mainmasts stretching canvas. When we were right, we sailed up that glacier. We had to zigzag, often doubling back when a track ended at a fissure. I remember a feeling of passionate numbness. As long as my strength held, I was exuberant, the sun overhead, the light, wet snow swirling in updrafts right and left. The farther we got from the shore, the easier our run, because the snow slackened off. There is little snowfall on the continent itself, the blizzards being the wind picking up crystals and flinging them. On the glacier, I was protected from the worst of the coastal winds, and the first few days felt myself climbing into an untracked world of white and compelling wonder.

It could not last. My journey was a lie. And I believe what happened to me there was luck. As I left behind Anvers, which I had made my tomb, I also left behind the turbulence in my mind. My heart was lightened by the beauty of Antarctica. I have emphasized the dread of the South. If a man ignores death, sheds Grandfather's and Longfaeroe's sense of weak flesh and holds to the might of the spirit, then he can stand back and appreciate God's creation. God made Antarctica as seriously as he made Eden. Before those gigantic blue-black mountains that tower to heaven, draped in mantles of gale-blown clouds pink and blue, made majestic by fingers of glaciers that rippled the exposed rock, what is adequate to be said? It can seem a dream.

The physical reward is pain. That pain overcame me after a week's run. My giddiness passed; a dull vertigo settled in. I anticipated my fall. The cold stiffened my limbs, my solitude slowed my step. I fed the dogs, made sloppy efforts to keep on. They were ready; I failed them. We stayed three days waiting for one blow to pass, lingered another two days farther up a new glacier for no reason. After that I lost sense of and care for time. At the top of the glacier, I was faced with a futile choice, either down into a valley of mountainous shadows pocked with deep drifts, or off onto a ridge the team might not have managed. I hesitated, camped at the crest, built a shelter of rock slabs and snow, kept a large fire, consumed too much of my coal. The dogs lay down in their holes, I in mine. We all knew I had quit.

My ice mausoleum was well set, a natural window to the south, opening onto crisscrossing mountain chains that heaved ever higher toward the gateway onto the Antarctica plateau itself. That was several hundred miles southward. There was more immediate spectacle: the stepping stones that surrounded the great smoking colossus, Satan's Seat. It dominated the landscape, master of Graham Land, set above the Wilkins Coast, between the Larsen Ice Shelf and the whale-shaped Alexander Island, and amid what is charted as the Eternity Mountains. I was at least one hundred miles upwind of the worst of the eruptions, yet the poisonous black clouds venting from the crater had splashed the snowfields with twisted geometric designs. It seemed a masterwork of a master abstracter, the master mystery-maker. The winds could sweep clear the slopes of the volcanoes, west to east, so from my vantage I could study the cycle. The earth would shrug; rockslides and ice ridges would jump once and then pour down the slopes in an avalanche that sent a gray-white wash into the valleys; the crater would then spew ever blacker smoke streams into the cloud cover above; finally, roars would pronounce a new episode, a glow building in the fumes. Instead of Satan's Seat then heaving ashen fire into the sky, one of the stepping stones would vent, a demon's seat evidencing obeisance. I saw this cycle once completely, saw it repeat just short of spewing continually. It was hypnotic, drew me into the process, humbled me, witness to a clockwork of ash and wind. I felt, feeding my own fire, eating the last of my food, that my end was privileged with secrets of creation. I watched myself die as I watched the earth tremble with cataclysmic renaissance.

It was humility before that splendor that returned me to cold reason. My delusions about conspiracies, treacheries, imminent world wars, gradually came to seem to me to be trivial, mean-spirited, proceeding from my vanity. More to the point of my being camped on that glacier, my deranged notions that Satan was my ally came to humiliate me. I saw my gibberish and was mortified. I taunted myself, told my team that their master was a pitiable, pitiless fool, unworthy of their muscle and devotion. I did talk to my wolves, but not as a berserker, nor as a madman, instead as a simple sinner, low and regretful, sane and ironic in reflection.

"Satan's Seat, we call that one," I told Iceberg's great-grandson. "That gives more to Satan than to that mountain. No devil could ever be so grand! Look at the size!"

(This should be explained: On Anvers Island, the fumes from

Satan's Seat could appear an enormous figure, such as Christmas Muir had once described to me, a great ram's head, horned and grinning. I had first dismissed this as sealer talk, then, as warlord of murder, embraced it as fitting judgment on the evils of men, as if Satan ruled the camps. Now, I rejected it again and for all time as gab. It was a volcano, a grotesque and terrifying one, and no more. It was the world in motion, only that, vomiting up the goods of elemental nature. If one were to look down into that volcano, one would not see Hell, or evil; one would see the future fields of bounty. And the cloud that billowed and glowed above it was merely windblown ash, in the shape of nothing but metaphor.)

"I called my master the God of Hate," I told my wheel dog. "Israel, he would groan at me, call me a brat. God, yes, God most tender. The hate is my invention. God created this lovely world. Man made hatred, did so out of disgust for his own ingratitude. And what man has done wrong, he can do right. The God of Love, I see that, Israel, a lesson so simple."

With my reason, I regained also one of the keenest defenses with which man is blessed, fear of death. I understood that a good measure of sanity is an acceptance of such a fear. I emptied of folly as I filled with fear. I did not want to die. I was cold and alone, yet wanted more of life, even if it was to be torment. I saw my end and wept. This journey had been suicide, I realized, and I was sorry for it. More, I blamed myself for my presumption to defy the knowable limits of nature, for my pride to be more than a man. Of all the sins I committed, this seems the worst. God had graced me with life; Lamba had given me birth; Peregrine, Israel, Guy, Earle, Thord, Orri, Molly, had given me childhood; Grandfather had given me chance; the Furores and the South Georgians and the wretched of the camps had given me everything they had. What right had I to return this trust with smug blasphemy? My fear of death blended with my anger at myself. I turned the fury that I had lavished on the Charity Factor onto myself.

"Stupid, extreme, cruel, lustful, faithless, small, small man!" I shouted to the dogs. "That is what sits here! All of life was before me! Look at the heavens, look at the earth, for me, all could have been for me! Selfish, rash, blundering Grim! You wolves have more dignity in your teeth than I ever managed in my life!

Would you have come up here to quit? Before your sensible wants my learning is waste. I know why you don't answer me. What could you tell such an ignoramus? You are beasts, and happy for it! I am a man, and sad for it! Not for good cause! Out of contrariness! Ludicrous, trivial, vain, spiteful, greedy Grim! The only decent thing I can do for you now is make myself your last meal. What is a man who feeds himself to wolves? A bootless fool, sour meat!"

I stress that though this seems ranting, it was not. I had to shout over the wind and the barking. Otherwise it was intimate intercourse, self-indulgent, true, yet it was my last meal and I permitted a feast of woe. I acted accordingly. I was despondent, not overmuch. I felt stupid, also very sanely ridiculous.

As I lay restless and chatting, the cold and the solitude joined to give me that phenomenon of life in Antarctica that is best described here as useful melancholia. I lost perspective. The window on Satan's Seat closed. A new window opened onto my past. Memories beckoned me. I walked forgotten paths and met forgotten acquaintances. I turned from talking with my wolves to conversing with my history. The same experience I endured then, I reiterate, is what has made it possible for me to recall so much of my story here in the ice prison, with a minor difference. Then, I was clumsy at travel in my mind's museum, and images blurred, scenes collapsed out of chronology. I stumbled through my life both seeker and fugitive. It did not then lead to clarity, as I can make it do now. Of consequence, I can only report my melancholy, save for one conversation that was not reminiscence but prescient revelation.

"You were my best friend," I said.

"No long face there, Grim," said Germanicus.

"All those dear folk, our South Georgians, why did they have to die like that?" I said.

"We none of us ken that," said Germanicus.

"Are they happy in Heaven?" I said.

"O aye, be sure that the pastor sees to it. They be released. Give way, now, Grim, look to yourself," said Germanicus.

"Abbie said that, do you remember? Save yourself, she said. I've always thought that was what she told Robby. 'Save himself,' she told Robby to tell me."

"Aye, bonnie words," said Germanicus.

"I've made a mess of it. And if I couldn't save me, who would want to?" I said, looking away from Germanicus and down into the snow. I saw there Germanicus as he had been the winter before in my hall, broken and white, dead from wounds, a tired and good man released. He was the last of the sealers to leave me. No stories are equal for his courage, especially after Jane was murdered, and their baby boy. I mourned him so completely that I had denied my grief until then on the glacier. How happy I felt to be able to look up from the snow and find his black beard flecked with ice, his smile giving me warmth. I was not deceived. I knew he was a ghost, or whatever he should be called—a realized memory. It still gave me great comfort. I built my fire up with my sled and the food containers, then cut free the team, keeping Iceberg's great-grandson tethered near me to hold back the team's hunger until it ruled them. By then, I would not need protection.

I lay down to die. There is no surprise as to the failure of that presumption. There is a final and small puzzle to my last days as King of Antarctica. I mean to say, I fell, but I was soon enough scooped up and returned to destiny. It was not just that way. I have waited twenty-nine years to figure out just what it was, however, and if it is not the most intriguing confusion in my narrative, it remains for me the queerest of inexplicable surprises. What was her mind? I have already rejected the one motive that would seem to explain such conduct. She could not have loved me. She must have hated me. Perhaps there is more to love than anyone can bear to know. Was it womanly secret on a scale that I cannot conceive that moved her to urge me to, and then to retrieve me from, Satan's Seat? Love or hate, then, in all a great and abiding passion in the human heart, moved Cleopatra Furore to retrieve Grim Fiddle, moved the queen to dispatch her knave to fetch the king from his chatty, morbid, beauteous sanctuary. I report it as flatly as it happened. I lay down to die and Babe Furore walked out of the wind. I could not ask him, mute witness, so for the thrill it still means to me I shall close this abridged confession with a question that I shall endeavor to pursue after life: "Why Cleopatra, why did you save Grim Fiddle?"

My Sam

I cannot murder Grim Fiddle. This last writing has shown me what I have become in my ice prison, a curious old pilgrim, game for more, luxurious with memories that crowd my manuscript. It is six weeks since I pronounced my imminent departure from this life. I renounce my plan. No Babe Furore had to walk out of the wind this time. I have been nursed back to health by my delivery of the story of the People's Republic of Antarctica. The patient is again patient with his destiny. Denial of the life I have been given, by love and accident, would be the most foolish sort of ingratitude. I forbid it. There is more to my decision, less philosophically abstract. I am now palpably reminded of Abigail's advice to me to save myself, and of Cleopatra's one queer assistance to the same end. It is time that Grim Fiddle took charge of that effort, the delivered stood up his own deliverer.

This is not to say that my apprehension about Diomedes's letter was unfounded. A new letter has finally arrived, yesterday, obliging me to finish my fall from Satan's Seat without detail. I had hoped to report my arrest and trial. There were some fine speeches. I suppress that now. Diomedes announces more immediate noise. I do not care to give the One World Reunion a voice in my last testimony. The sum of their endeavor is that, according to Diomedes, Grim Fiddle is reborn in green history. The Reunionists threaten the worst of my anticipations. Along with Diomedes's letter, the supply ship—long delayed by happy storms—brought communication to Gardiner to prepare this place for extinction. They are all expecting momentary recall. The excitement here is cluttered, does not interest me. Grim Fiddle the goat becomes Grim Fiddle the lamb; it is the same, a lie.

What recourse for me? I am lucky for my genius. I talked with Gardiner this morning. He could not have been more obliging. I sense my conceit colors this report. I should scold myself for my deception of such a well-meaning, hopeful man. I shall not. I told Gardiner that I wanted the freedom of the quay; he

agreed. I told Gardiner that I wanted his promise that this manuscript would reach Diomedes no matter what happens to me or
my pending reawakening; he promised. I made him swear; he
swore, on the Fiddle Bible.

The door to my prison is open. The path to my future is
clear. I intend to become a fugitive. I am sixty-four years old. I
have a savvy wolf, and know the Antarctic as well as any man who
ever lived. The fortress on Anvers Island beckons me. There I
was criminally king. There again I shall be—not regent of but
brother to ghosts and possibilities. The volcanoes are silent. I shall
make thunder in my hall. It will be my paradise. I realize now
that I have also spoken prematurely of the death of the People's
Republic of Antarctica. I am the last citizen, and it lives on with
me, the tyrant become the keeper of the flame.

And if this seems an imperiled fantasy, I note that the stores
on Anvers were never destroyed, the fens and caves stand inviolate. How long will I have? Perhaps ten years in the flesh; Grandfather lived till seventy-four. And perhaps eternity as a ghost;
Skallagrim Strider does live on in this place, Elephant Island, so
why not Grim Fiddle at Anvers Island? I answer best any worry
for my future by reworking Norse wisdom: Dare is better than
caution for any man who goes out on the ice, for the length of
my life and the day of my death were foretold long ago, and by
an intimate of mine, whom I fancy spied her son sanguine and
serendipitous on the ice when she looked into that magic hand-
mirror late in the evening of the spring equinox of 1973. I boast
I am predetermined, then, back to the wall of blizzards and behemoths. I shall have my wolves, the descendants of Iceberg and
Goldberg, for the glacier at Anvers Island is a wolf-keep. I shall
have my runic carvings, magical histories. I have considered taking this work with me, to continue the interrupted chronicle. It is
better not. I have dim premonition, as if a whisper in my ear, that
I shall be preoccupied with long vigilance. The ice camps might
be empty of the wretched now. The world remains full of shame.

There is a last detail. I want to believe that my Sam survived,
that someday he shall read his father's confession, this odyssey of
proverbial ruin. I have no power to thieve time, like Mother. I

guess at his looks and whereabouts. It suits me. Orlando the Black was no defeatist. He was a Furore, the one of them I concerned myself with least; it follows that I entrusted my Sam, my abiding concern, to him. I have my high dream that Sam thrives; more, that he has sons and daughters, and that they thrive. I have asked Diomedes, by a letter that introduces this manuscript to him, to seek Radar Fiddle, if he lives, and to enlist his aid in locating my Sam. I would urge Diomedes also to seek Sam's grandmother, but he is a properly superstitious Greek and would never risk ensnaring a pale albatross.

When they do find you, Sam, you shall know you are my son. I suppose that you bear the scars of our parting. I think of those burns as your birthmark. Forgive me for them, forgive me for permitting your legacy to be exile and abandonment. You are not alone. There should be two others about your age whom I ask you to find and to embrace: Cesare, son of Grootgibeon and Cleopatra; and Solomon, son of Israel and Molly. Start your search in America. The landmark is Cleopatra. And when you find them, show them what I have written of your births, and of the birth of the People's Republic of Antarctica.

Do more; tell them that if there is not a single moral to my story—what sort of life has one theme—there is this: The path to truth is to be fair-minded; never set yourself above another and you cannot fall. The hoard to discover on this path, as a good man, is that you should never bend to a master. Beware of charity. Charity is the grin of slavery. Any man in a position to give charity—not to share, not to distribute equitably—but to give from his largesse charitably, attained that lordly position by first becoming a master of the earth, and of men, a slave-master. Be a bold man, and stick the masters. Look into the face of kings and tell them they are doomed to fall. Carry the assurance that there is only one country from which exile is insufferable. Its name is Heart's Truth. Remember that you are Grim Fiddle's only son, and Peregrine Ide's only grandson, and Mord Fiddle's only great-grandson, and so your heritage is exodus as much as it is truth-seeking.

This is the truth. I was not a savior. I was not a David. I was not a hero. I was a man who did wrong by stealing trust and taking rank, knowingly and criminally, and who repented, continues to repent, for my prideful misconduct. I was vain, eager, angry, and vengeful. I have learned to be grateful and patient. I still have hope to be wise, and to make right by doing right. In all, I was not a legend, I was a man. I was Grim Fiddle. No, I owe more to Israel's sense of humor than that. I am Grim Fiddle, and in a hurry, and very, very lucky for it.

About the Author

John Calvin Batchelor was born in Bryn Mawr, Pennsylvania, in 1948, and now lives in New York City. He was graduated from Princeton University and Union Theological Seminary. He is a member of the National Book Critics Circle and the author of a previous novel, *The Further Adventures of Halley's Comet*.